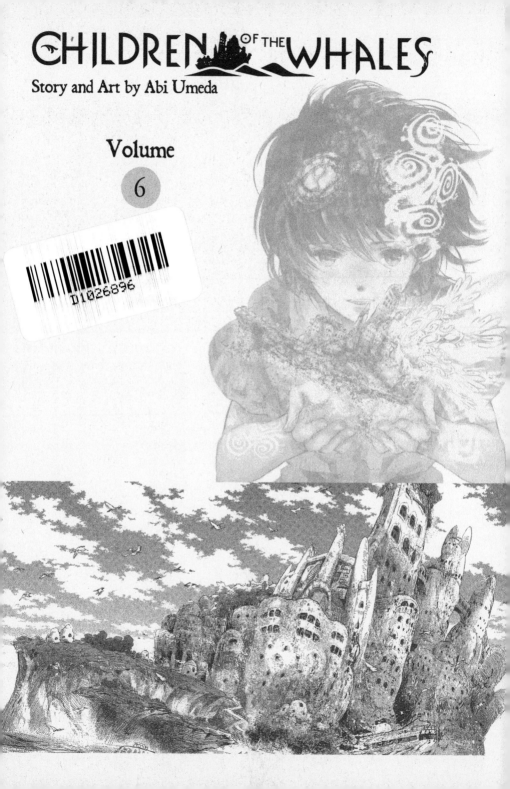

CHILDREN OF THE WHALES

Story and Art by Abi Umeda

Volume

6

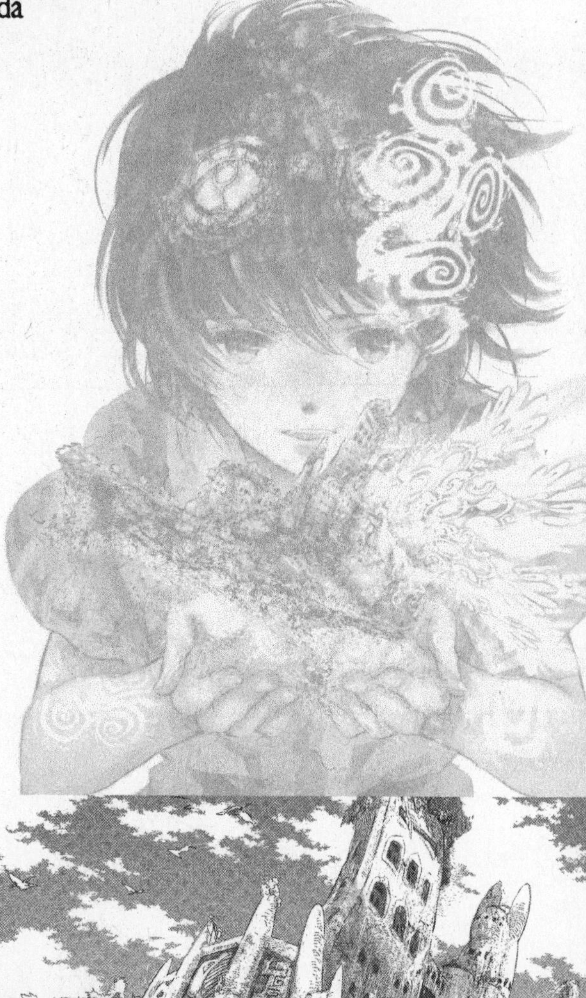

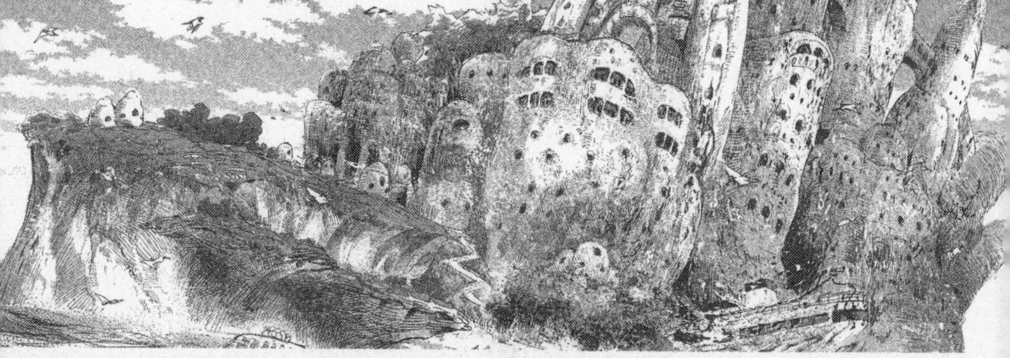

On the Mud Whale

Ouni
(Marked, 16 years old)

A very powerful thymia user. He has the power to destroy Nouses and is called the daímonas by the Allied Empire.

Lykos
(Marked, 14 years old)

A girl from the Allied Empire who comes aboard the Mud Whale. She has a connection with Chakuro and tells him the secret of Fálaina.

Chakuro
(Marked, 14 years old)

The young archivist of the Mud Whale. He has hypergraphia, a disorder that compels him to record everything.

Aíma
(???)

She appears to Chakuro after Neri disappears. She gave Chakuro the Mud Whale's rudder.

Neri
(???)

A girl with superhuman powers who disappears when Aíma appears.

Suou
(Unmarked, 17 years old)

The new mayor of the Mud Whale. He is a very compassionate person who hopes to find a remedy for the shortened life spans of the Marked.

Kuchiba
(Unmarked, 39 years old)

An adviser to the mayor. He had feelings for the previous mayor, Taisha.

Ginshu
(Marked, 16 years old)

Serves in the Vigilante Corps. She played an important role in the battle against Skyros and survived the mission.

Commander
(Marked, 25 years old)

Head of the Vigilante Corps. He defeated Liontari, a powerful apátheia soldier, during the battle against the Skyros forces.

The United Kingdom of Suidelasia

Rochalízo

He appears out of the blue while the Mud Whale is recovering from the battle with Skyros. Who is he, and what does he want?

The Empire

Orca

Commander of the apátheia forces that attacked the Mud Whale. He was tried for his role in the sinking of the Skyros but managed to evade punishment by spinning a convincing tale of Kataklysmós, the end of the world. He is Lykos's older brother.

A Record of the Mud Whale and the Sea of Sand

Year 93 of the Sand Exile.

The Mud Whale drifts endlessly through the Sea of Sand, home to about 500 people who know nothing of the outside world.

The Marked are those who can wield thymia, a psychic power fueled by emotion. They die young, around the age of 30. Those who have no thymia are called the Unmarked.

Chakuro, the Mud Whale archivist, meets Lykos one day on an abandoned island-ship found floating near theirs. She eventually opens up to the children on the Mud Whale, but her homeland, the Allied Empire, brutally attacks them twice before the Mud Whale is able to leave the prison-like currents that trap it.

With the aid of the mysterious Aíma, the rudder for the Mud Whale is discovered. Powered by a song that comes to the Marked in their dreams, the Mud Whale sails forth into an unknown world. In the midst of this excitement, Lykos finally reveals one of the secrets of Fálaina: this Nous is not consuming emotions in exchange for thymia—it is devouring the very life force of the Marked.

"The Mud Whale was our entire world."

Table of Contents

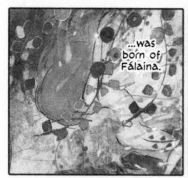

Aíma...
...was born of Fálaina.
Chéris grow...
...from the lachrymose trails of her dákry.
Chéris mix with motes of sand...
...and become faint, earth-toned dérma.
These are the walls of the Mud Whale.

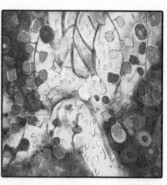

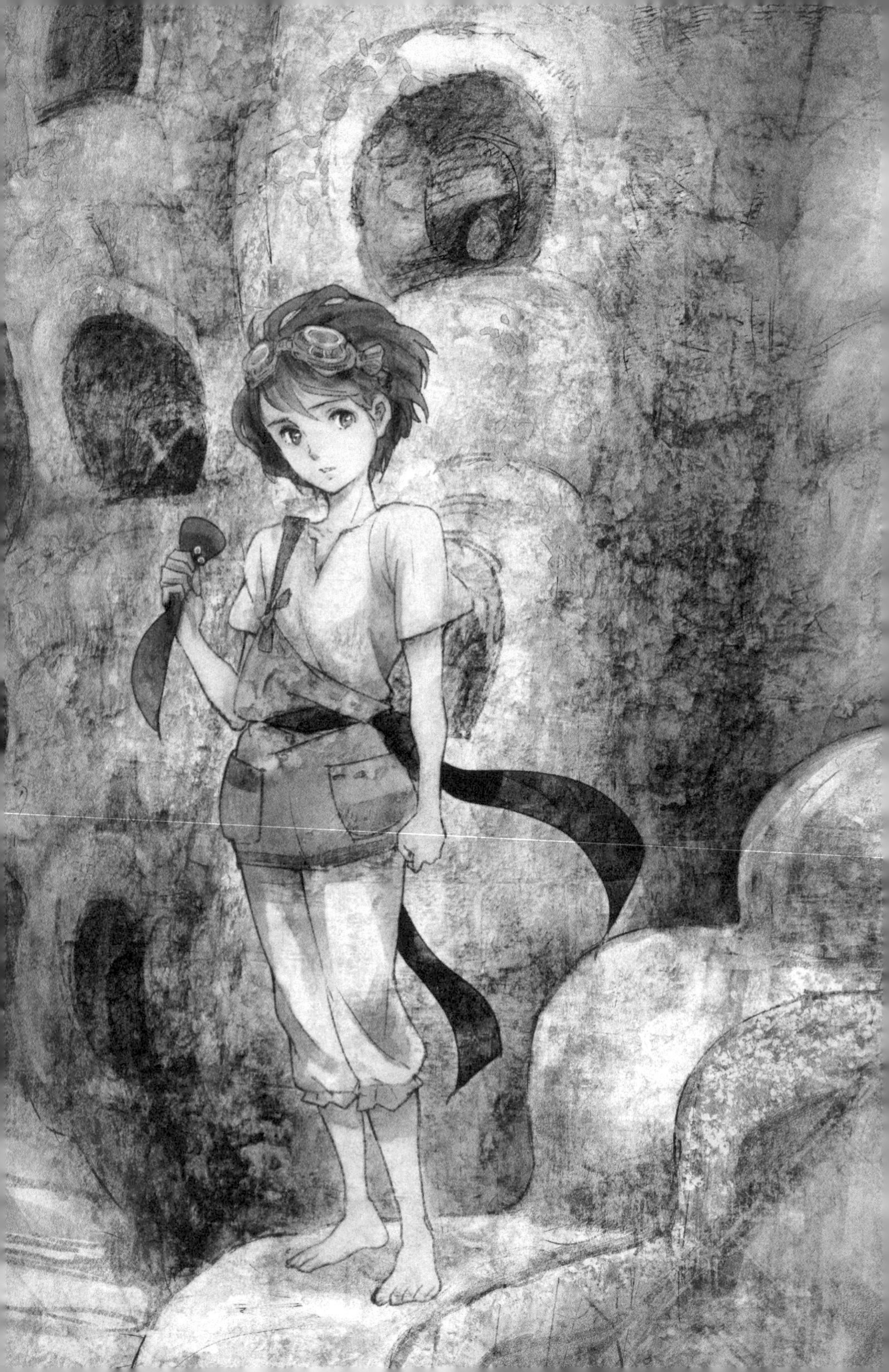

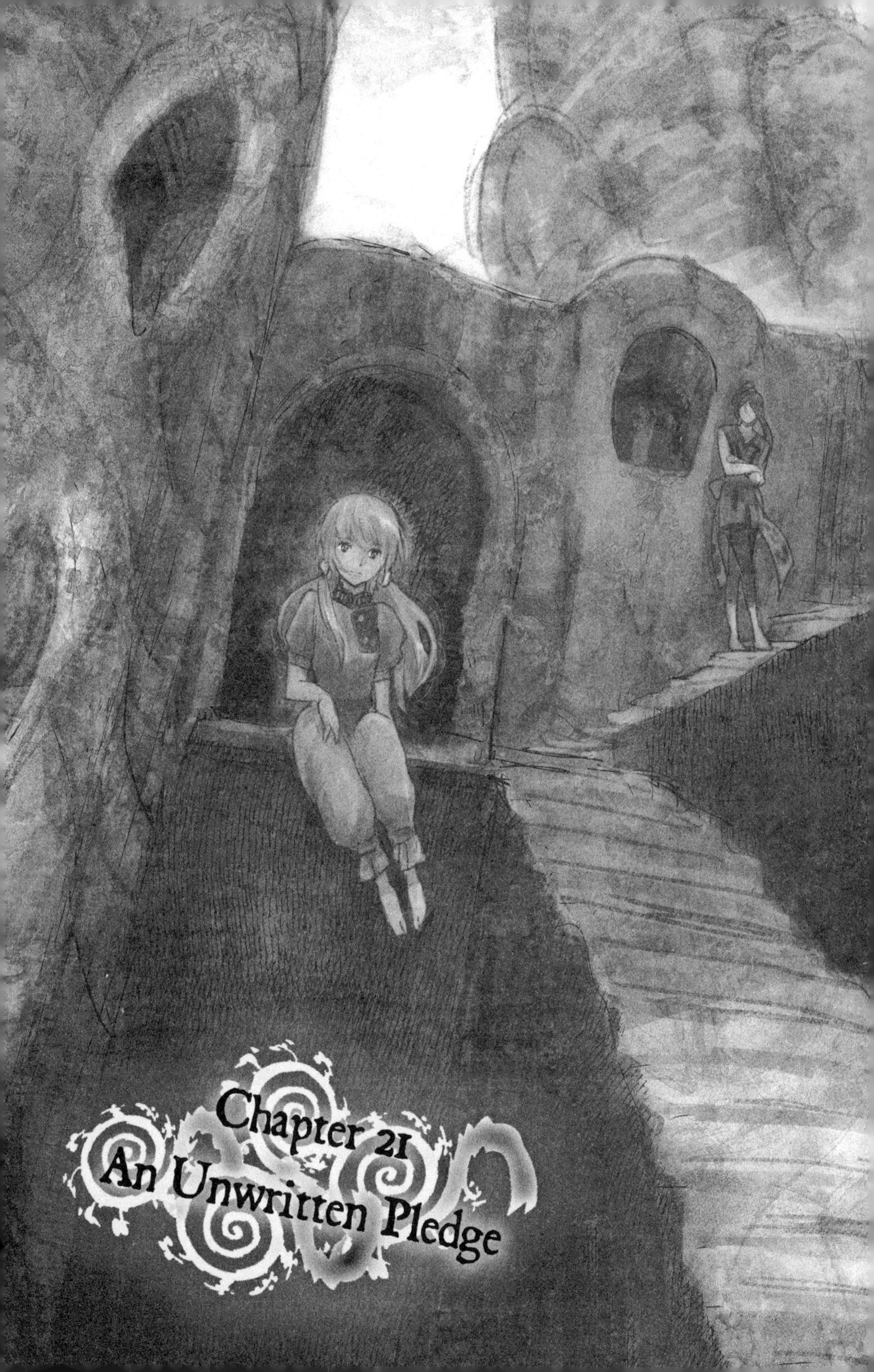
Chapter 21
An Unwritten Pledge

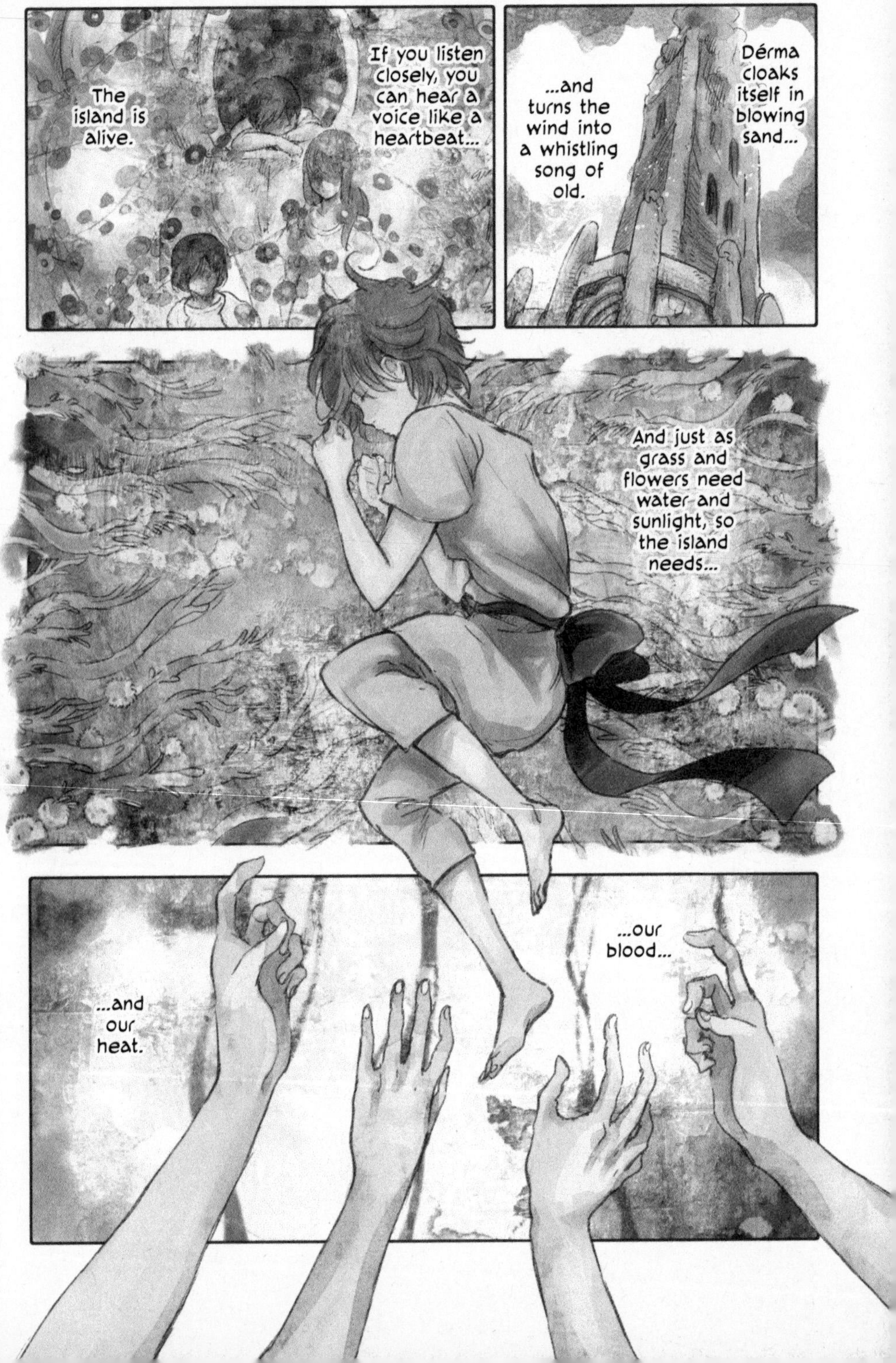
Dérma cloaks itself in blowing sand...
...and turns the wind into a whistling song of old.
If you listen closely, you can hear a voice like a heartbeat...
The island is alive.
And just as grass and flowers need water and sunlight, so the island needs...
...our blood...
...and our heat.

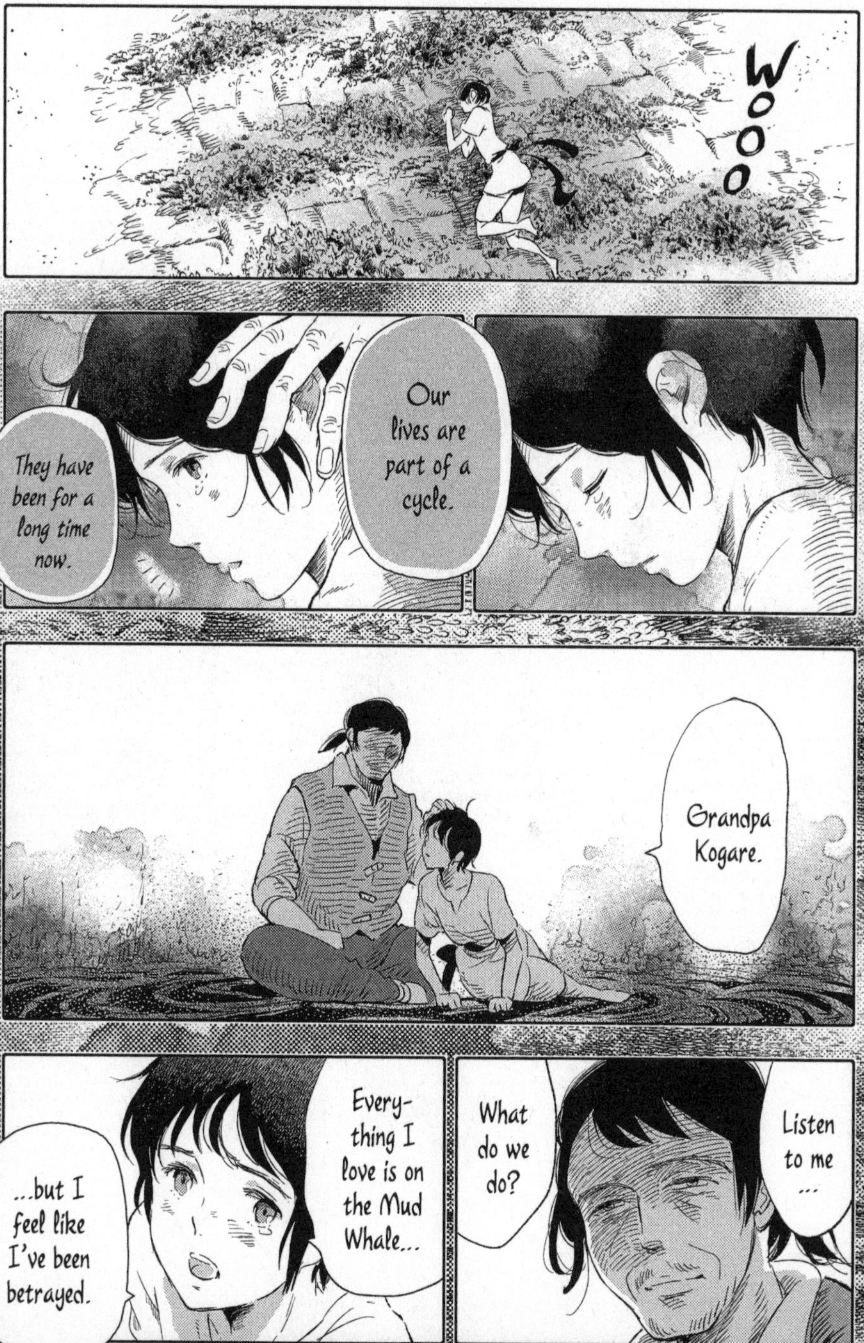
WOOOO
Our lives are part of a cycle.
They have been for a long time now.
Grandpa Kogare.
Listen to me...
What do we do?
Everything I love is on the Mud Whale...
...but I feel like I've been betrayed.

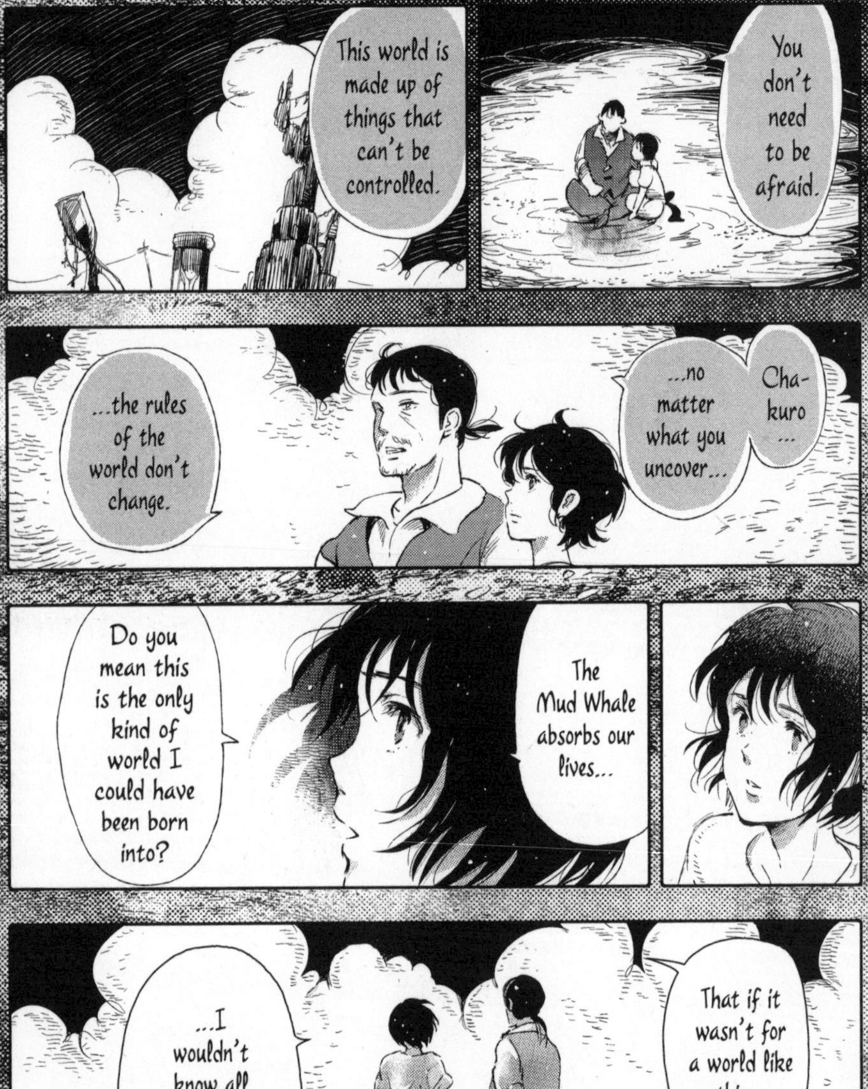
You don't need to be afraid.
This world is made up of things that can't be controlled.
Cha-kuro...
...no matter what you uncover...
...the rules of the world don't change.
The Mud Whale absorbs our lives...
Do you mean this is the only kind of world I could have been born into?
That if it wasn't for a world like this...
...I wouldn't know all the people and things that I love?

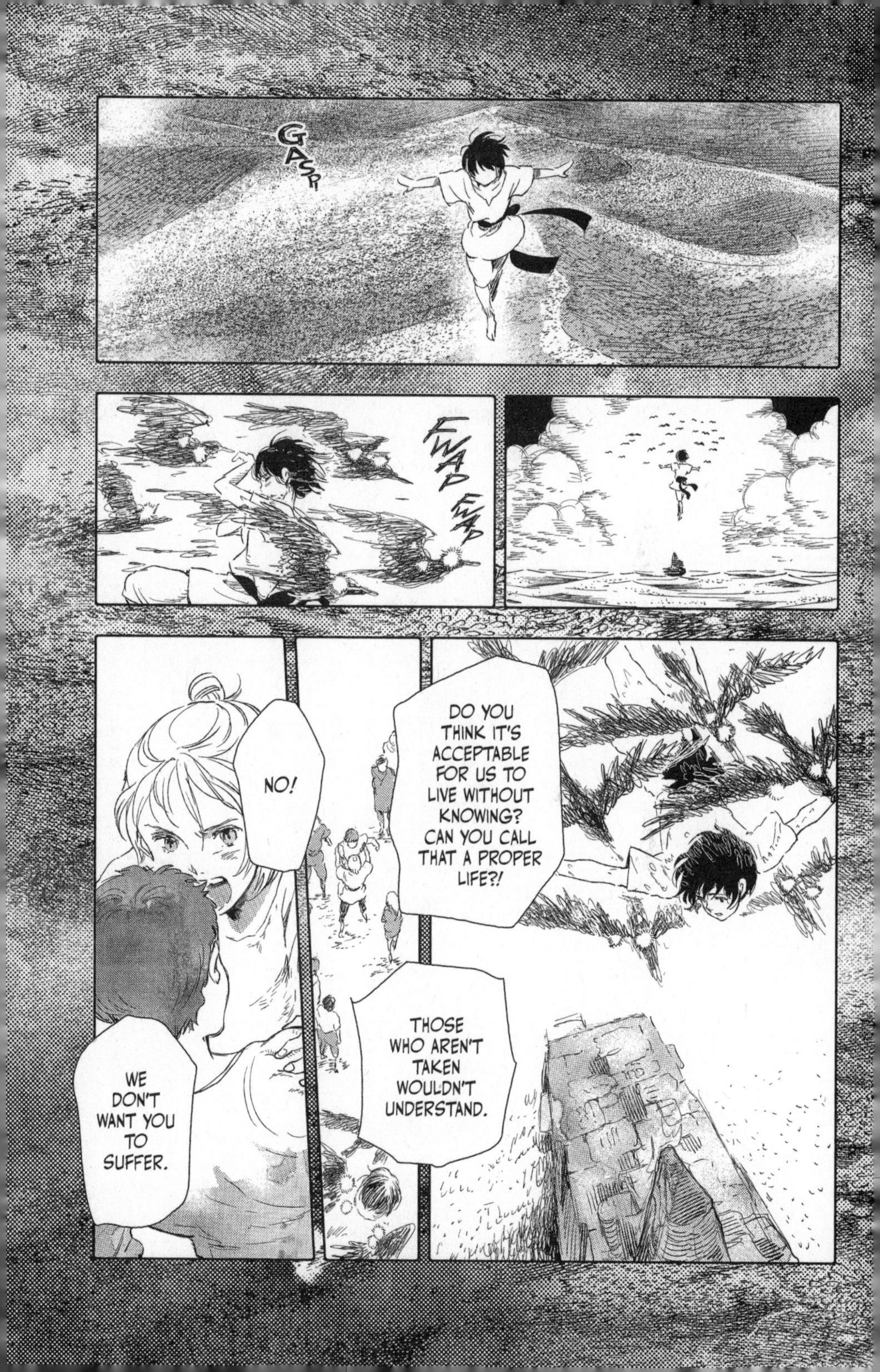
GASP!
FWAP FWAP
DO YOU THINK IT'S ACCEPTABLE FOR US TO LIVE WITHOUT KNOWING? CAN YOU CALL THAT A PROPER LIFE?!
THOSE WHO AREN'T TAKEN WOULDN'T UNDERSTAND.
NO!
WE DON'T WANT YOU TO SUFFER.

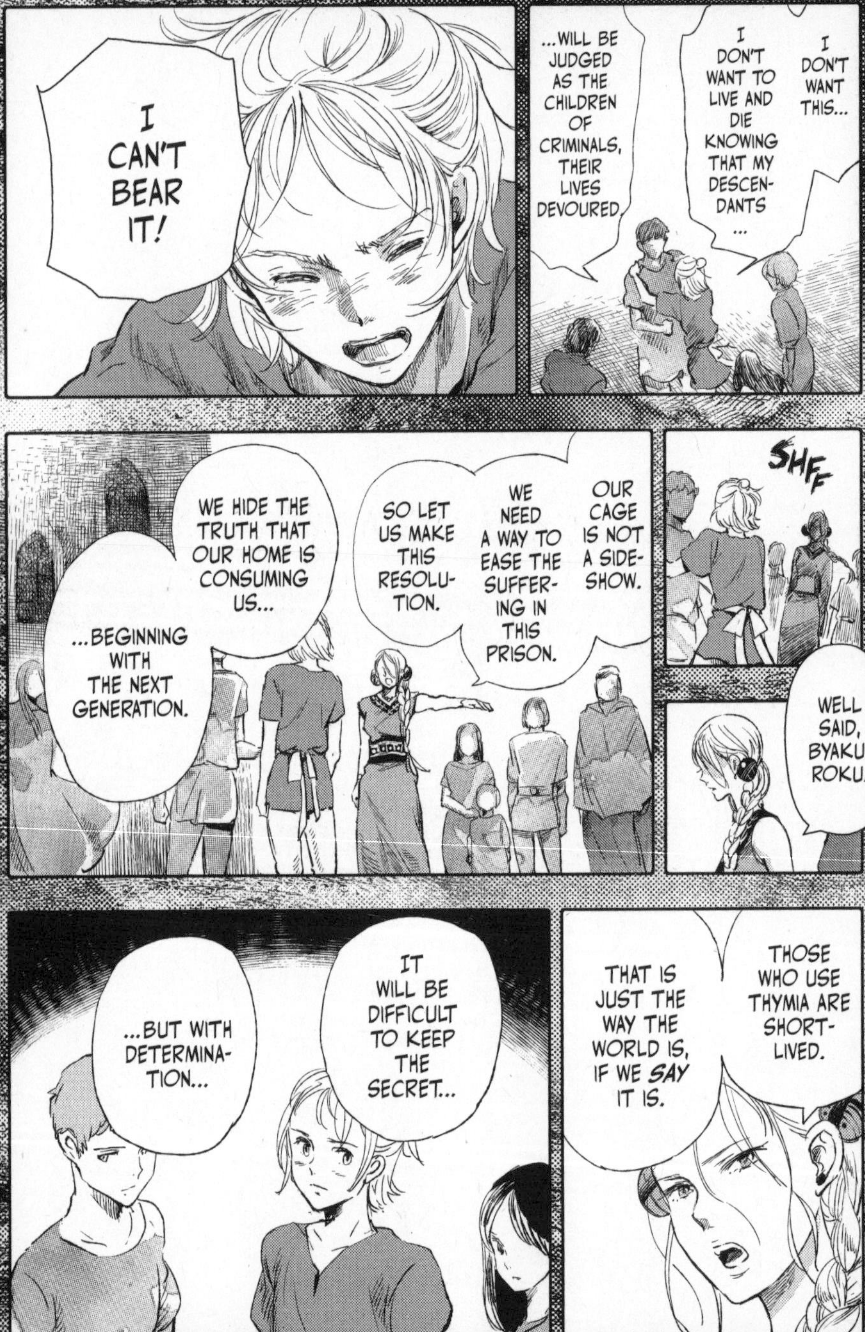
I DON'T WANT THIS...
I DON'T WANT TO LIVE AND DIE KNOWING THAT MY DESCENDANTS ...
...WILL BE JUDGED AS THE CHILDREN OF CRIMINALS, THEIR LIVES DEVOURED.
I CAN'T BEAR IT!
SHFF
WELL SAID, BYAKUROKU.
OUR CAGE IS NOT A SIDESHOW.
WE NEED A WAY TO EASE THE SUFFERING IN THIS PRISON.
SO LET US MAKE THIS RESOLUTION.
WE HIDE THE TRUTH THAT OUR HOME IS CONSUMING US...
...BEGINNING WITH THE NEXT GENERATION.
THOSE WHO USE THYMIA ARE SHORT-LIVED.
THAT IS JUST THE WAY THE WORLD IS, IF WE *SAY* IT IS.
IT WILL BE DIFFICULT TO KEEP THE SECRET...
...BUT WITH DETERMINATION...

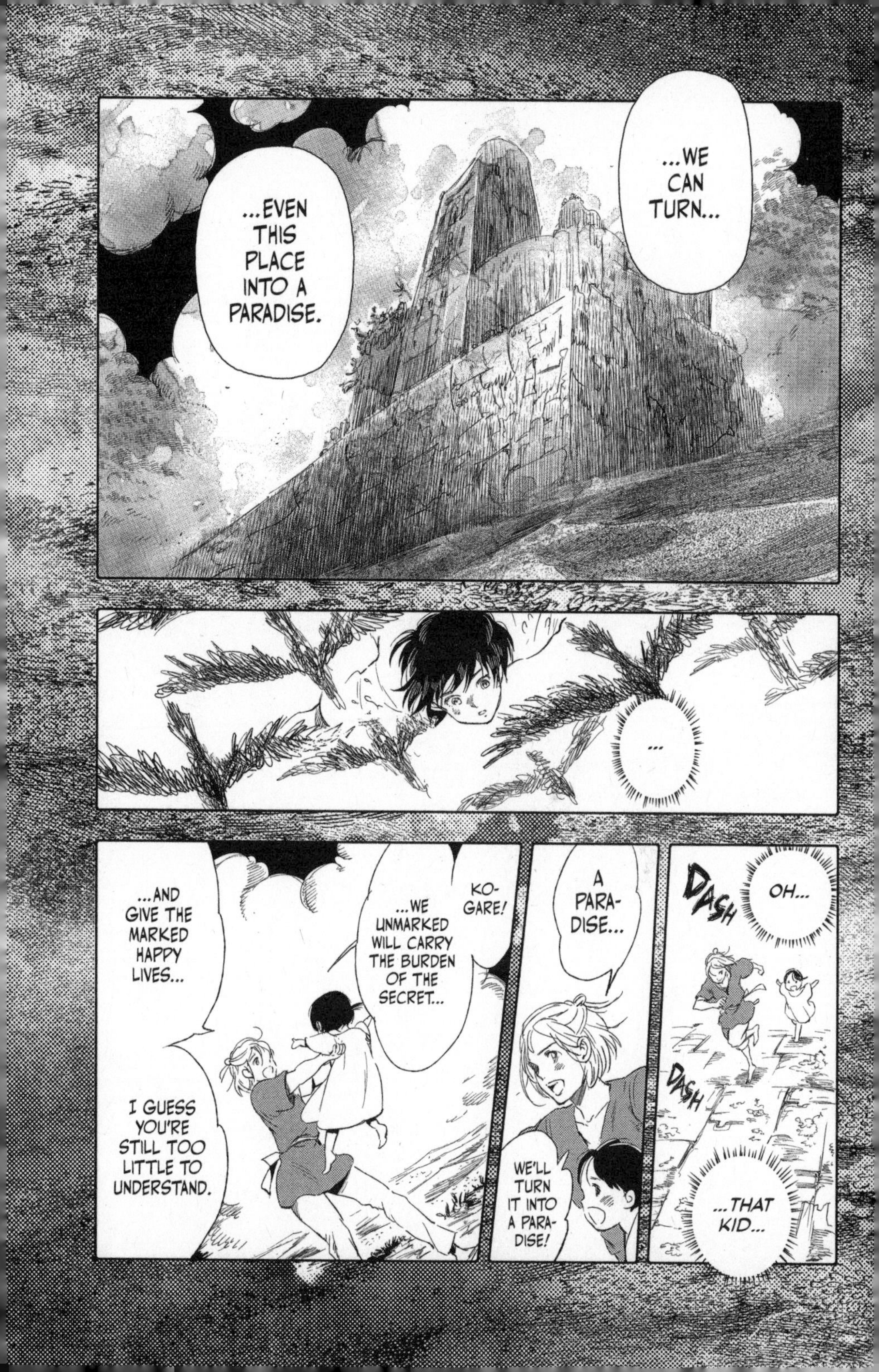
...WE CAN TURN...
...EVEN THIS PLACE INTO A PARADISE.
...
DASH
OH...
DASH
...THAT KID...
A PARA-DISE...
WE'LL TURN IT INTO A PARA-DISE!
KO-GARE!
...WE UNMARKED WILL CARRY THE BURDEN OF THE SECRET...
...AND GIVE THE MARKED HAPPY LIVES...
I GUESS YOU'RE STILL TOO LITTLE TO UNDERSTAND.

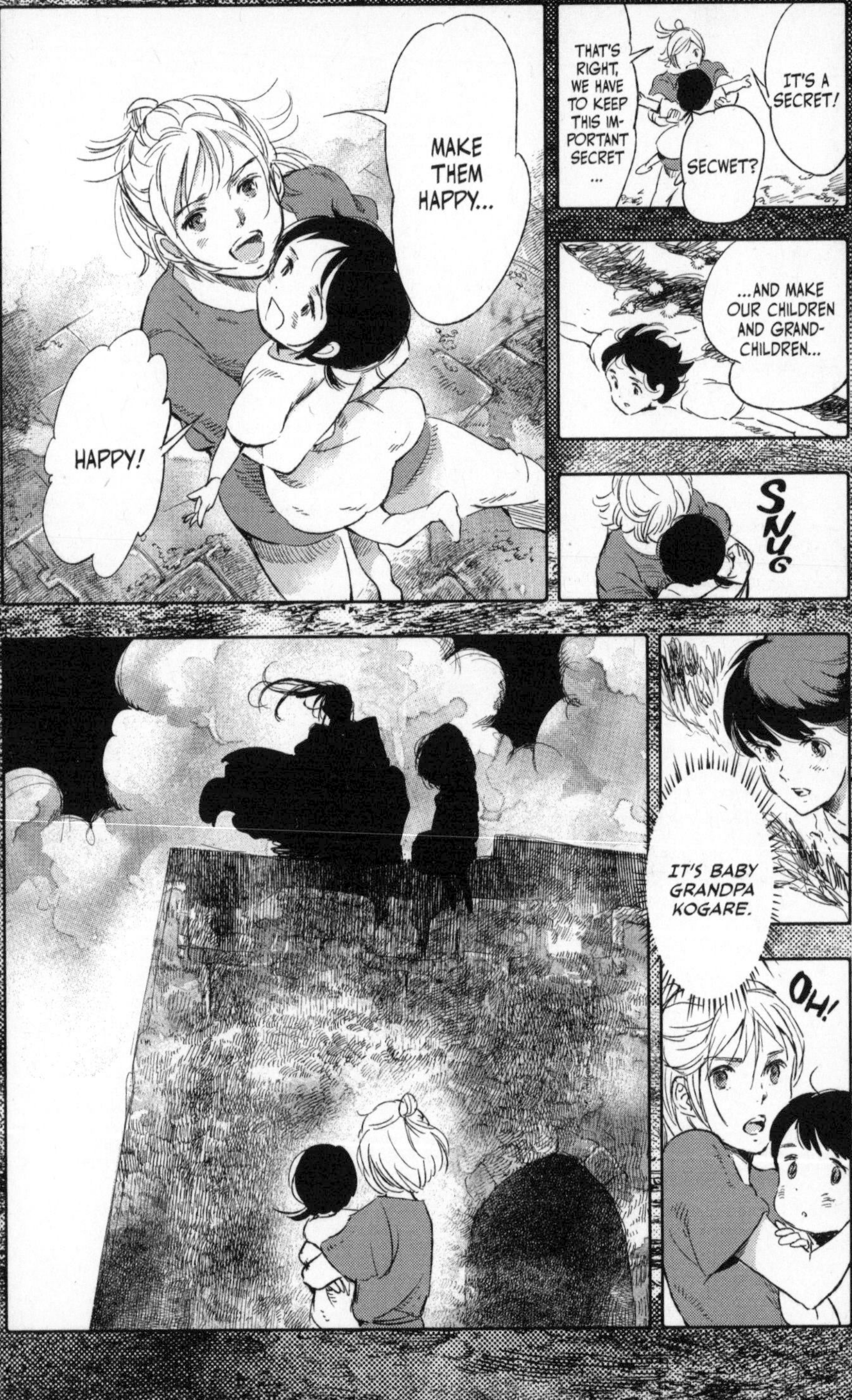
IT'S A SECRET!
SECWET?
THAT'S RIGHT, WE HAVE TO KEEP THIS IMPORTANT SECRET...
...AND MAKE OUR CHILDREN AND GRAND-CHILDREN...
SNUG
MAKE THEM HAPPY...
HAPPY!
IT'S BABY GRANDPA KOGARE.
OH!

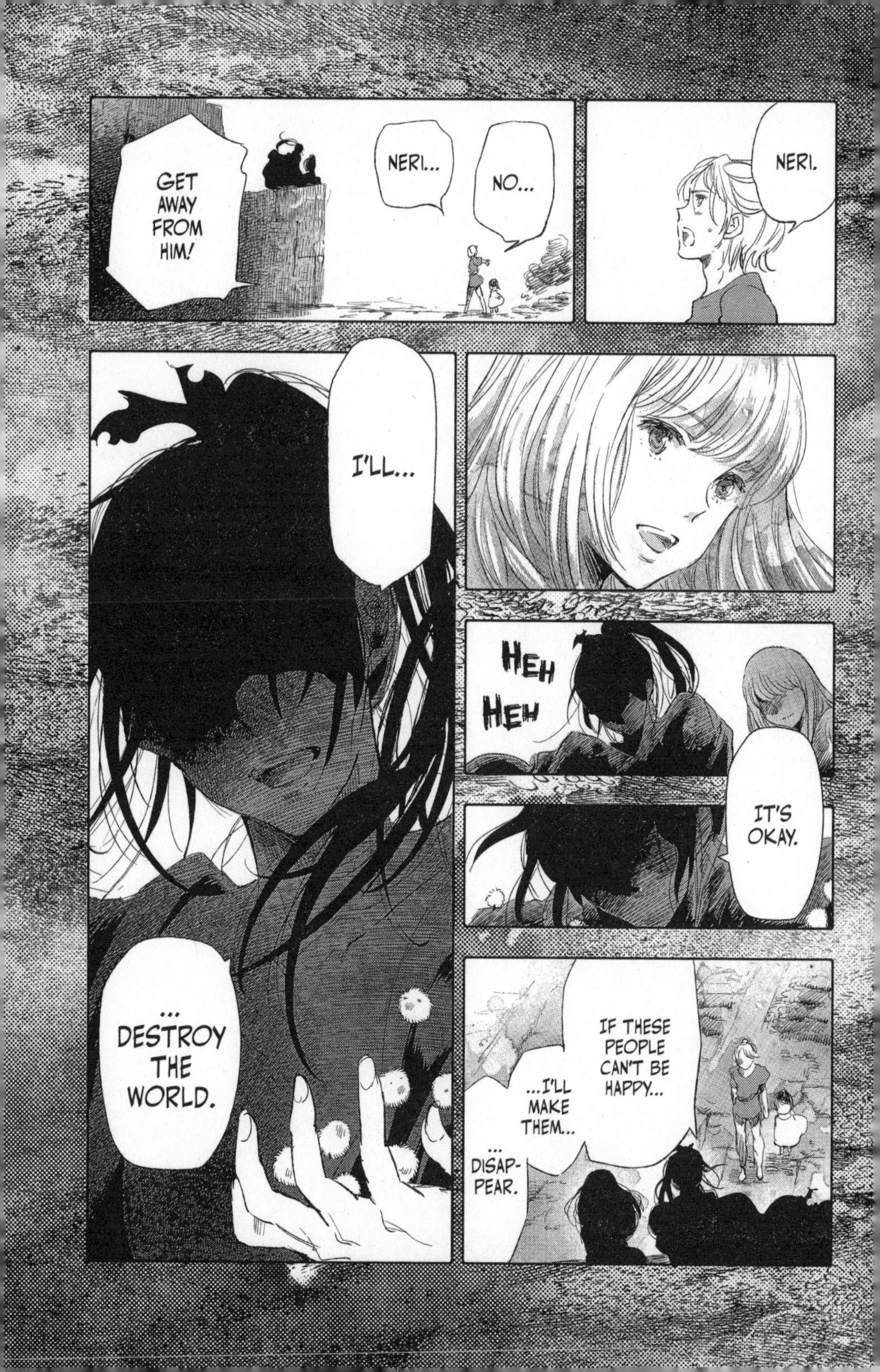
NERI.
NO...
NERI...
GET AWAY FROM HIM!
HEH HEH
IT'S OKAY.
IF THESE PEOPLE CAN'T BE HAPPY...
...I'LL MAKE THEM...
...DISAPPEAR.
I'LL...
...DESTROY THE WORLD.

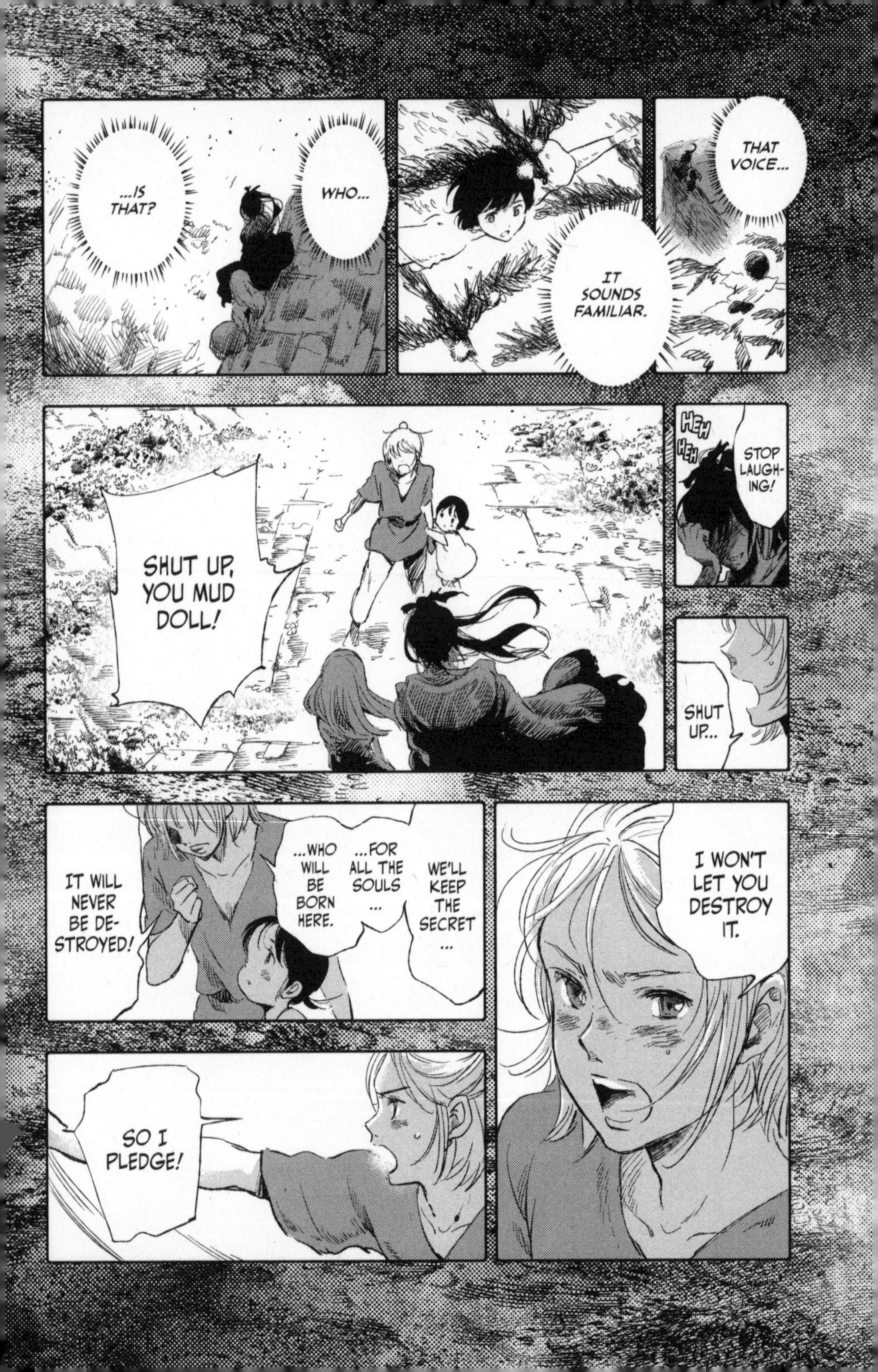
THAT VOICE...
IT SOUNDS FAMILIAR.
WHO...
...IS THAT?
HEH HEH
STOP LAUGHING!
SHUT UP...
SHUT UP, YOU MUD DOLL!
I WON'T LET YOU DESTROY IT.
WE'LL KEEP THE SECRET...
...FOR ALL THE SOULS...
...WHO WILL BE BORN HERE.
IT WILL NEVER BE DESTROYED!
SO I PLEDGE!

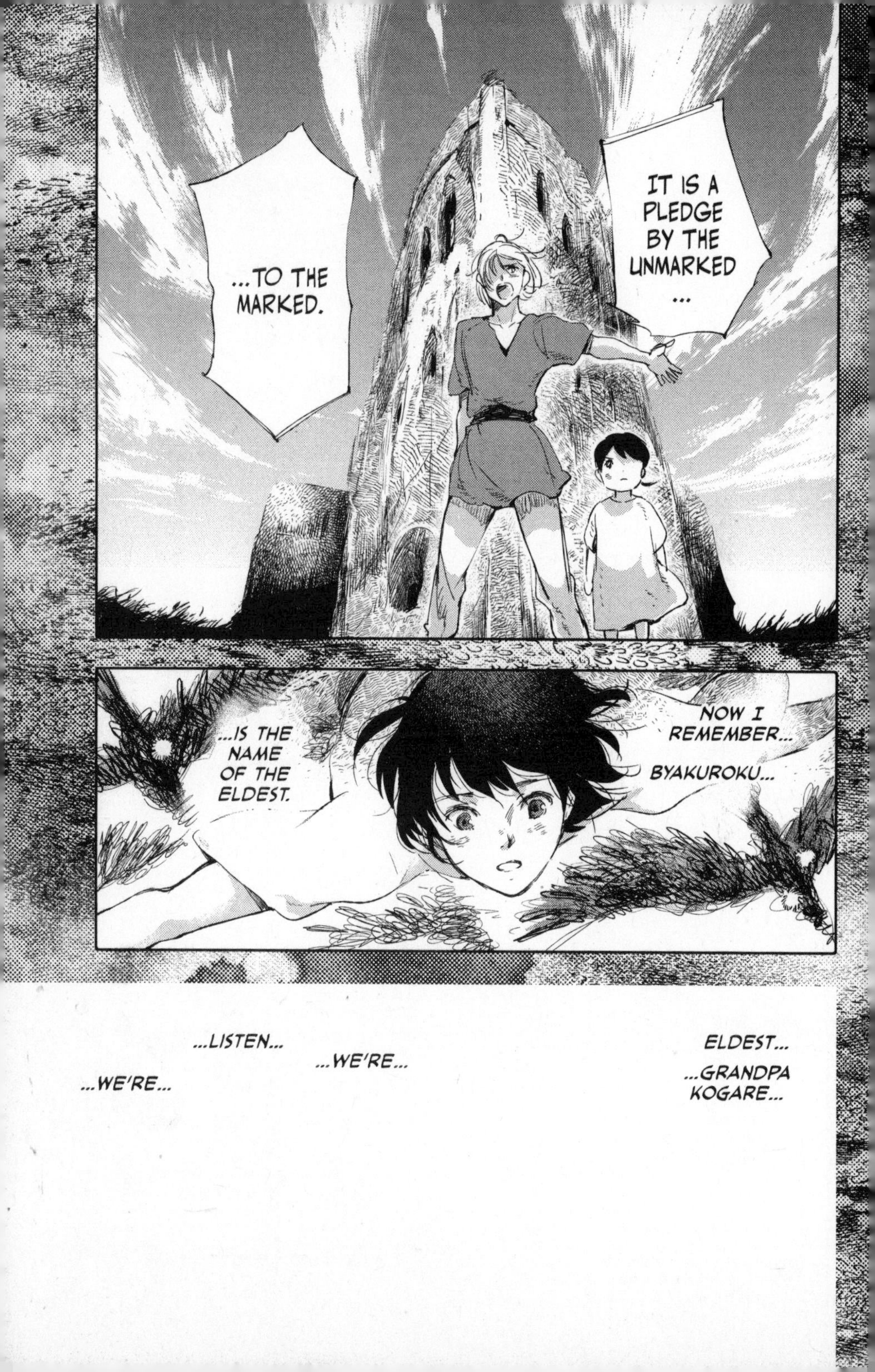
IT IS A PLEDGE BY THE UNMARKED ...
...TO THE MARKED.
NOW I REMEMBER...
BYAKUROKU...
...IS THE NAME OF THE ELDEST.
ELDEST...
...GRANDPA KOGARE...
...WE'RE...
...LISTEN...
...WE'RE...

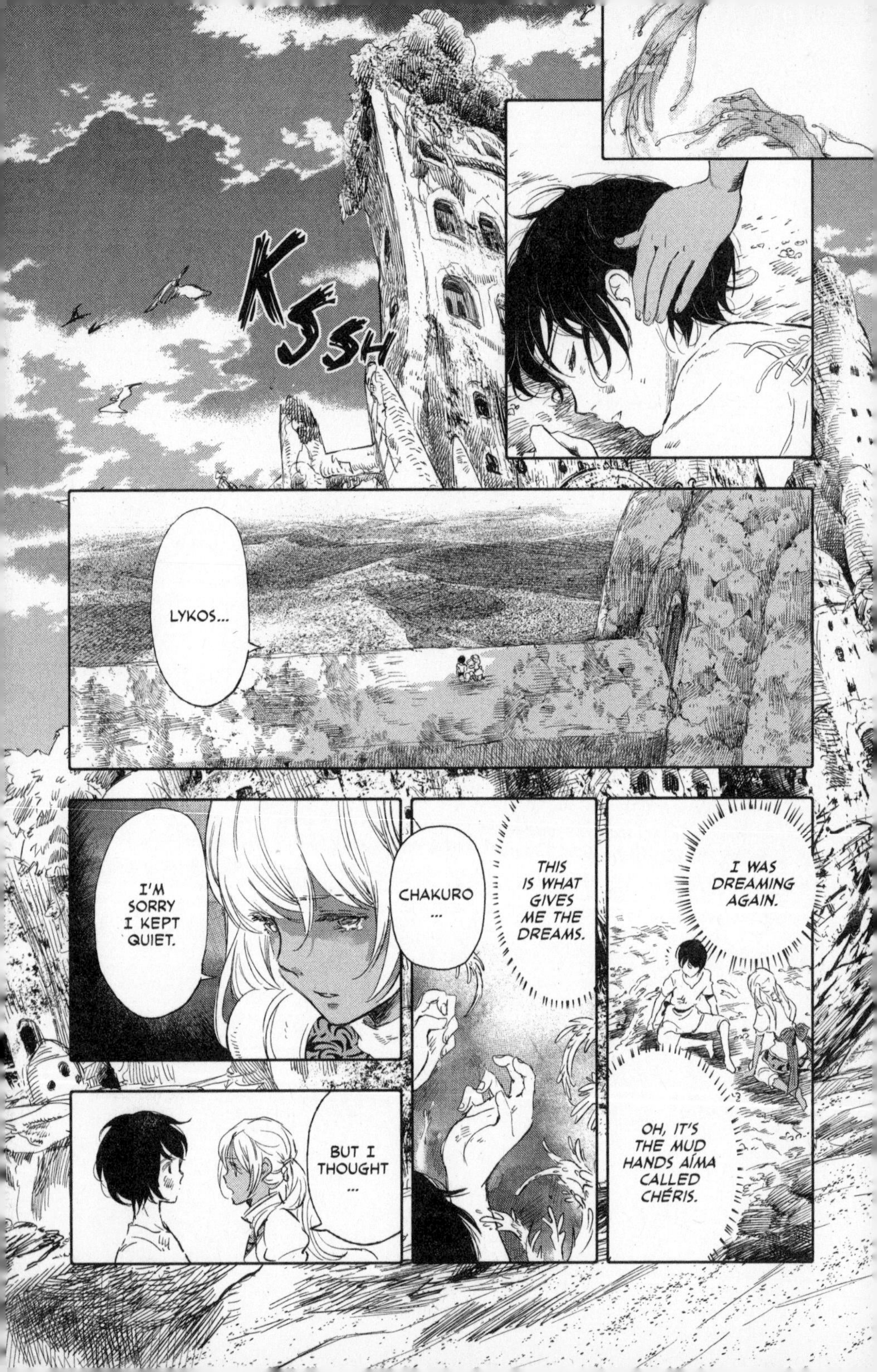
KSSH
LYKOS...
I WAS DREAMING AGAIN.
OH, IT'S THE MUD HANDS AÍMA CALLED CHÉRIS.
THIS IS WHAT GIVES ME THE DREAMS.
CHAKURO ...
I'M SORRY I KEPT QUIET.
BUT I THOUGHT ...

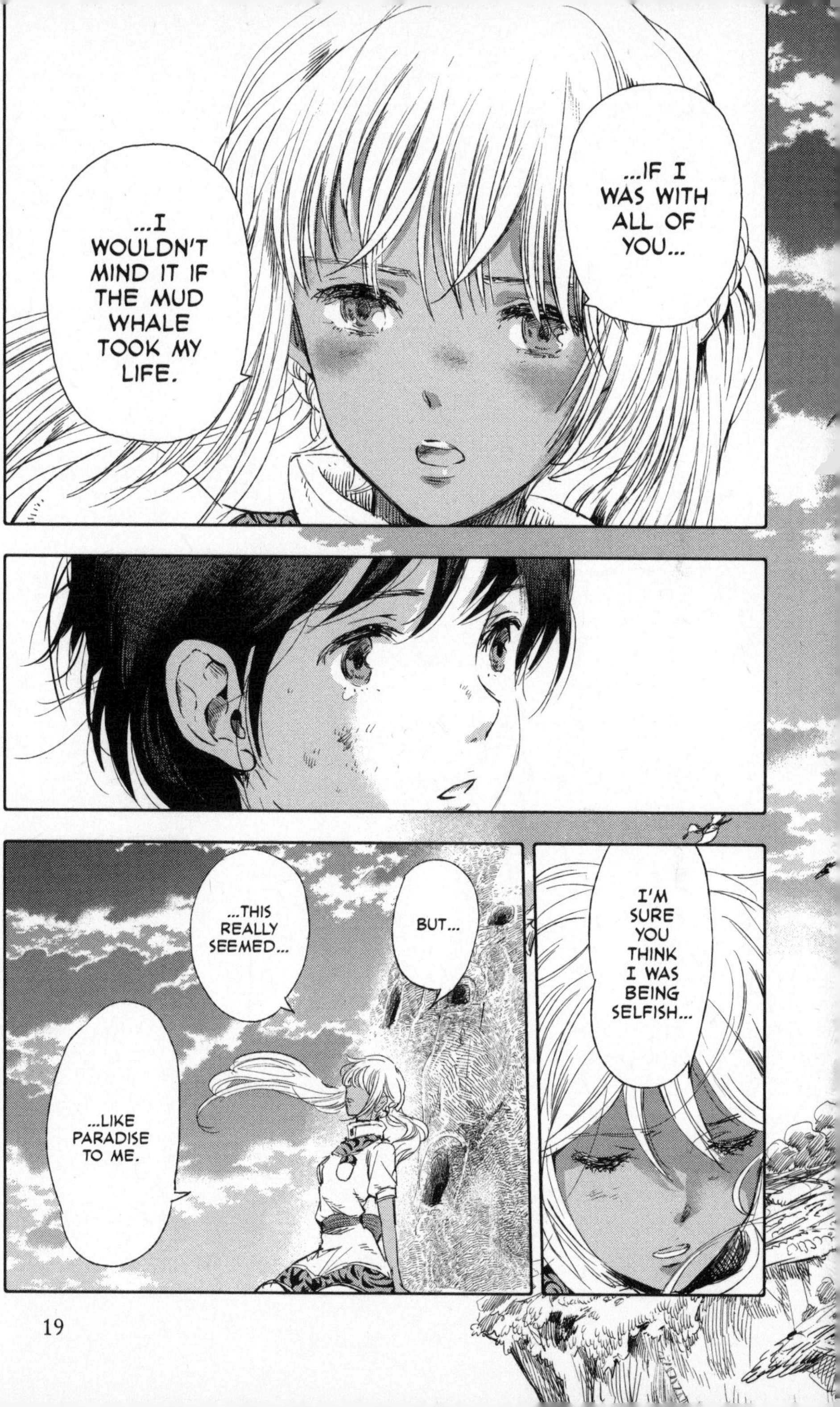
...IF I WAS WITH ALL OF YOU...
...I WOULDN'T MIND IT IF THE MUD WHALE TOOK MY LIFE.
I'M SURE YOU THINK I WAS BEING SELFISH...
BUT...
...THIS REALLY SEEMED...
...LIKE PARADISE TO ME.

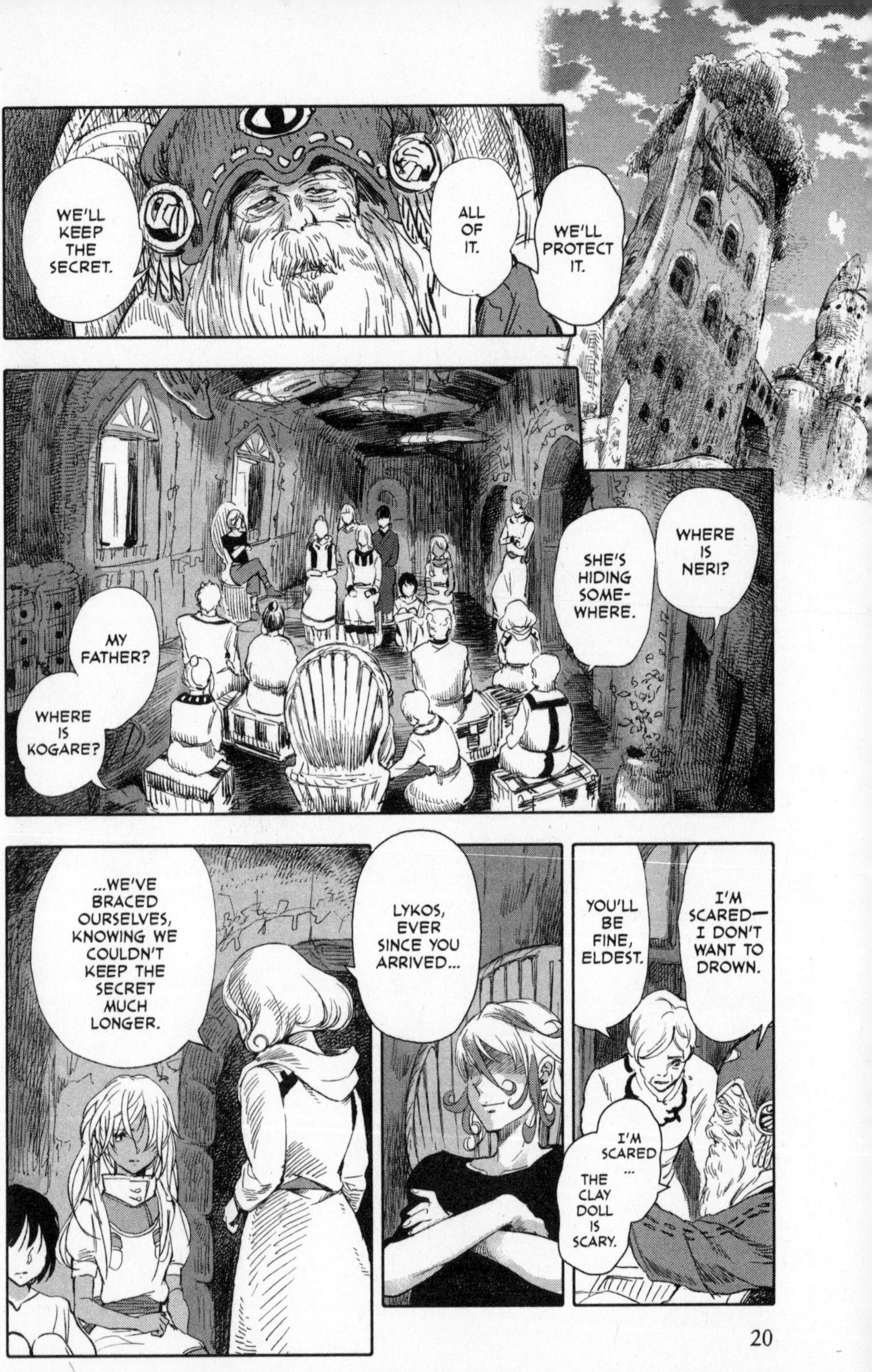
WE'LL PROTECT IT.
ALL OF IT.
WE'LL KEEP THE SECRET.
WHERE IS NERI?
SHE'S HIDING SOMEWHERE.
MY FATHER?
WHERE IS KOGARE?
I'M SCARED— I DON'T WANT TO DROWN.
YOU'LL BE FINE, ELDEST.
I'M SCARED...
THE CLAY DOLL IS SCARY.
LYKOS, EVER SINCE YOU ARRIVED...
...WE'VE BRACED OURSELVES, KNOWING WE COULDN'T KEEP THE SECRET MUCH LONGER.

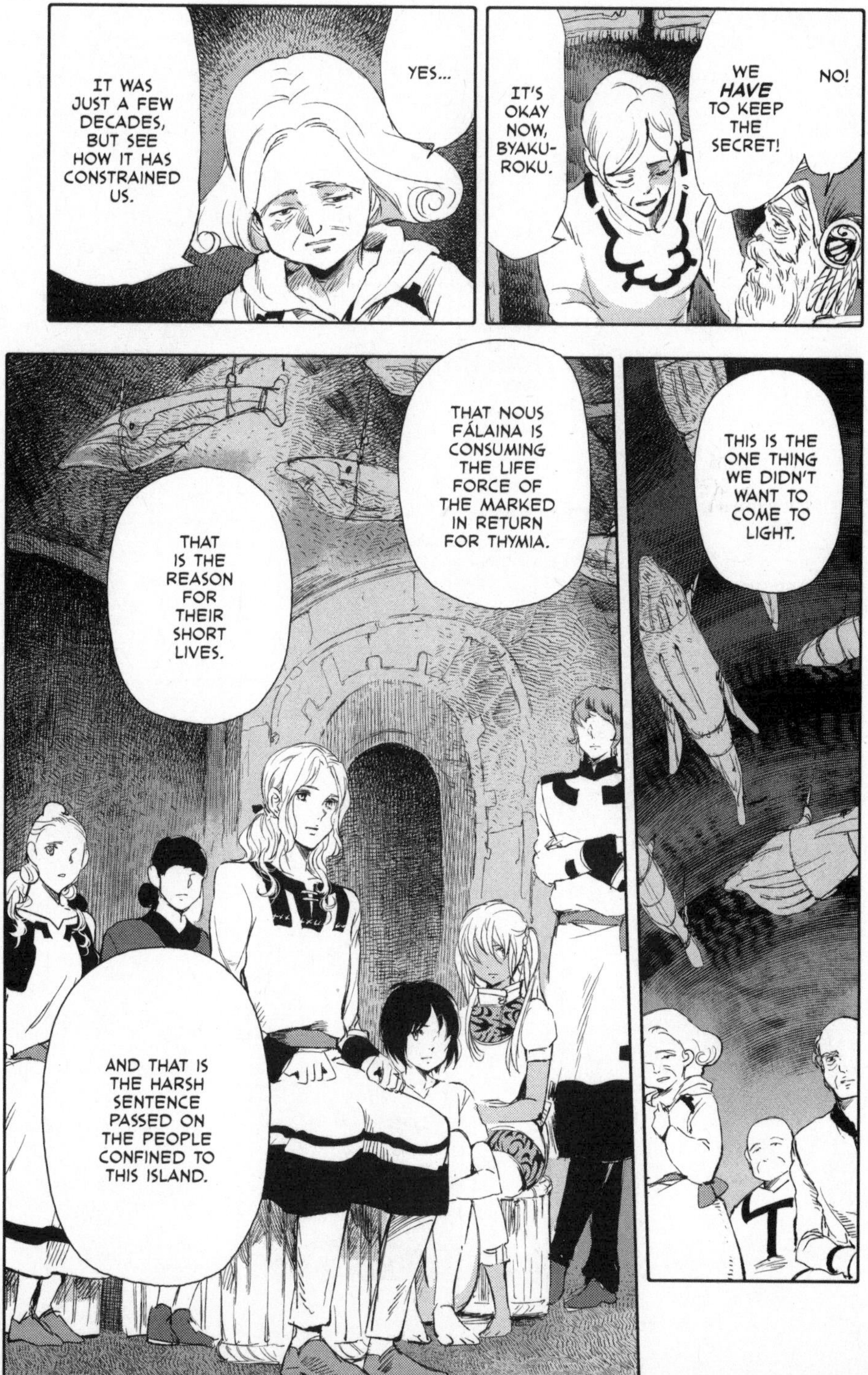
NO!
WE *HAVE* TO KEEP THE SECRET!
IT'S OKAY NOW, BYAKU-ROKU.
YES...
IT WAS JUST A FEW DECADES, BUT SEE HOW IT HAS CONSTRAINED US.
THIS IS THE ONE THING WE DIDN'T WANT TO COME TO LIGHT.
THAT NOUS FÁLAINA IS CONSUMING THE LIFE FORCE OF THE MARKED IN RETURN FOR THYMIA.
THAT IS THE REASON FOR THEIR SHORT LIVES.
AND THAT IS THE HARSH SENTENCE PASSED ON THE PEOPLE CONFINED TO THIS ISLAND.

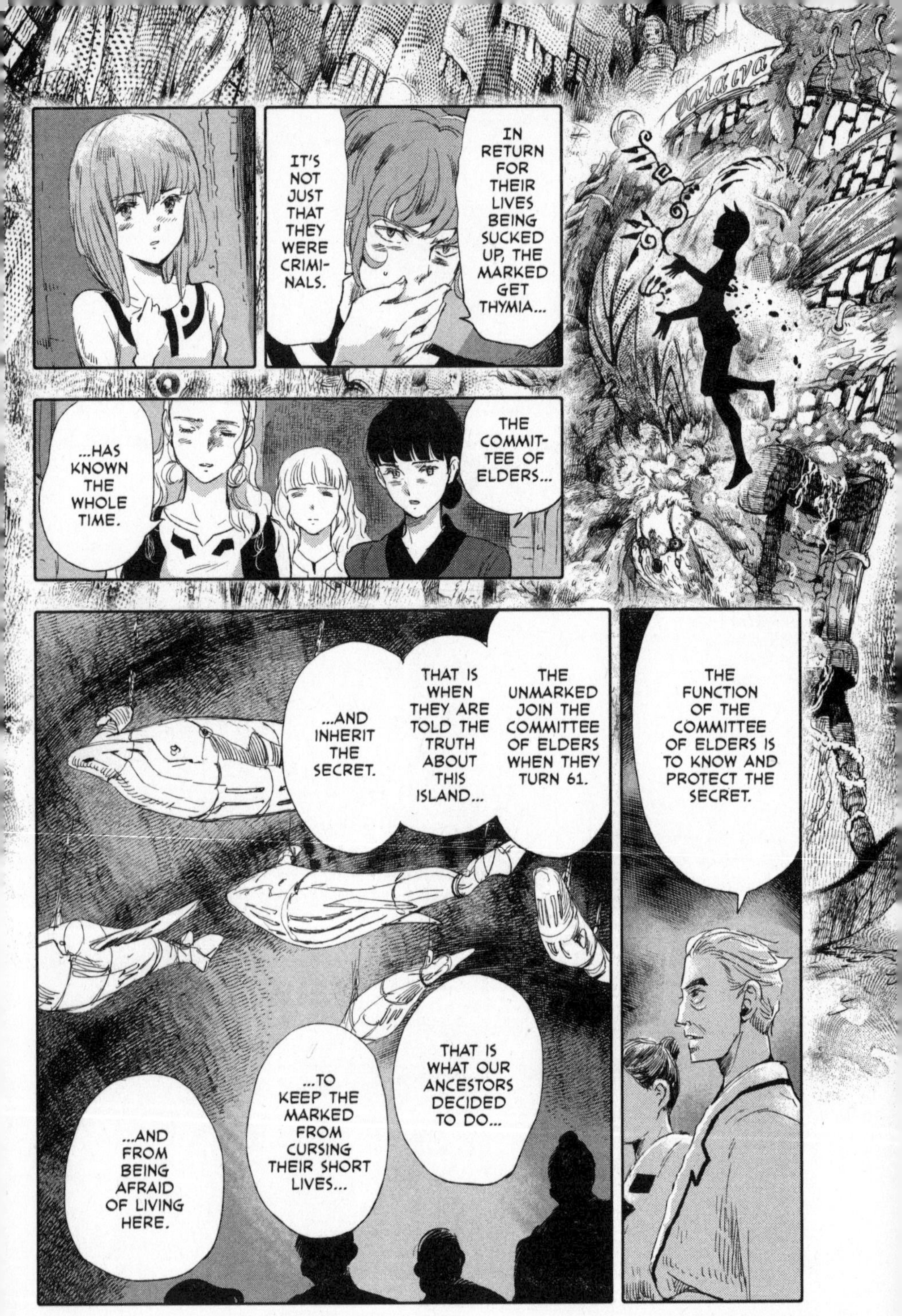

IN RETURN FOR THEIR LIVES BEING SUCKED UP, THE MARKED GET THYMIA...
IT'S NOT JUST THAT THEY WERE CRIMI-NALS.
THE COMMIT-TEE OF ELDERS...
...HAS KNOWN THE WHOLE TIME.
THE FUNCTION OF THE COMMITTEE OF ELDERS IS TO KNOW AND PROTECT THE SECRET.
THE UNMARKED JOIN THE COMMITTEE OF ELDERS WHEN THEY TURN 61.
THAT IS WHEN THEY ARE TOLD THE TRUTH ABOUT THIS ISLAND...
...AND INHERIT THE SECRET.
THAT IS WHAT OUR ANCESTORS DECIDED TO DO...
...TO KEEP THE MARKED FROM CURSING THEIR SHORT LIVES...
...AND FROM BEING AFRAID OF LIVING HERE.

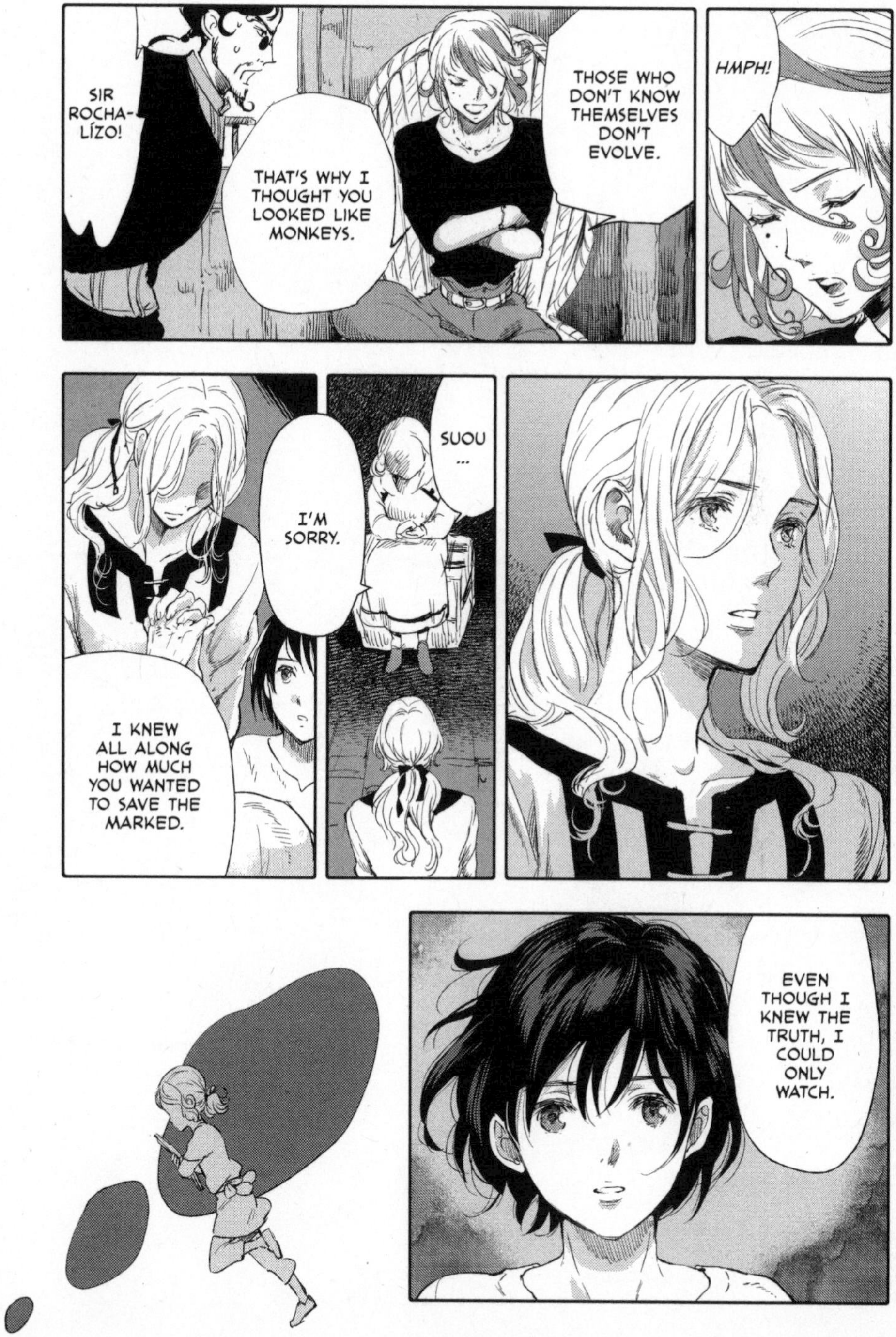
HMPH!
THOSE WHO DON'T KNOW THEMSELVES DON'T EVOLVE.
THAT'S WHY I THOUGHT YOU LOOKED LIKE MONKEYS.
SIR ROCHA-LÍZO!
SUOU ...
I'M SORRY.
I KNEW ALL ALONG HOW MUCH YOU WANTED TO SAVE THE MARKED.
EVEN THOUGH I KNEW THE TRUTH, I COULD ONLY WATCH.

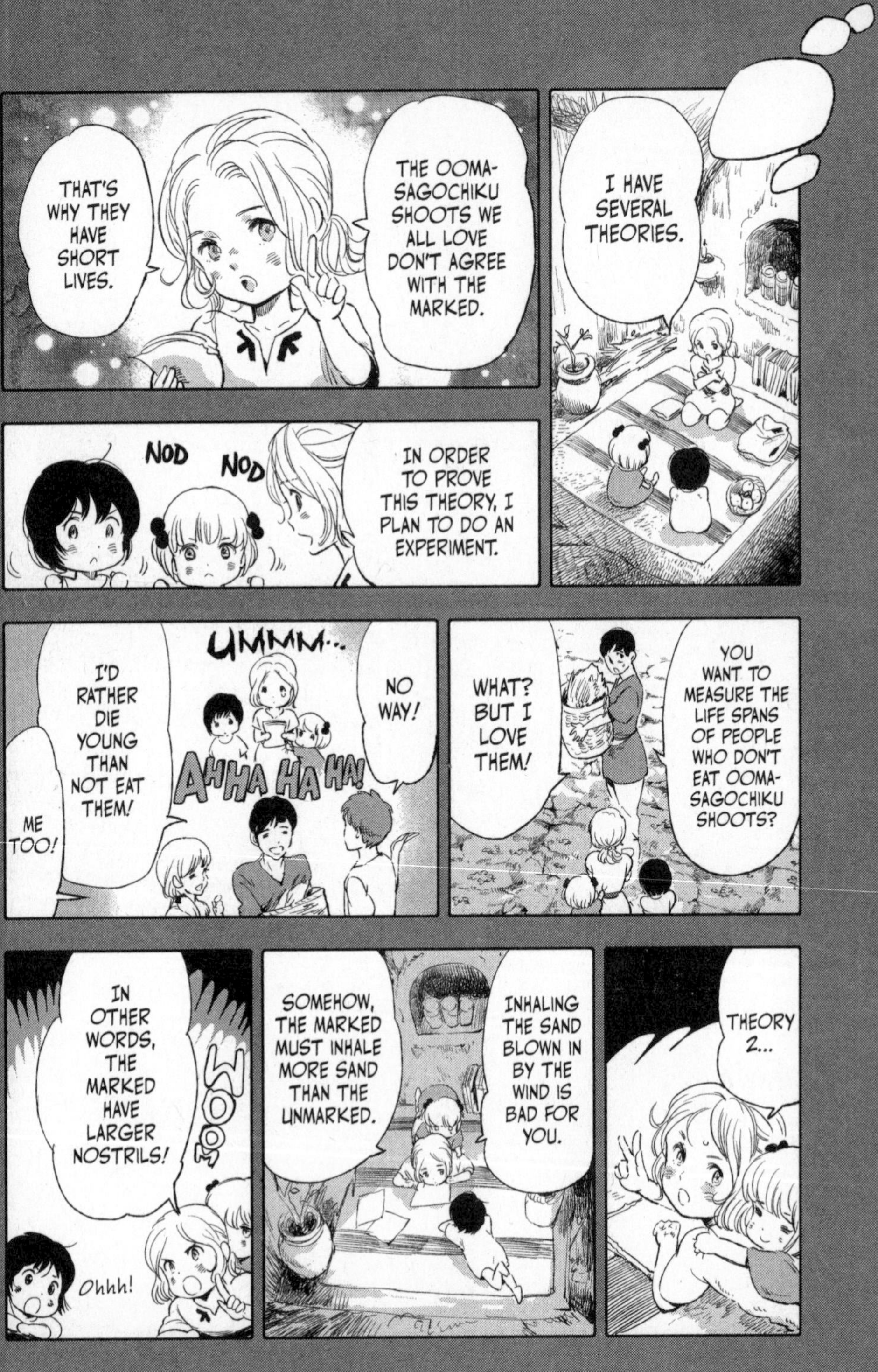
I HAVE SEVERAL THEORIES.
THE OOMA-SAGOCHIKU SHOOTS WE ALL LOVE DON'T AGREE WITH THE MARKED.
THAT'S WHY THEY HAVE SHORT LIVES.
IN ORDER TO PROVE THIS THEORY, I PLAN TO DO AN EXPERIMENT.
NOD
NOD
YOU WANT TO MEASURE THE LIFE SPANS OF PEOPLE WHO DON'T EAT OOMA-SAGOCHIKU SHOOTS?
WHAT? BUT I LOVE THEM!
NO WAY!
UMMM...
I'D RATHER DIE YOUNG THAN NOT EAT THEM!
AHHA HA HA!
ME TOO!
THEORY 2...
INHALING THE SAND BLOWN IN BY THE WIND IS BAD FOR YOU.
SOMEHOW, THE MARKED MUST INHALE MORE SAND THAN THE UNMARKED.
IN OTHER WORDS, THE MARKED HAVE LARGER NOSTRILS!
WOOM
Ohhh!

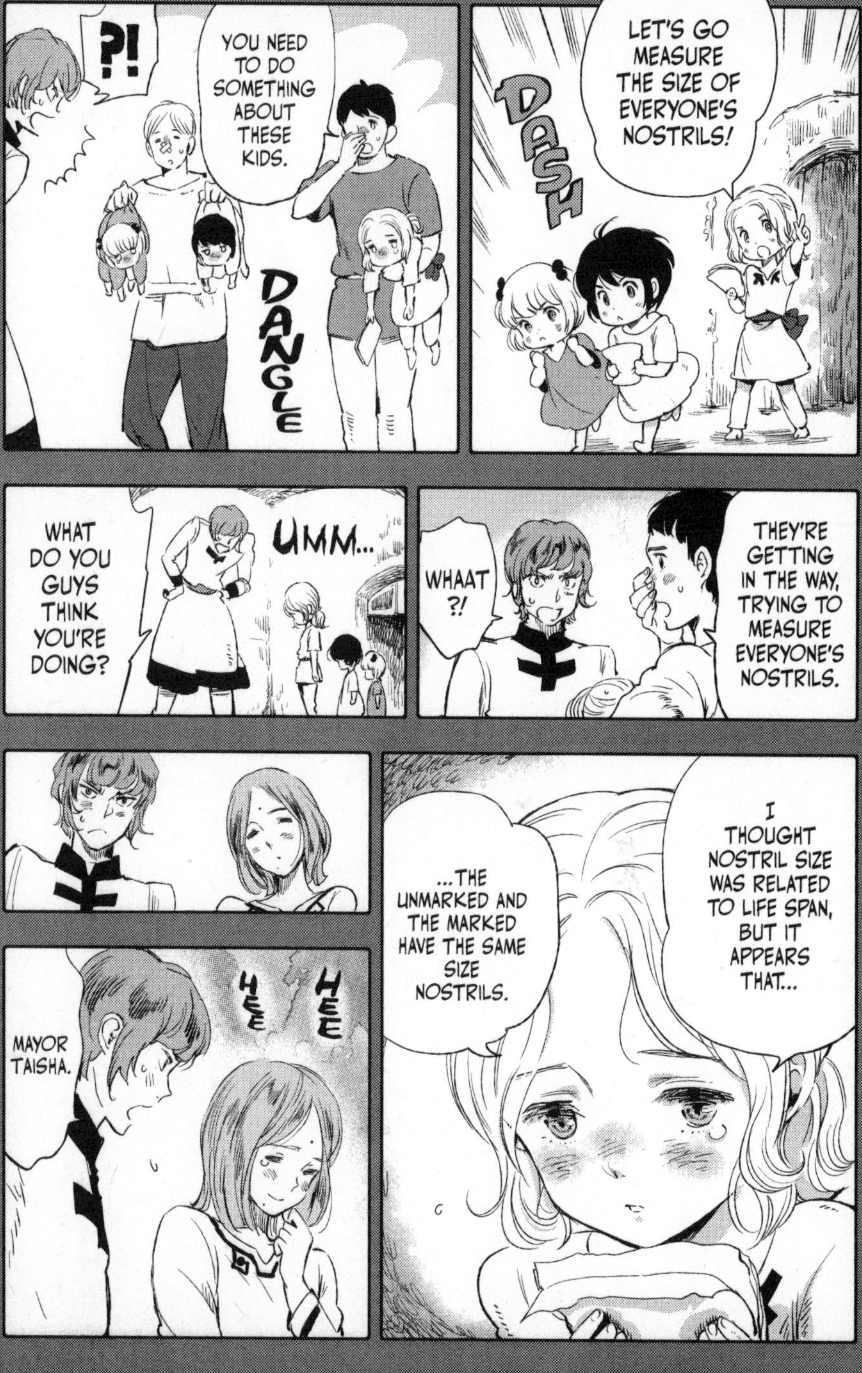
LET'S GO MEASURE THE SIZE OF EVERYONE'S NOSTRILS!
DASH
?!
YOU NEED TO DO SOMETHING ABOUT THESE KIDS.
DANGLE
THEY'RE GETTING IN THE WAY, TRYING TO MEASURE EVERYONE'S NOSTRILS.
WHAAT ?!
UMM...
WHAT DO YOU GUYS THINK YOU'RE DOING?
I THOUGHT NOSTRIL SIZE WAS RELATED TO LIFE SPAN, BUT IT APPEARS THAT...
...THE UNMARKED AND THE MARKED HAVE THE SAME SIZE NOSTRILS.
HEE HEE
MAYOR TAISHA.

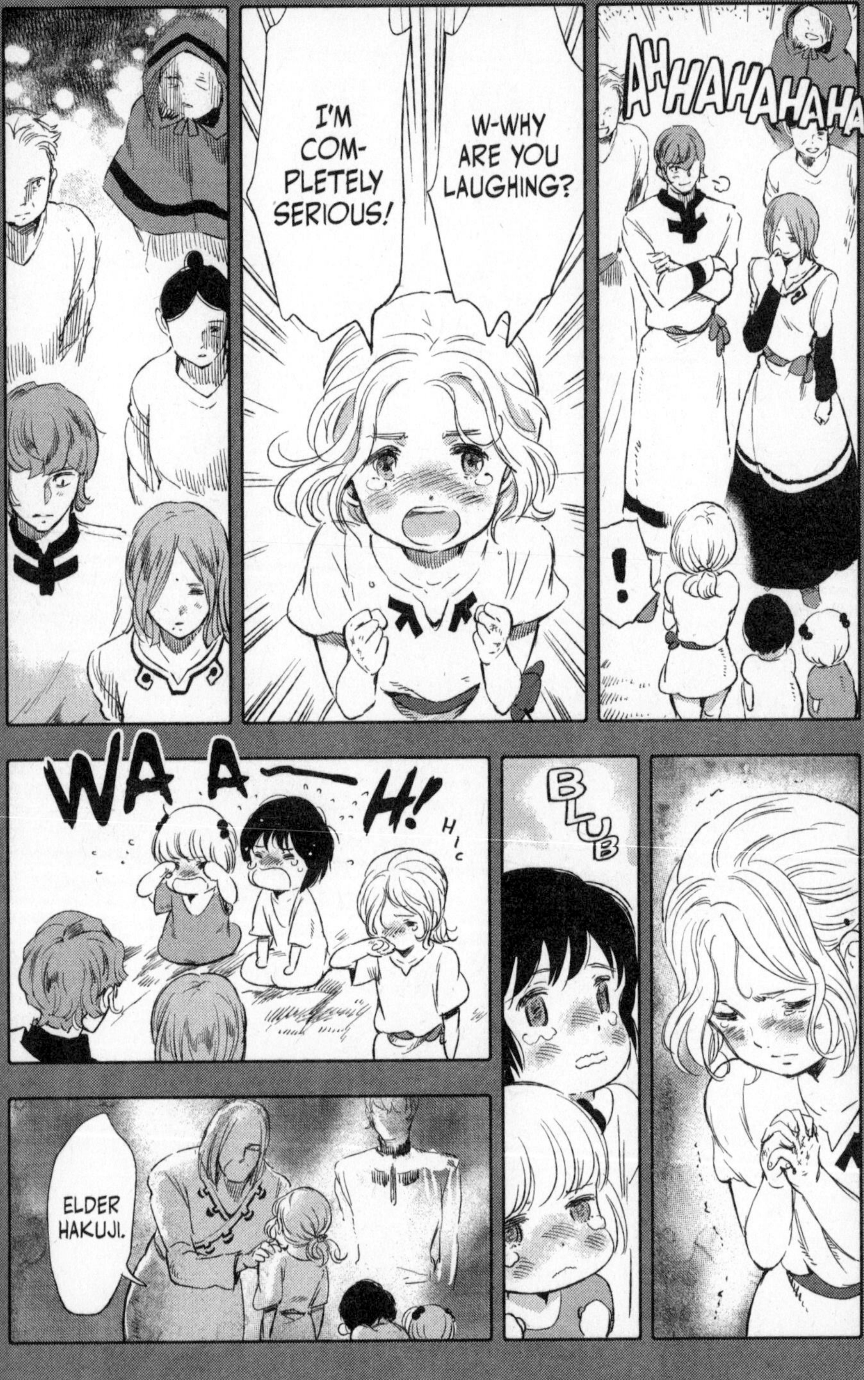
AHHAHAHAHAHA
!
W-WHY ARE YOU LAUGHING?
I'M COM-PLETELY SERIOUS!
BLUB
WA A—H!
HIC
ELDER HAKUJI.

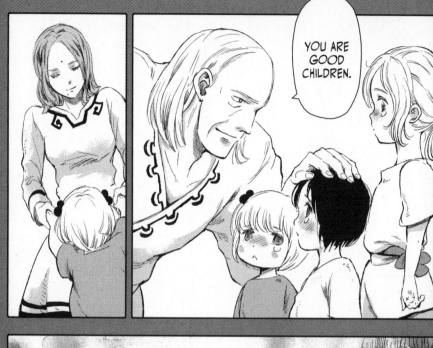

YOU ARE
GOOD
CHILDREN.

I'M
SORRY,
SUOU.

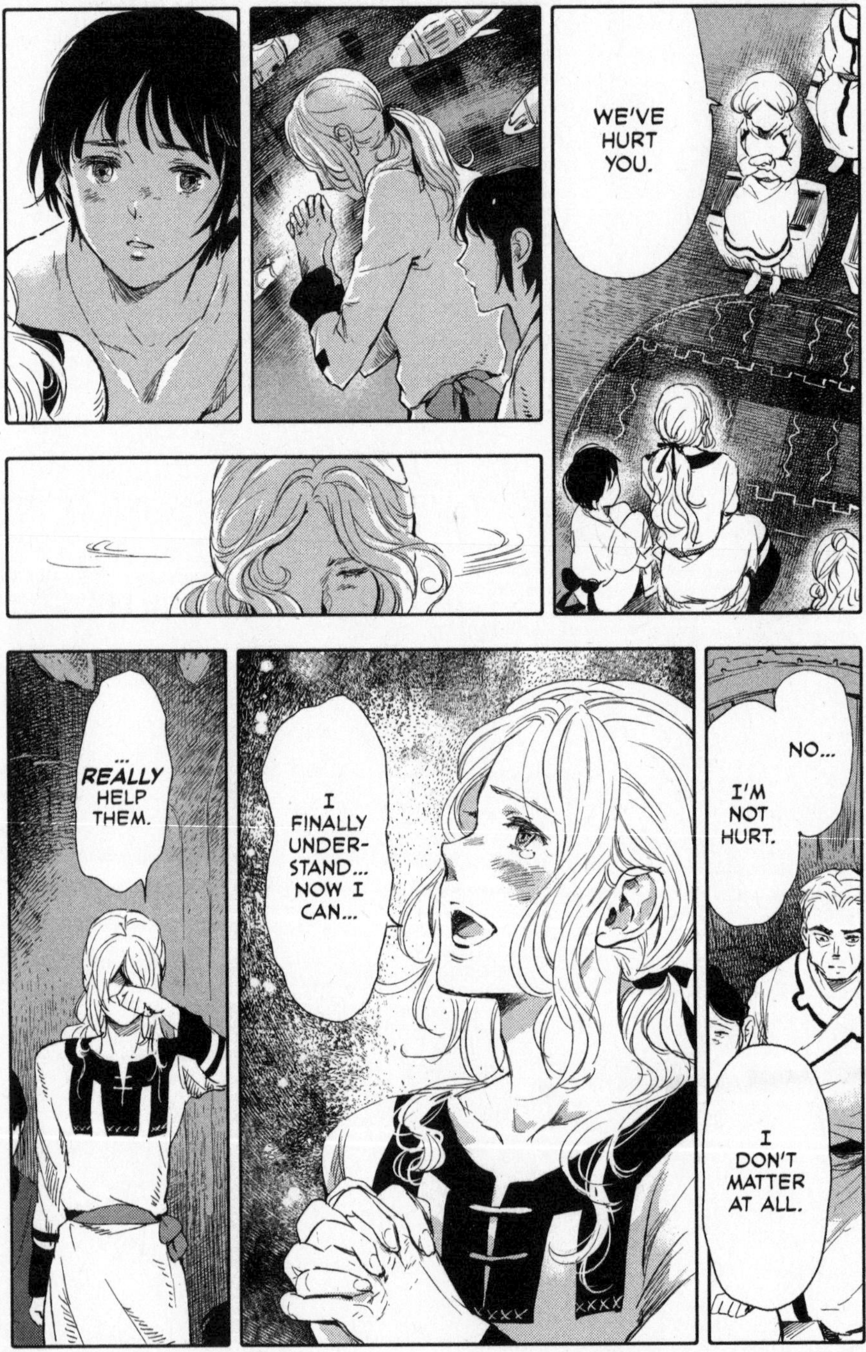
WE'VE HURT YOU.
NO...
I'M NOT HURT.
I DON'T MATTER AT ALL.
I FINALLY UNDER-STAND... NOW I CAN...
...REALLY HELP THEM.

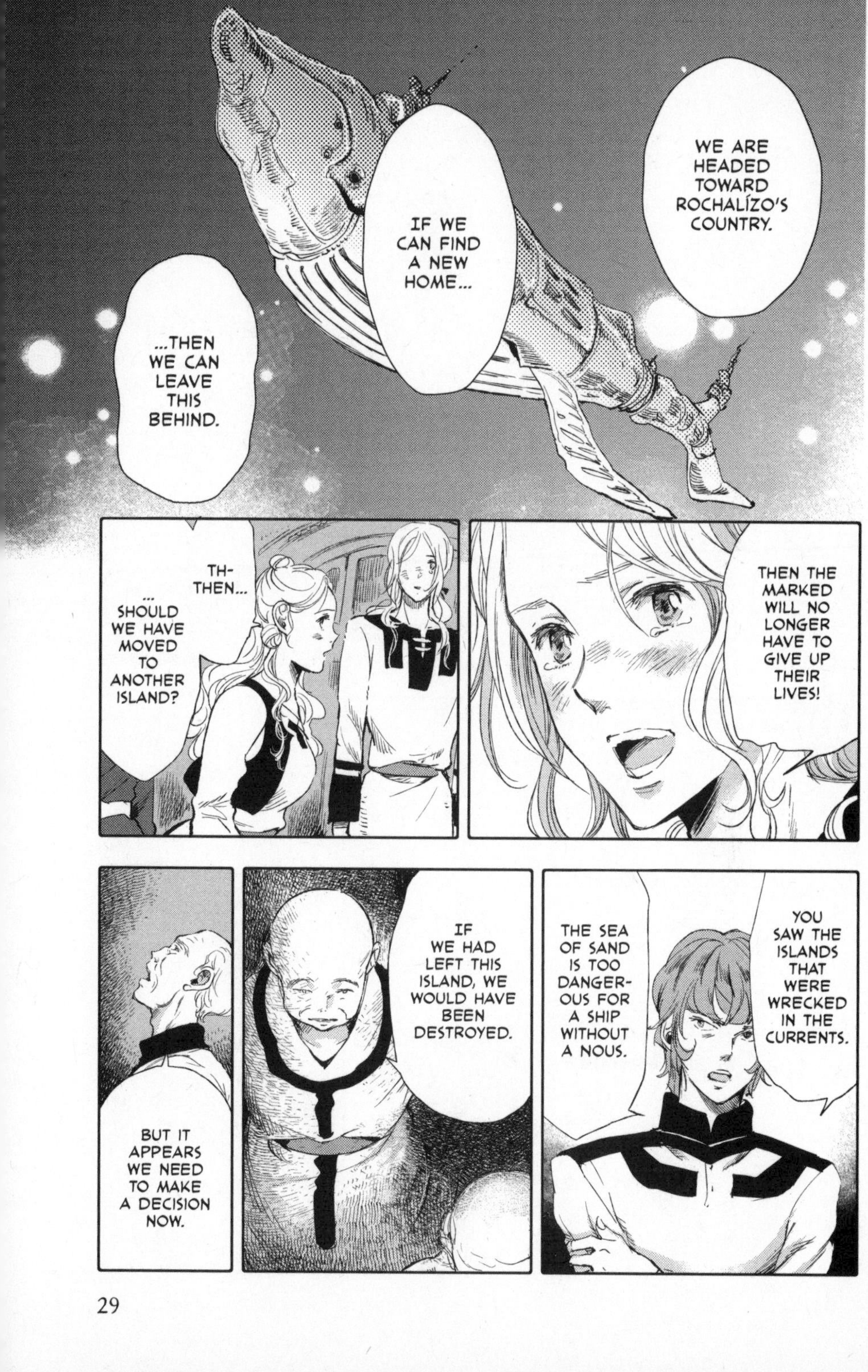
WE ARE HEADED TOWARD ROCHALÍZO'S COUNTRY.
IF WE CAN FIND A NEW HOME...
...THEN WE CAN LEAVE THIS BEHIND.
THEN THE MARKED WILL NO LONGER HAVE TO GIVE UP THEIR LIVES!
TH- THEN...
...SHOULD WE HAVE MOVED TO ANOTHER ISLAND?
YOU SAW THE ISLANDS THAT WERE WRECKED IN THE CURRENTS.
THE SEA OF SAND IS TOO DANGER-OUS FOR A SHIP WITHOUT A NOUS.
IF WE HAD LEFT THIS ISLAND, WE WOULD HAVE BEEN DESTROYED.
BUT IT APPEARS WE NEED TO MAKE A DECISION NOW.

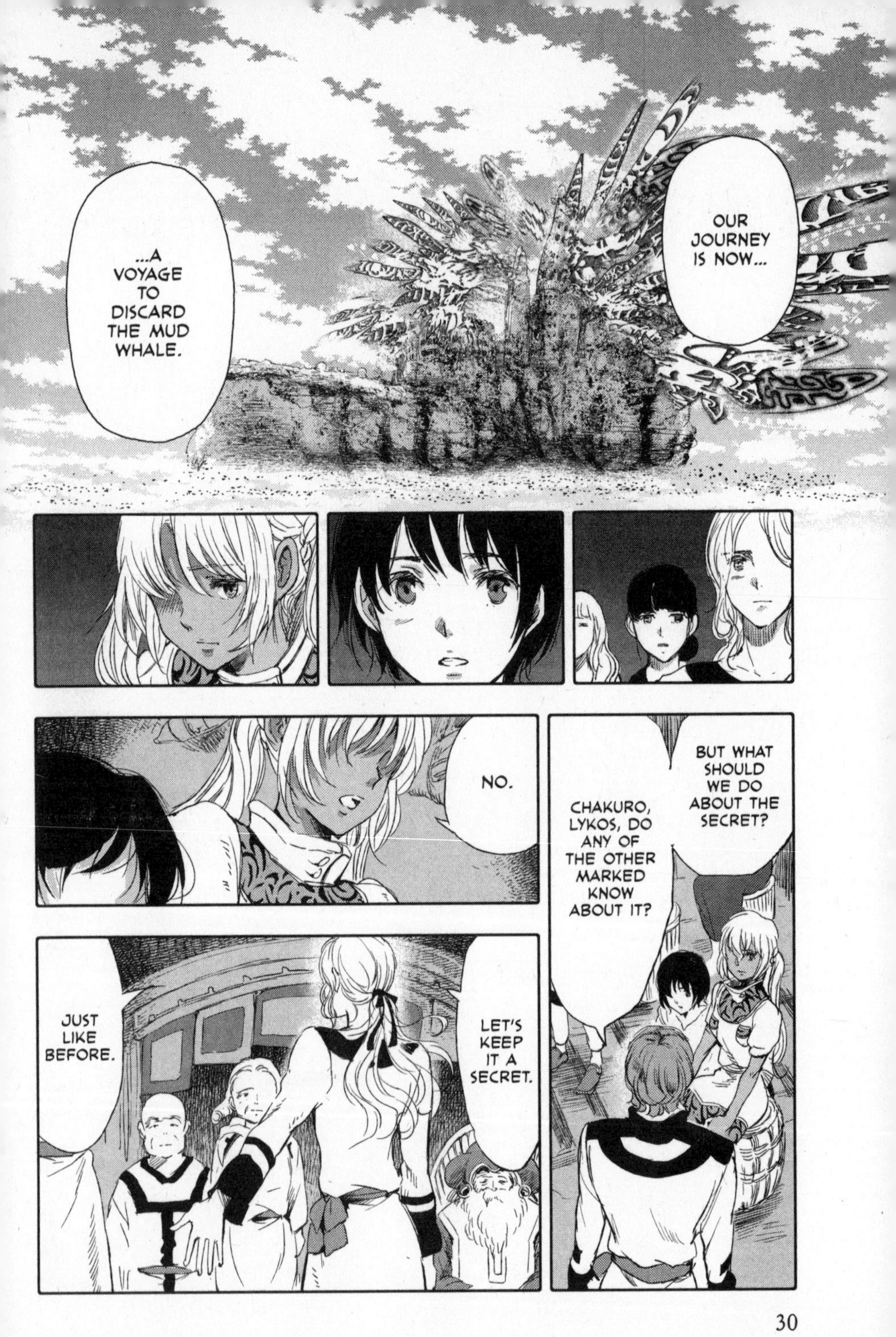
OUR JOURNEY IS NOW...
...A VOYAGE TO DISCARD THE MUD WHALE.
BUT WHAT SHOULD WE DO ABOUT THE SECRET?
CHAKURO, LYKOS, DO ANY OF THE OTHER MARKED KNOW ABOUT IT?
NO.
LET'S KEEP IT A SECRET.
JUST LIKE BEFORE.

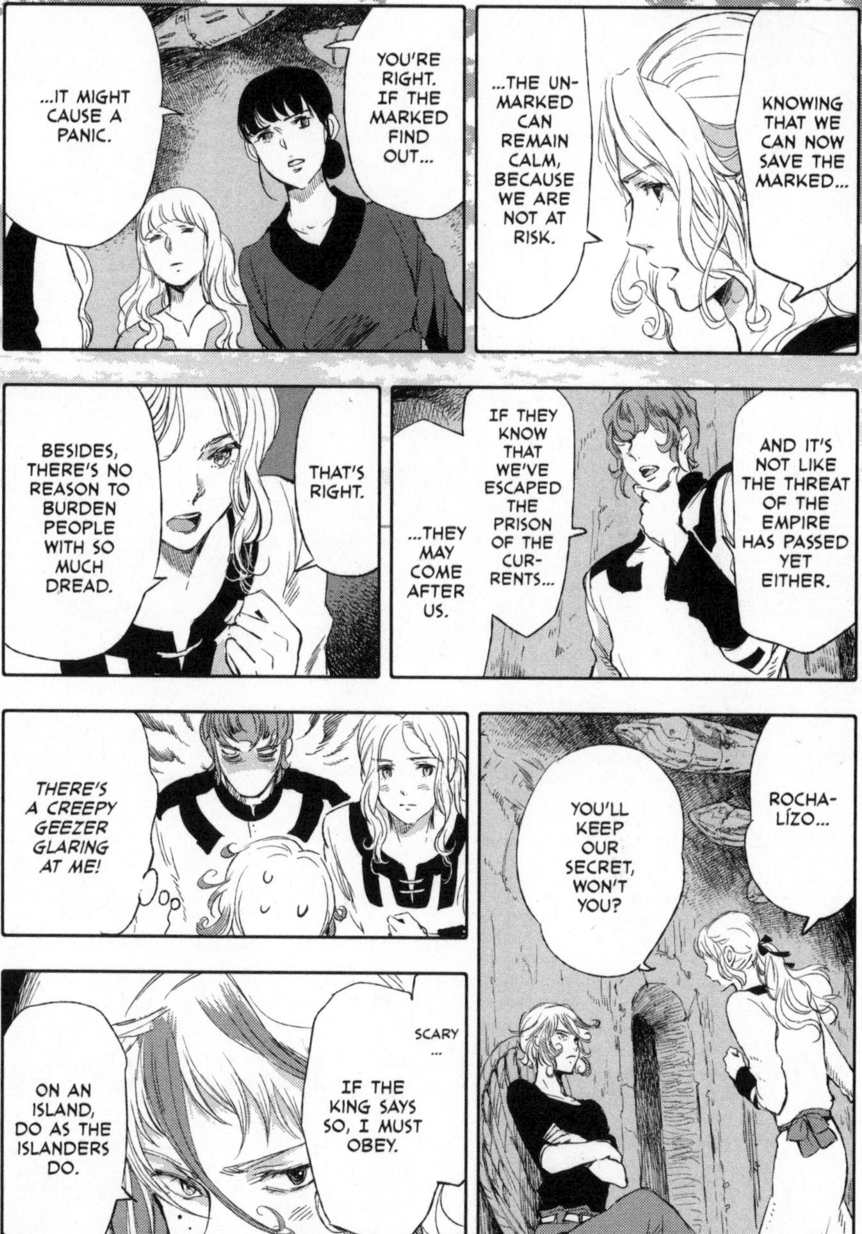
KNOWING THAT WE CAN NOW SAVE THE MARKED...
...THE UN-MARKED CAN REMAIN CALM, BECAUSE WE ARE NOT AT RISK.
YOU'RE RIGHT. IF THE MARKED FIND OUT...
...IT MIGHT CAUSE A PANIC.
AND IT'S NOT LIKE THE THREAT OF THE EMPIRE HAS PASSED YET EITHER.
IF THEY KNOW THAT WE'VE ESCAPED THE PRISON OF THE CUR-RENTS...
...THEY MAY COME AFTER US.
THAT'S RIGHT.
BESIDES, THERE'S NO REASON TO BURDEN PEOPLE WITH SO MUCH DREAD.
ROCHA-LÍZO...
YOU'LL KEEP OUR SECRET, WON'T YOU?
THERE'S A CREEPY GEEZER GLARING AT ME!
SCARY ...
IF THE KING SAYS SO, I MUST OBEY.
ON AN ISLAND, DO AS THE ISLANDERS DO.

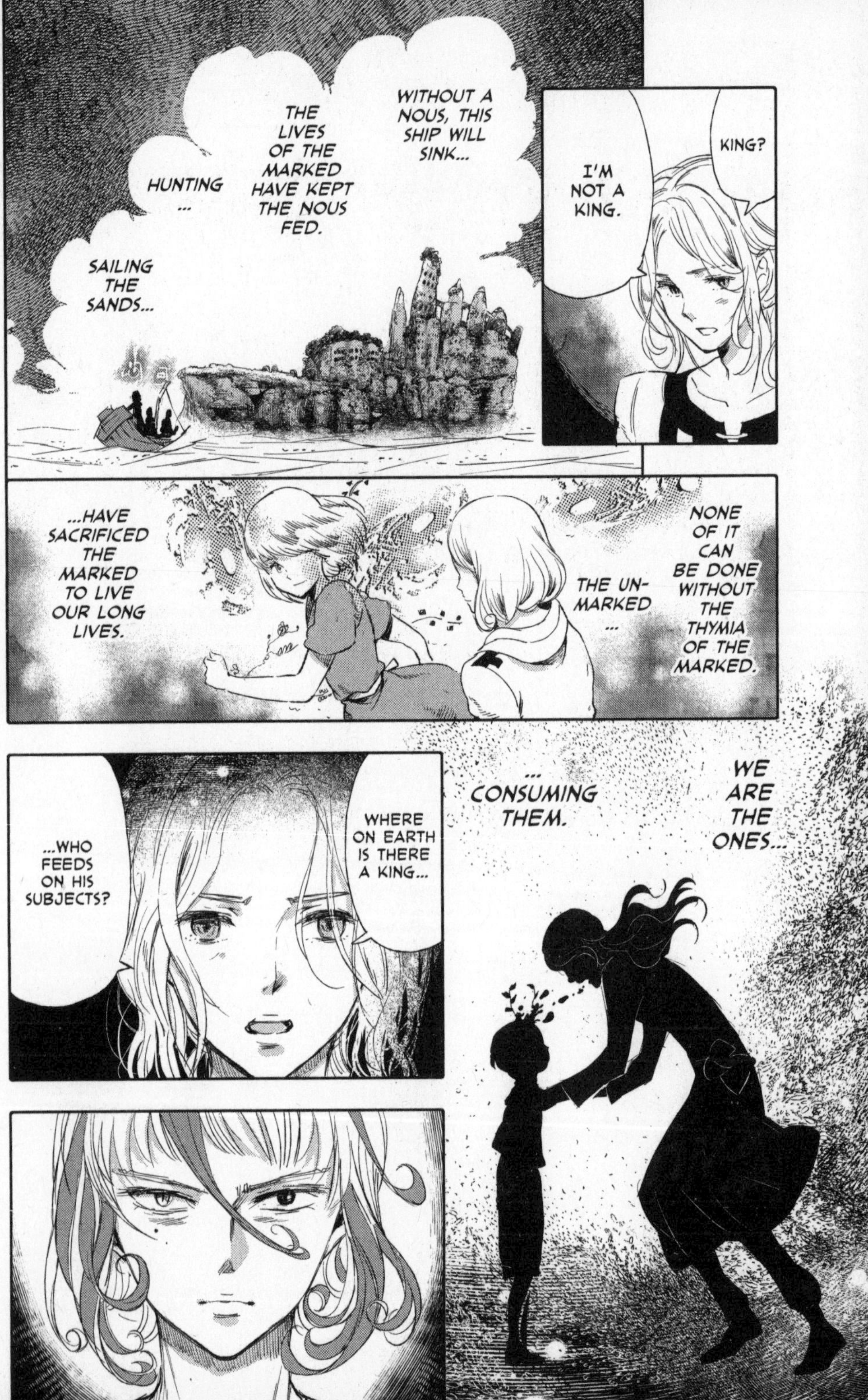
KING?
I'M NOT A KING.
WITHOUT A NOUS, THIS SHIP WILL SINK...
THE LIVES OF THE MARKED HAVE KEPT THE NOUS FED.
HUNTING...
SAILING THE SANDS...
NONE OF IT CAN BE DONE WITHOUT THE THYMIA OF THE MARKED.
THE UN-MARKED...
...HAVE SACRIFICED THE MARKED TO LIVE OUR LONG LIVES.
WE ARE THE ONES...
...CONSUMING THEM.
WHERE ON EARTH IS THERE A KING...
...WHO FEEDS ON HIS SUBJECTS?

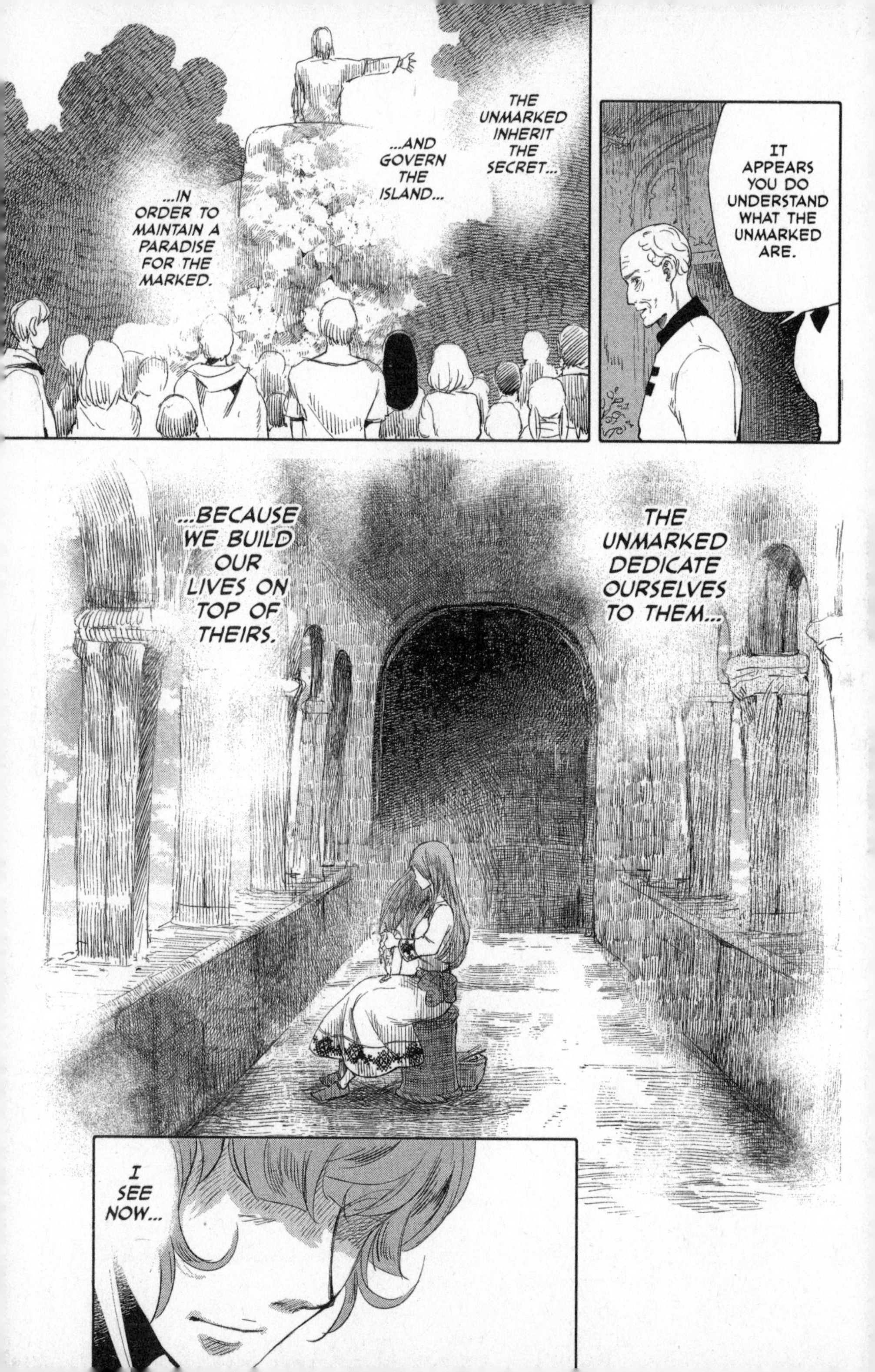
IT APPEARS YOU DO UNDERSTAND WHAT THE UNMARKED ARE.
THE UNMARKED INHERIT THE SECRET...
...AND GOVERN THE ISLAND...
...IN ORDER TO MAINTAIN A PARADISE FOR THE MARKED.
THE UNMARKED DEDICATE OURSELVES TO THEM...
...BECAUSE WE BUILD OUR LIVES ON TOP OF THEIRS.
I SEE NOW...

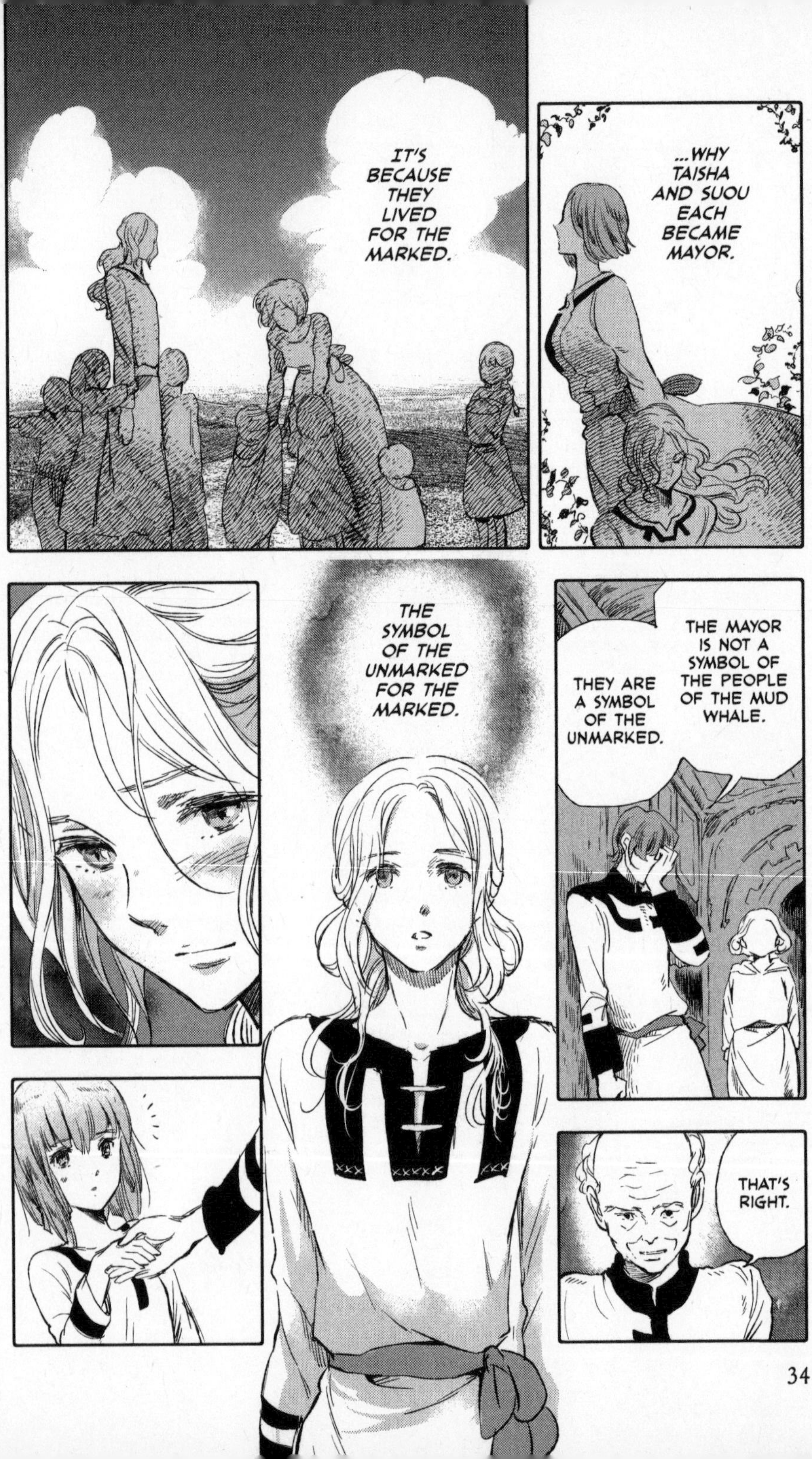
...WHY TAISHA AND SUOU EACH BECAME MAYOR.
IT'S BECAUSE THEY LIVED FOR THE MARKED.
THE MAYOR IS NOT A SYMBOL OF THE PEOPLE OF THE MUD WHALE.
THEY ARE A SYMBOL OF THE UNMARKED.
THAT'S RIGHT.
THE SYMBOL OF THE UNMARKED FOR THE MARKED.

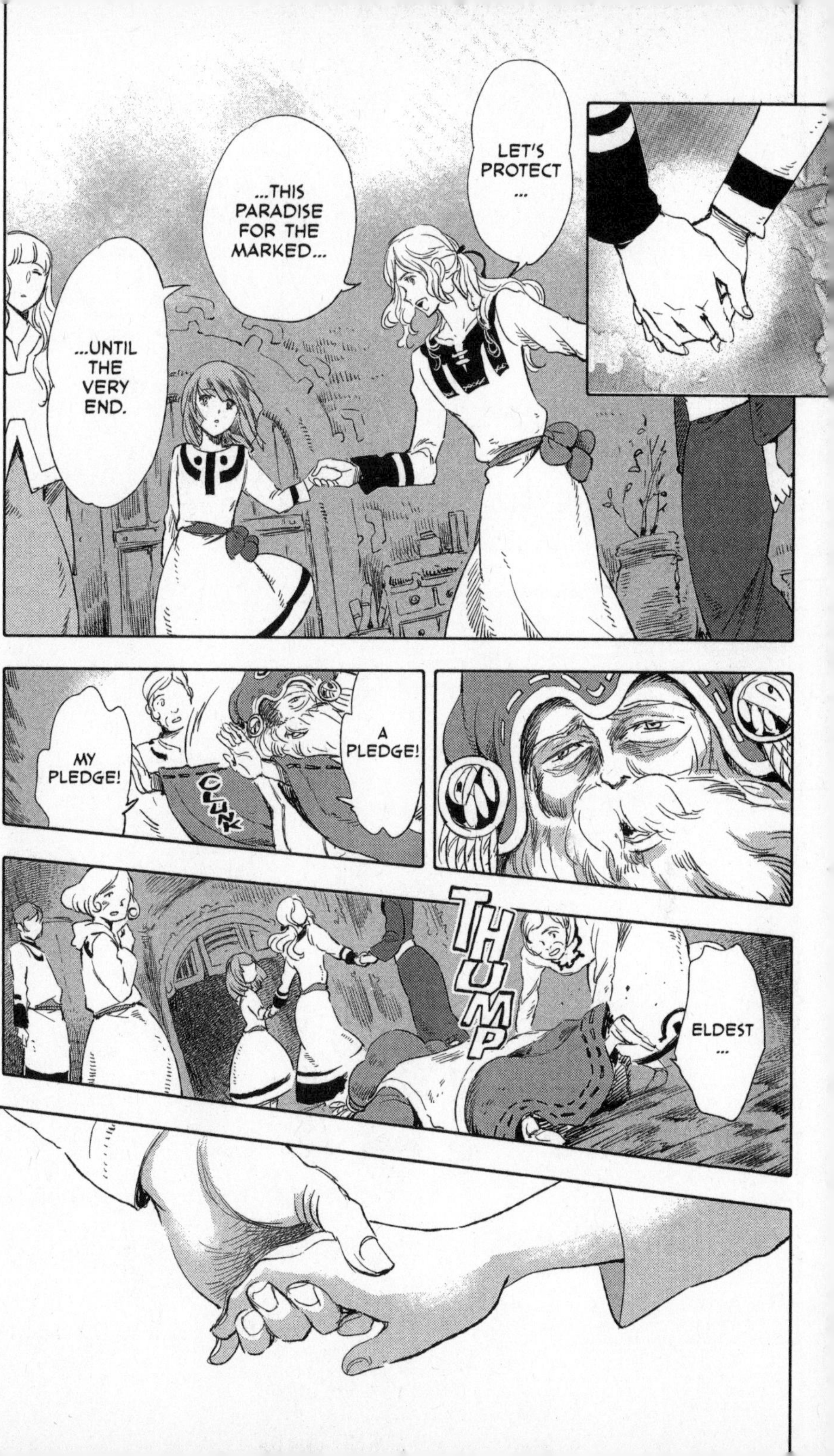
LET'S PROTECT ...
...THIS PARADISE FOR THE MARKED...
...UNTIL THE VERY END.
A PLEDGE!
CLUNK
MY PLEDGE!
ELDEST ...
THUMP

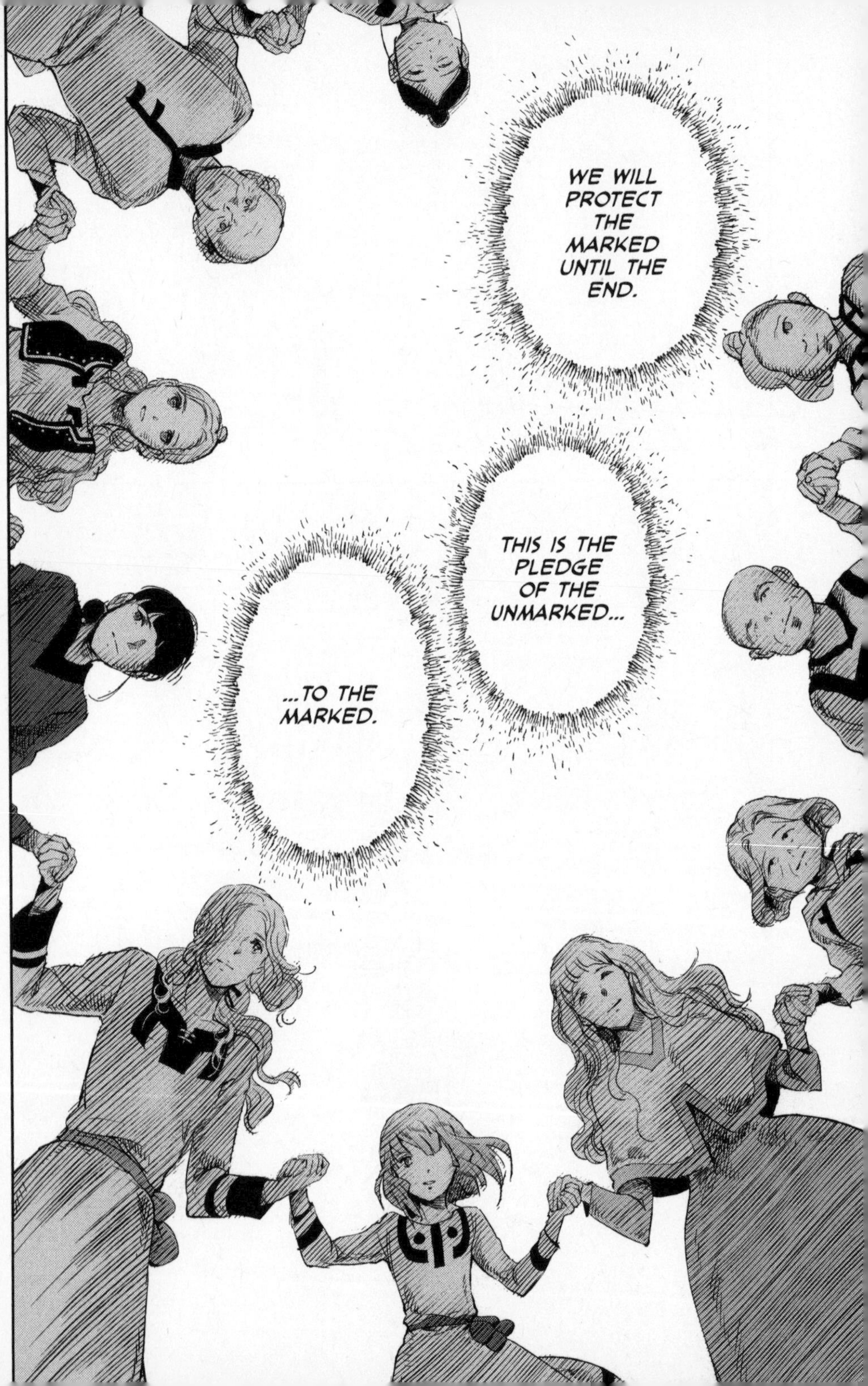
WE WILL PROTECT THE MARKED UNTIL THE END.
THIS IS THE PLEDGE OF THE UNMARKED...
...TO THE MARKED.

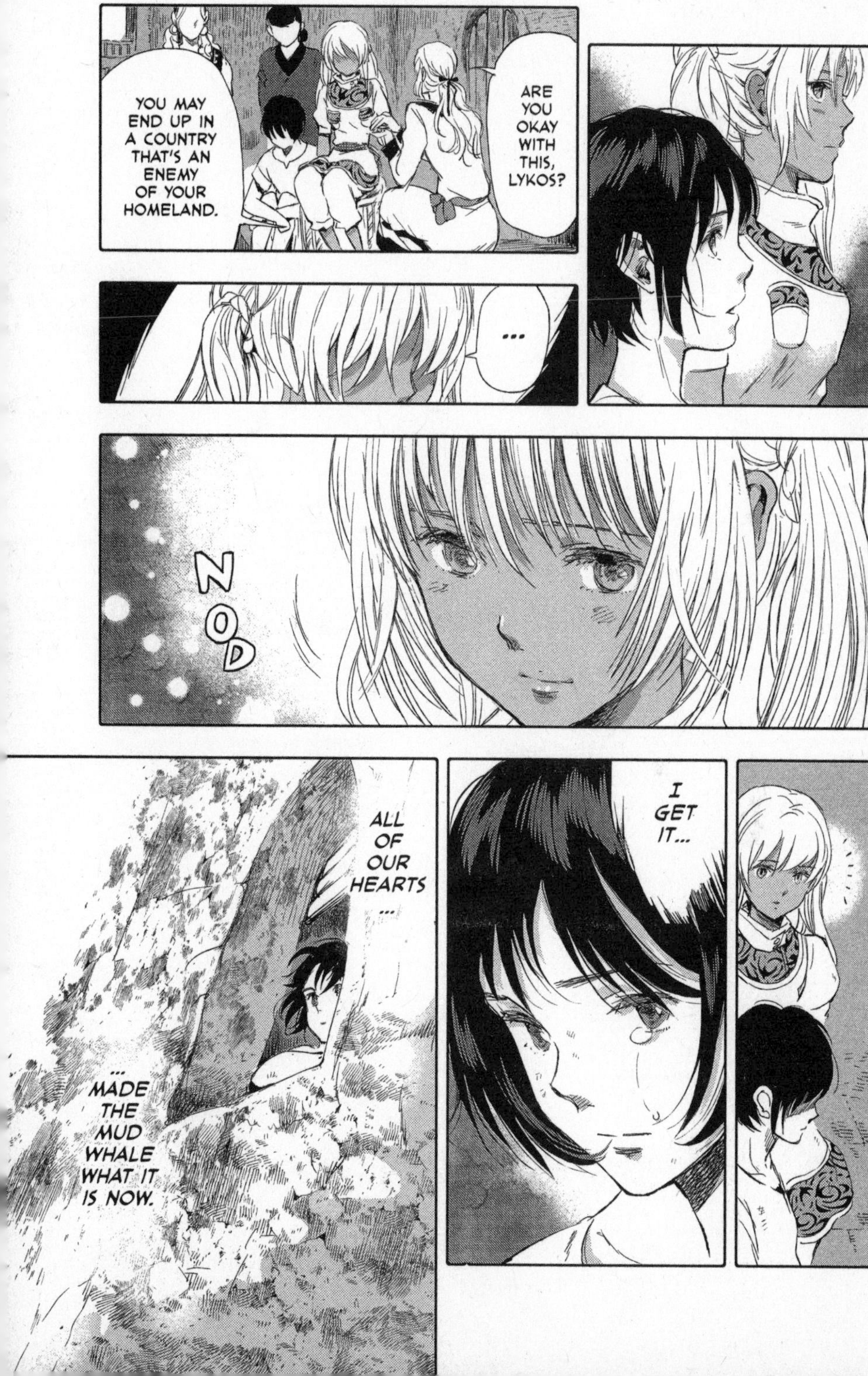
ARE YOU OKAY WITH THIS, LYKOS?
YOU MAY END UP IN A COUNTRY THAT'S AN ENEMY OF YOUR HOMELAND.
...
NOD
I GET IT...
ALL OF OUR HEARTS...
...MADE THE MUD WHALE WHAT IT IS NOW.

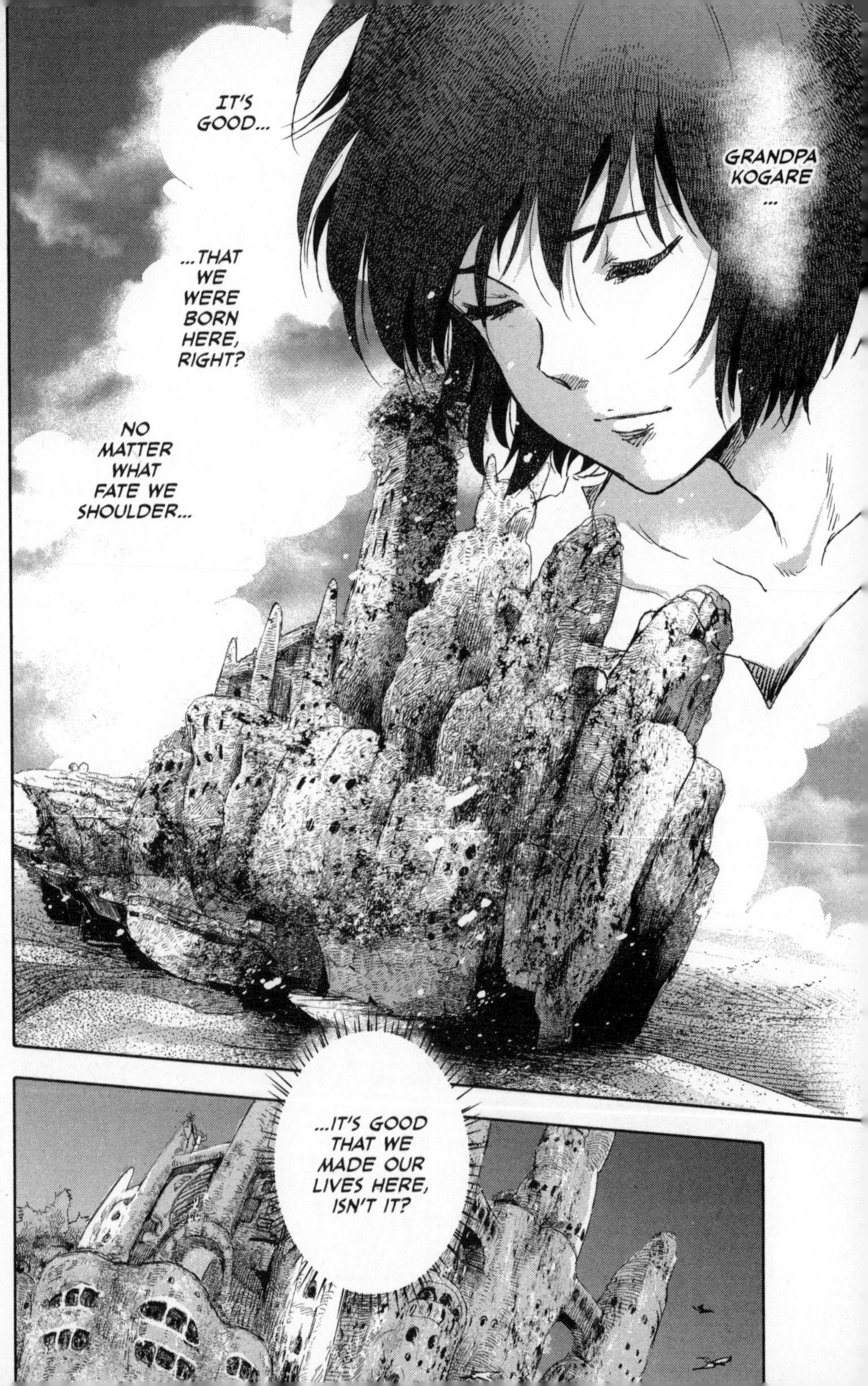
GRANDPA KOGARE...
IT'S GOOD...
...THAT WE WERE BORN HERE, RIGHT?
NO MATTER WHAT FATE WE SHOULDER...
...IT'S GOOD THAT WE MADE OUR LIVES HERE, ISN'T IT?

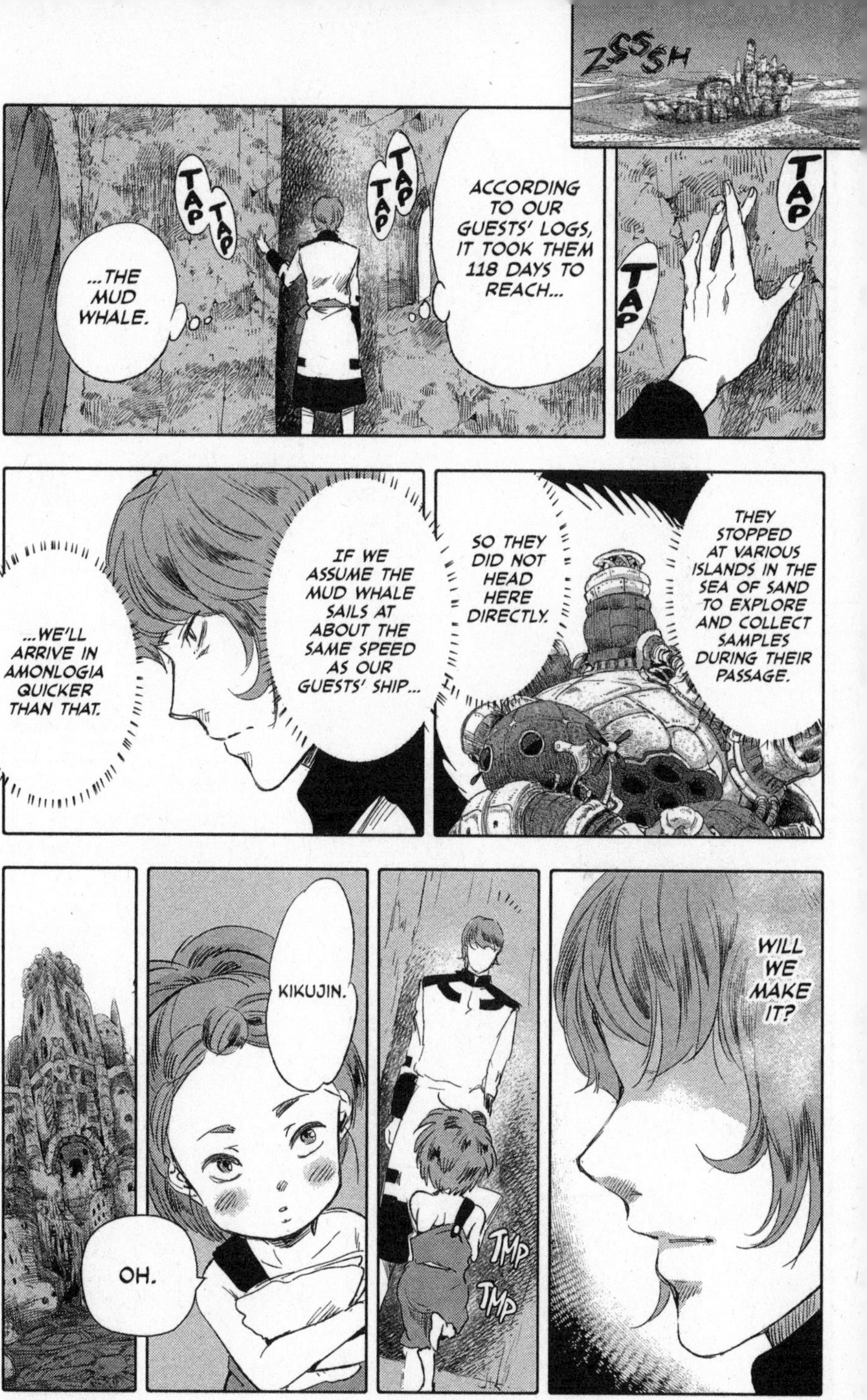
ZSSSH
TAP
TAP
ACCORDING TO OUR GUESTS' LOGS, IT TOOK THEM 118 DAYS TO REACH...
TAP TAP
TAP TAP
...THE MUD WHALE.
THEY STOPPED AT VARIOUS ISLANDS IN THE SEA OF SAND TO EXPLORE AND COLLECT SAMPLES DURING THEIR PASSAGE.
SO THEY DID NOT HEAD HERE DIRECTLY.
IF WE ASSUME THE MUD WHALE SAILS AT ABOUT THE SAME SPEED AS OUR GUESTS' SHIP...
...WE'LL ARRIVE IN AMONLOGIA QUICKER THAN THAT.
WILL WE MAKE IT?
TMP
TMP
KIKUJIN.
OH.

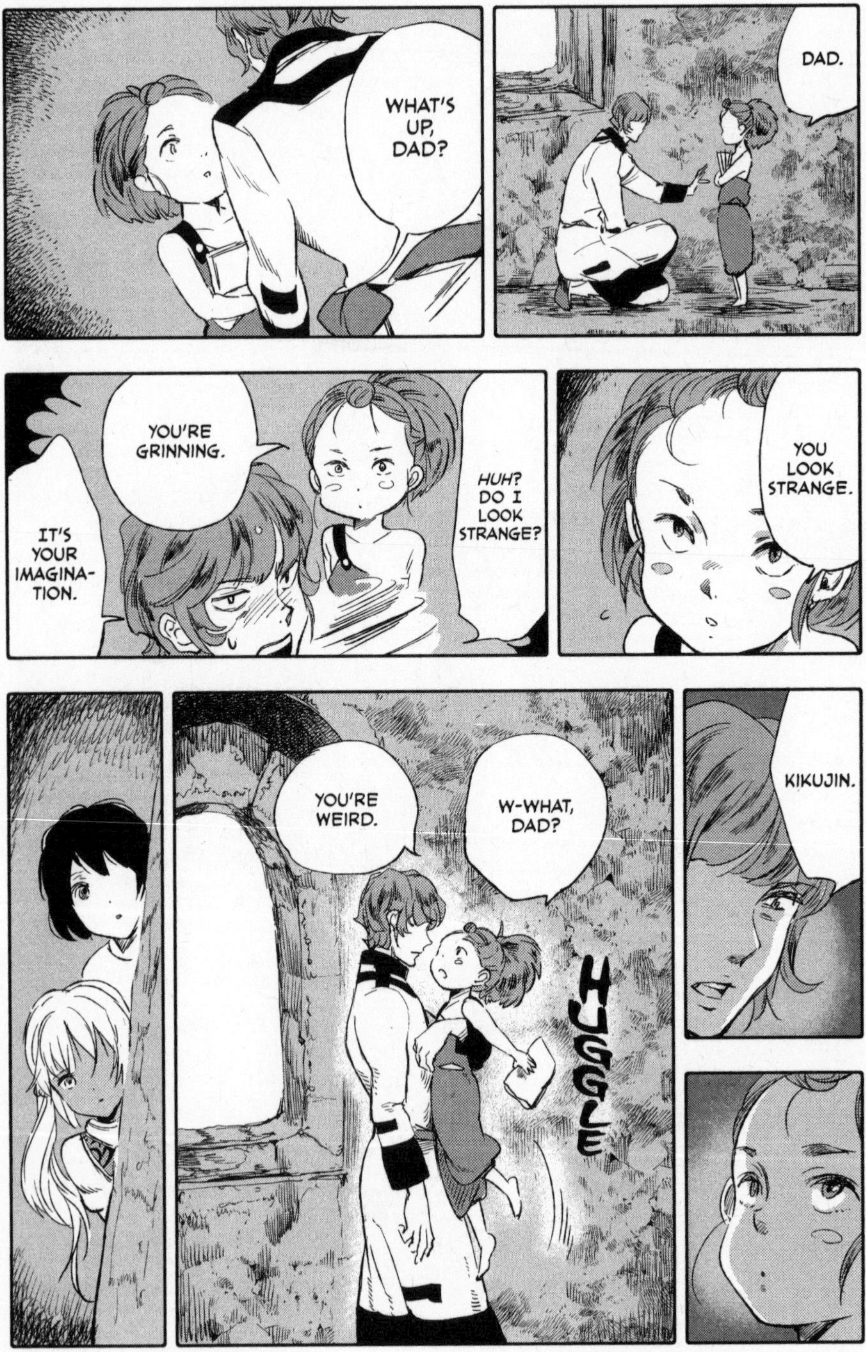
DAD.
WHAT'S UP, DAD?
YOU LOOK STRANGE.
HUH? DO I LOOK STRANGE?
YOU'RE GRINNING.
IT'S YOUR IMAGINATION.
KIKUJIN.
W-WHAT, DAD?
YOU'RE WEIRD.
HUGGLE

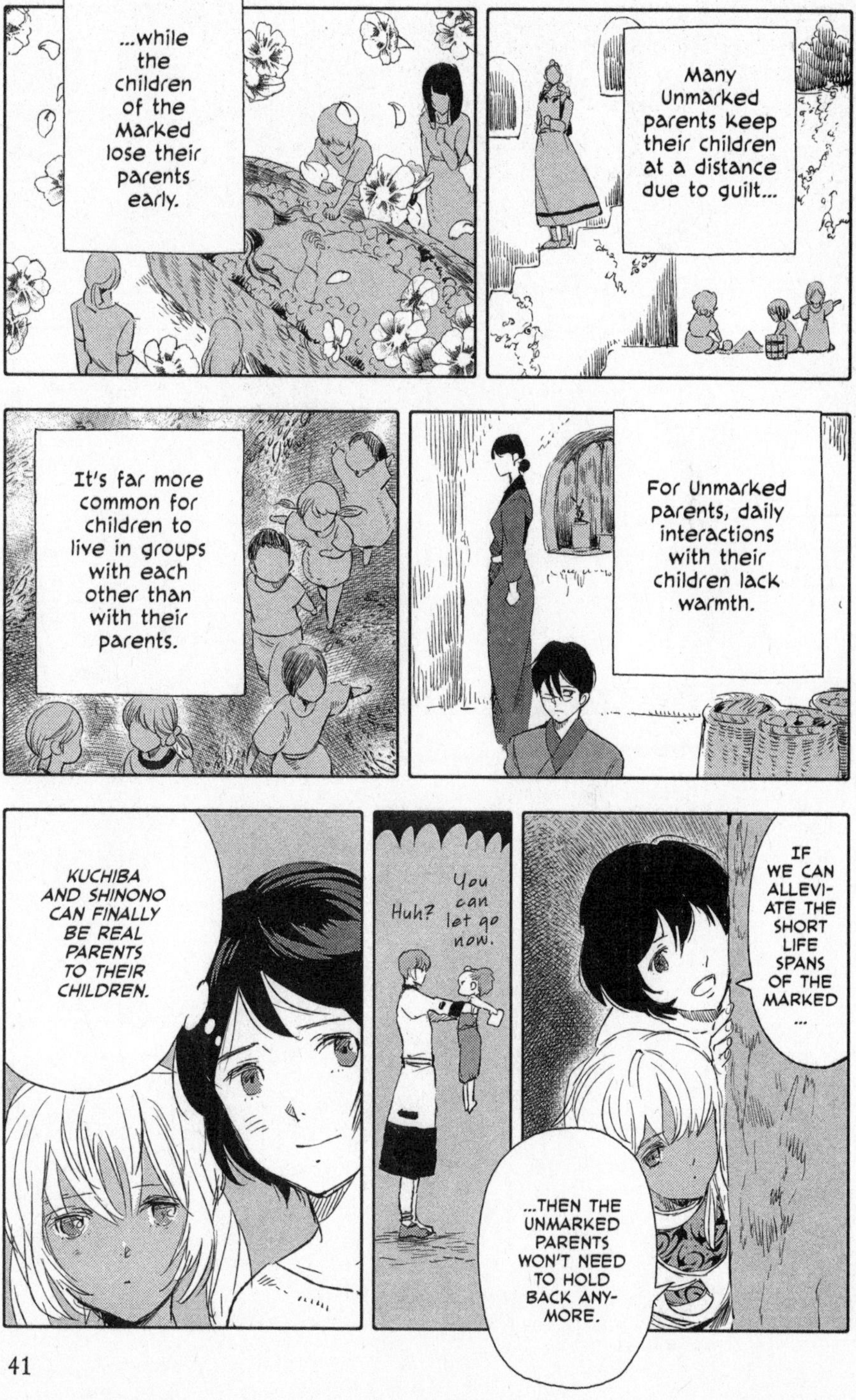

Many Unmarked parents keep their children at a distance due to guilt...
...while the children of the Marked lose their parents early.
For Unmarked parents, daily interactions with their children lack warmth.
It's far more common for children to live in groups with each other than with their parents.
IF WE CAN ALLEVIATE THE SHORT LIFE SPANS OF THE MARKED...
...THEN THE UNMARKED PARENTS WON'T NEED TO HOLD BACK ANYMORE.
You can let go now.
Huh?
KUCHIBA AND SHINONO CAN FINALLY BE REAL PARENTS TO THEIR CHILDREN.

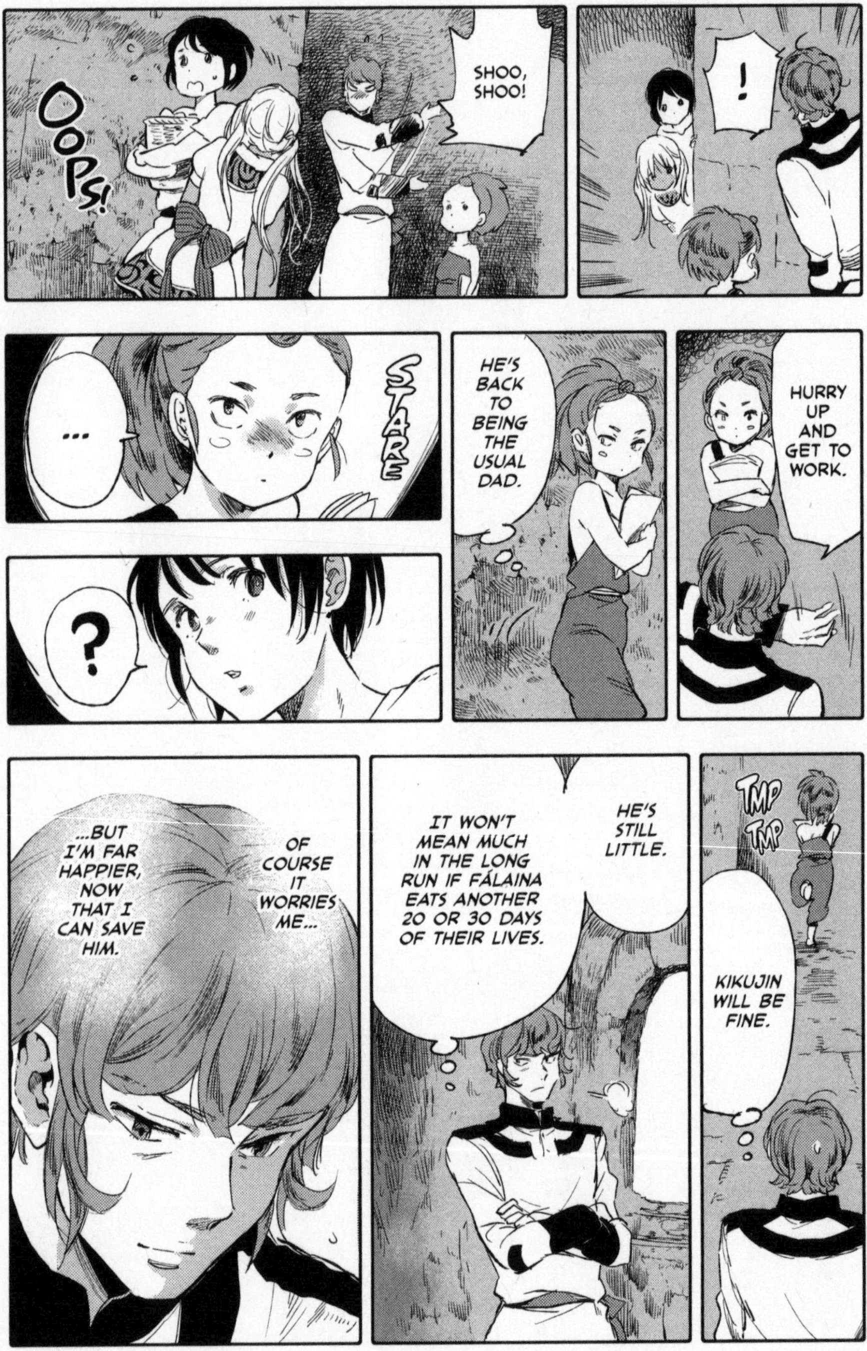
!
SHOO, SHOO!
OOPS!
HURRY UP AND GET TO WORK.
HE'S BACK TO BEING THE USUAL DAD.
STARE
...
?
TMP TMP
KIKUJIN WILL BE FINE.
HE'S STILL LITTLE.
IT WON'T MEAN MUCH IN THE LONG RUN IF FÁLAINA EATS ANOTHER 20 OR 30 DAYS OF THEIR LIVES.
OF COURSE IT WORRIES ME...
...BUT I'M FAR HAPPIER, NOW THAT I CAN SAVE HIM.

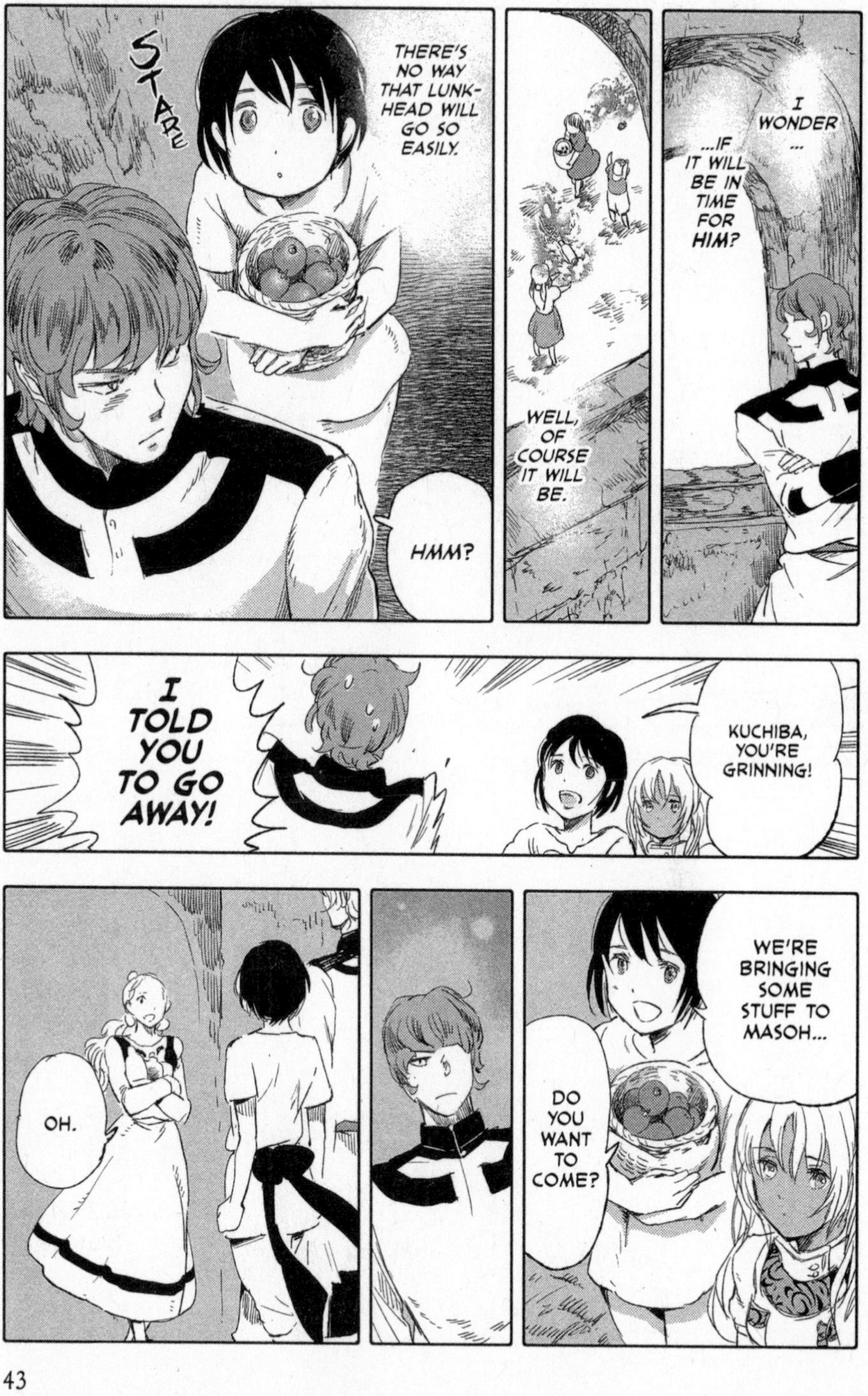
I WONDER ...
...IF IT WILL BE IN TIME FOR HIM?
WELL, OF COURSE IT WILL BE.
THERE'S NO WAY THAT LUNK-HEAD WILL GO SO EASILY.
STARE
HMM?
KUCHIBA, YOU'RE GRINNING!
I TOLD YOU TO GO AWAY!
WE'RE BRINGING SOME STUFF TO MASOH...
DO YOU WANT TO COME?
OH.

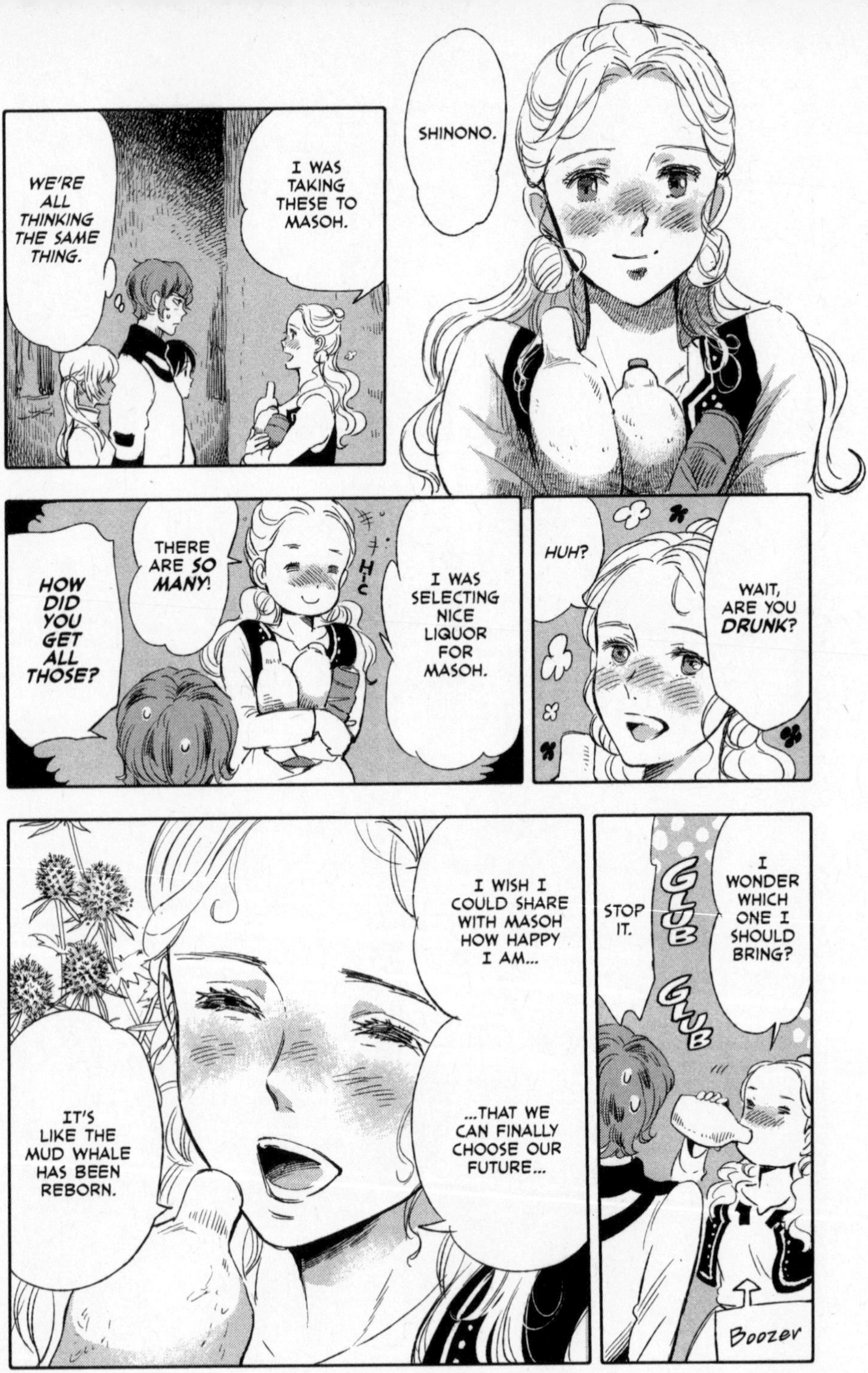
SHINONO.
I WAS TAKING THESE TO MASOH.
WE'RE ALL THINKING THE SAME THING.
HUH?
WAIT, ARE YOU DRUNK?
I WAS SELECTING NICE LIQUOR FOR MASOH.
HIC
THERE ARE SO MANY!
HOW DID YOU GET ALL THOSE?
I WONDER WHICH ONE I SHOULD BRING?
GLUB
GLUB
STOP IT.
Boozer
I WISH I COULD SHARE WITH MASOH HOW HAPPY I AM...
...THAT WE CAN FINALLY CHOOSE OUR FUTURE...
IT'S LIKE THE MUD WHALE HAS BEEN REBORN.

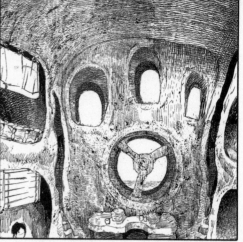

IT'S GETTING HARDER TO WALK.
IT LOOKS LIKE THE MUD WHALE HAS ESCAPED THE CURRENT...
...BUT I'M GRADUALLY LOSING MY FREEDOM.
I WONDER IF IT'S PUNISHMENT FOR KILLING THAT GIRL?
OR MAYBE IT CAN'T BE HELPED, IF WE'RE CRIMINALS.
I GUESS I'LL HAVE A LOOK AROUND ...
...WHILE I CAN STILL WALK.
SKWIK
THAT'S ENOUGH.

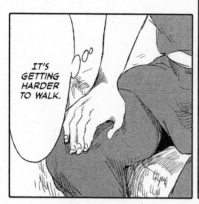

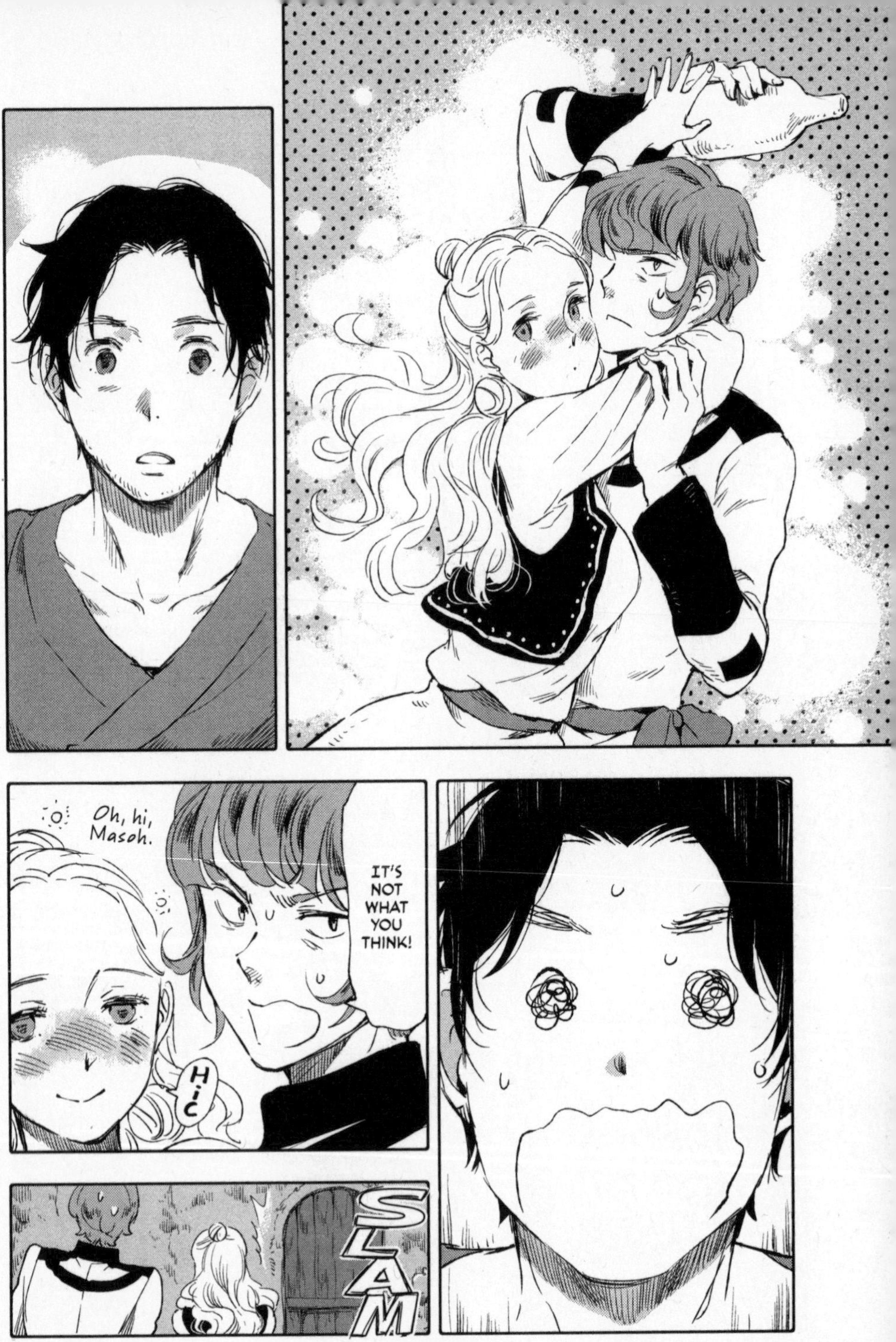
IT'S NOT WHAT YOU THINK!
Oh, hi, Masoh.
Hic
SLAM

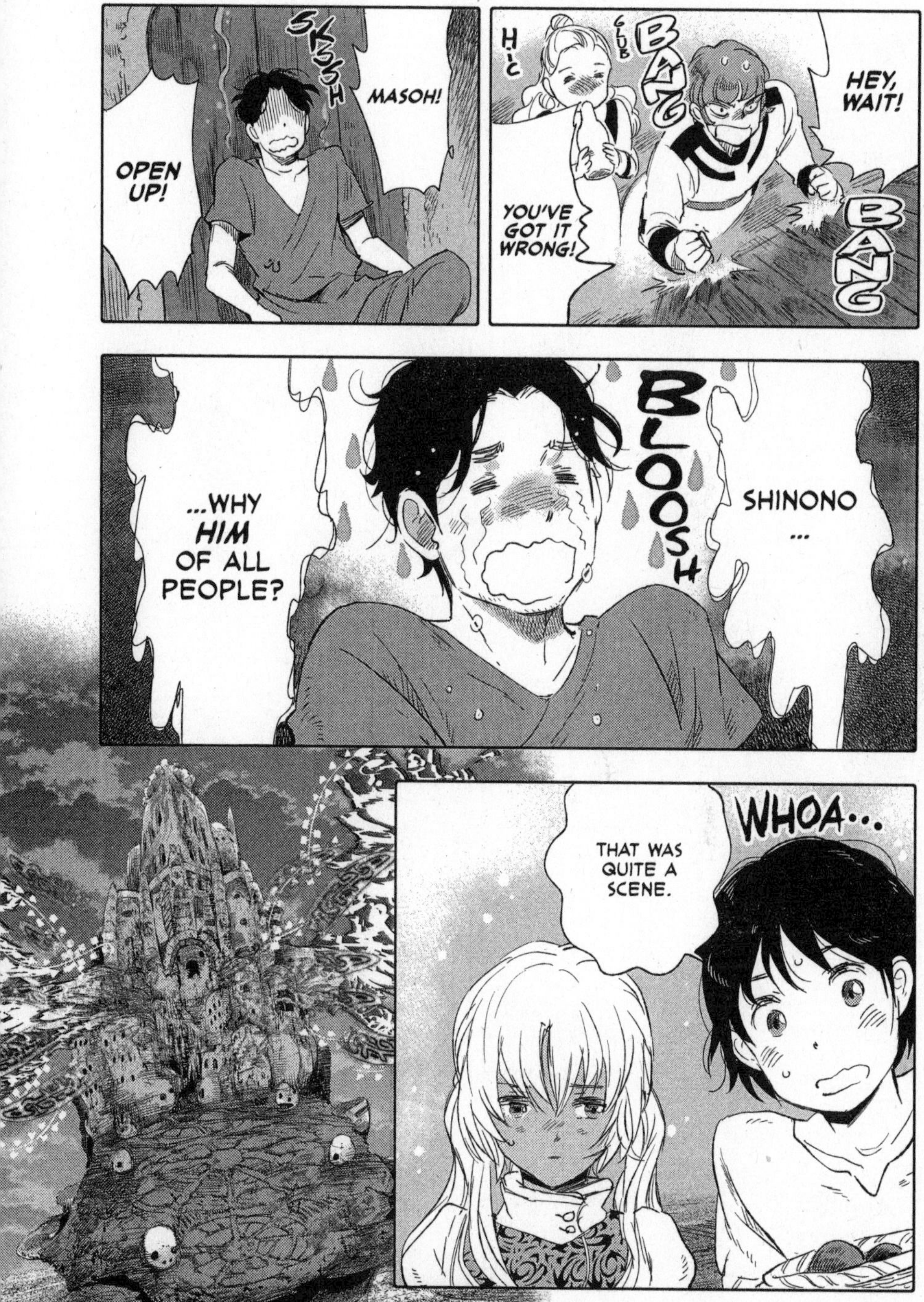
HEY, WAIT!
BANG BANG
BANG
GLUB
HIC
YOU'VE GOT IT WRONG!
MASOH!
SKSSH
OPEN UP!
SHINONO ...
BLOOSH
...WHY *HIM* OF ALL PEOPLE?
WHOA...
THAT WAS QUITE A SCENE.

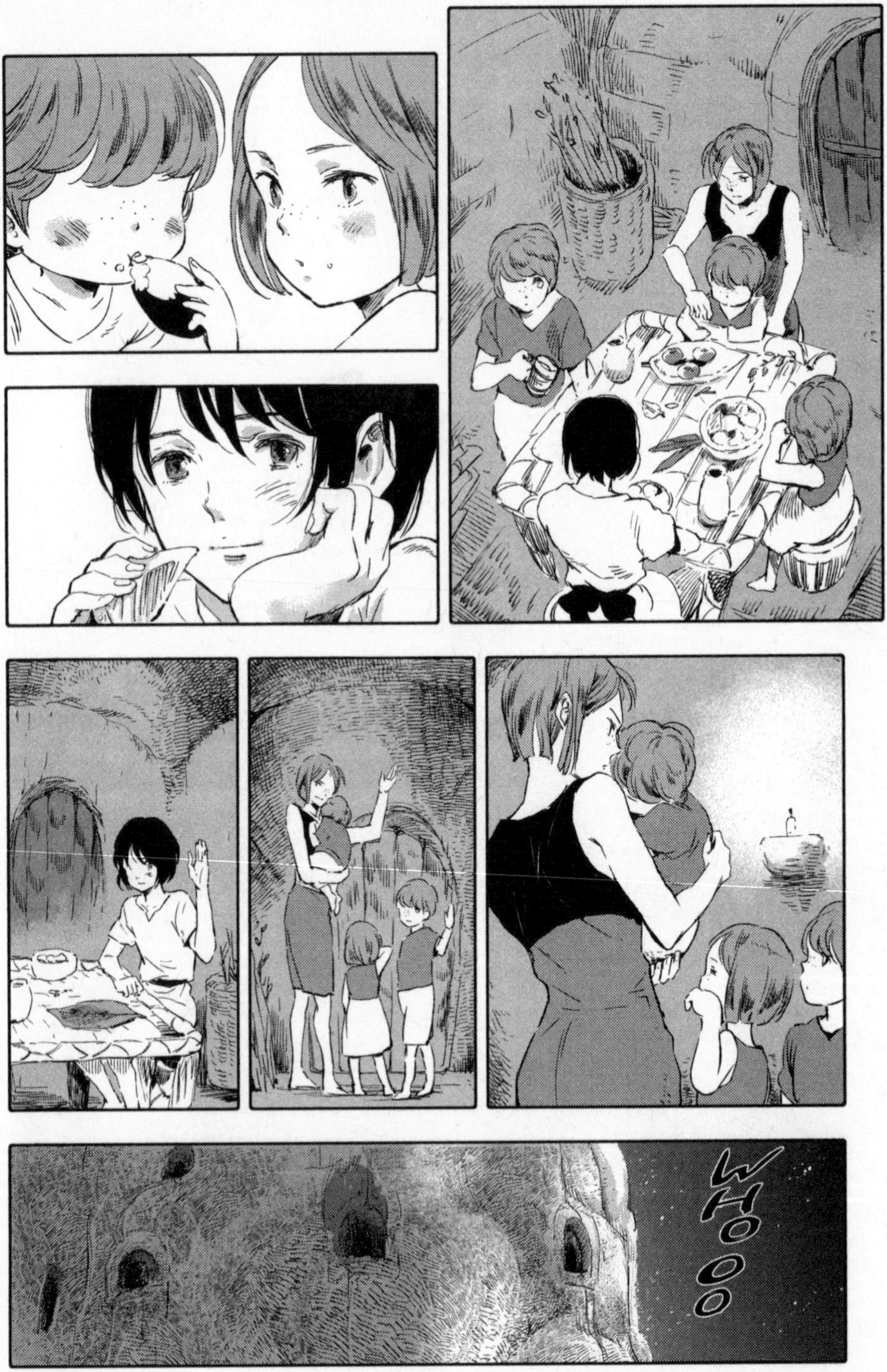
WHOOOO

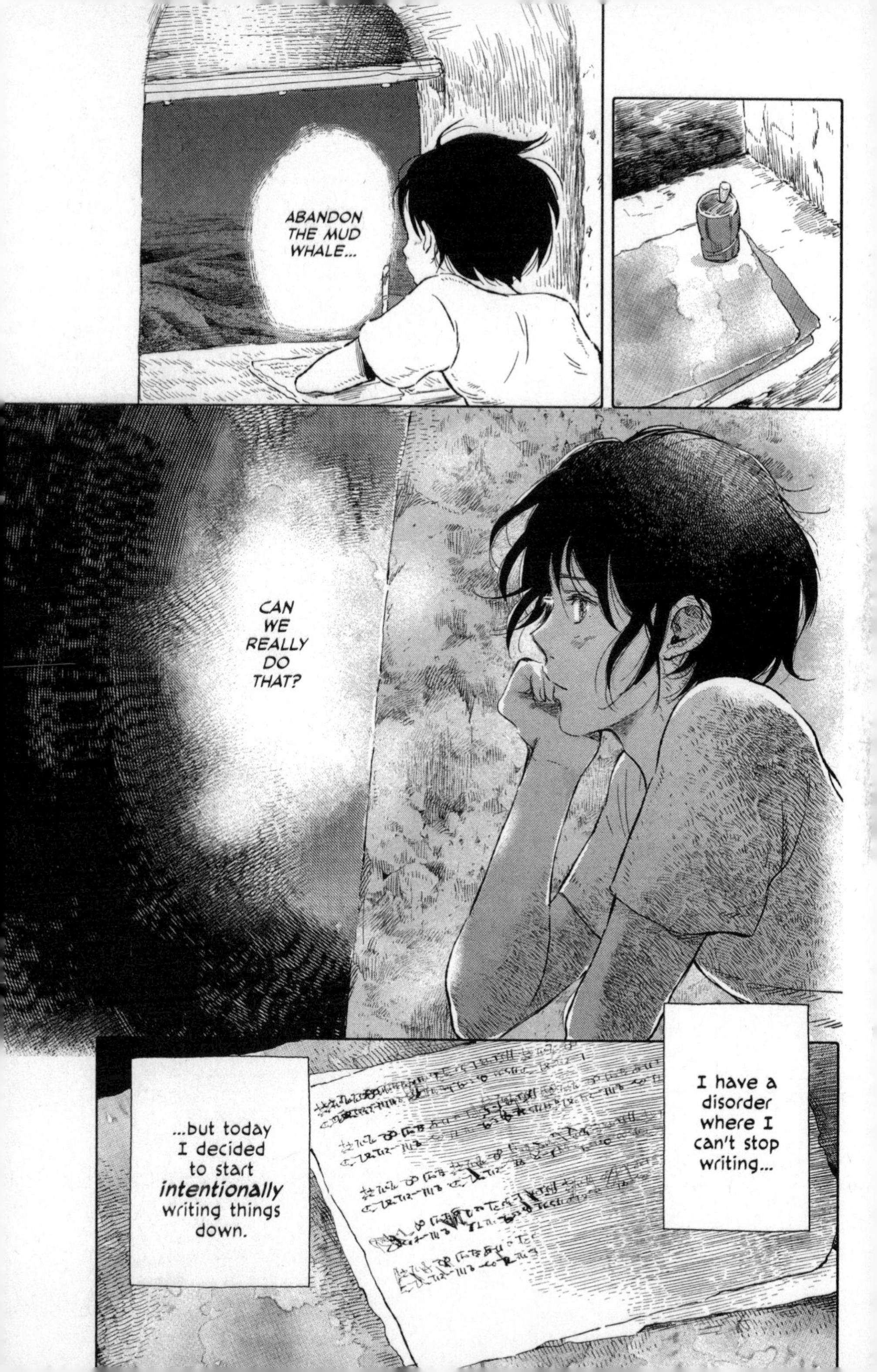
ABANDON THE MUD WHALE...
CAN WE REALLY DO THAT?
I have a disorder where I can't stop writing...
...but today I decided to start *intentionally* writing things down.

That's why...

One day I want someone to read this record of the Mud Whale and its people...

A LADDER... OF *LIGHT*?

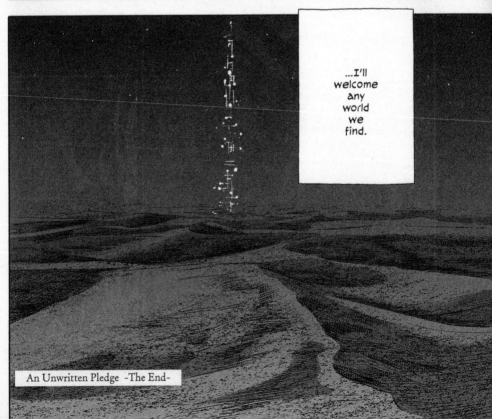

...I'll welcome any world we find.

An Unwritten Pledge -The End-

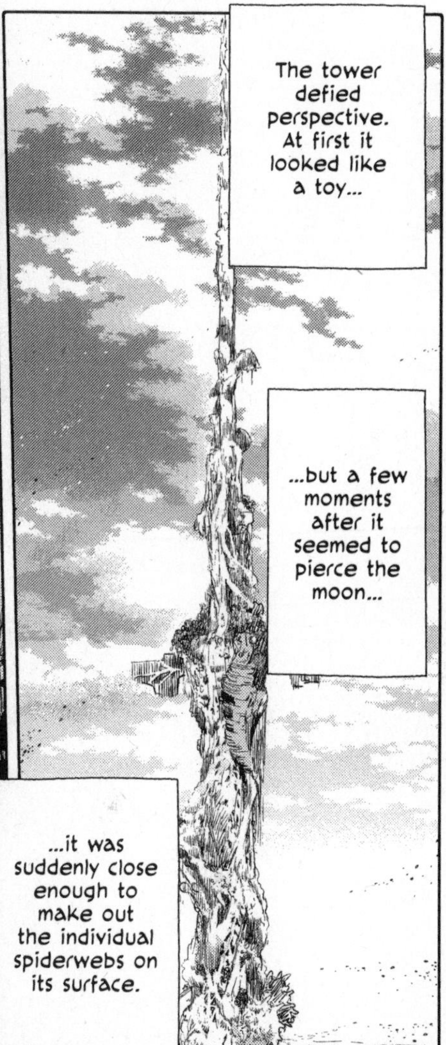
The tower defied perspective. At first it looked like a toy...
...but a few moments after it seemed to pierce the moon...
...it was suddenly close enough to make out the individual spiderwebs on its surface.

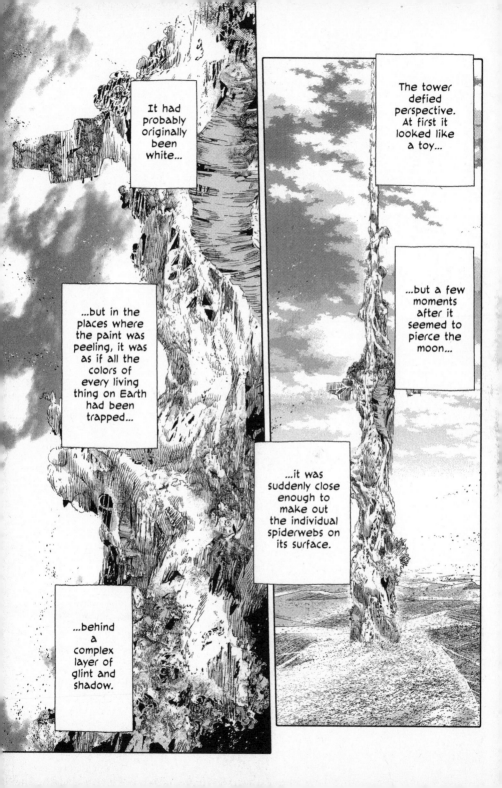

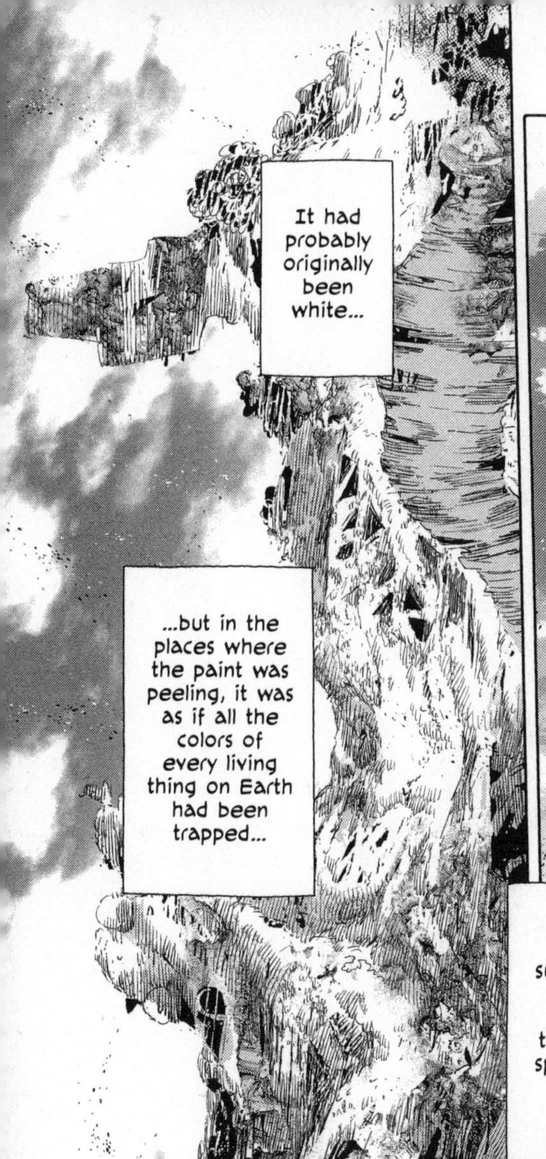
It had probably originally been white...
...but in the places where the paint was peeling, it was as if all the colors of every living thing on Earth had been trapped...
...behind a complex layer of glint and shadow.

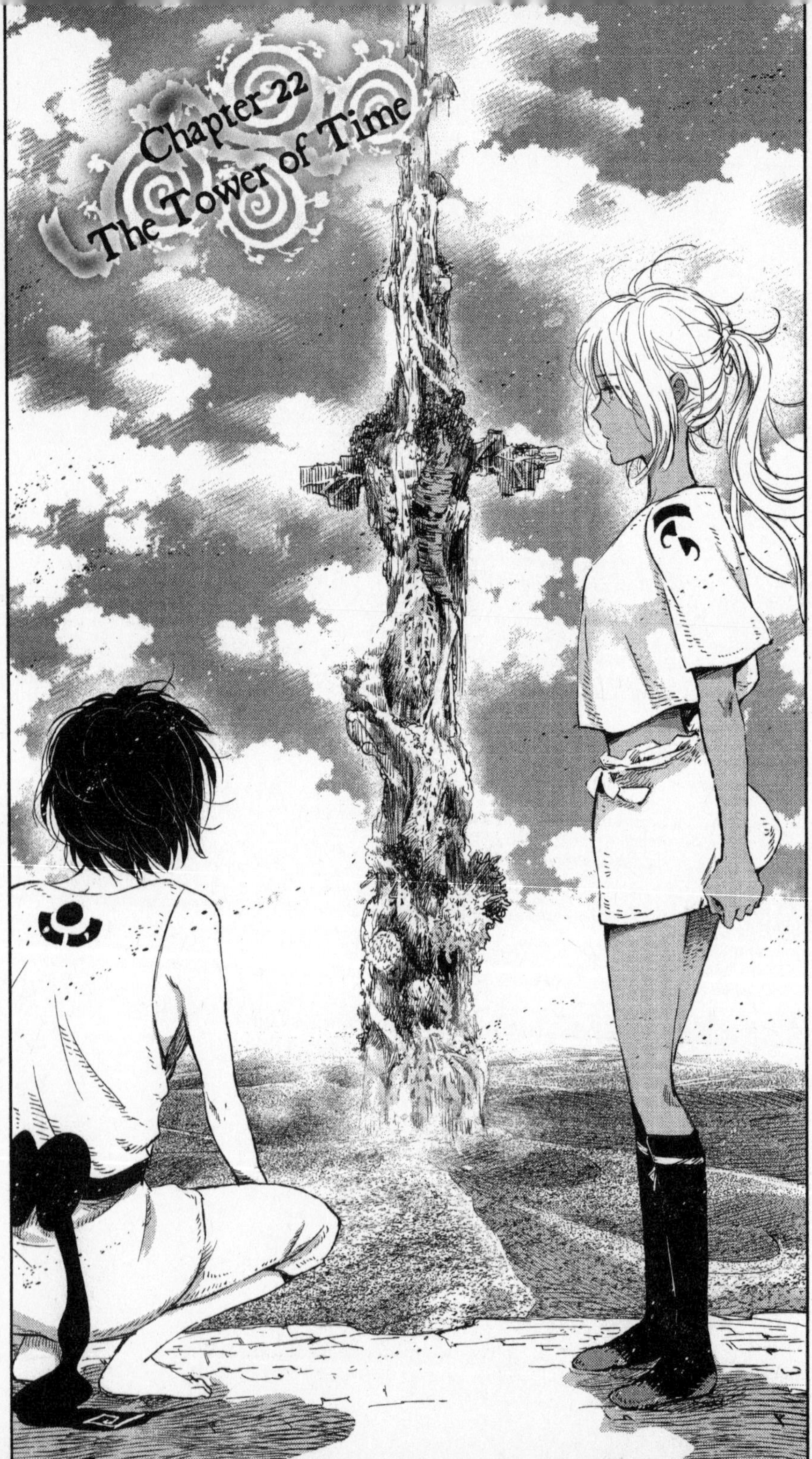
Chapter 22
The Tower of Time

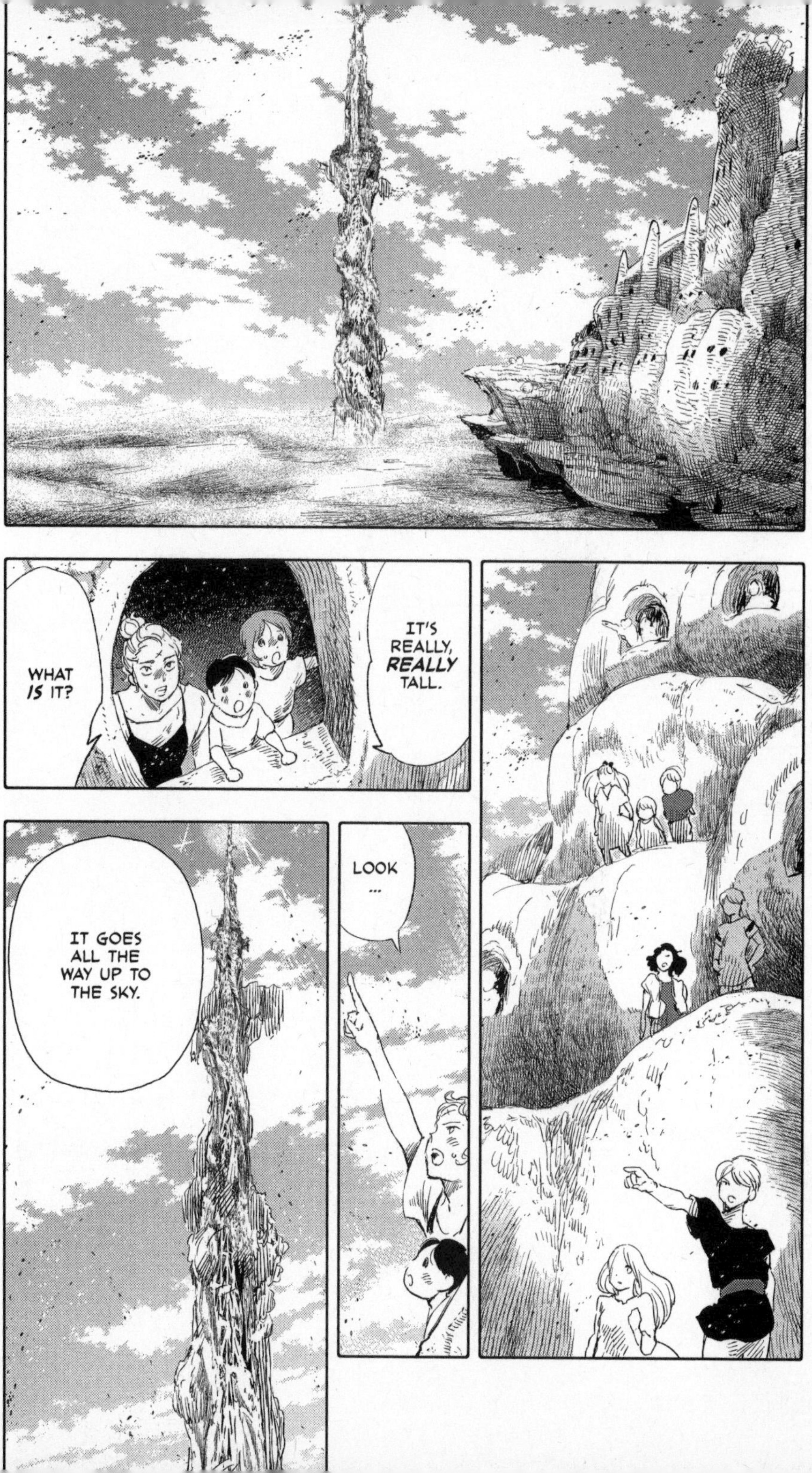
IT'S REALLY, *REALLY* TALL.
WHAT *IS* IT?
LOOK ...
IT GOES ALL THE WAY UP TO THE SKY.

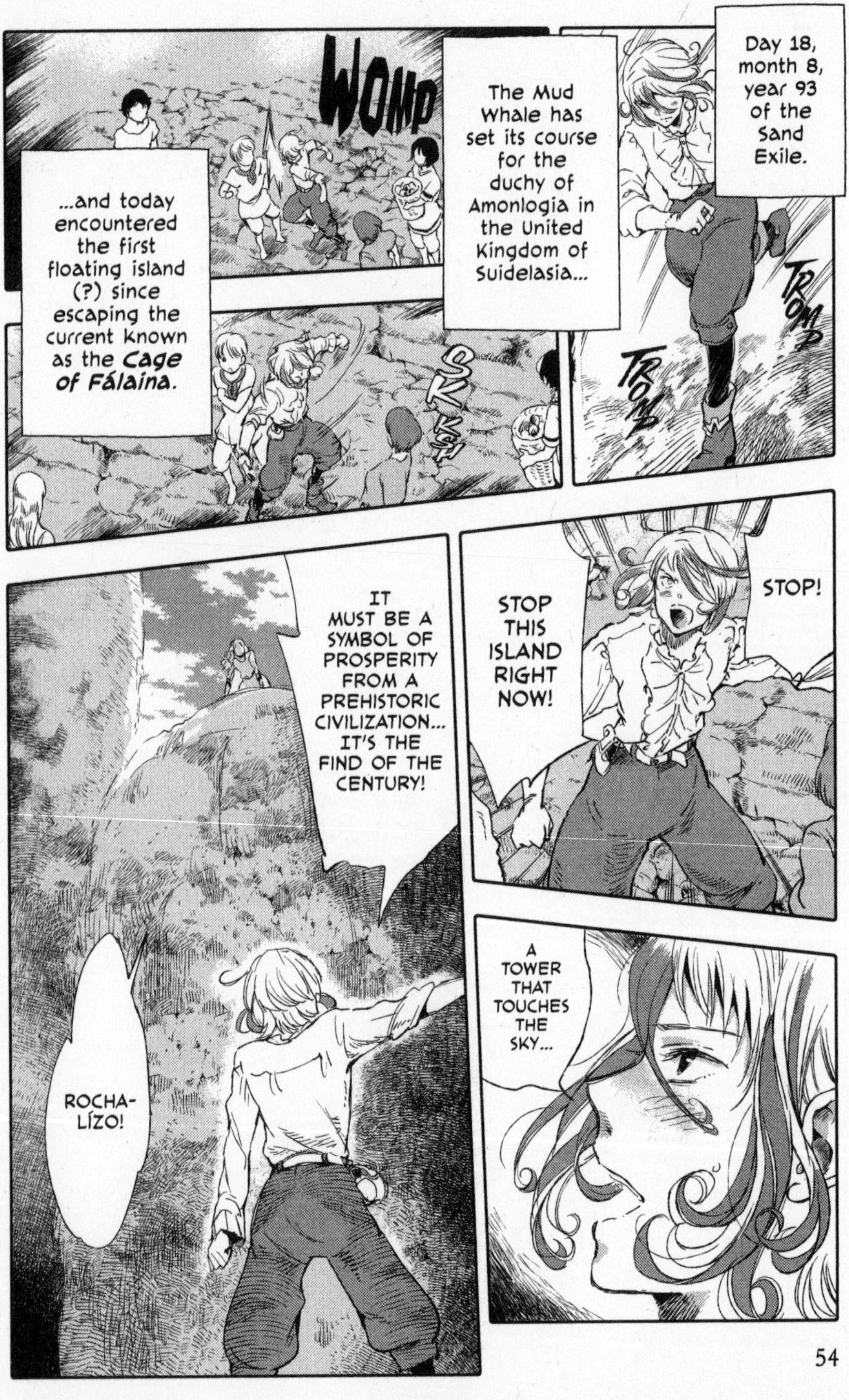
Day 18, month 8, year 93 of the Sand Exile.
TROMP
TROMP
The Mud Whale has set its course for the duchy of Amonlogia in the United Kingdom of Suidelasia...
...and today encountered the first floating island (?) since escaping the current known as the *Cage of Fálaina*.
WOMP
SKRSH
STOP!
STOP THIS ISLAND RIGHT NOW!
A TOWER THAT TOUCHES THE SKY...
IT MUST BE A SYMBOL OF PROSPERITY FROM A PREHISTORIC CIVILIZATION... IT'S THE FIND OF THE CENTURY!
ROCHA-LÍZO!

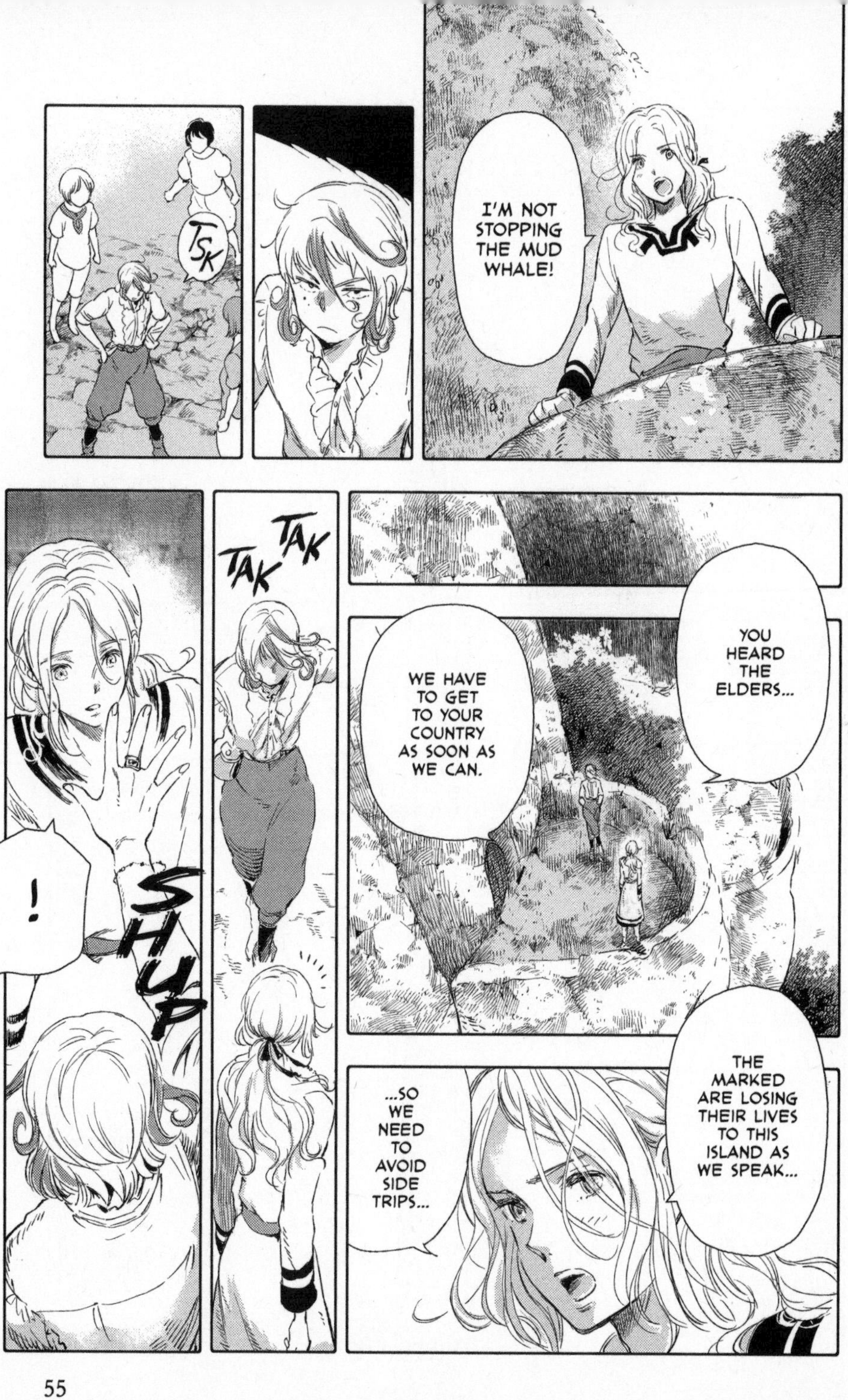
I'M NOT STOPPING THE MUD WHALE!
TSK
YOU HEARD THE ELDERS...
WE HAVE TO GET TO YOUR COUNTRY AS SOON AS WE CAN.
THE MARKED ARE LOSING THEIR LIVES TO THIS ISLAND AS WE SPEAK...
...SO WE NEED TO AVOID SIDE TRIPS...
TAK TAK
!
SHUP

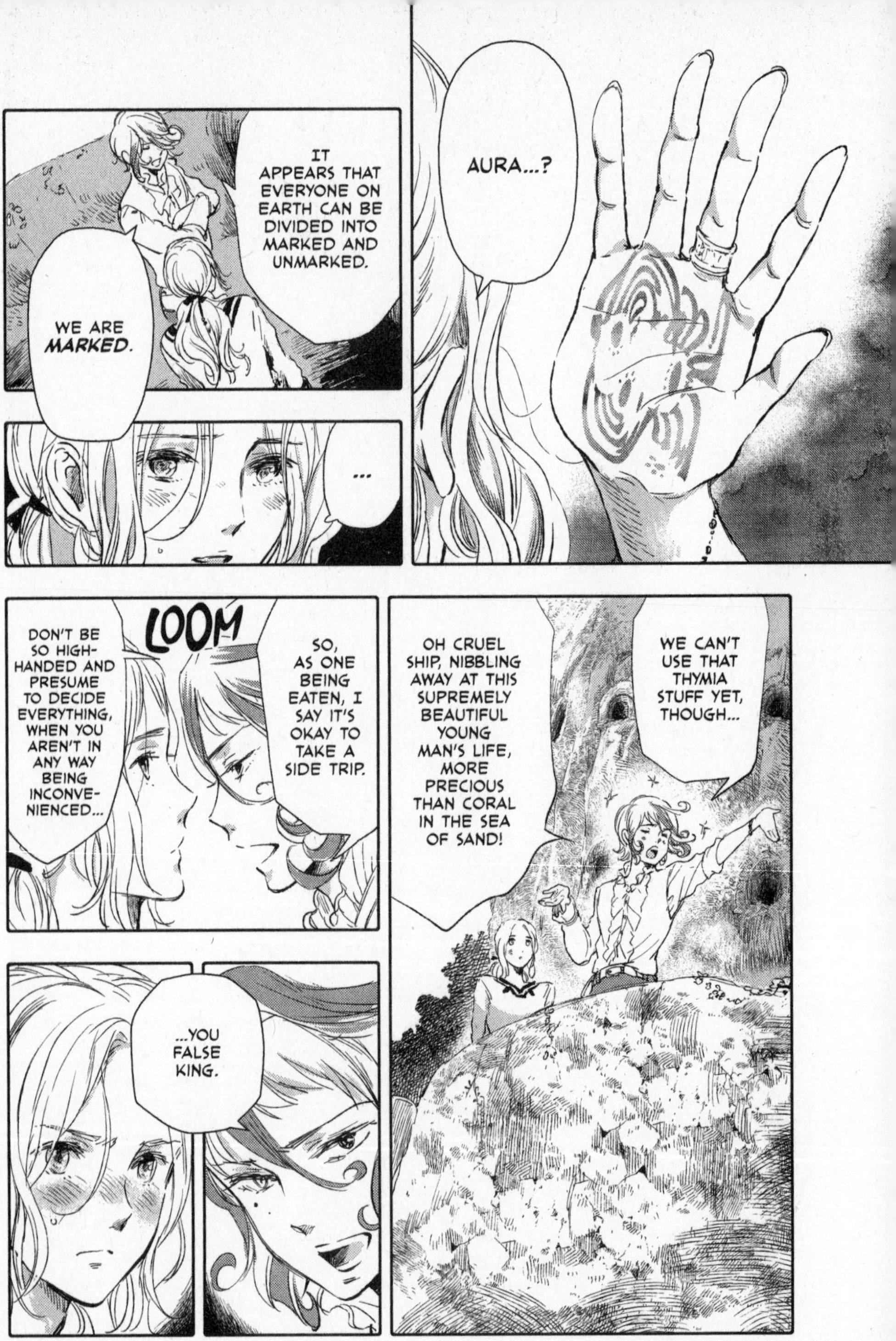
AURA...?
IT APPEARS THAT EVERYONE ON EARTH CAN BE DIVIDED INTO MARKED AND UNMARKED.
WE ARE *MARKED*.
...
WE CAN'T USE THAT THYMIA STUFF YET, THOUGH...
OH CRUEL SHIP, NIBBLING AWAY AT THIS SUPREMELY BEAUTIFUL YOUNG MAN'S LIFE, MORE PRECIOUS THAN CORAL IN THE SEA OF SAND!
SO, AS ONE BEING EATEN, I SAY IT'S OKAY TO TAKE A SIDE TRIP.
LOOM
DON'T BE SO HIGH-HANDED AND PRESUME TO DECIDE EVERYTHING, WHEN YOU AREN'T IN ANY WAY BEING INCONVENIENCED...
...YOU FALSE KING.

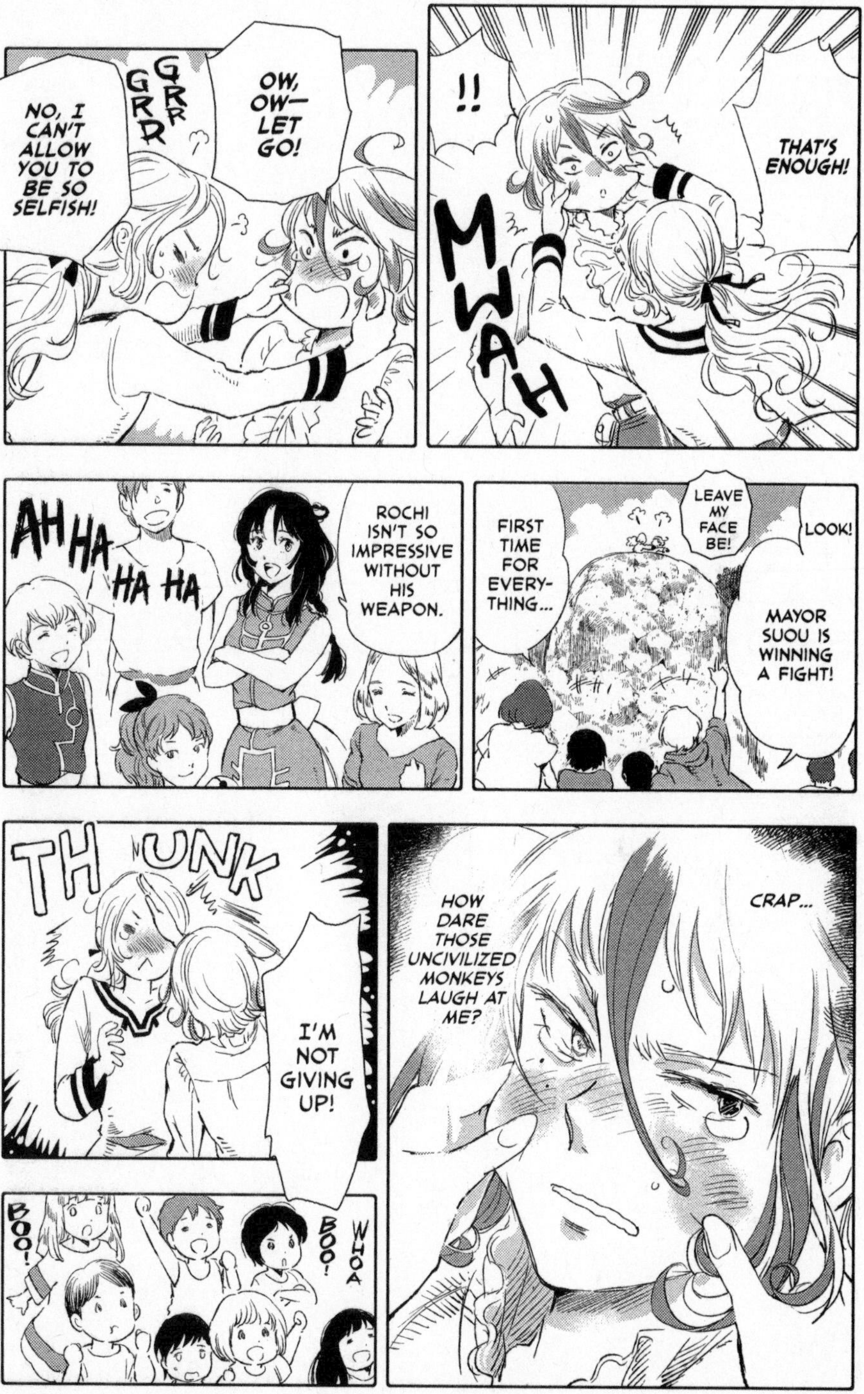
!!
THAT'S ENOUGH!
MWAH
OW, OW— LET GO!
GRR GRR
NO, I CAN'T ALLOW YOU TO BE SO SELFISH!
LOOK!
MAYOR SUOU IS WINNING A FIGHT!
LEAVE MY FACE BE!
FIRST TIME FOR EVERY-THING...
ROCHI ISN'T SO IMPRESSIVE WITHOUT HIS WEAPON.
AH HA HA HA HA
CRAP...
HOW DARE THOSE UNCIVILIZED MONKEYS LAUGH AT ME?
THUNK
I'M NOT GIVING UP!
WHOA
BOO!
BOO!

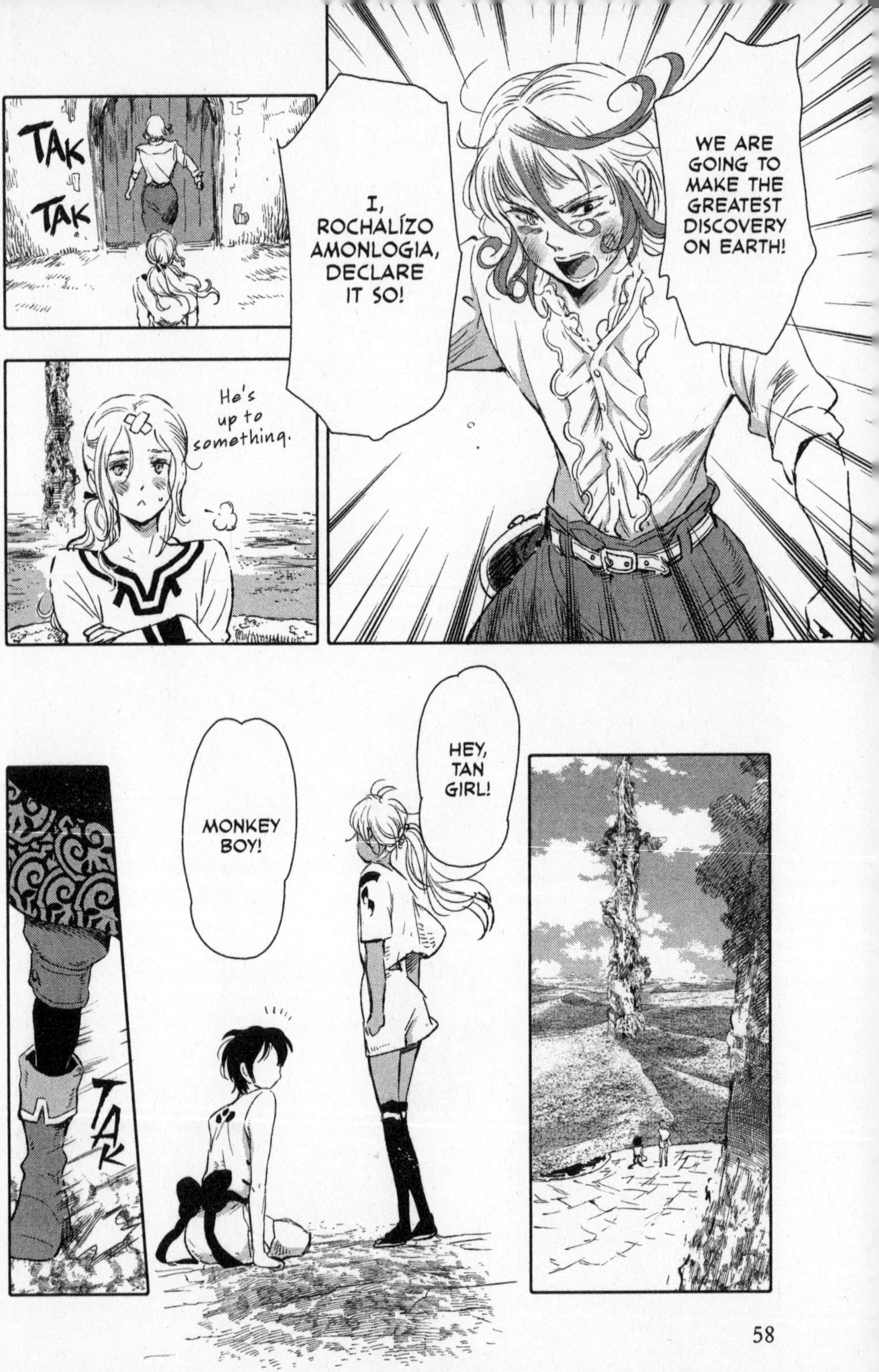
WE ARE GOING TO MAKE THE GREATEST DISCOVERY ON EARTH!
I, ROCHALÍZO AMONLOGIA, DECLARE IT SO!
TAK TAK
He's up to something.
HEY, TAN GIRL!
MONKEY BOY!
TAK

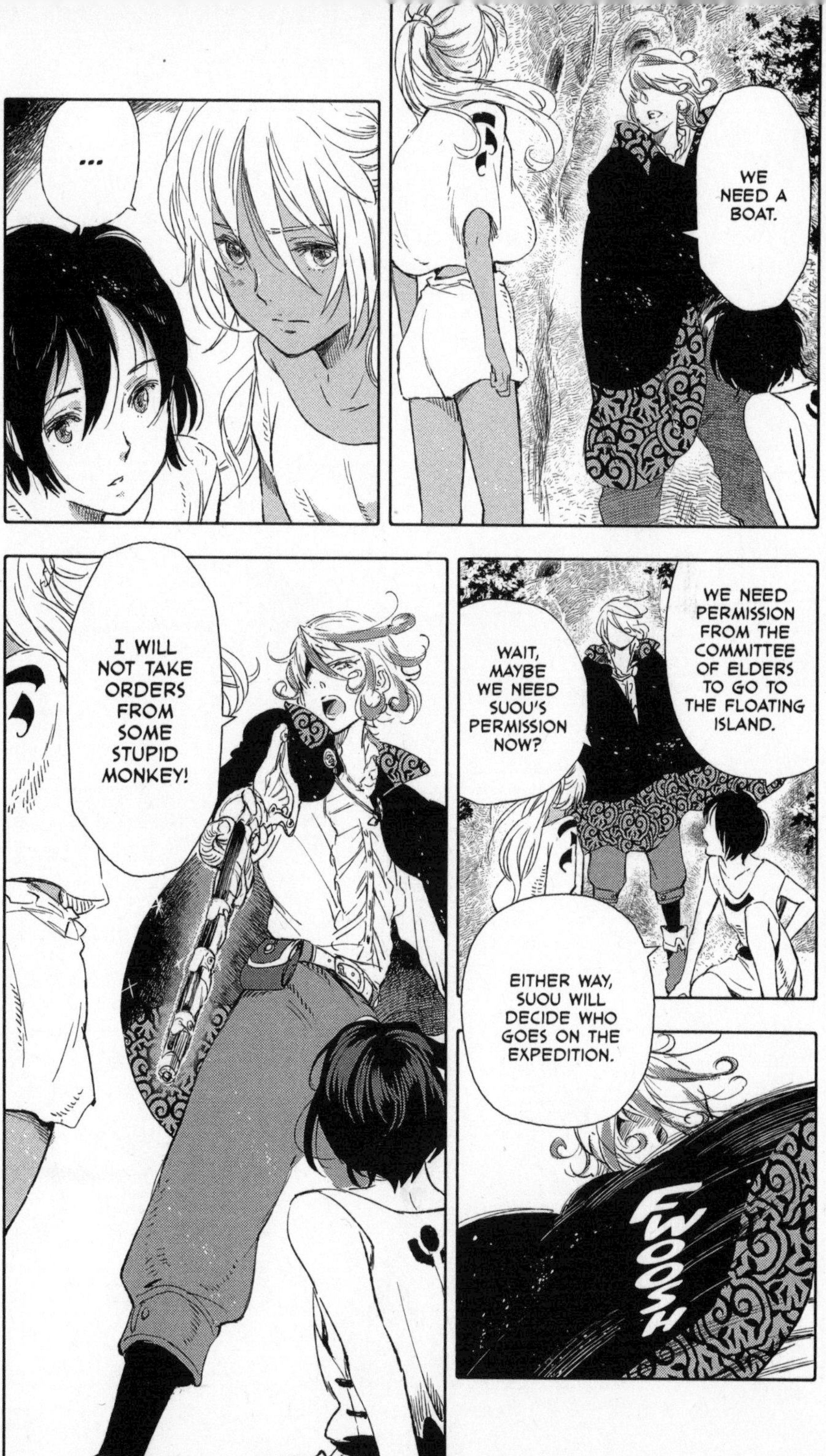
WE NEED A BOAT.
...
WE NEED PERMISSION FROM THE COMMITTEE OF ELDERS TO GO TO THE FLOATING ISLAND.
WAIT, MAYBE WE NEED SUOU'S PERMISSION NOW?
EITHER WAY, SUOU WILL DECIDE WHO GOES ON THE EXPEDITION.
FWOOSH
I WILL NOT TAKE ORDERS FROM SOME STUPID MONKEY!

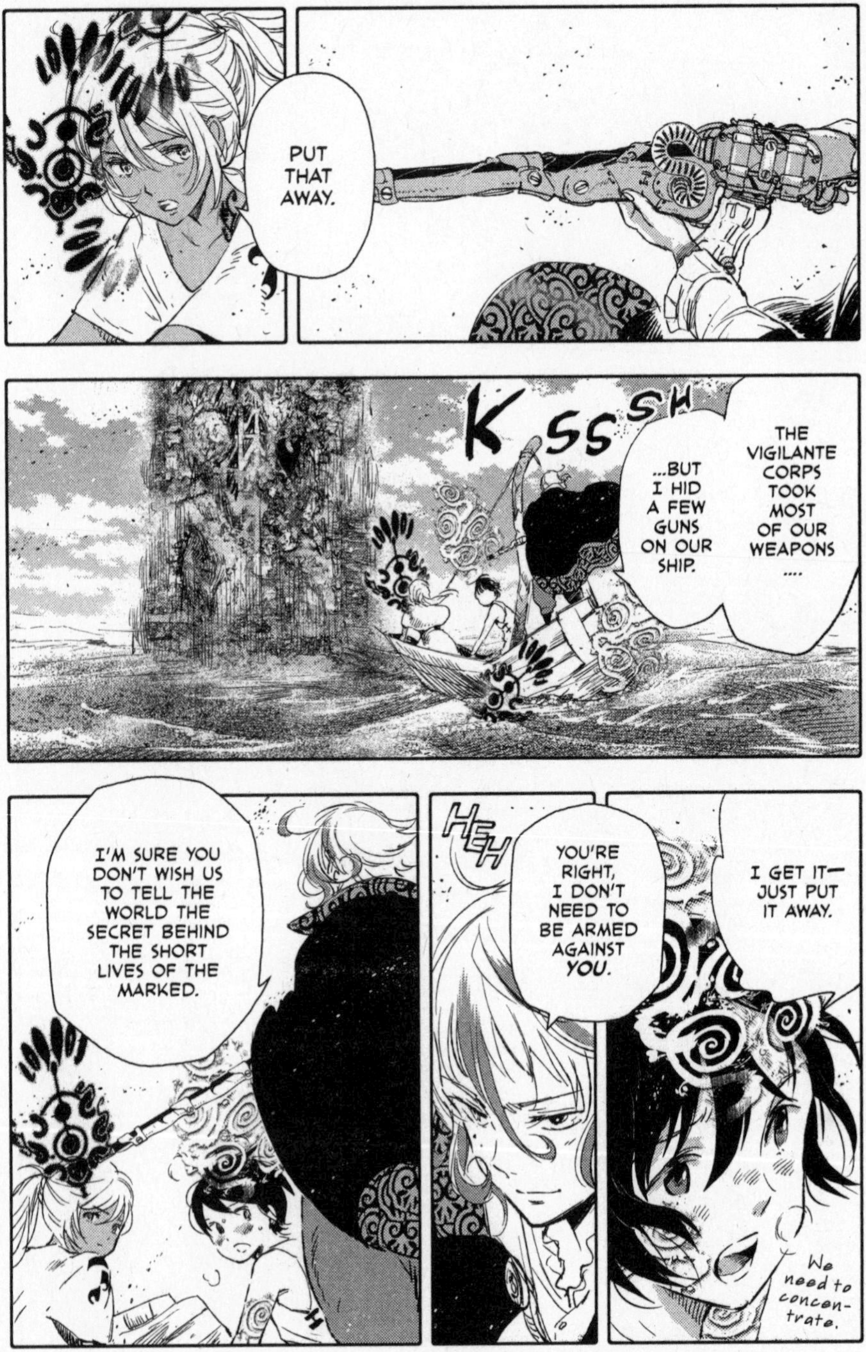
PUT THAT AWAY.
KSSSH
THE VIGILANTE CORPS TOOK MOST OF OUR WEAPONS....
...BUT I HID A FEW GUNS ON OUR SHIP.
I GET IT— JUST PUT IT AWAY.
We need to concen-trate.
HEH
YOU'RE RIGHT, I DON'T NEED TO BE ARMED AGAINST *YOU*.
I'M SURE YOU DON'T WISH US TO TELL THE WORLD THE SECRET BEHIND THE SHORT LIVES OF THE MARKED.

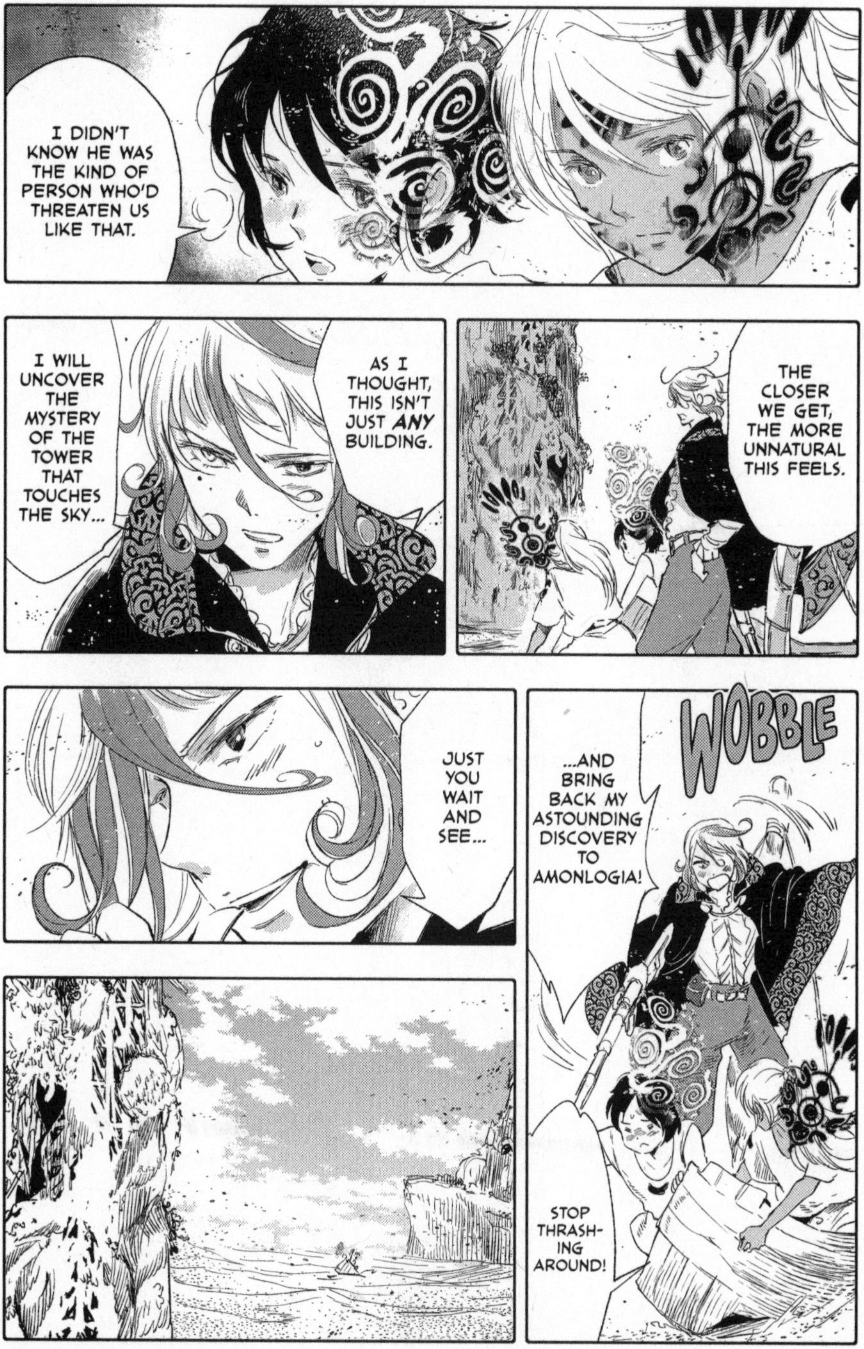
I DIDN'T KNOW HE WAS THE KIND OF PERSON WHO'D THREATEN US LIKE THAT.
THE CLOSER WE GET, THE MORE UNNATURAL THIS FEELS.
AS I THOUGHT, THIS ISN'T JUST *ANY* BUILDING.
I WILL UNCOVER THE MYSTERY OF THE TOWER THAT TOUCHES THE SKY...
WOBBLE
...AND BRING BACK MY ASTOUNDING DISCOVERY TO AMONLOGIA!
STOP THRASH-ING AROUND!
JUST YOU WAIT AND SEE...

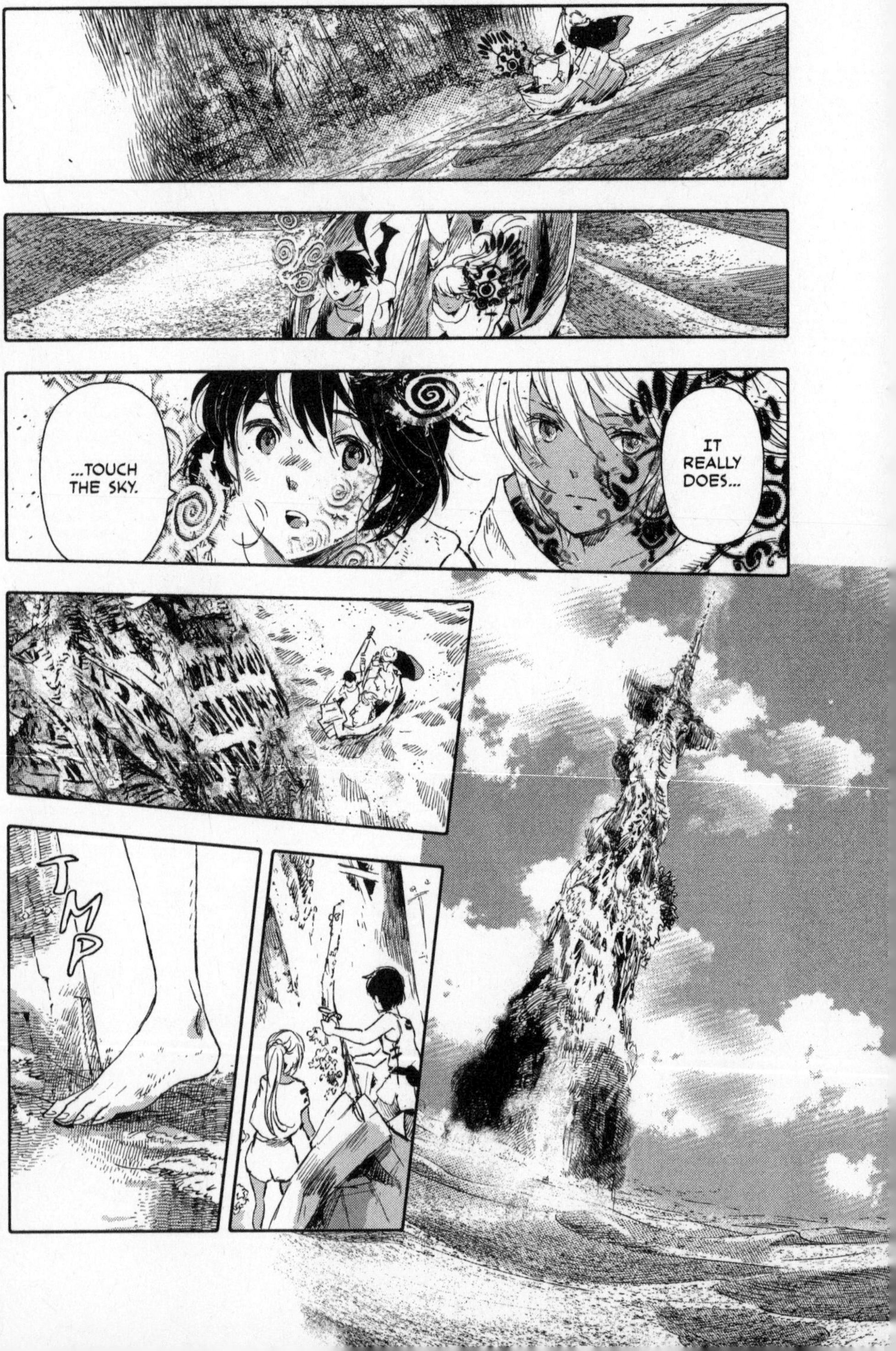
IT REALLY DOES...
...TOUCH THE SKY.
TMP

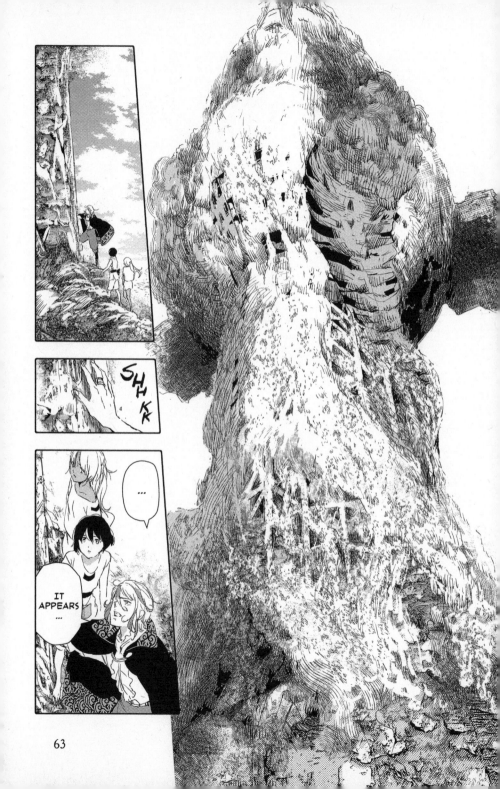

SHHKK

...

IT
APPEARS
...

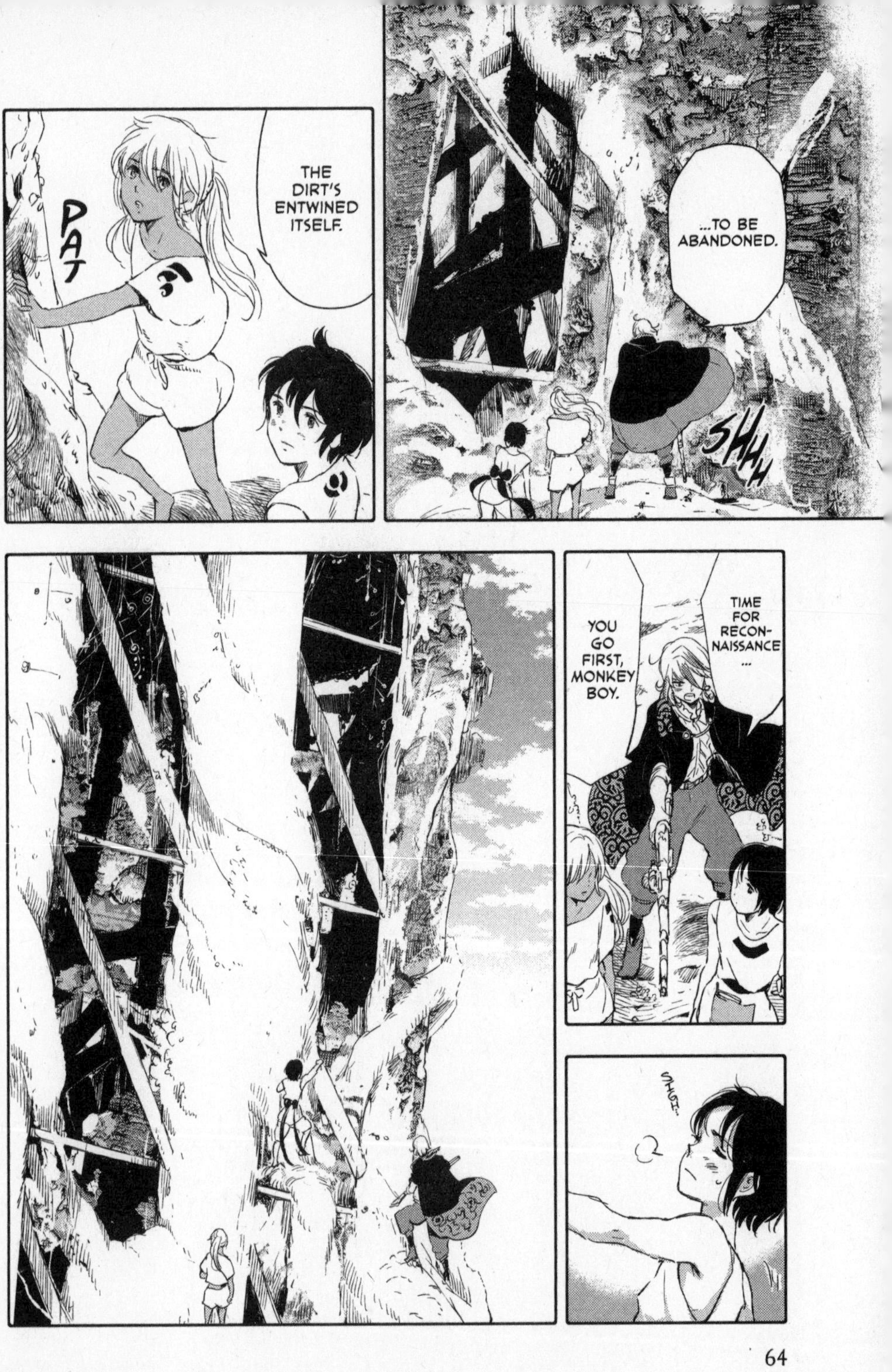
...TO BE ABANDONED.
SHHH
THE DIRT'S ENTWINED ITSELF.
PAT
TIME FOR RECONNAISSANCE...
YOU GO FIRST, MONKEY BOY.
SIGH...

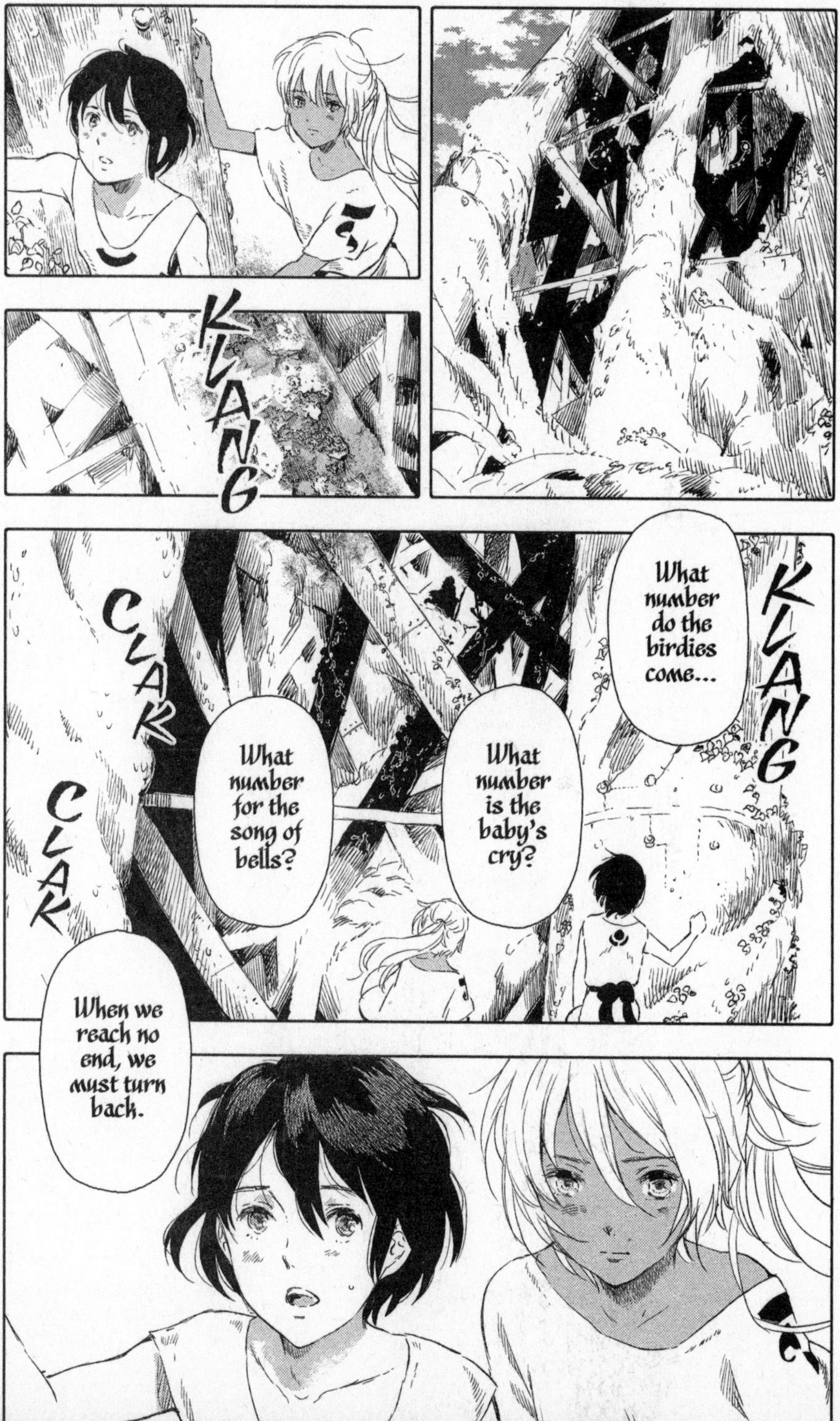
KLANG
KLANG
What number do the birdies come...
What number is the baby's cry?
What number for the song of bells?
CLAK
CLAK
When we reach no end, we must turn back.

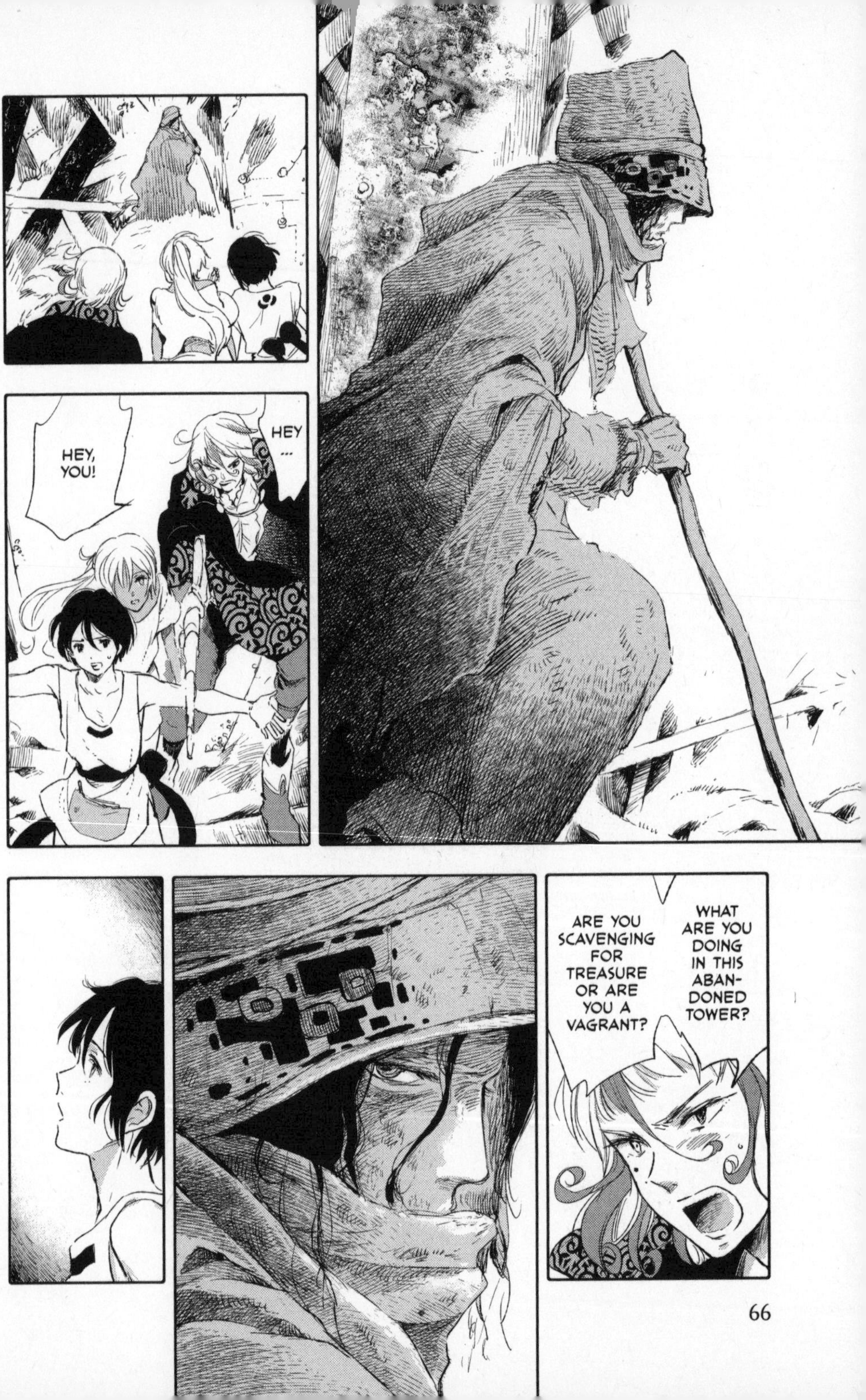
HEY ...
HEY, YOU!
WHAT ARE YOU DOING IN THIS ABAN-DONED TOWER?
ARE YOU SCAVENGING FOR TREASURE OR ARE YOU A VAGRANT?

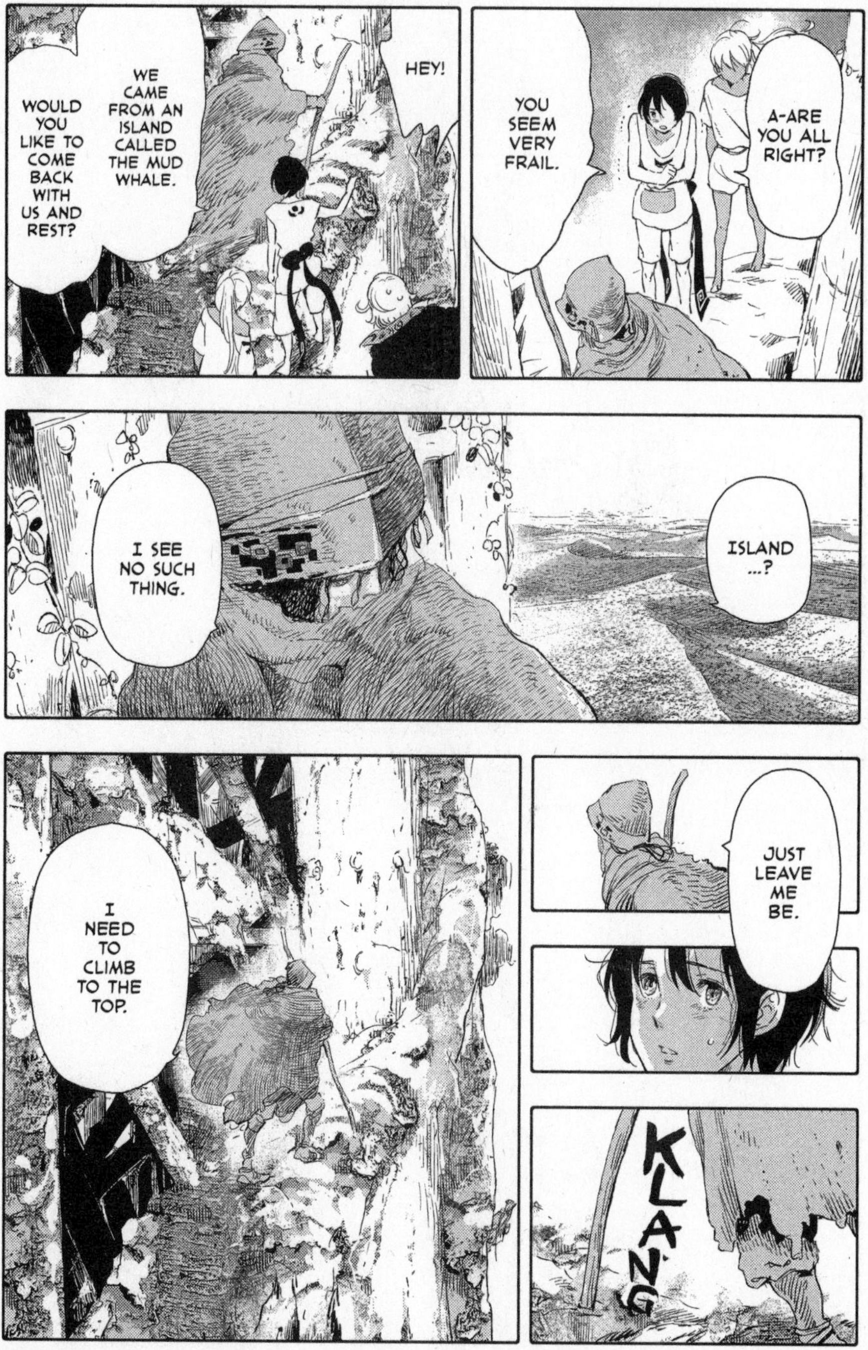
A-ARE YOU ALL RIGHT?
YOU SEEM VERY FRAIL.
HEY!
WE CAME FROM AN ISLAND CALLED THE MUD WHALE.
WOULD YOU LIKE TO COME BACK WITH US AND REST?
ISLAND ...?
I SEE NO SUCH THING.
JUST LEAVE ME BE.
KLANG
I NEED TO CLIMB TO THE TOP.

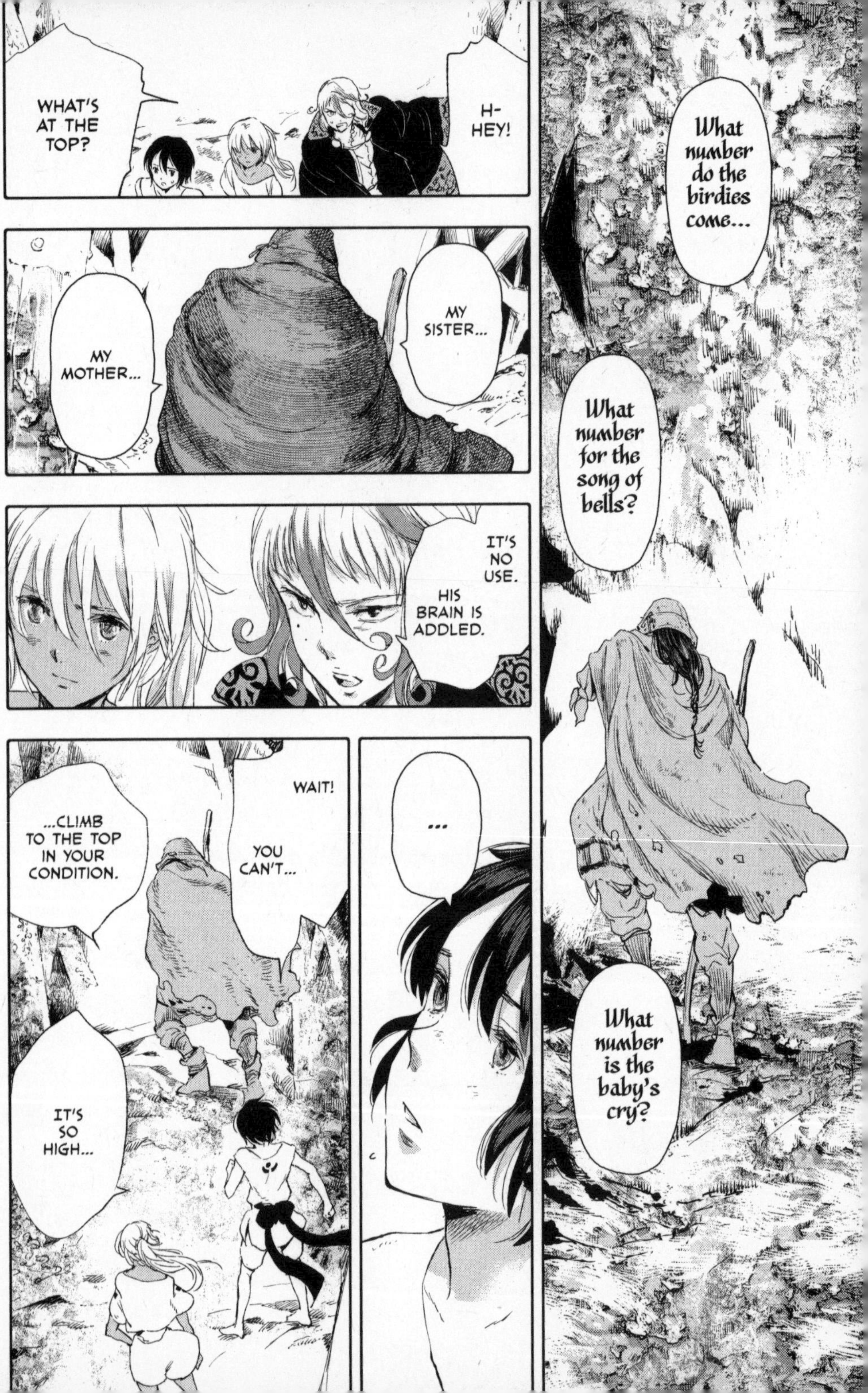
What number do the birdies come...
What number for the song of bells?
What number is the baby's cry?
H-HEY!
WHAT'S AT THE TOP?
MY SISTER...
MY MOTHER...
IT'S NO USE.
HIS BRAIN IS ADDLED.
...
WAIT!
YOU CAN'T...
...CLIMB TO THE TOP IN YOUR CONDITION.
IT'S SO HIGH...

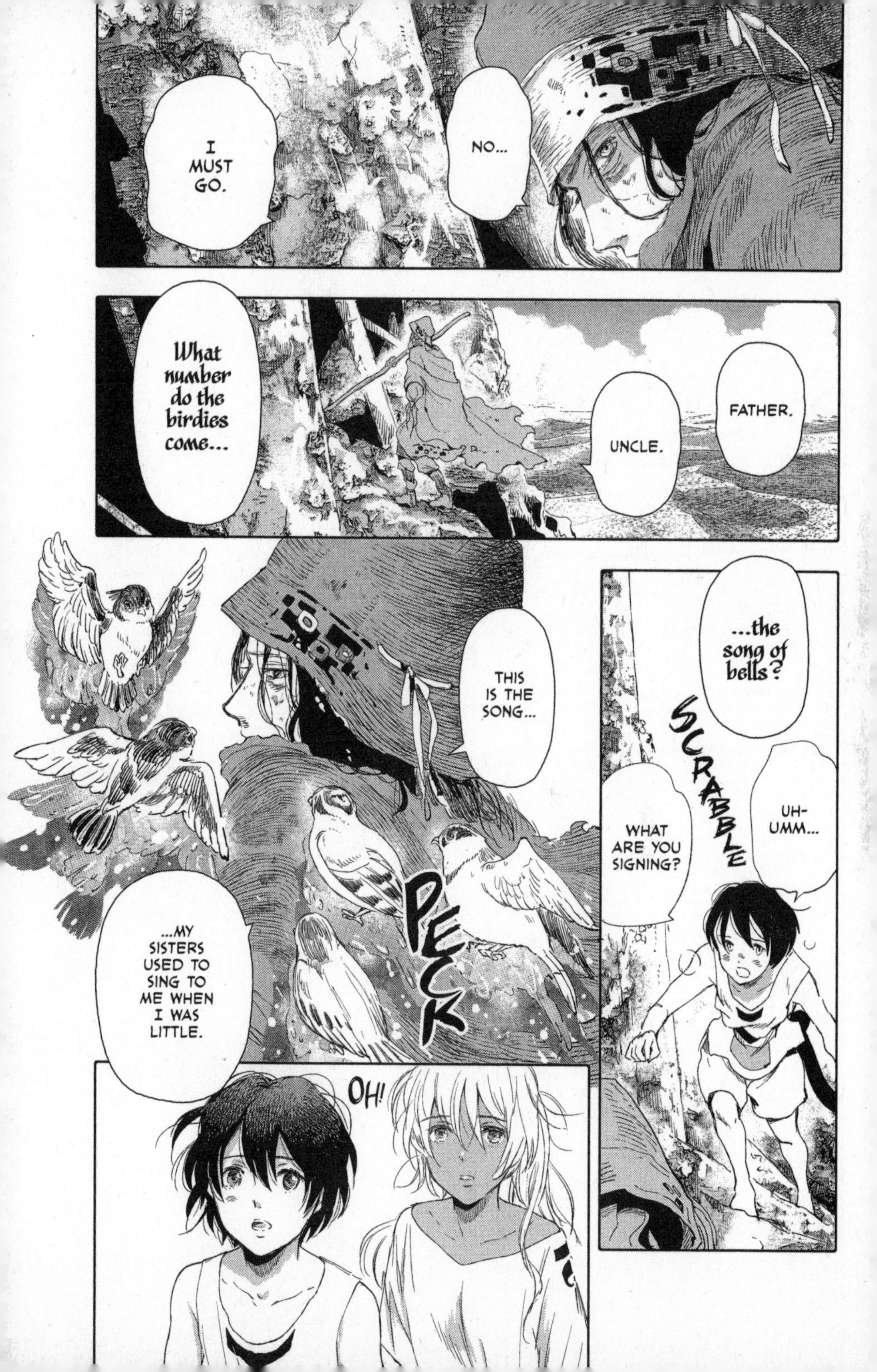
NO...
I MUST GO.
FATHER.
UNCLE.
What number do the birdies come...
...the song of bells?
SCRABBLE
UH-UMM...
WHAT ARE YOU SIGNING?
THIS IS THE SONG...
PECK
...MY SISTERS USED TO SING TO ME WHEN I WAS LITTLE.
OH!

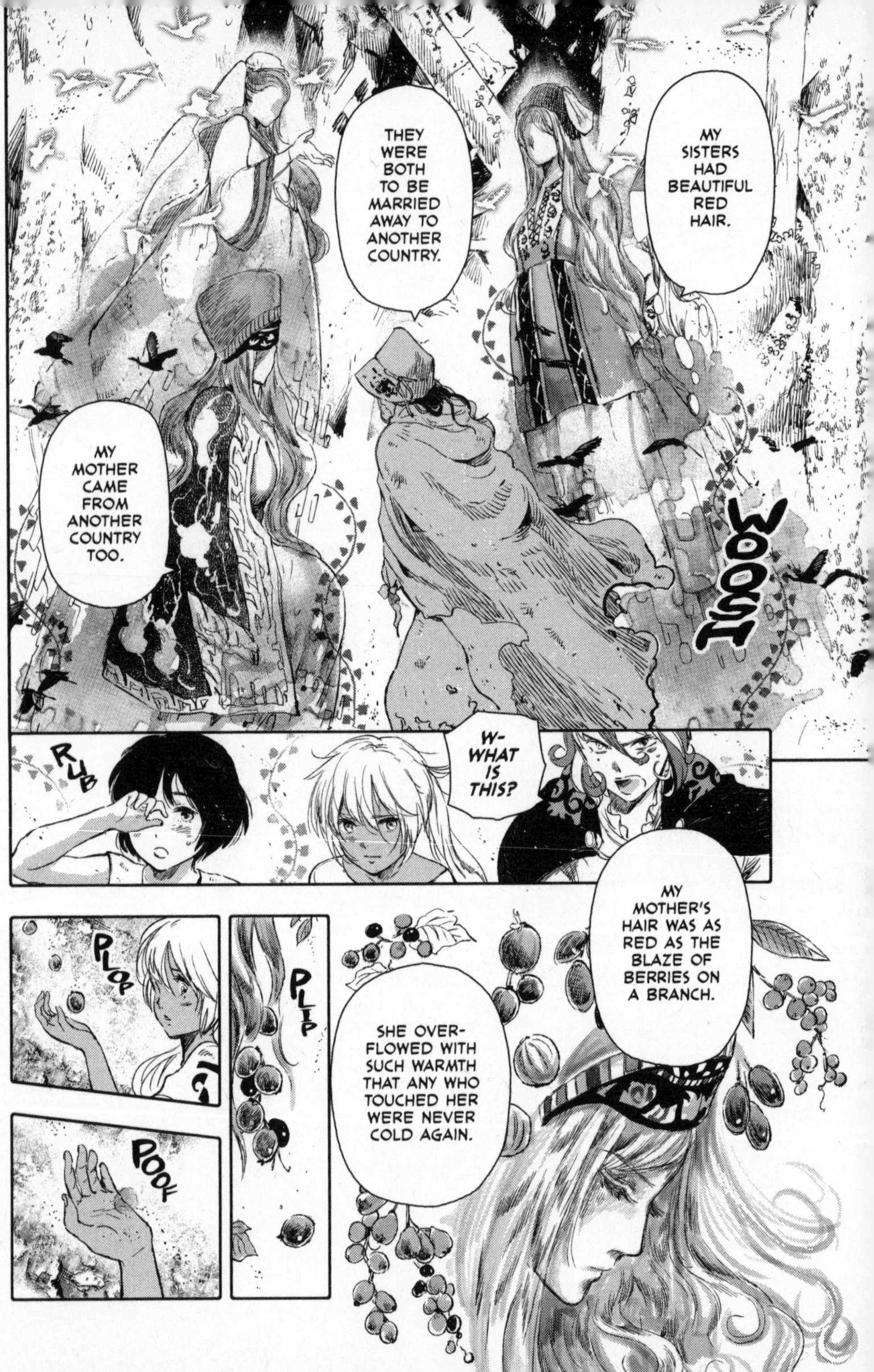
MY SISTERS HAD BEAUTIFUL RED HAIR.
THEY WERE BOTH TO BE MARRIED AWAY TO ANOTHER COUNTRY.
WOOSH
MY MOTHER CAME FROM ANOTHER COUNTRY TOO.
W-WHAT IS THIS?
RUB
MY MOTHER'S HAIR WAS AS RED AS THE BLAZE OF BERRIES ON A BRANCH.
SHE OVER-FLOWED WITH SUCH WARMTH THAT ANY WHO TOUCHED HER WERE NEVER COLD AGAIN.
PLIP
PLOP
POOF

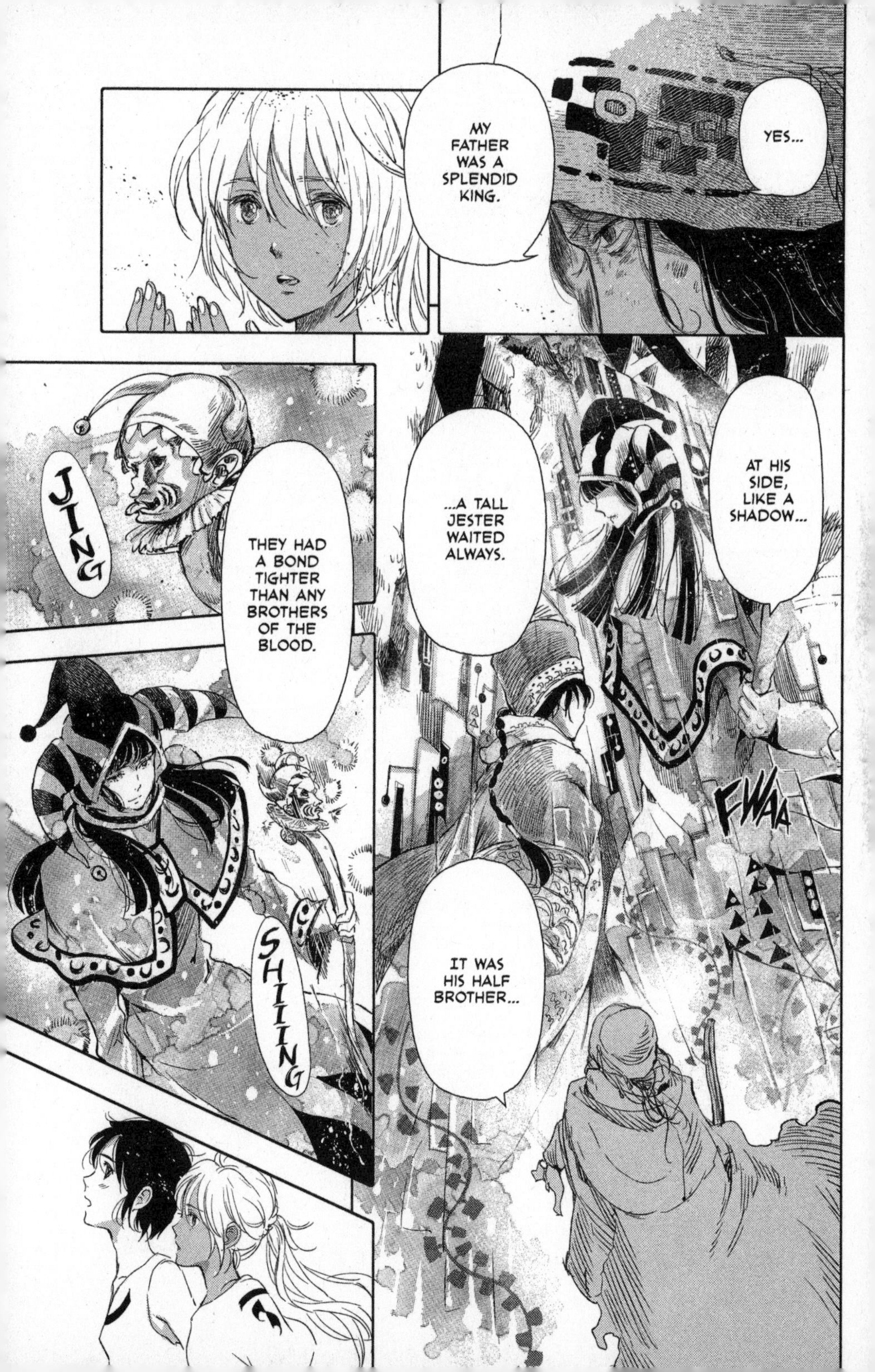
YES...
MY FATHER WAS A SPLENDID KING.
AT HIS SIDE, LIKE A SHADOW...
...A TALL JESTER WAITED ALWAYS.
FWAA
IT WAS HIS HALF BROTHER...
JING
THEY HAD A BOND TIGHTER THAN ANY BROTHERS OF THE BLOOD.
SHIIING

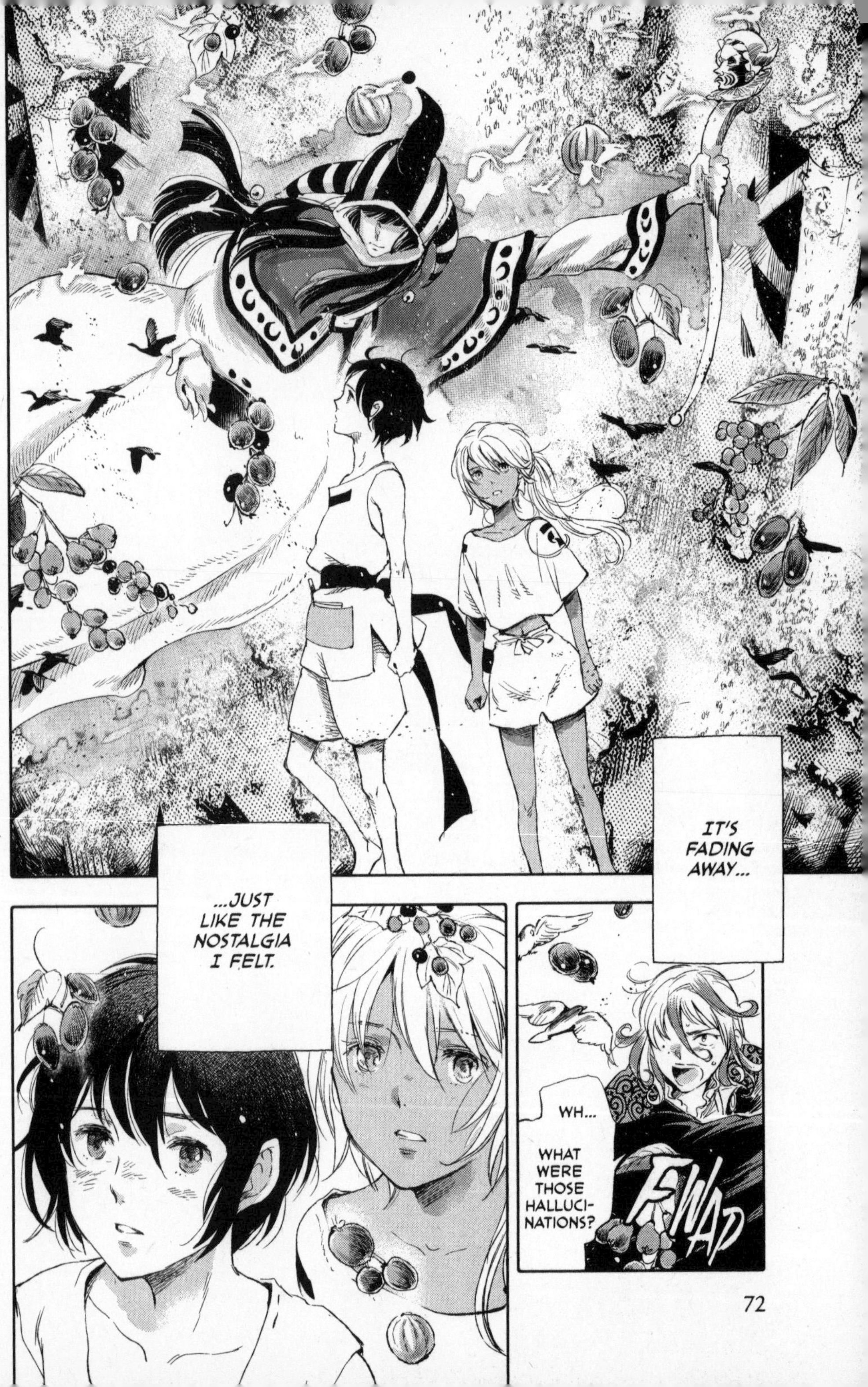
IT'S FADING AWAY...
...JUST LIKE THE NOSTALGIA I FELT.
WH...
WHAT WERE THOSE HALLUCI-NATIONS?
FWAP

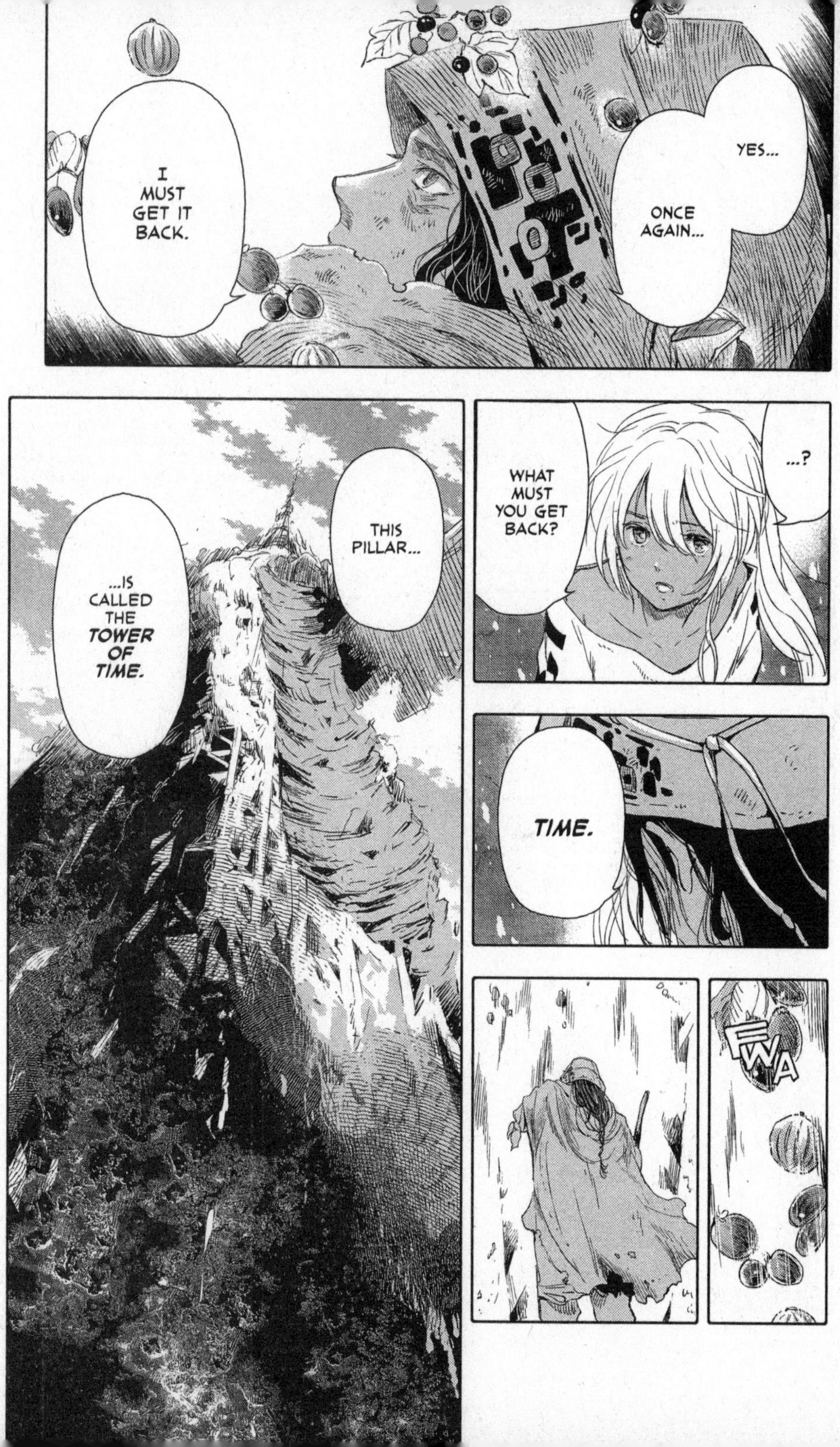
YES... ONCE AGAIN...
I MUST GET IT BACK.
...?
WHAT MUST YOU GET BACK?
TIME.
FWA
THIS PILLAR...
...IS CALLED THE *TOWER OF TIME.*

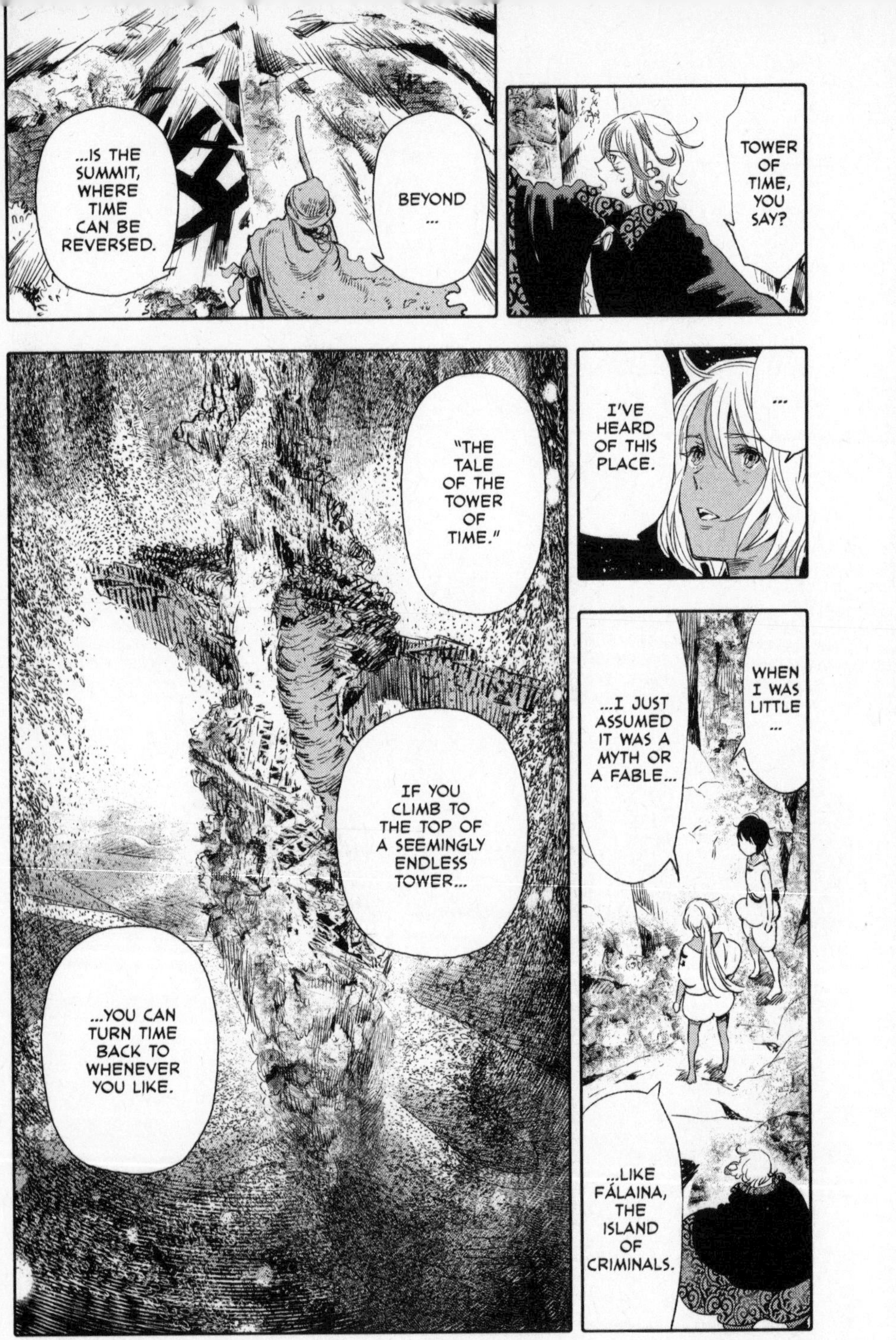
TOWER OF TIME, YOU SAY?
BEYOND ...
...IS THE SUMMIT, WHERE TIME CAN BE REVERSED.
...
I'VE HEARD OF THIS PLACE.
WHEN I WAS LITTLE ...
...I JUST ASSUMED IT WAS A MYTH OR A FABLE...
...LIKE FÁLAINA, THE ISLAND OF CRIMINALS.
"THE TALE OF THE TOWER OF TIME."
IF YOU CLIMB TO THE TOP OF A SEEMINGLY ENDLESS TOWER...
...YOU CAN TURN TIME BACK TO WHENEVER YOU LIKE.

HOW IDIOTIC!

?!

YOU CAN GO BACK IN TIME.

YOU'RE RIGHT...

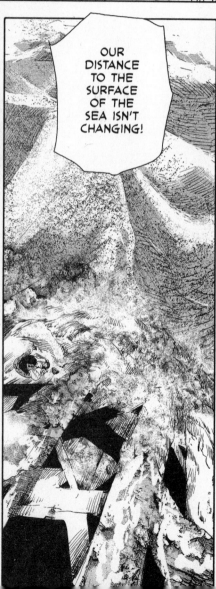

OUR DISTANCE TO THE SURFACE OF THE SEA ISN'T CHANGING!

BUT WE'VE BEEN CLIMBING ALL THIS TIME.

ZSSSH

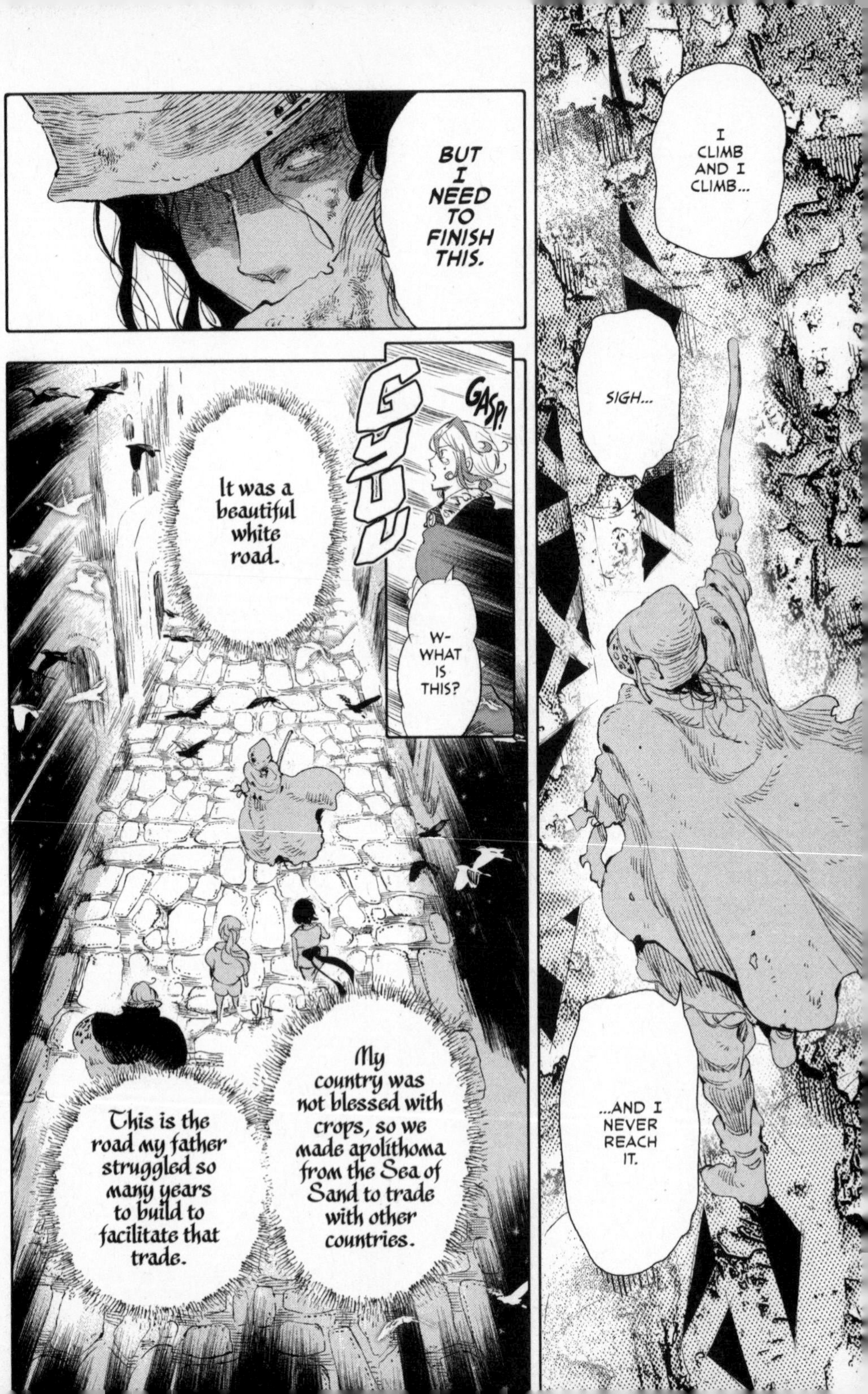
I CLIMB AND I CLIMB...
SIGH...
...AND I NEVER REACH IT.
BUT I NEED TO FINISH THIS.
GASP!
GYU
W-WHAT IS THIS?
It was a beautiful white road.
My country was not blessed with crops, so we made apolithoma from the Sea of Sand to trade with other countries.
This is the road my father struggled so many years to build to facilitate that trade.

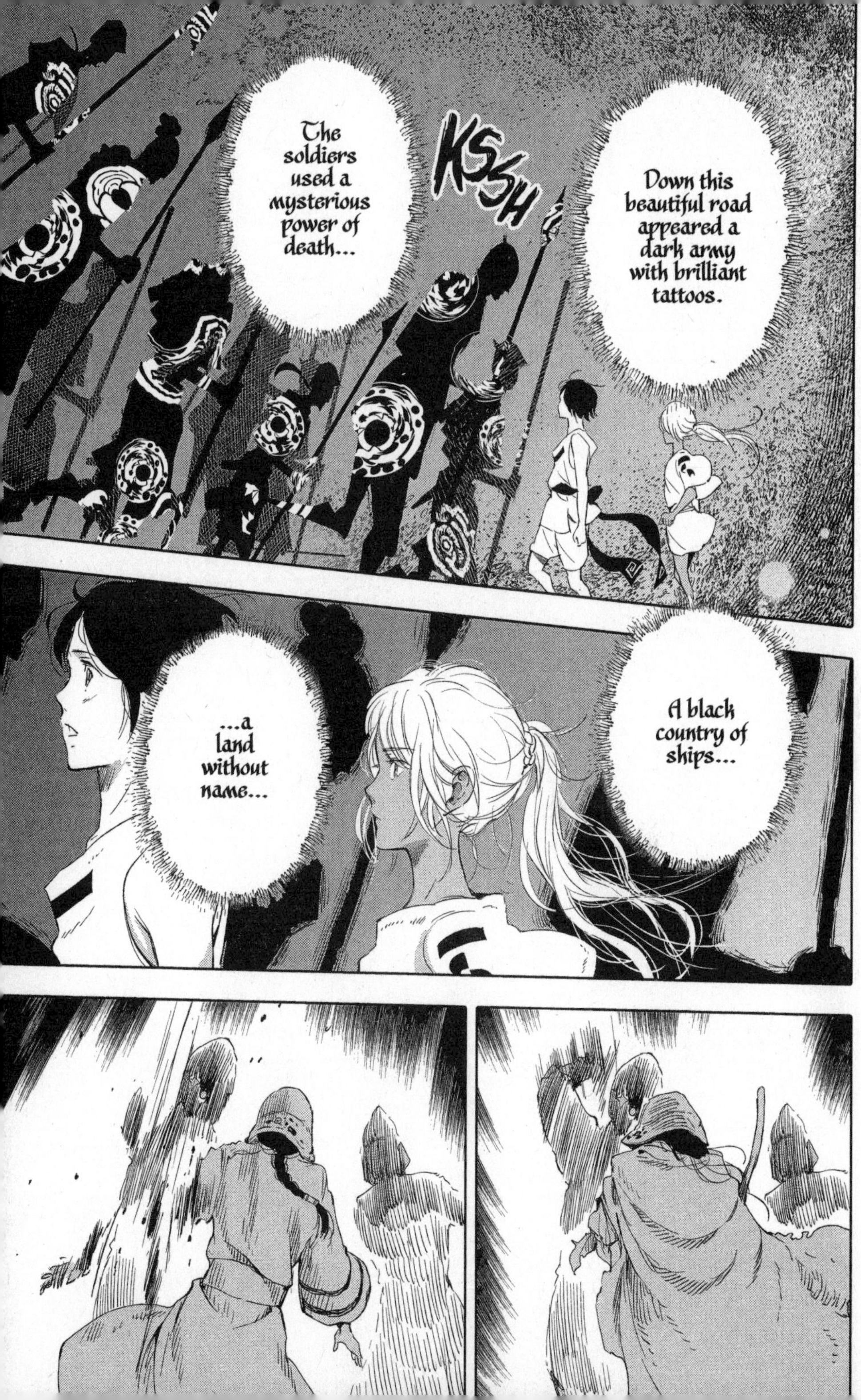
Down this beautiful road appeared a dark army with brilliant tattoos.
KSSH
The soldiers used a mysterious power of death...
A black country of ships...
...a land without name...

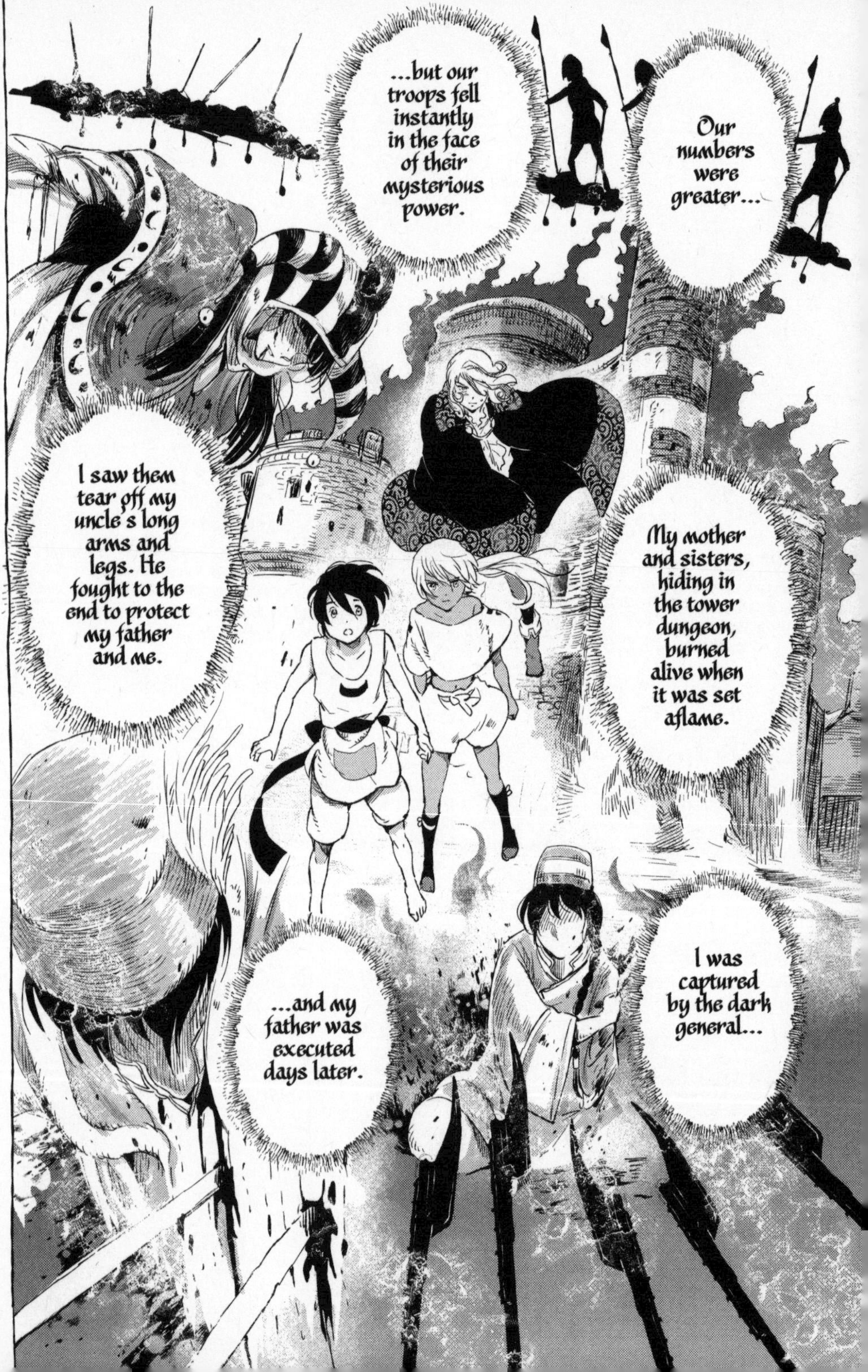
Our numbers were greater...
...but our troops fell instantly in the face of their mysterious power.
I saw them tear off my uncle's long arms and legs. He fought to the end to protect my father and me.
My mother and sisters, hiding in the tower dungeon, burned alive when it was set aflame.
I was captured by the dark general...
...and my father was executed days later.

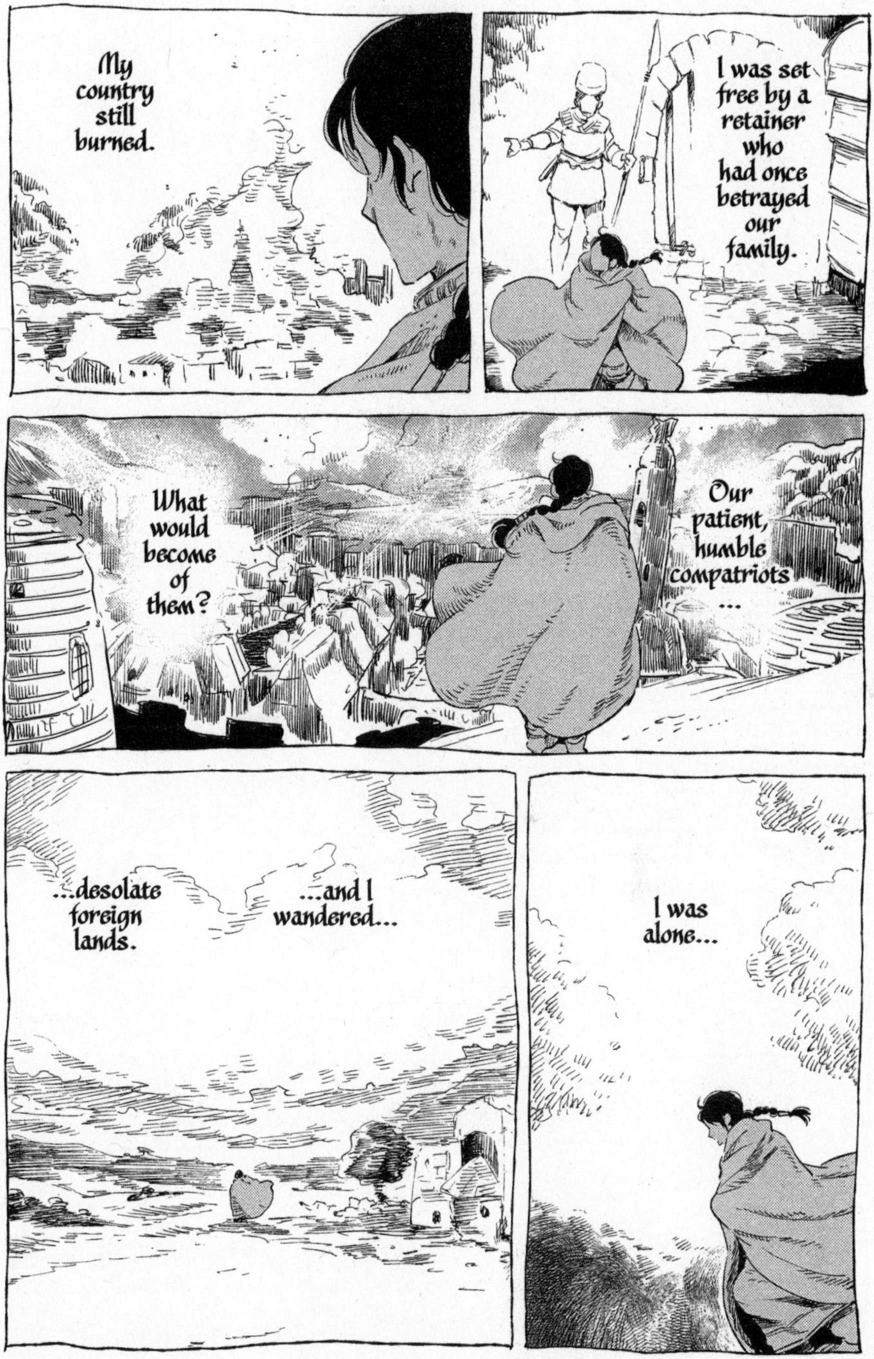
I was set free by a retainer who had once betrayed our family.
My country still burned.
Our patient, humble compatriots...
What would become of them?
I was alone...
...and I wandered...
...desolate foreign lands.

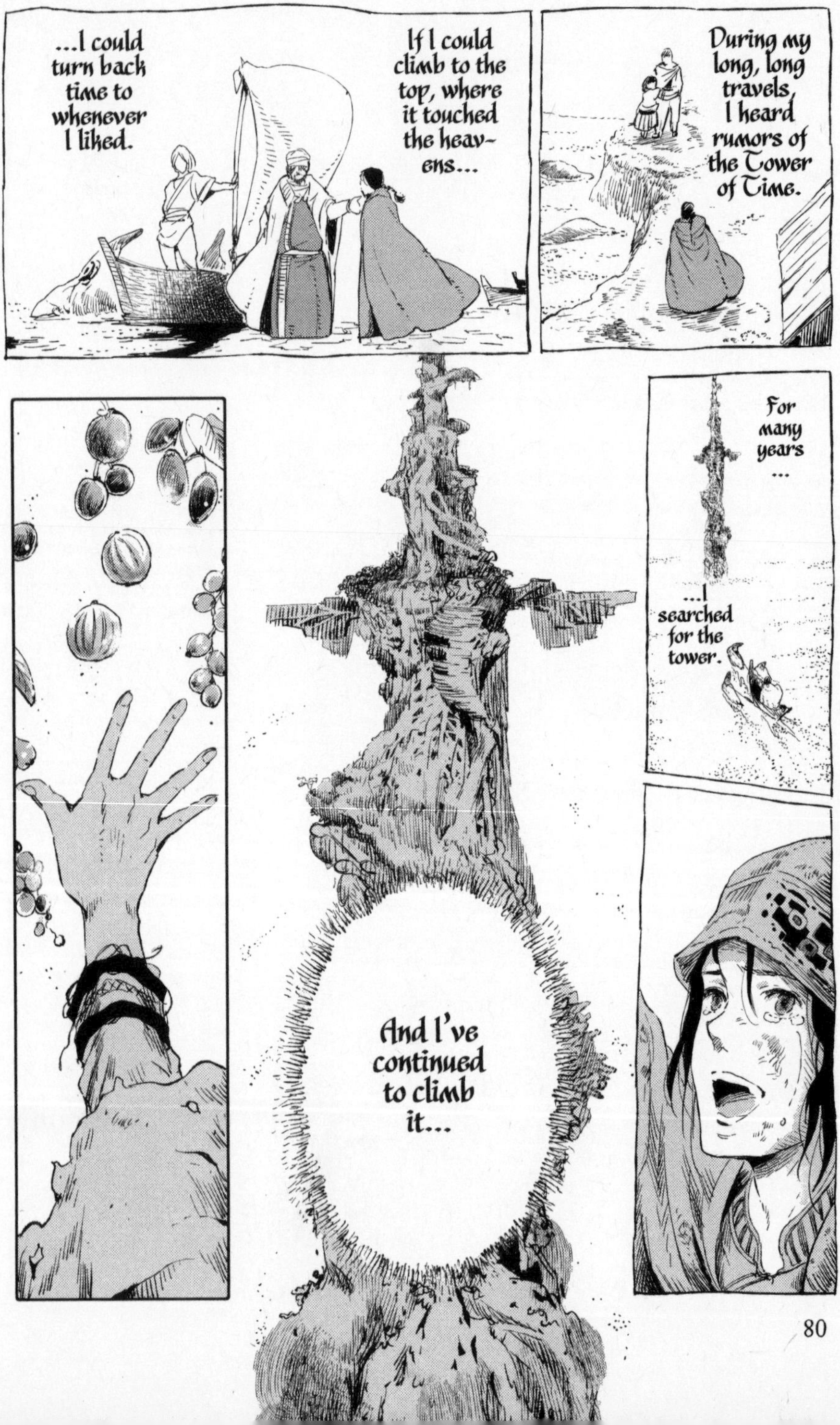
During my long, long travels, I heard rumors of the Tower of Time.
If I could climb to the top, where it touched the heav-ens...
...I could turn back time to whenever I liked.
For many years...
...I searched for the tower.
And I've continued to climb it...

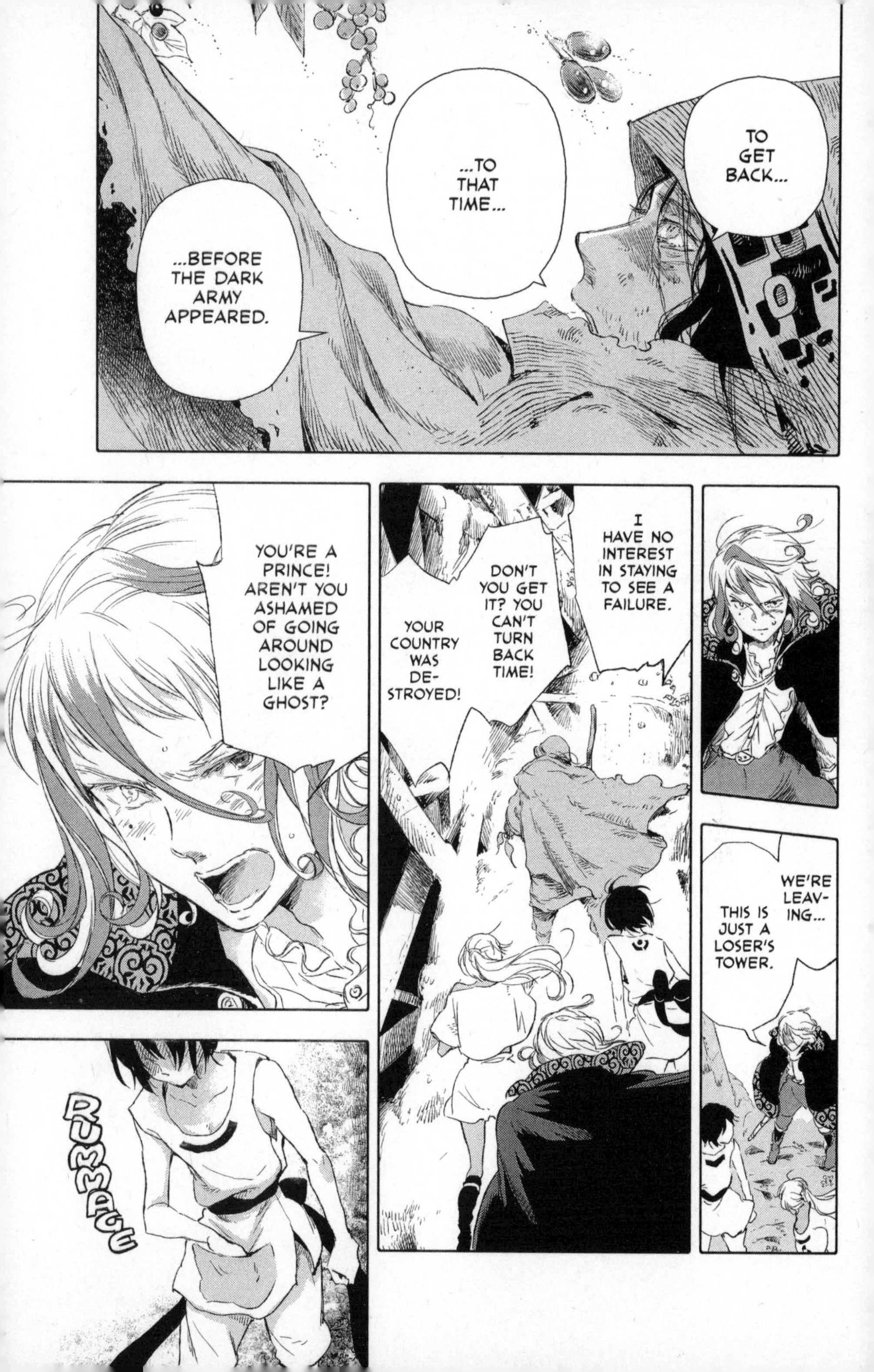
TO GET BACK...
...TO THAT TIME...
...BEFORE THE DARK ARMY APPEARED.
WE'RE LEAV-ING...
THIS IS JUST A LOSER'S TOWER.
I HAVE NO INTEREST IN STAYING TO SEE A FAILURE.
DON'T YOU GET IT? YOU CAN'T TURN BACK TIME!
YOUR COUNTRY WAS DE-STROYED!
YOU'RE A PRINCE! AREN'T YOU ASHAMED OF GOING AROUND LOOKING LIKE A GHOST?
RUMMAGE

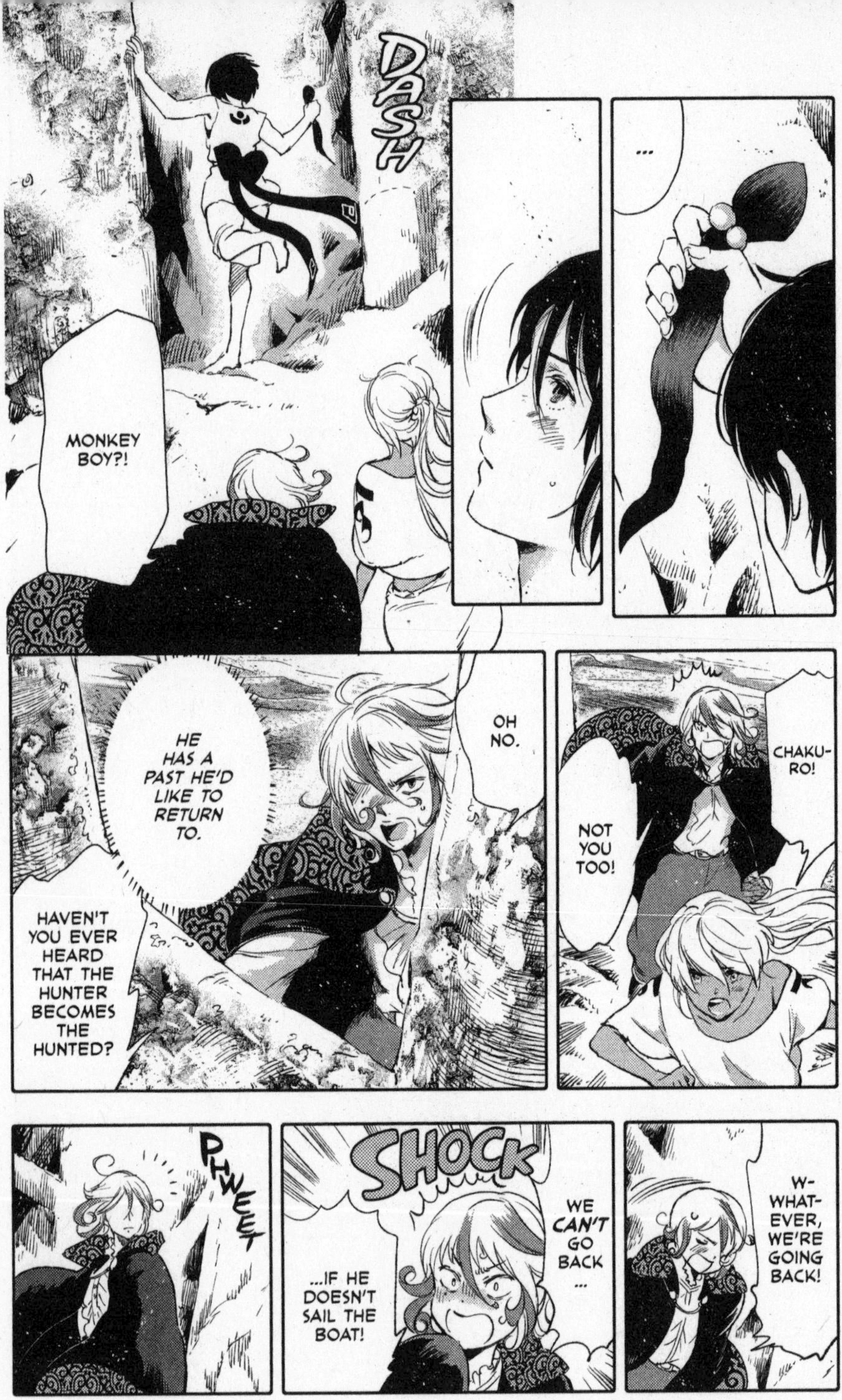
...
DASH
MONKEY BOY?!
CHAKU-RO!
NOT YOU TOO!
OH NO.
HE HAS A PAST HE'D LIKE TO RETURN TO.
HAVEN'T YOU EVER HEARD THAT THE HUNTER BECOMES THE HUNTED?
W-WHAT-EVER, WE'RE GOING BACK!
SHOCK
WE CAN'T GO BACK...
...IF HE DOESN'T SAIL THE BOAT!
PHWEET

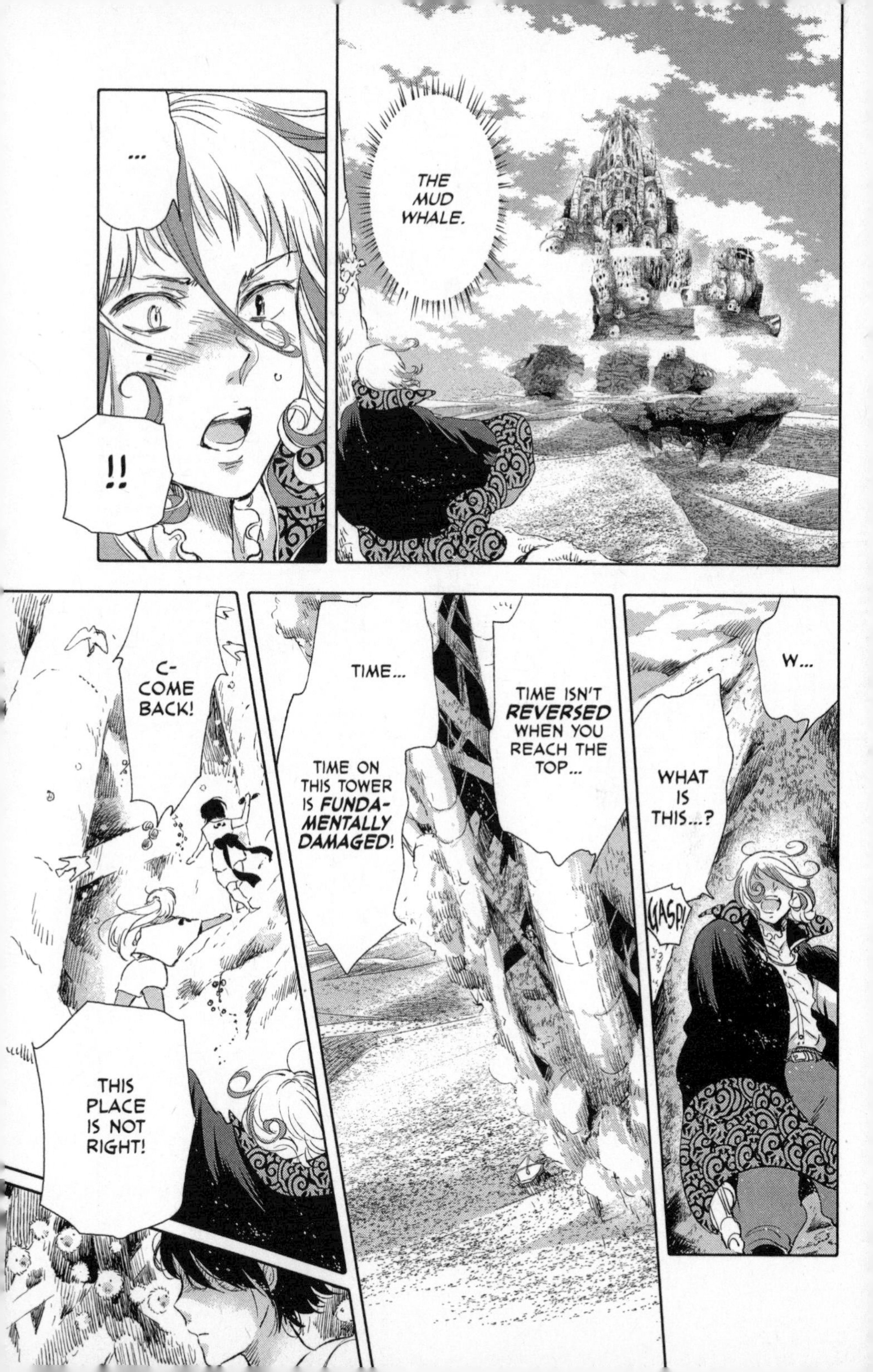
THE MUD WHALE.
...
!!
W...
WHAT IS THIS...?
GASP!
TIME...
TIME ISN'T REVERSED WHEN YOU REACH THE TOP...
TIME ON THIS TOWER IS FUNDAMENTALLY DAMAGED!
C-COME BACK!
THIS PLACE IS NOT RIGHT!

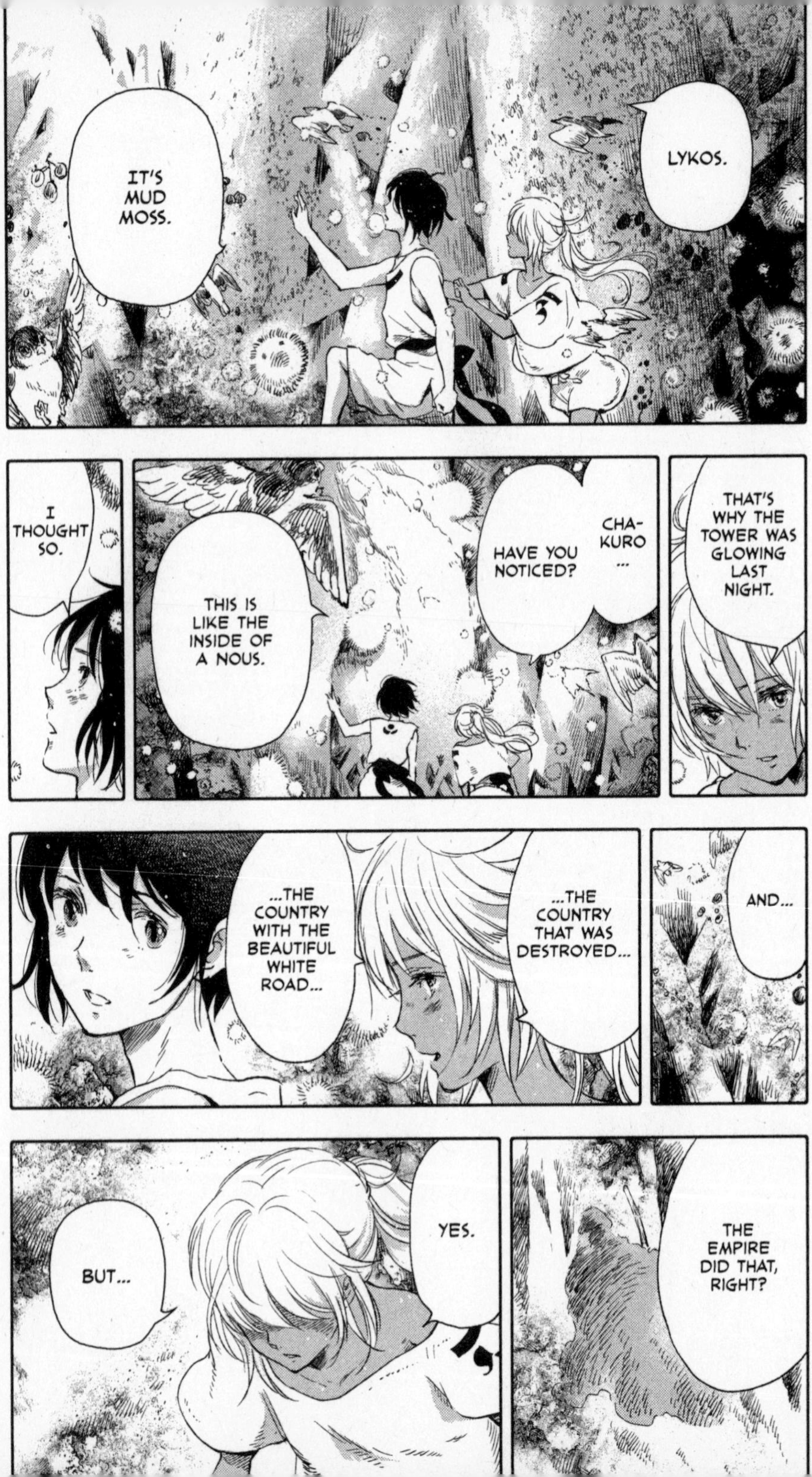
LYKOS.
IT'S MUD MOSS.
THAT'S WHY THE TOWER WAS GLOWING LAST NIGHT.
CHA-KURO...
HAVE YOU NOTICED?
THIS IS LIKE THE INSIDE OF A NOUS.
I THOUGHT SO.
AND...
...THE COUNTRY THAT WAS DESTROYED...
...THE COUNTRY WITH THE BEAUTIFUL WHITE ROAD...
THE EMPIRE DID THAT, RIGHT?
YES.
BUT...

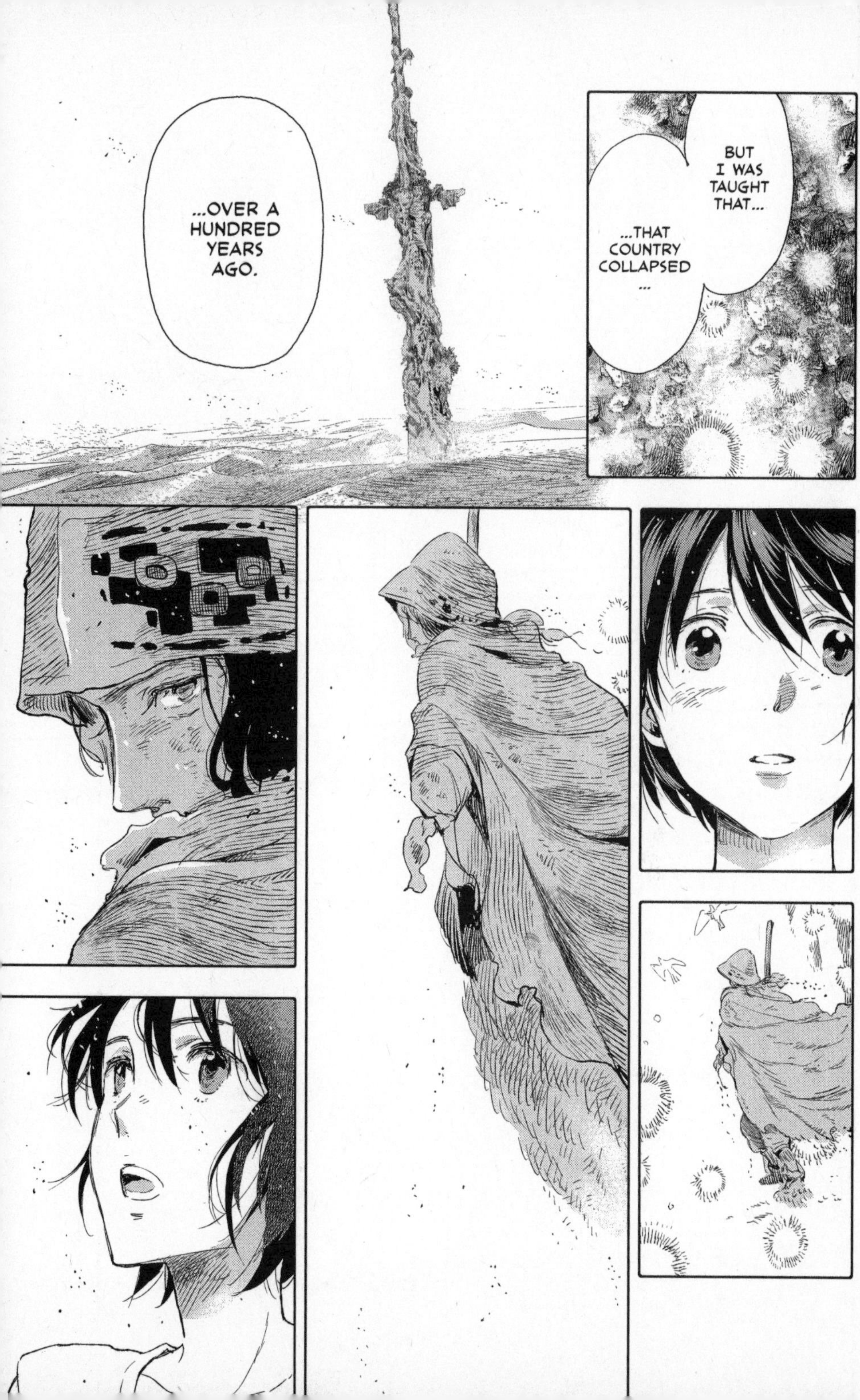
BUT I WAS TAUGHT THAT...
...THAT COUNTRY COLLAPSED ...
...OVER A HUNDRED YEARS AGO.

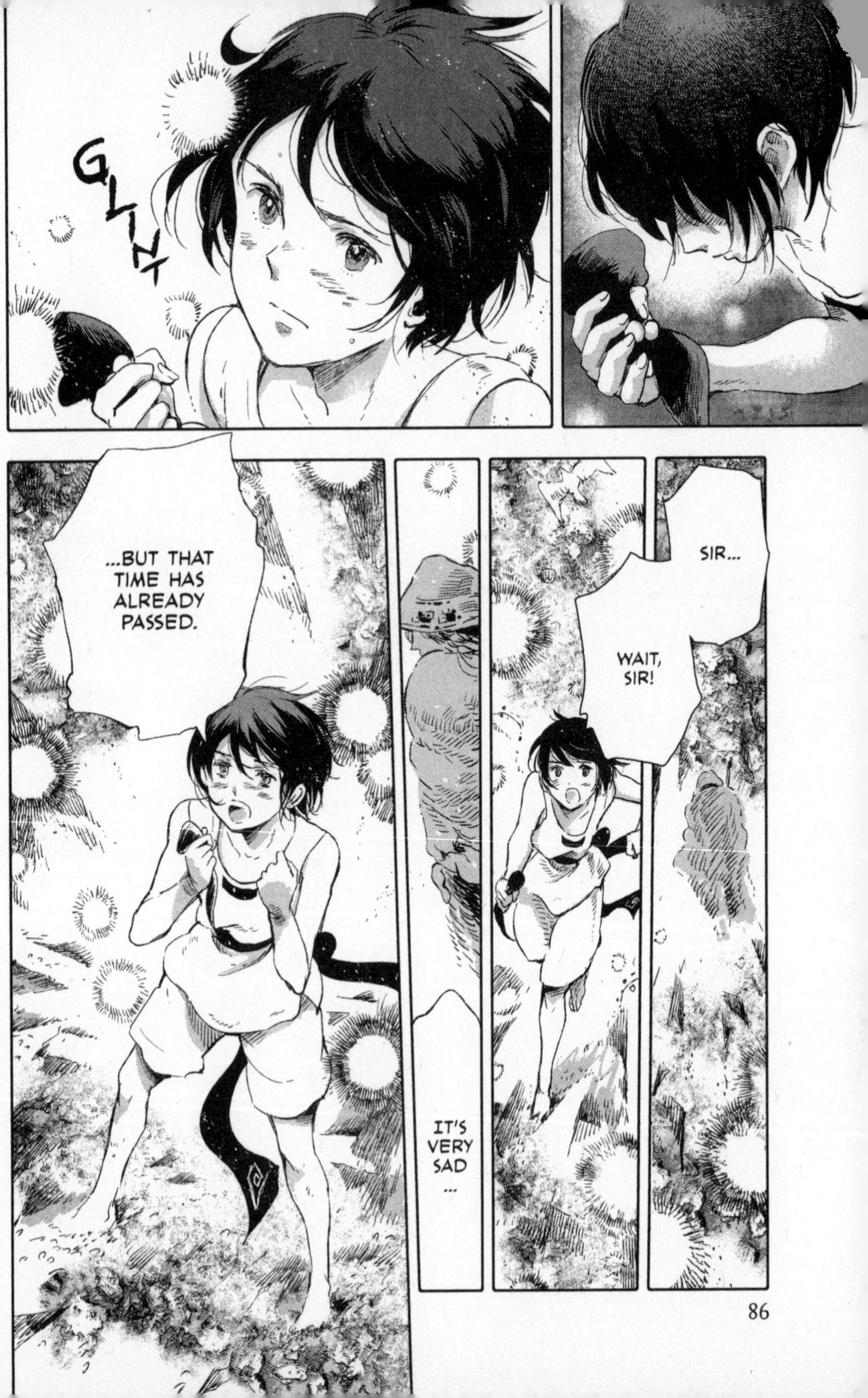
GLINT
SIR...
WAIT, SIR!
IT'S VERY SAD ...
...BUT THAT TIME HAS ALREADY PASSED.

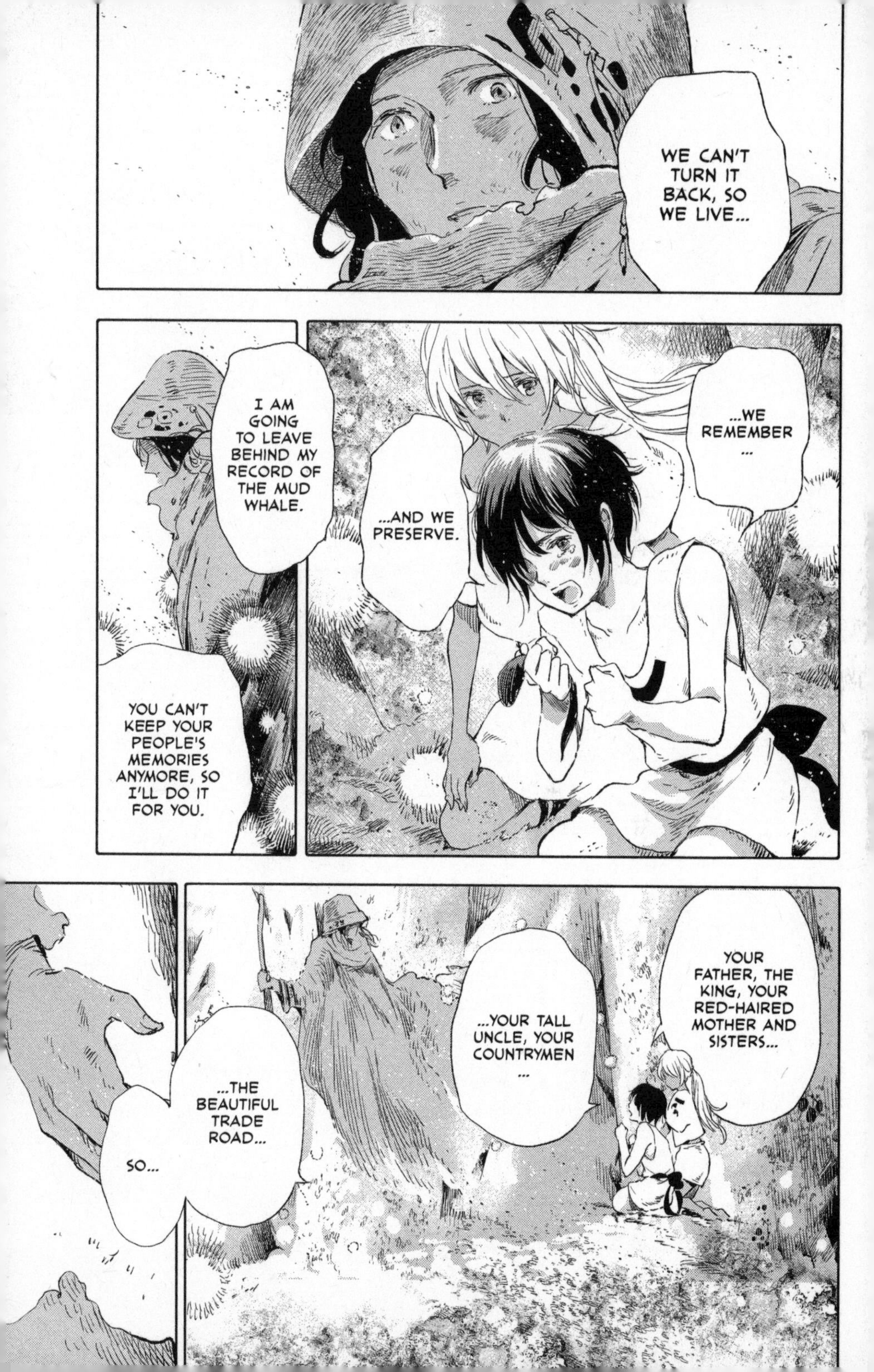
WE CAN'T TURN IT BACK, SO WE LIVE...
...WE REMEMBER ...
...AND WE PRESERVE.
I AM GOING TO LEAVE BEHIND MY RECORD OF THE MUD WHALE.
YOU CAN'T KEEP YOUR PEOPLE'S MEMORIES ANYMORE, SO I'LL DO IT FOR YOU.
YOUR FATHER, THE KING, YOUR RED-HAIRED MOTHER AND SISTERS...
...YOUR TALL UNCLE, YOUR COUNTRYMEN ...
...THE BEAUTIFUL TRADE ROAD...
SO...

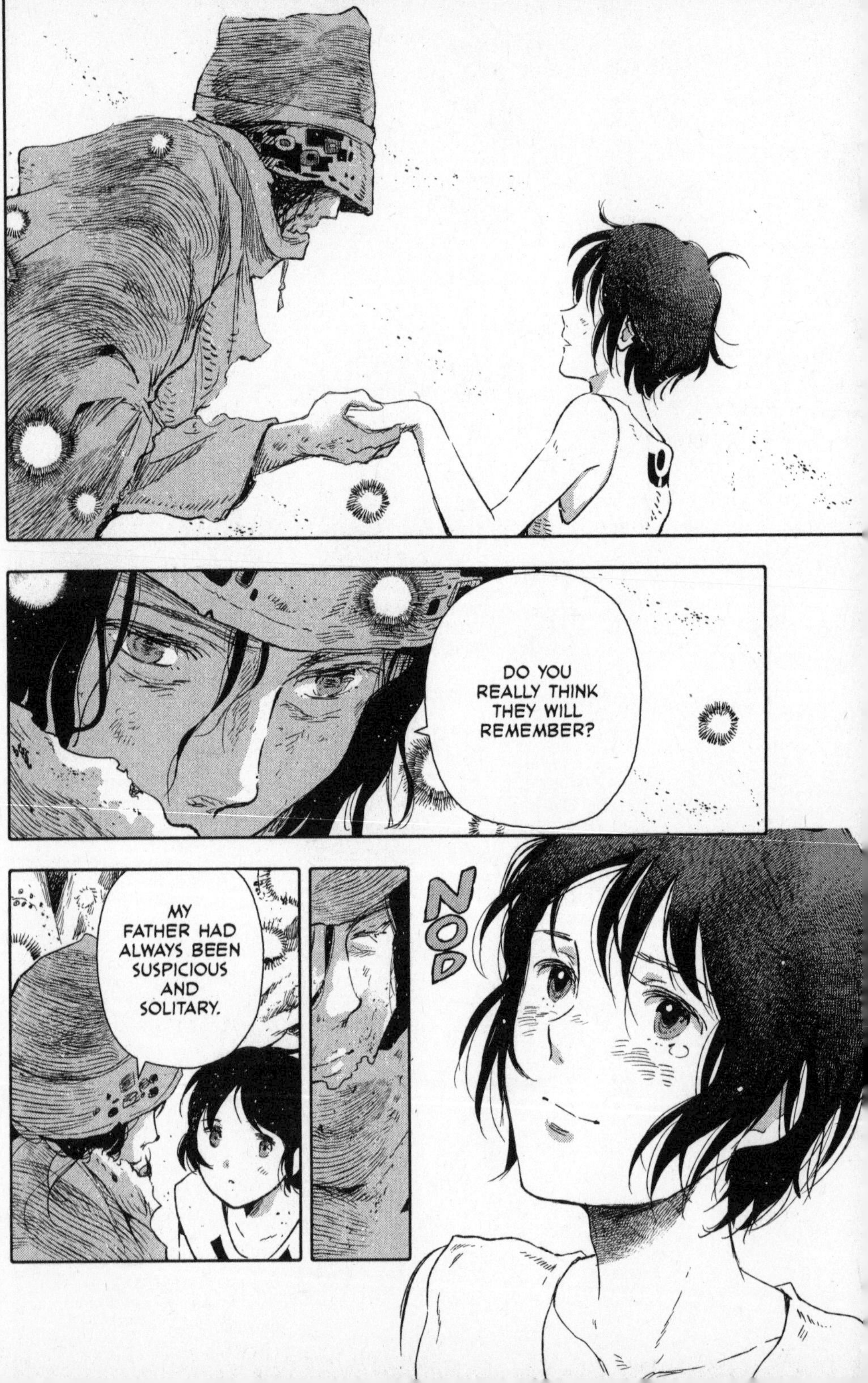
DO YOU REALLY THINK THEY WILL REMEMBER?
NOD
MY FATHER HAD ALWAYS BEEN SUSPICIOUS AND SOLITARY.

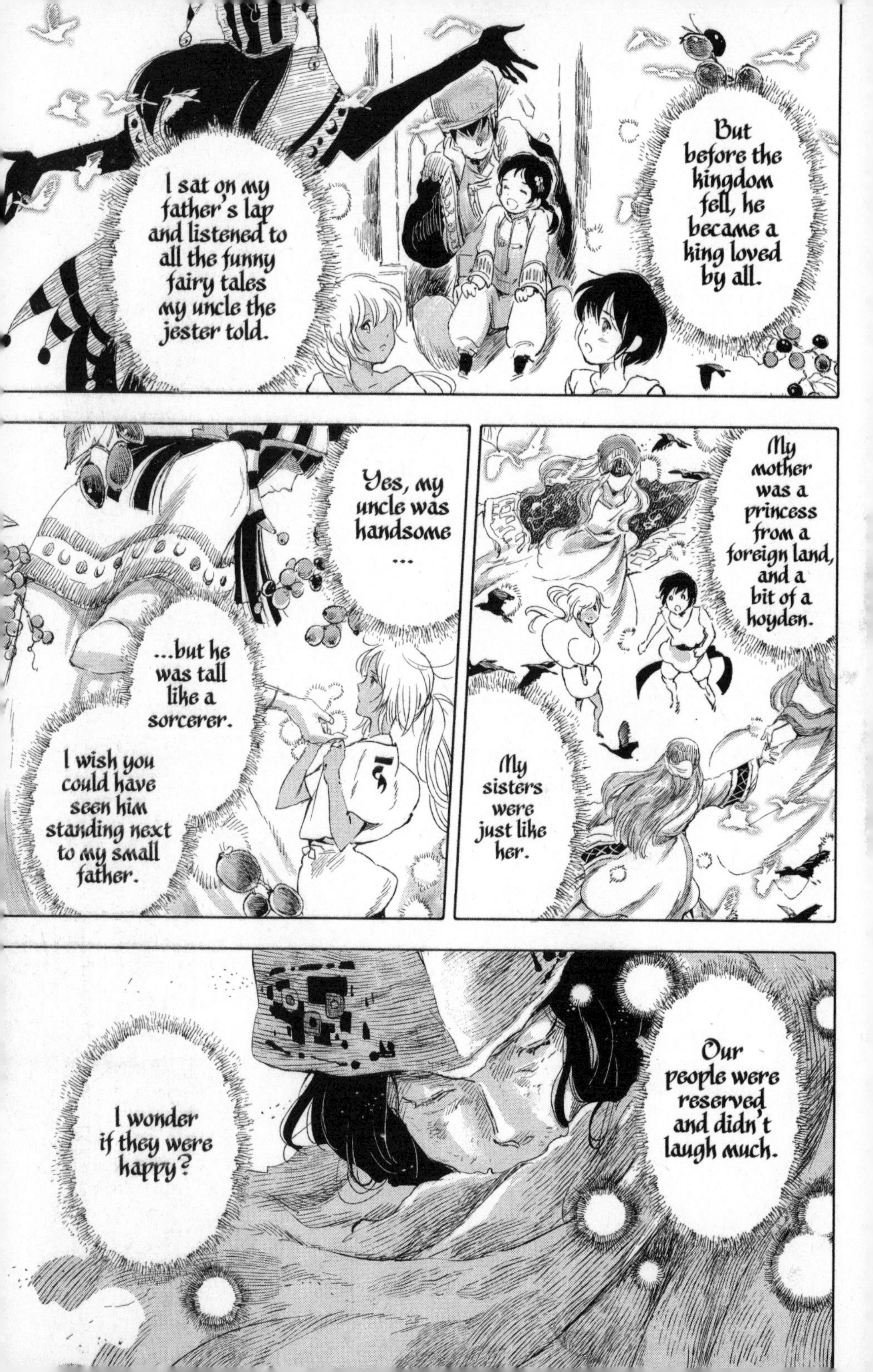
But before the kingdom fell, he became a king loved by all.
I sat on my father's lap and listened to all the funny fairy tales my uncle the jester told.
My mother was a princess from a foreign land, and a bit of a hoyden.
My sisters were just like her.
Yes, my uncle was handsome...
...but he was tall like a sorcerer.
I wish you could have seen him standing next to my small father.
Our people were reserved and didn't laugh much.
I wonder if they were happy?

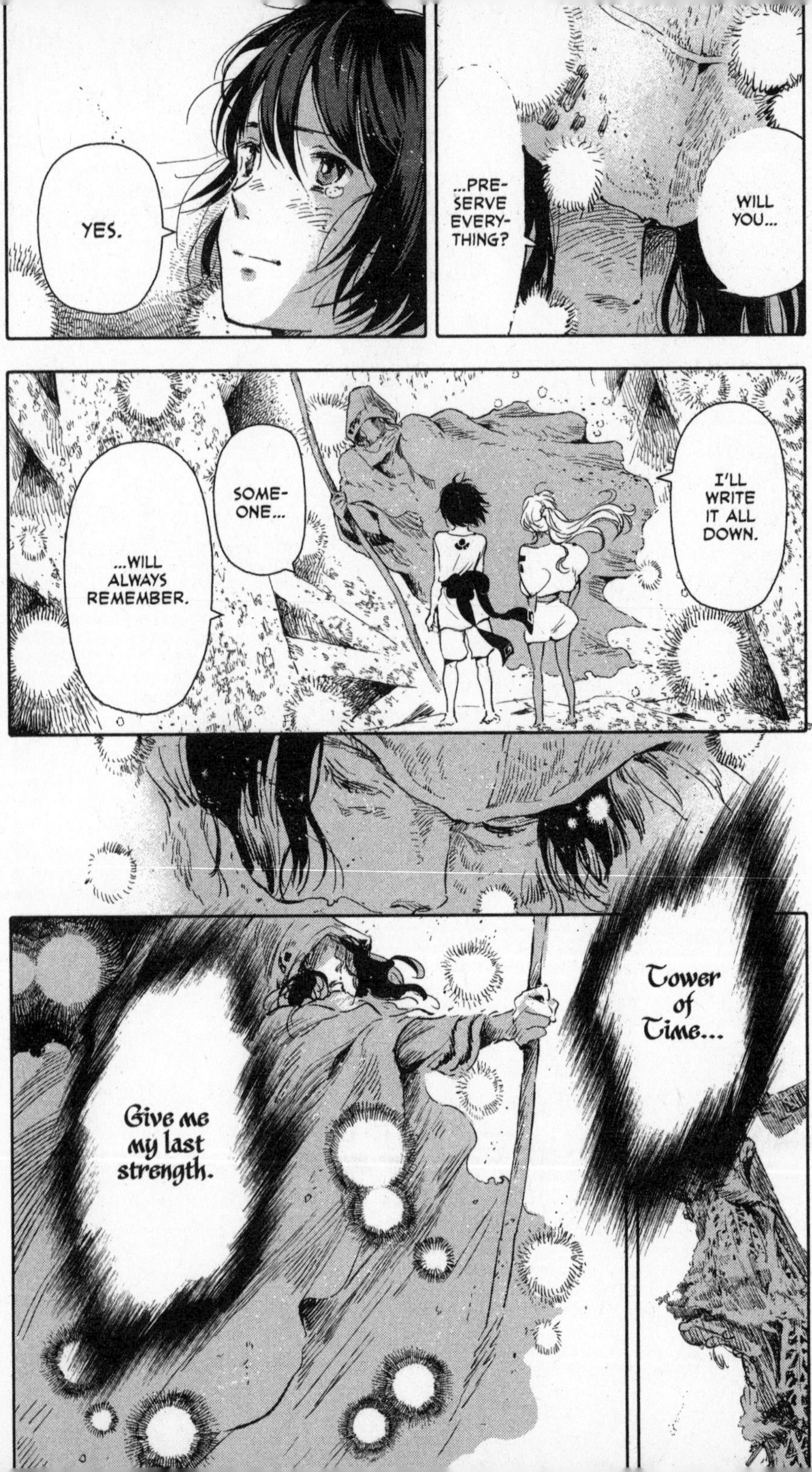
WILL YOU...
...PRE-SERVE EVERYTHING?
YES.
I'LL WRITE IT ALL DOWN.
SOME-ONE...
...WILL ALWAYS REMEMBER.
Tower of Time...
Give me my last strength.

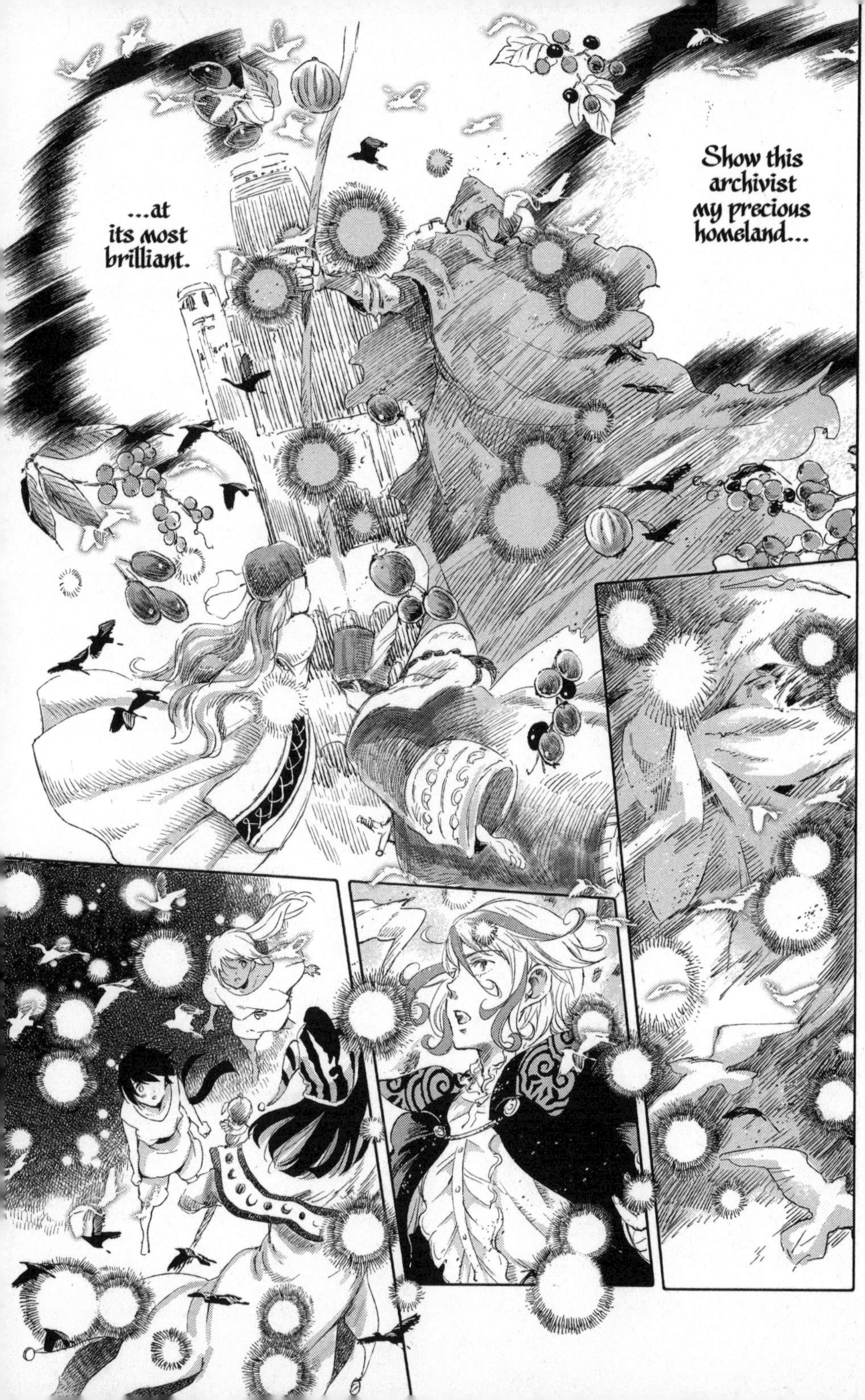
Show this archivist my precious homeland...
...at its most brilliant.

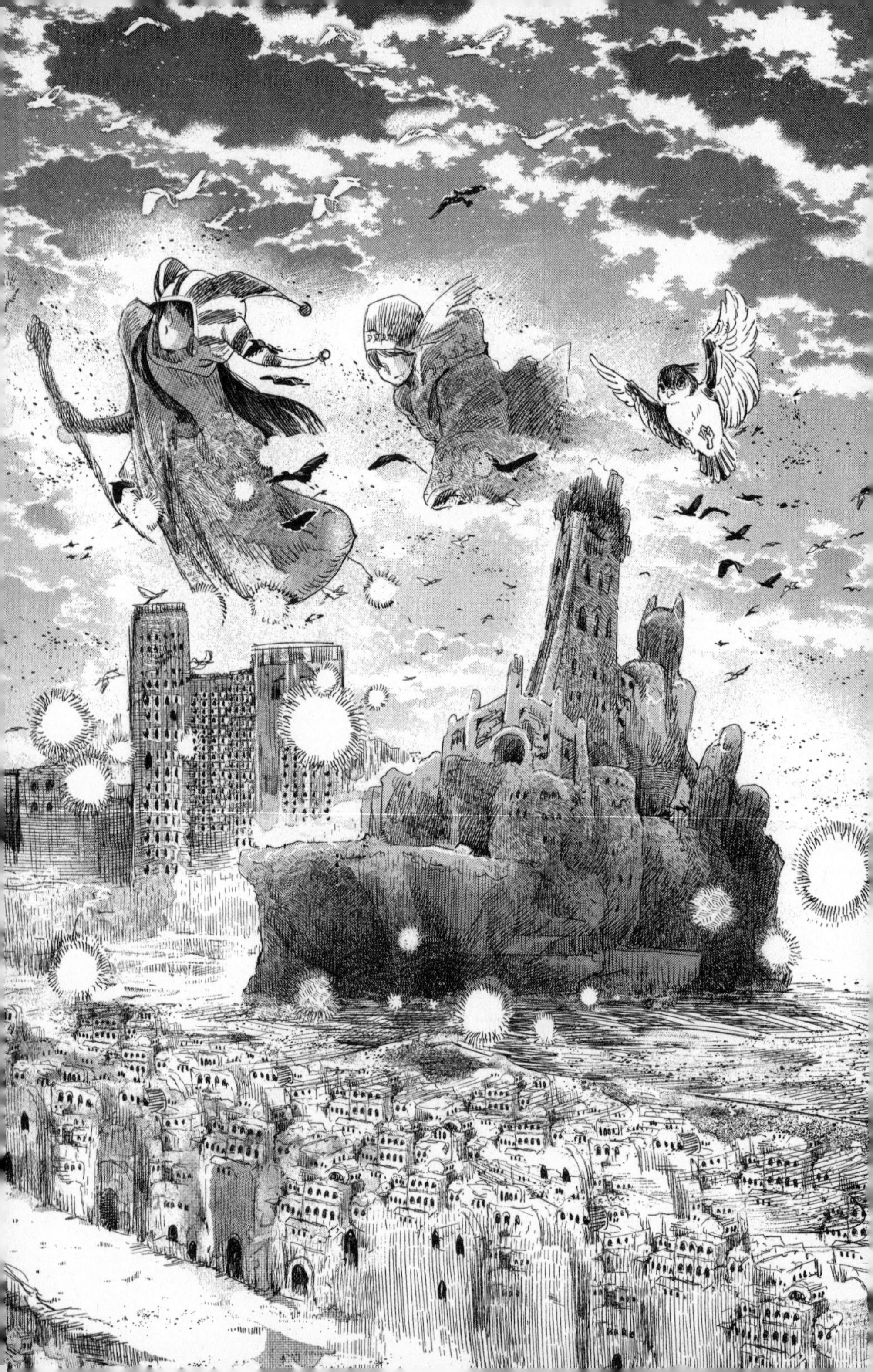

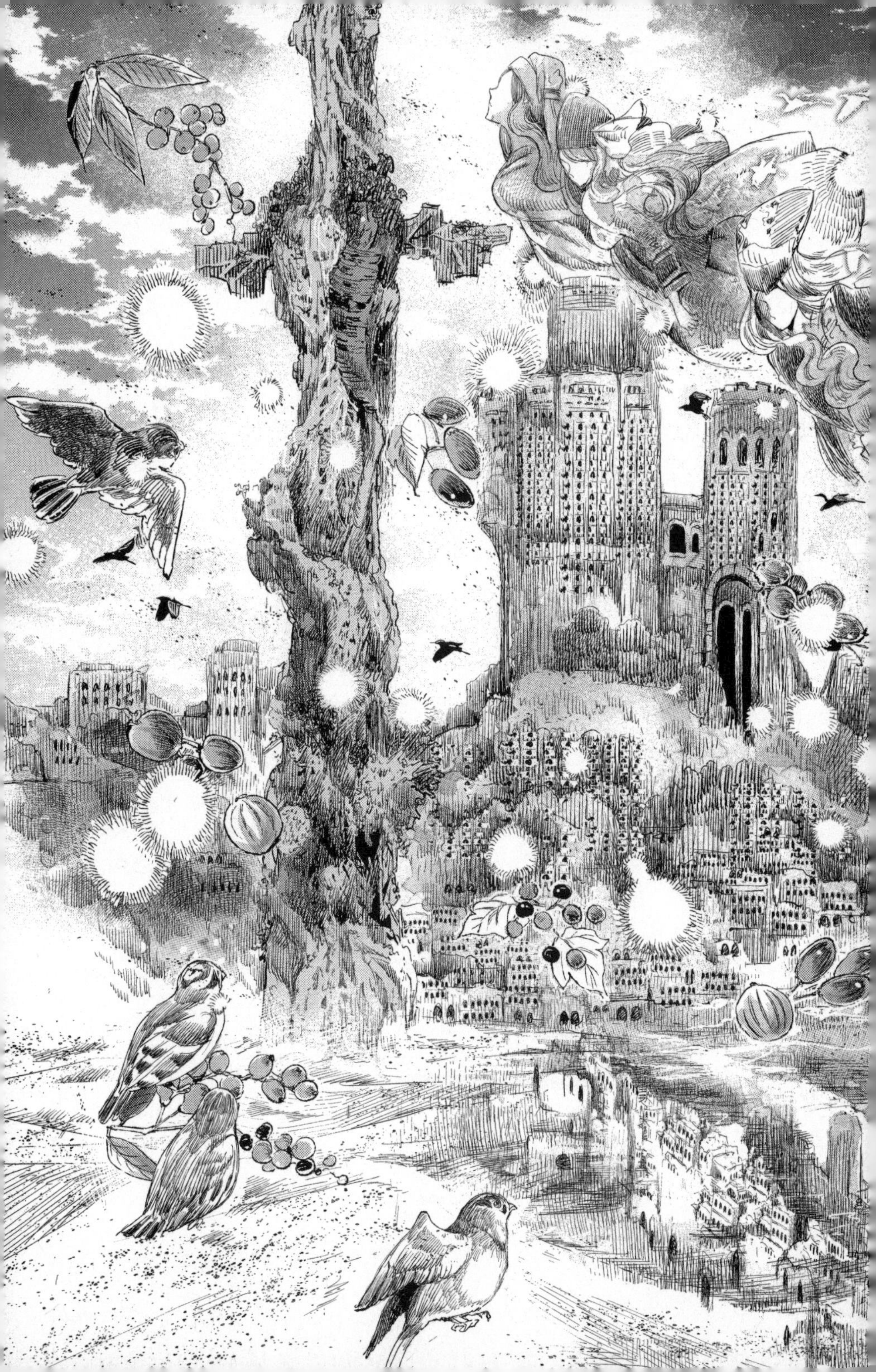

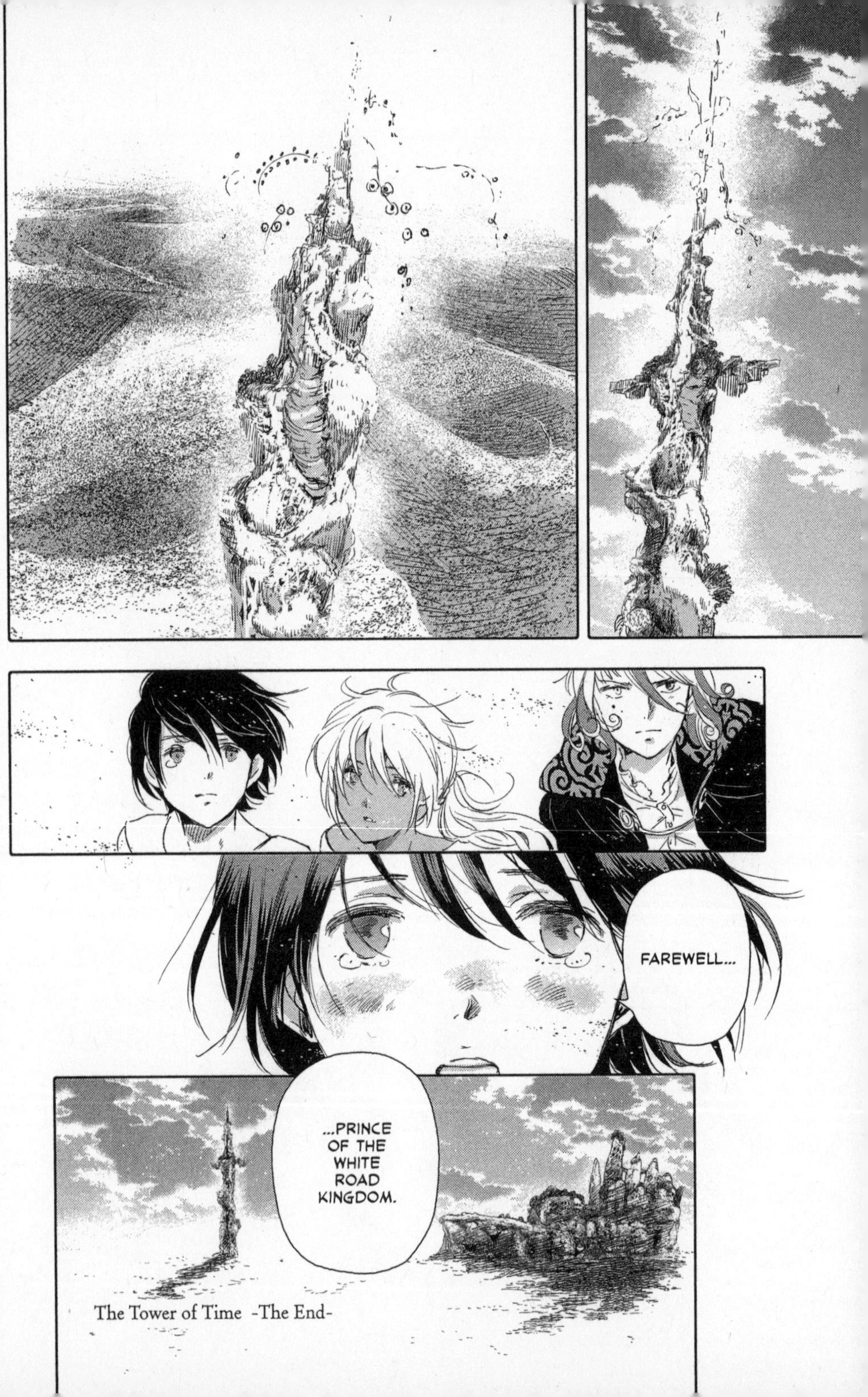
FAREWELL...
...PRINCE OF THE WHITE ROAD KINGDOM.
The Tower of Time -The End-

Sketch ⑧

Resources and Supplies:

The Mud Whale was resource poor, so supplies and food were strictly managed and distributed with painstaking equality. The necessity of keeping detailed accounts of crops and supplies is why there was an official archivist.

The unmarked leaders who were entrusted with keeping the peace on the Mud Whale were very careful that no one starved or had complaints about being treated unfairly.

The management of salt is a great example of their efforts. The only salt available was what had been gleaned from a salt island and a large quantity of refined salt scavenged from an abandoned ship. Since they had no way of knowing when or if they would find more, it was strictly rationed. Someone was once even sent to the Belly for taking more than their ration of salt.

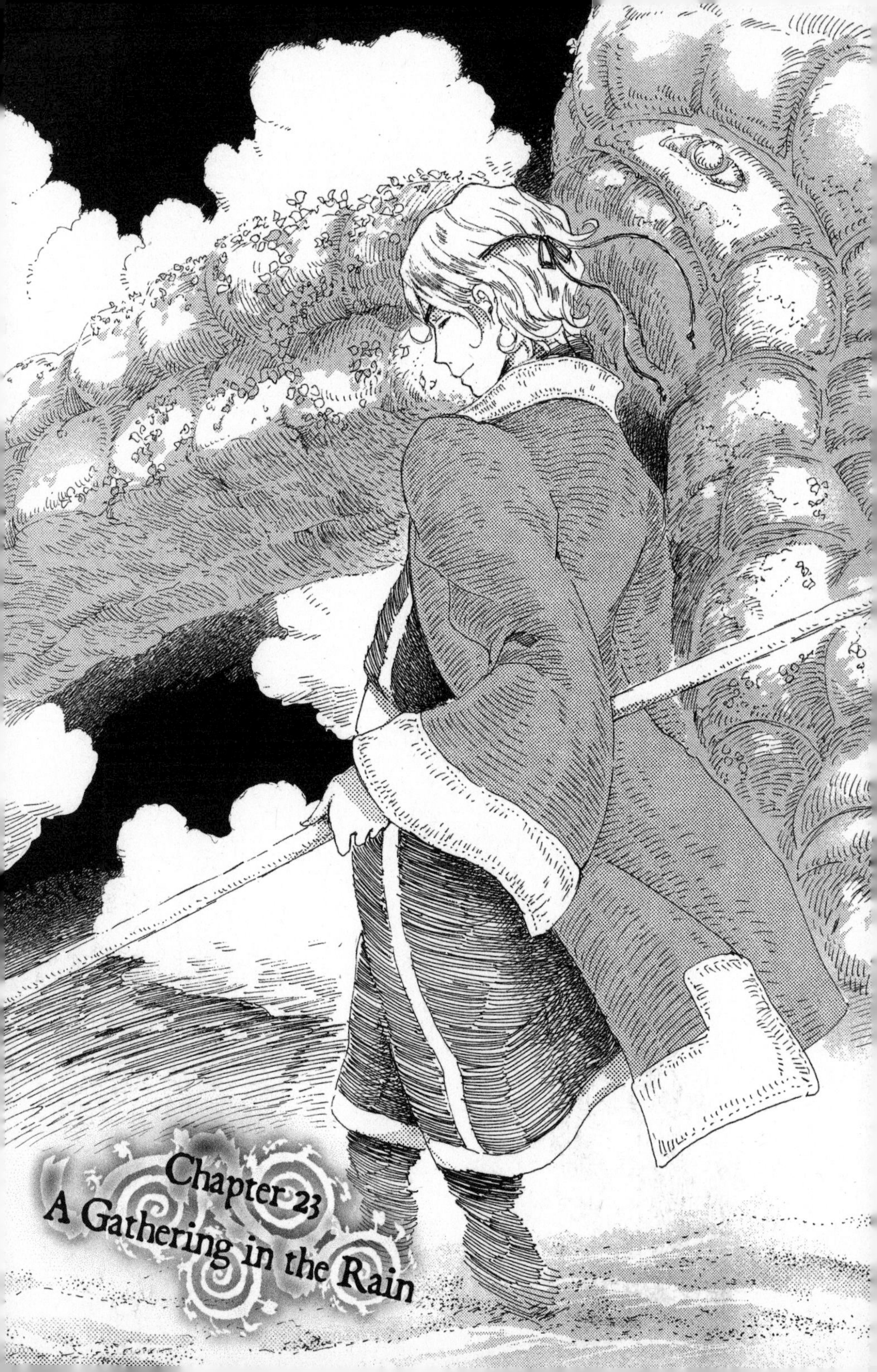
Chapter 23
A Gathering in the Rain

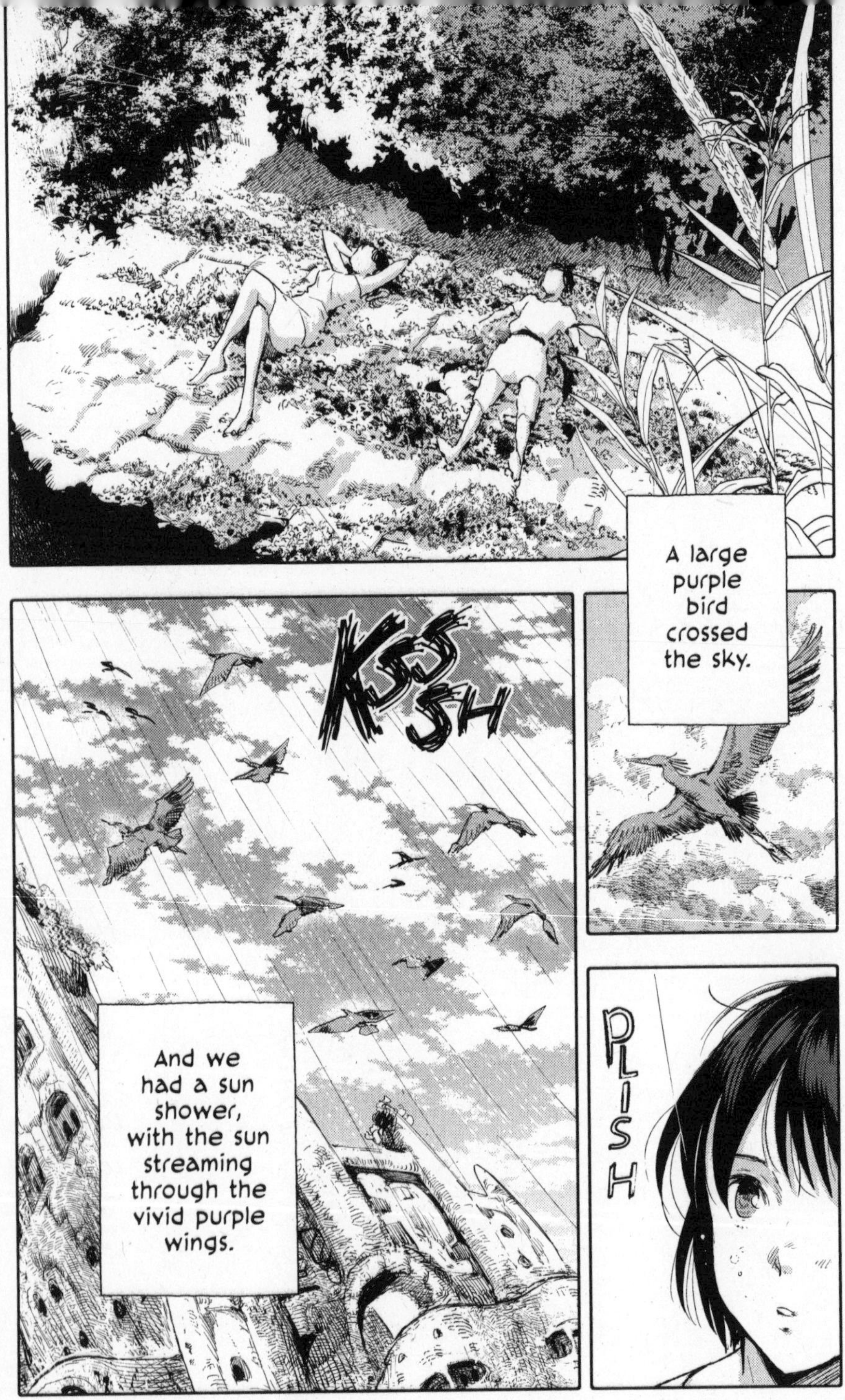
A large purple bird crossed the sky.
PLISH
KSSSH
And we had a sun shower, with the sun streaming through the vivid purple wings.

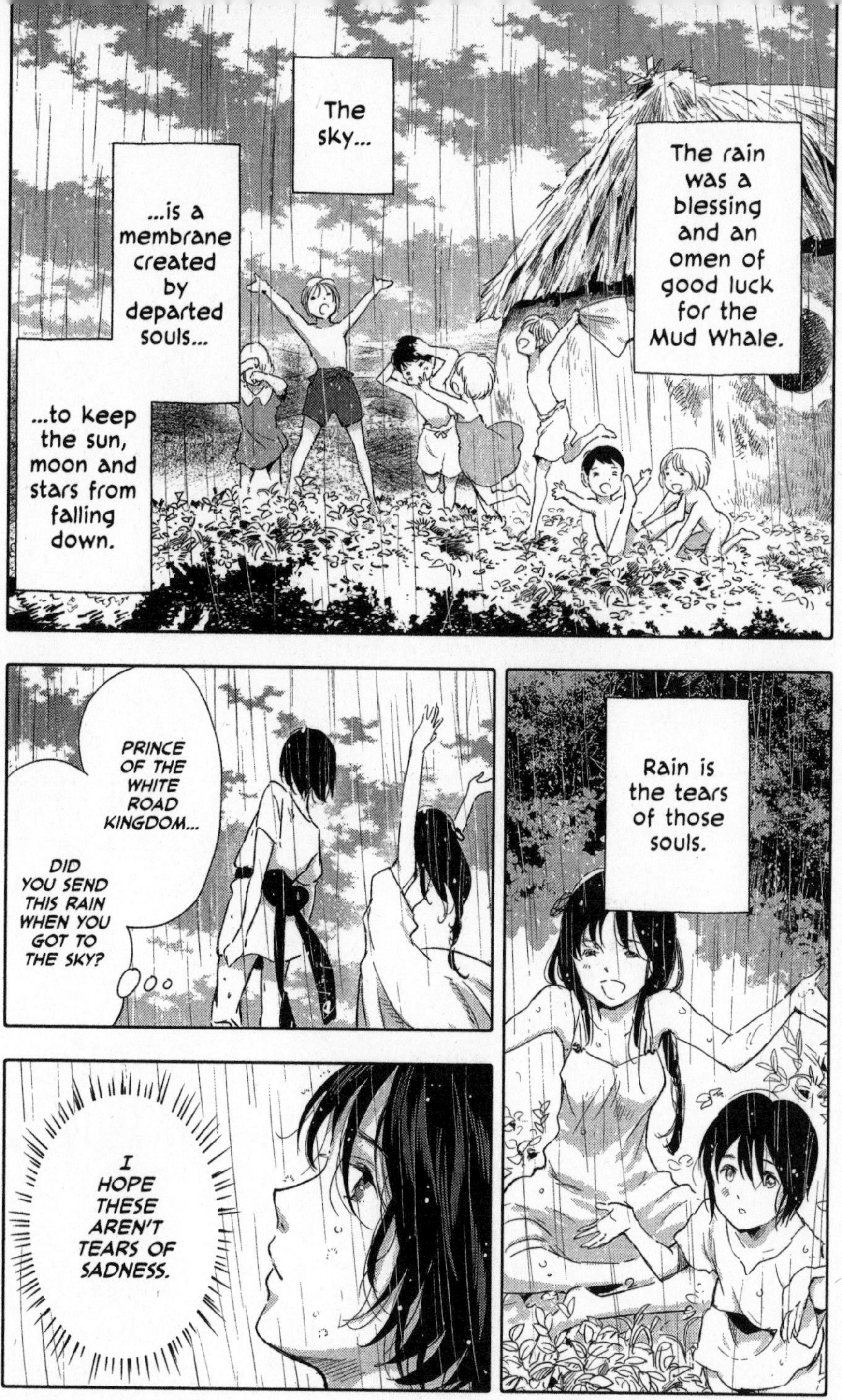
The rain was a blessing and an omen of good luck for the Mud Whale.
The sky...
...is a membrane created by departed souls...
...to keep the sun, moon and stars from falling down.
Rain is the tears of those souls.
PRINCE OF THE WHITE ROAD KINGDOM...
DID YOU SEND THIS RAIN WHEN YOU GOT TO THE SKY?
I HOPE THESE AREN'T TEARS OF SADNESS.

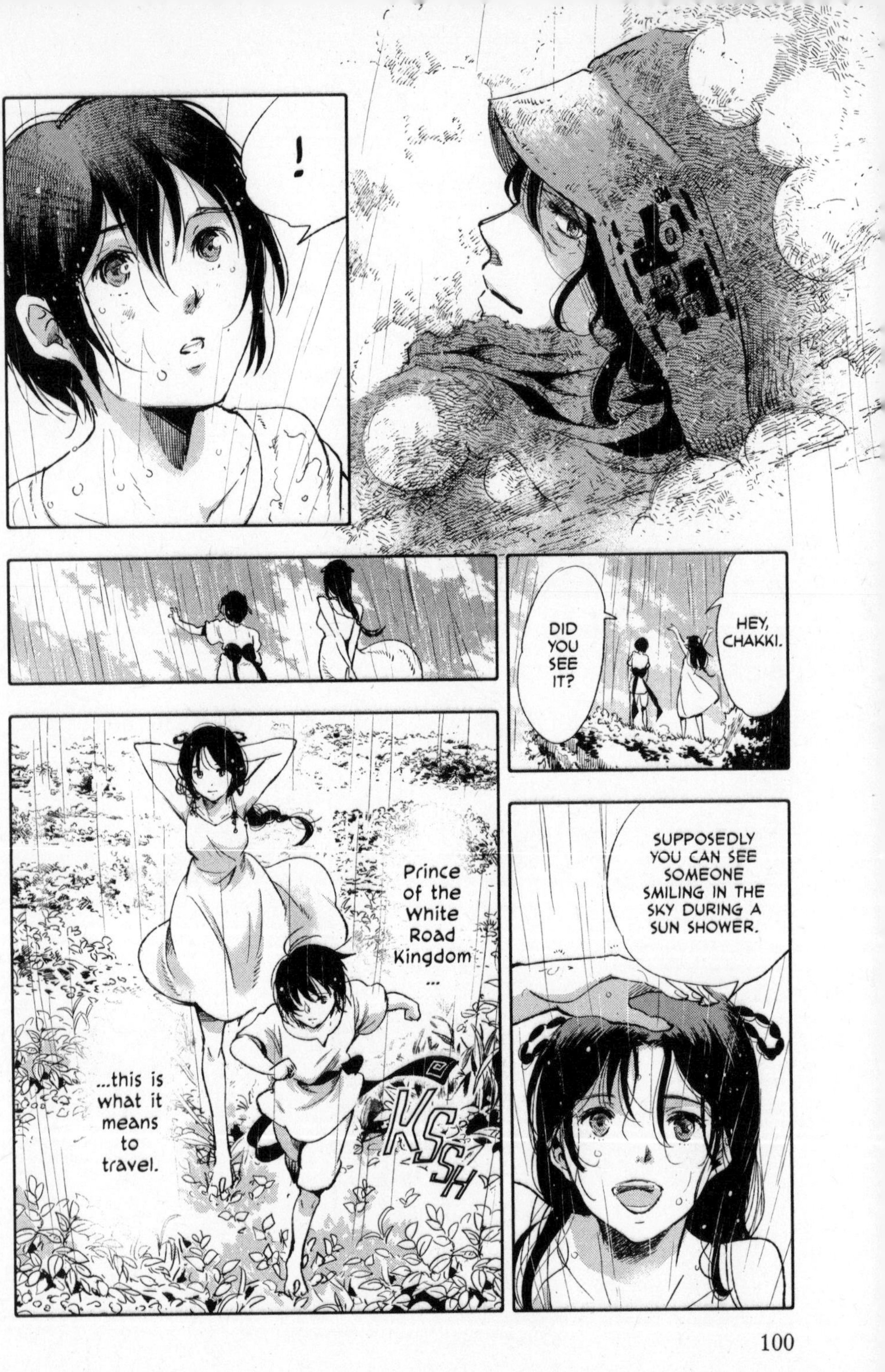
!
HEY, CHAKKI.
DID YOU SEE IT?
SUPPOSEDLY YOU CAN SEE SOMEONE SMILING IN THE SKY DURING A SUN SHOWER.
Prince of the White Road Kingdom ...
...this is what it means to travel.
KSSH

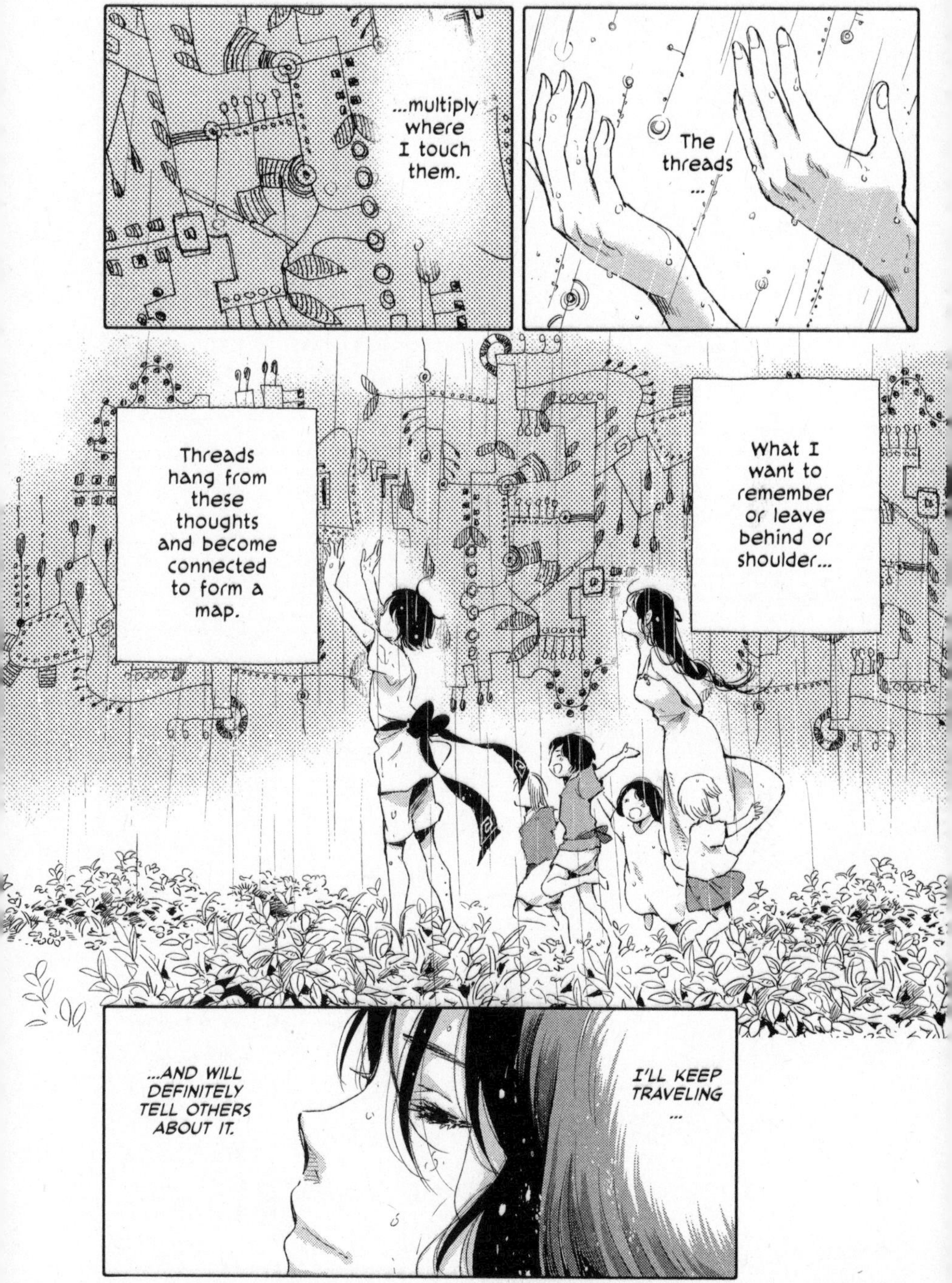
The threads ...
...multiply where I touch them.
What I want to remember or leave behind or shoulder...
Threads hang from these thoughts and become connected to form a map.
I'LL KEEP TRAVELING ...
...AND WILL DEFINITELY TELL OTHERS ABOUT IT.

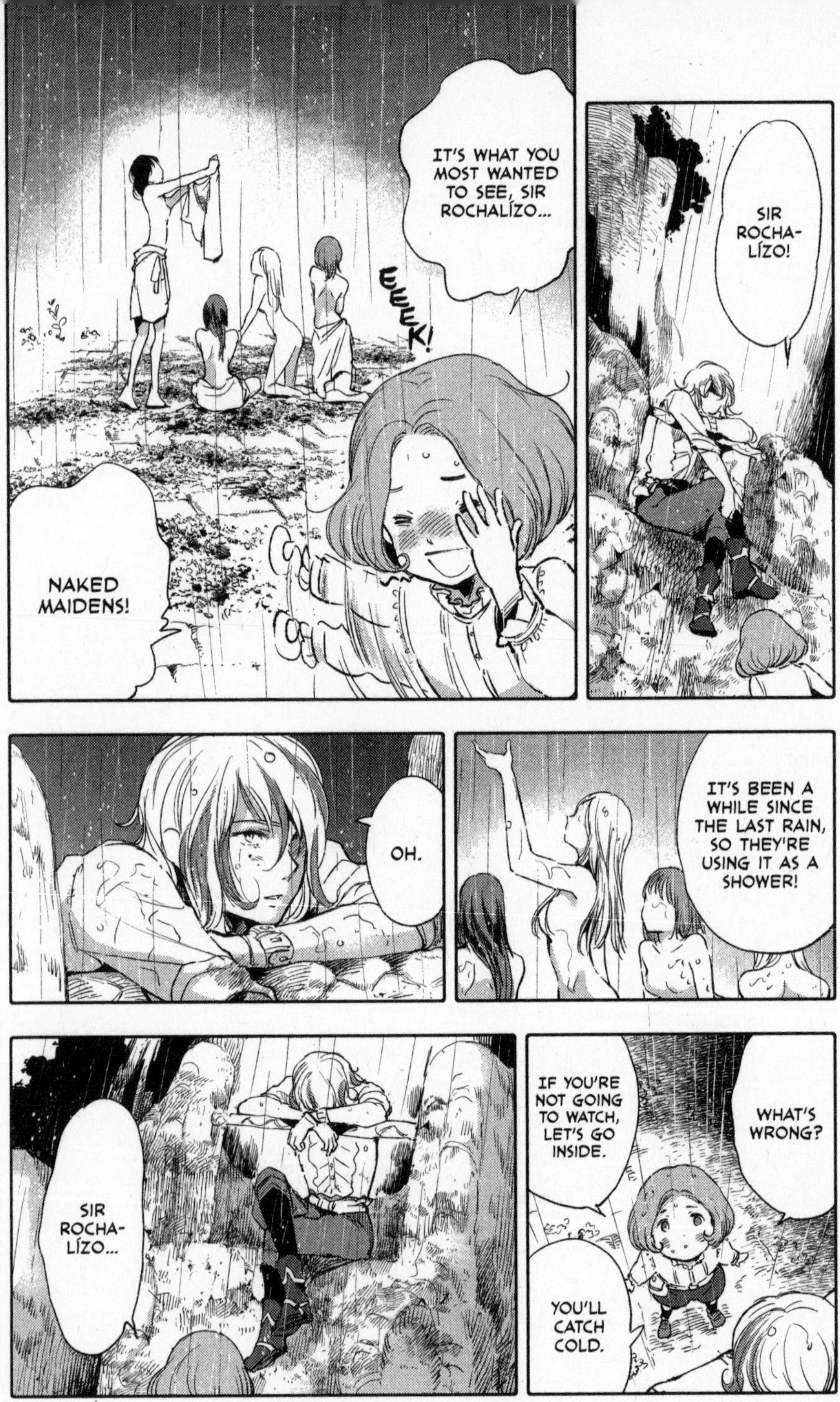
SIR ROCHA-LÍZO!
IT'S WHAT YOU MOST WANTED TO SEE, SIR ROCHALÍZO...
EEEK!
NAKED MAIDENS!
IT'S BEEN A WHILE SINCE THE LAST RAIN, SO THEY'RE USING IT AS A SHOWER!
OH.
WHAT'S WRONG?
IF YOU'RE NOT GOING TO WATCH, LET'S GO INSIDE.
YOU'LL CATCH COLD.
SIR ROCHA-LÍZO...

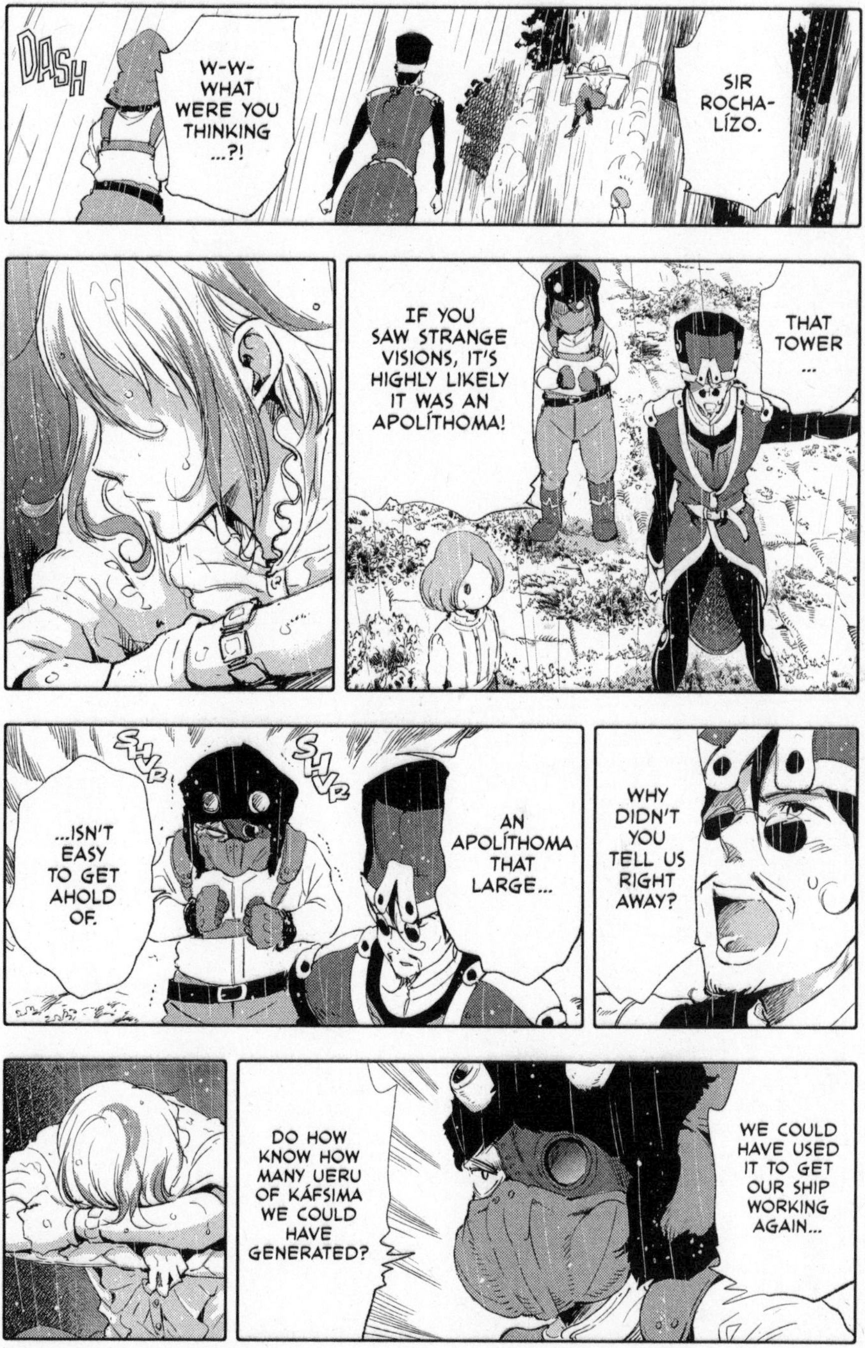
SIR ROCHA-LÍZO.
W-W-WHAT WERE YOU THINKING ...?!
DASH
THAT TOWER ...
IF YOU SAW STRANGE VISIONS, IT'S HIGHLY LIKELY IT WAS AN APOLÍTHOMA!
WHY DIDN'T YOU TELL US RIGHT AWAY?
SHVR
AN APOLÍTHOMA THAT LARGE...
SHVR
...ISN'T EASY TO GET AHOLD OF.
WE COULD HAVE USED IT TO GET OUR SHIP WORKING AGAIN...
DO HOW KNOW HOW MANY UERU OF KÁFSIMA WE COULD HAVE GENERATED?

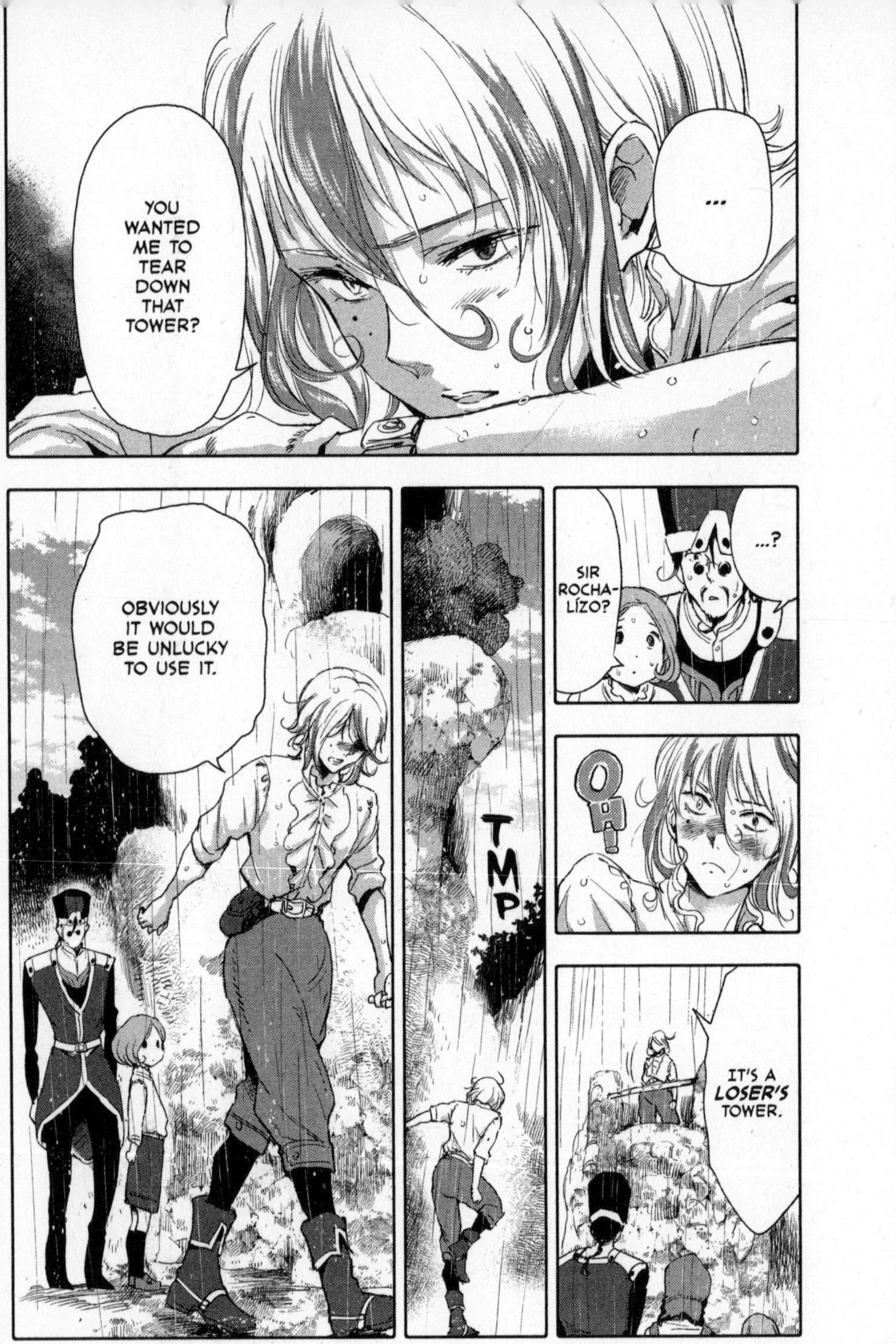
...
YOU WANTED ME TO TEAR DOWN THAT TOWER?
...?
SIR ROCHALÍZO?
OH!
IT'S A *LOSER'S* TOWER.
TMP
OBVIOUSLY IT WOULD BE UNLUCKY TO USE IT.

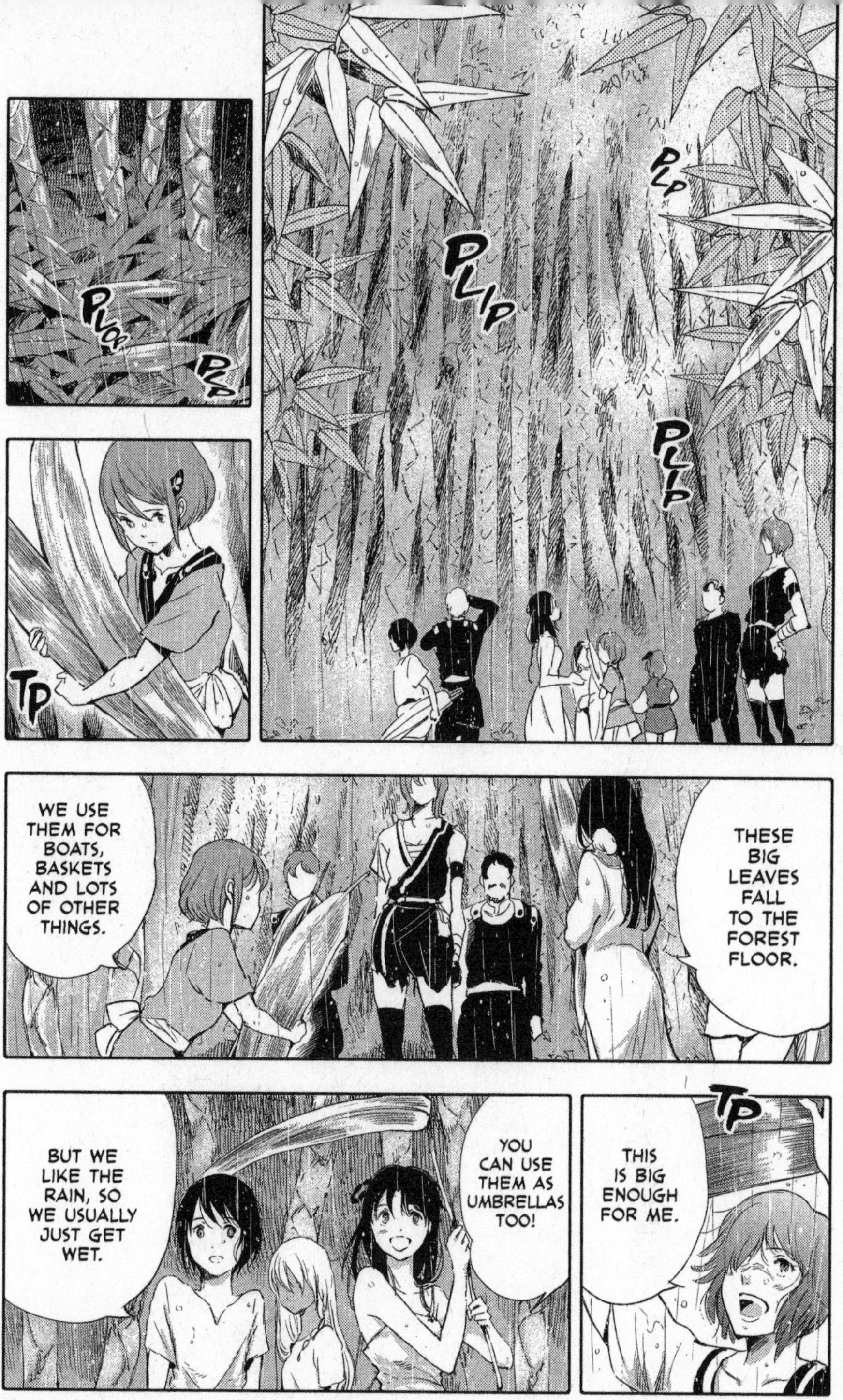
PLP
PLIP
PLIP
PLOP
PLP
TP
THESE BIG LEAVES FALL TO THE FOREST FLOOR.
WE USE THEM FOR BOATS, BASKETS AND LOTS OF OTHER THINGS.
TP
THIS IS BIG ENOUGH FOR ME.
YOU CAN USE THEM AS UMBRELLAS TOO!
BUT WE LIKE THE RAIN, SO WE USUALLY JUST GET WET.

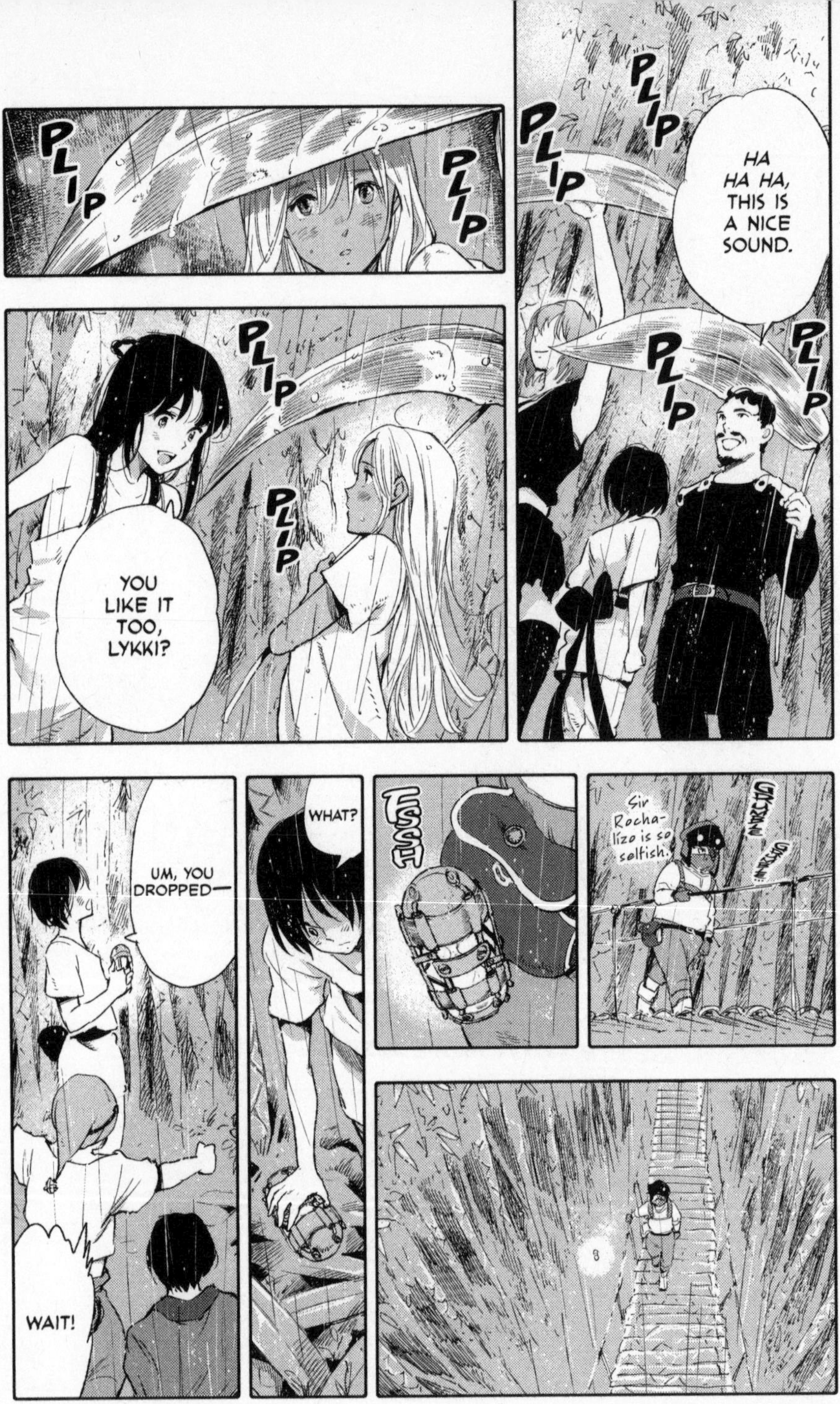
PLIP
PLIP
PLIP
HA HA HA, THIS IS A NICE SOUND.
PLIP
PLIP
PLIP
PLIP
PLIP
PLIP
PLIP
YOU LIKE IT TOO, LYKKI?
GRUMBLE
GRUMBLE...
Sir Rochalízo is so selfish.
FSSH
WHAT?
UM, YOU DROPPED—
WAIT!

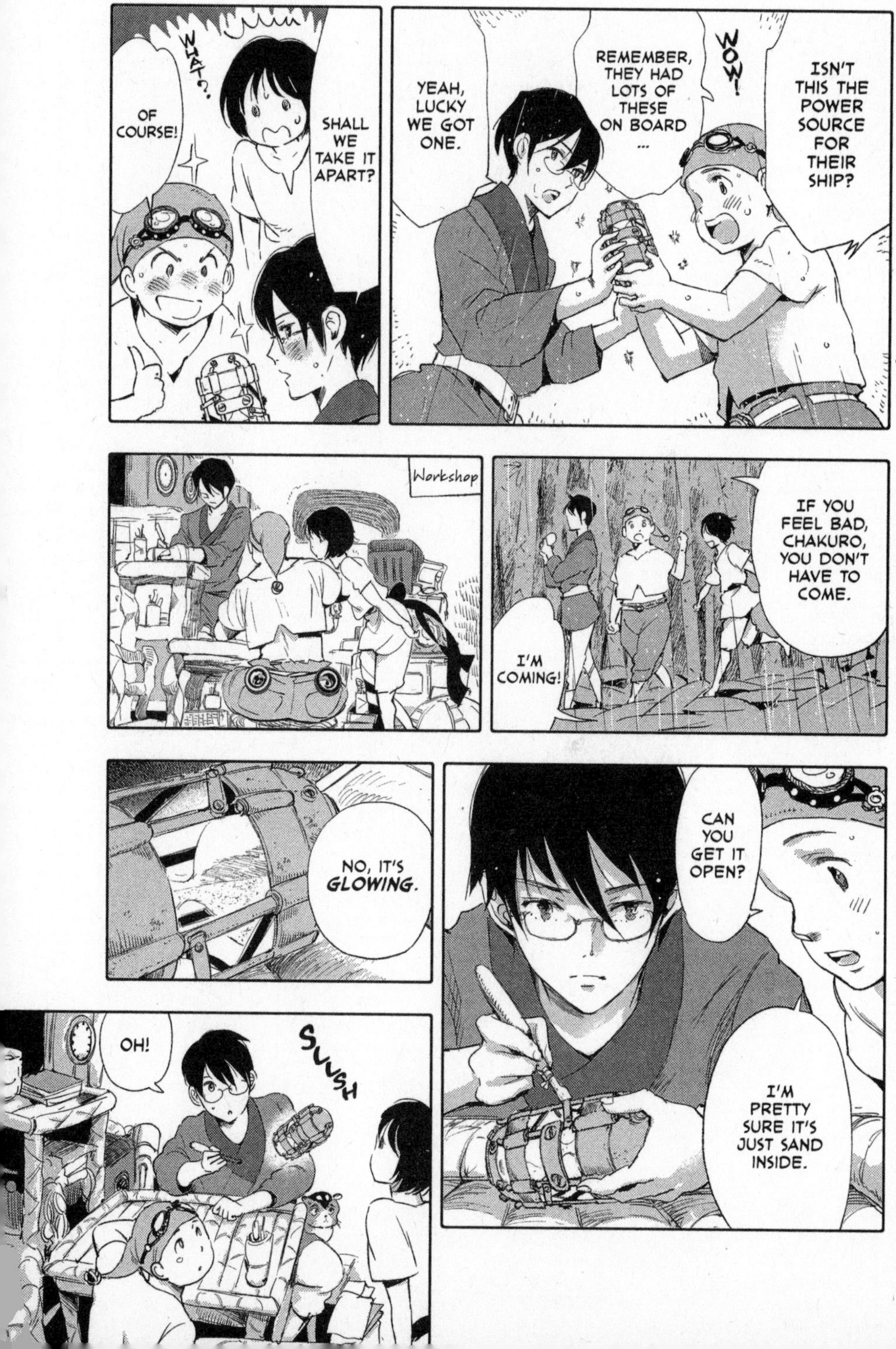
ISN'T THIS THE POWER SOURCE FOR THEIR SHIP?
WOW!
REMEMBER, THEY HAD LOTS OF THESE ON BOARD ...
YEAH, LUCKY WE GOT ONE.
SHALL WE TAKE IT APART?
WHAT?
OF COURSE!
IF YOU FEEL BAD, CHAKURO, YOU DON'T HAVE TO COME.
I'M COMING!
Workshop
CAN YOU GET IT OPEN?
I'M PRETTY SURE IT'S JUST SAND INSIDE.
NO, IT'S *GLOWING*.
SUUSH
OH!

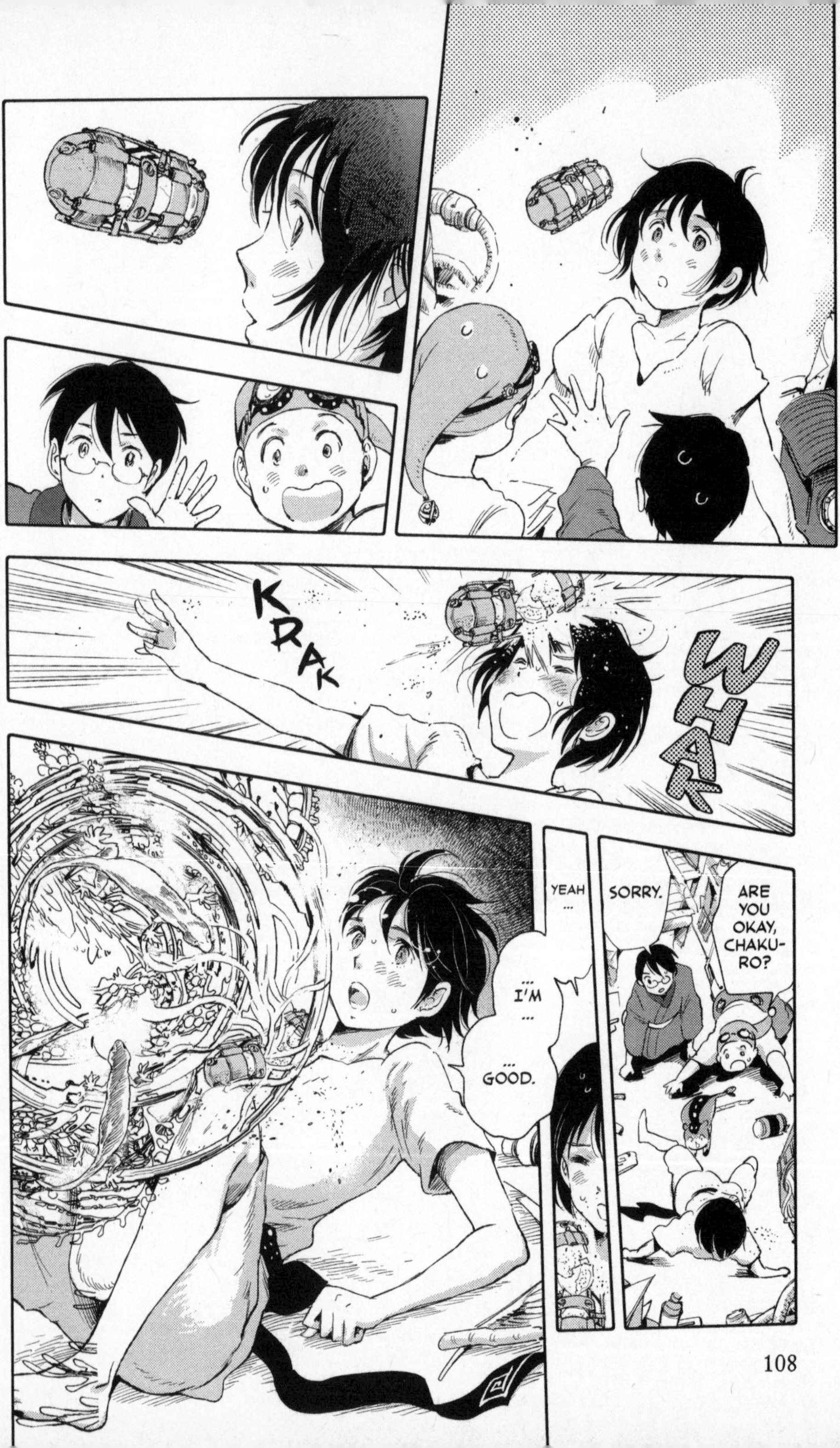
WHAK
KRAK
ARE YOU OKAY, CHAKU-RO?
SORRY.
YEAH ...
... I'M ...
... GOOD.

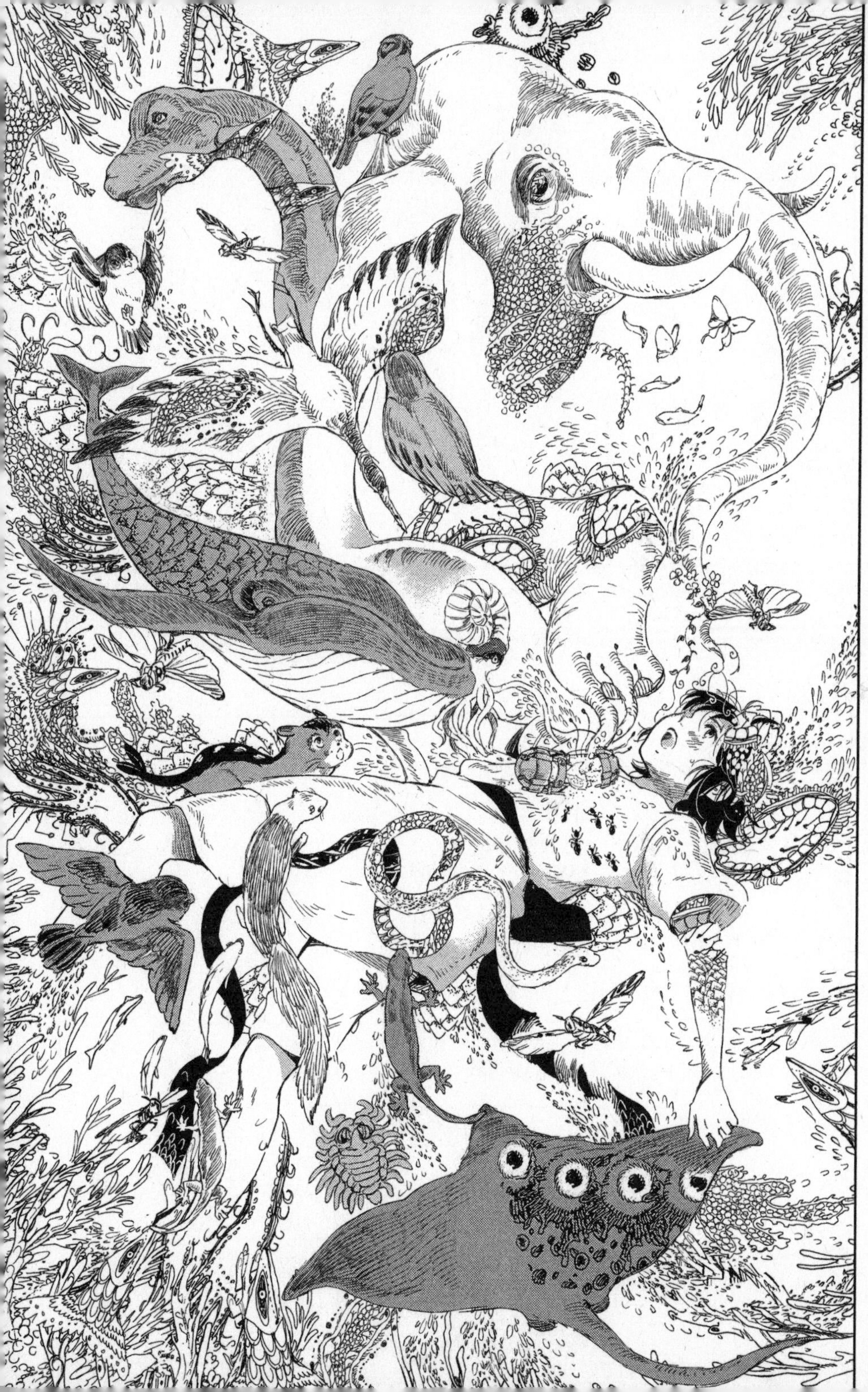

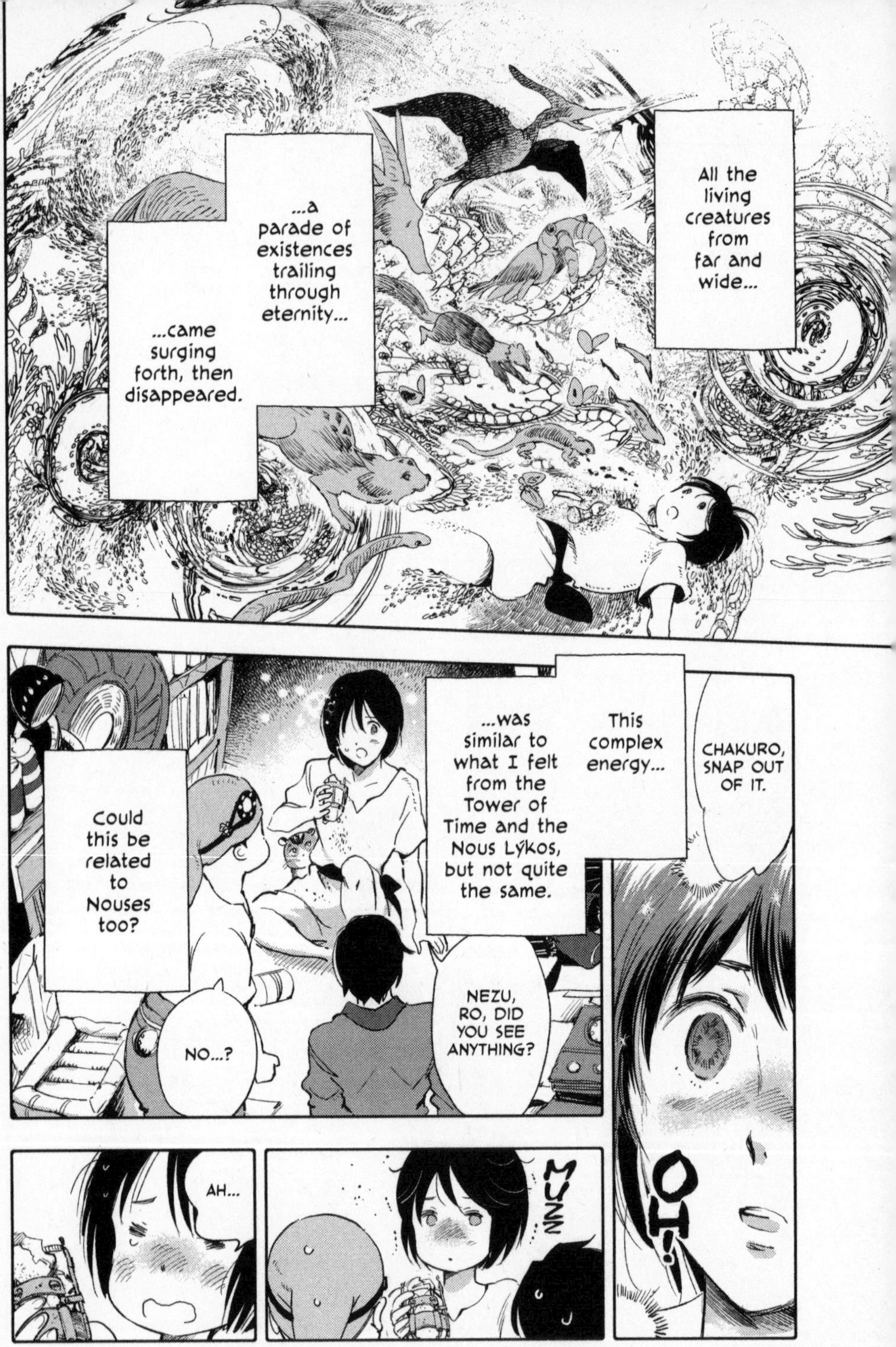
All the living creatures from far and wide...
...a parade of existences trailing through eternity...
...came surging forth, then disappeared.
CHAKURO, SNAP OUT OF IT.
OH!
This complex energy...
...was similar to what I felt from the Tower of Time and the Nous Lýkos, but not quite the same.
Could this be related to Nouses too?
NEZU, RO, DID YOU SEE ANYTHING?
NO...?
MUNN
AH...

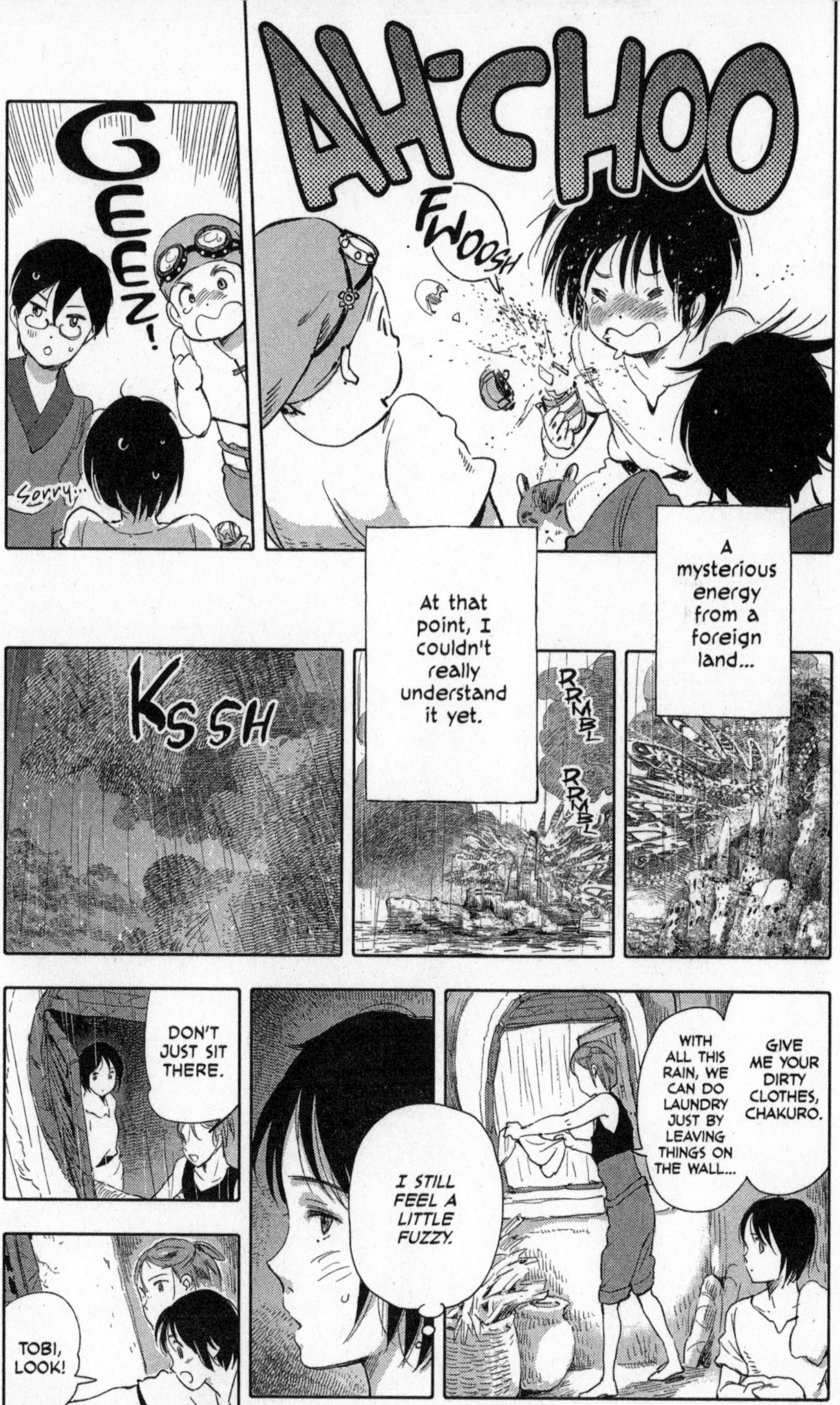
AH-CHOO
FWOOSH
GEEZ!
Sorry...
A mysterious energy from a foreign land...
At that point, I couldn't really understand it yet.
RRMBL
RRMBL
KSSH
GIVE ME YOUR DIRTY CLOTHES, CHAKURO.
WITH ALL THIS RAIN, WE CAN DO LAUNDRY JUST BY LEAVING THINGS ON THE WALL...
I STILL FEEL A LITTLE FUZZY.
DON'T JUST SIT THERE.
TOBI, LOOK!

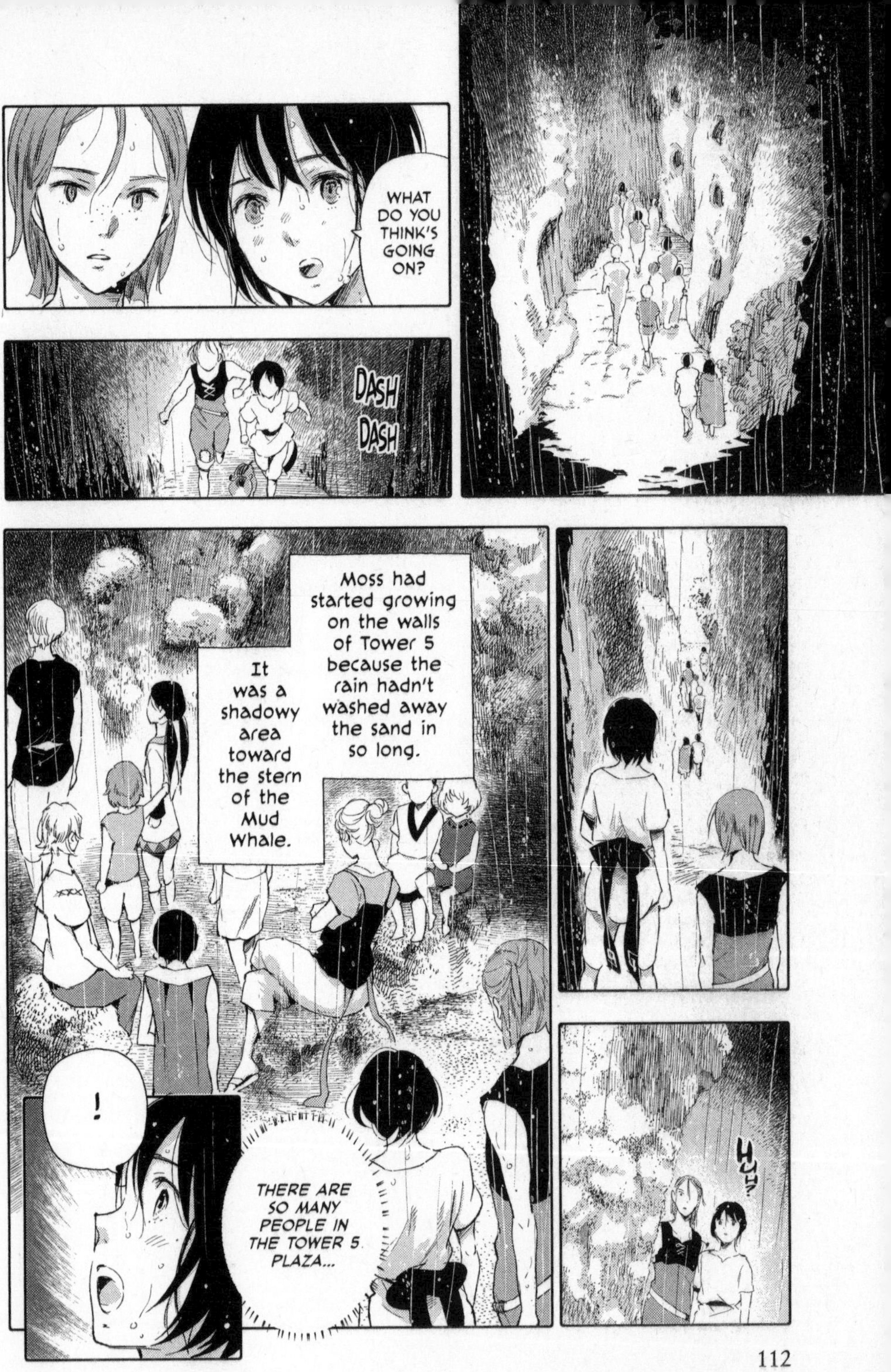
WHAT DO YOU THINK'S GOING ON?
DASH DASH
HUH?
Moss had started growing on the walls of Tower 5 because the rain hadn't washed away the sand in so long.
It was a shadowy area toward the stern of the Mud Whale.
THERE ARE SO MANY PEOPLE IN THE TOWER 5 PLAZA...
!

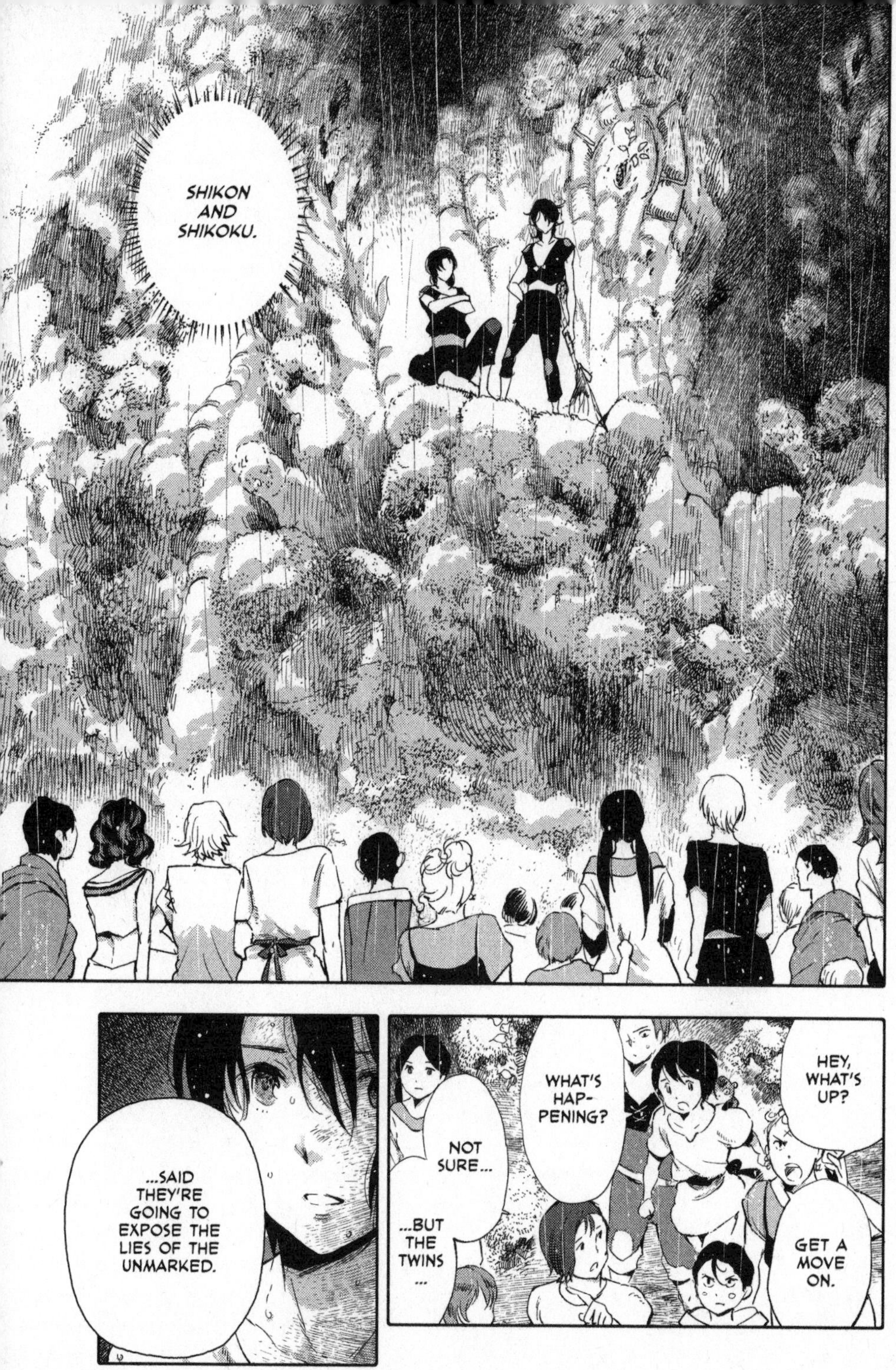
SHIKON AND SHIKOKU.
HEY, WHAT'S UP?
WHAT'S HAP-PENING?
GET A MOVE ON.
NOT SURE...
...BUT THE TWINS ...
...SAID THEY'RE GOING TO EXPOSE THE LIES OF THE UNMARKED.

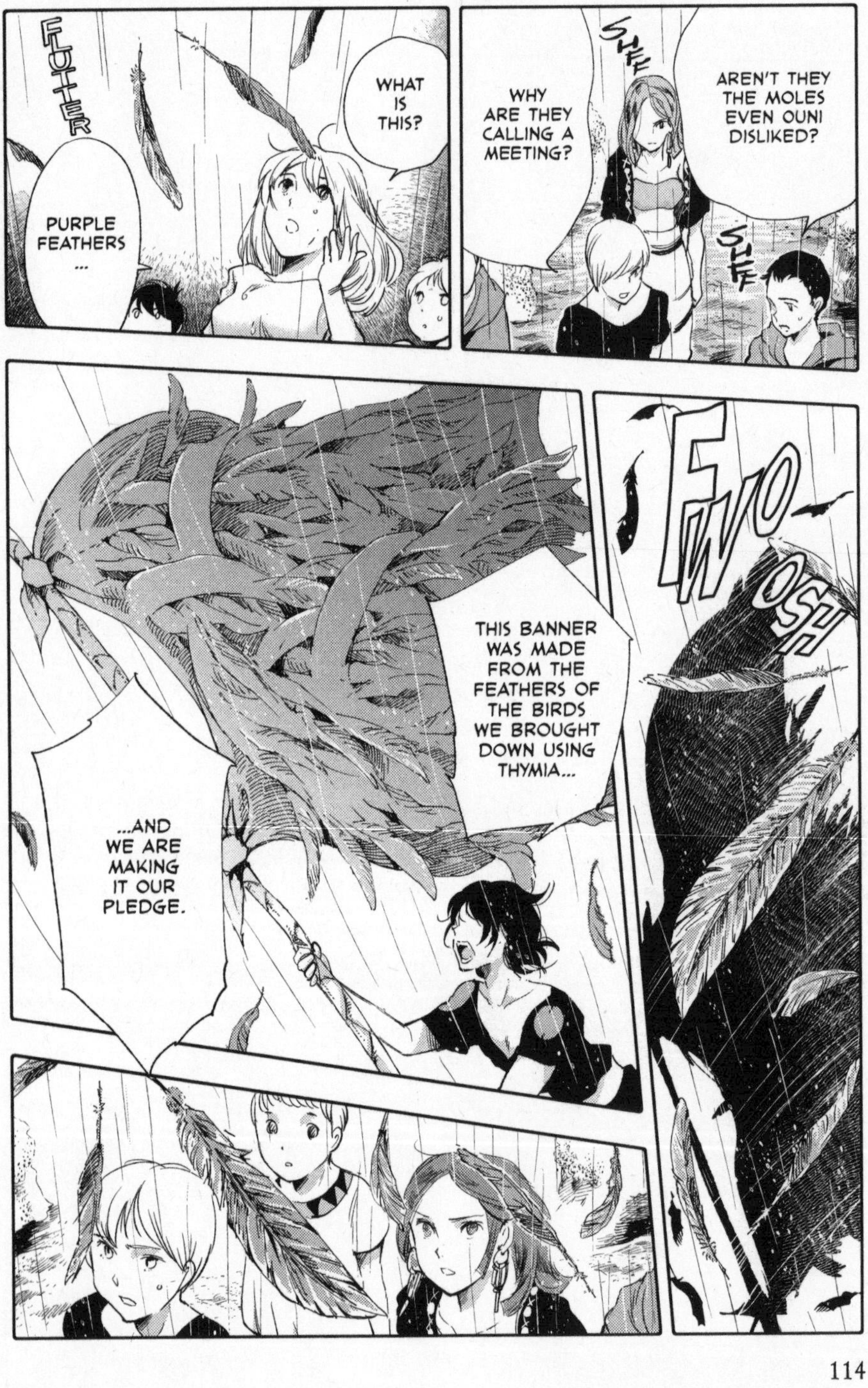
SHFF
AREN'T THEY THE MOLES EVEN OUNI DISLIKED?
WHY ARE THEY CALLING A MEETING?
SHFF
WHAT IS THIS?
FLUTTER
PURPLE FEATHERS ...
FWOOSH
THIS BANNER WAS MADE FROM THE FEATHERS OF THE BIRDS WE BROUGHT DOWN USING THYMIA...
...AND WE ARE MAKING IT OUR PLEDGE.

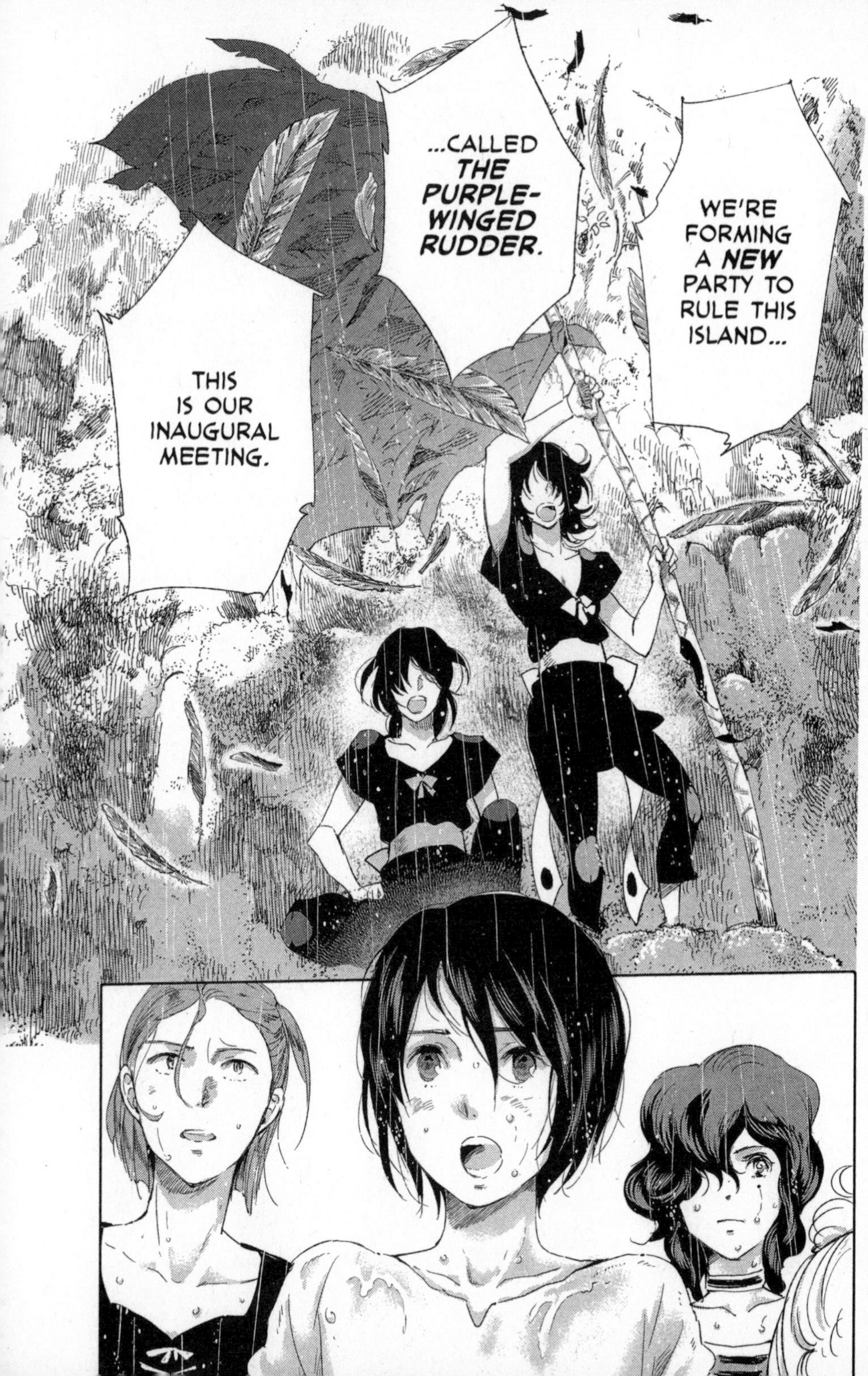
WE'RE FORMING A NEW PARTY TO RULE THIS ISLAND...
...CALLED THE PURPLE-WINGED RUDDER.
THIS IS OUR INAUGURAL MEETING.

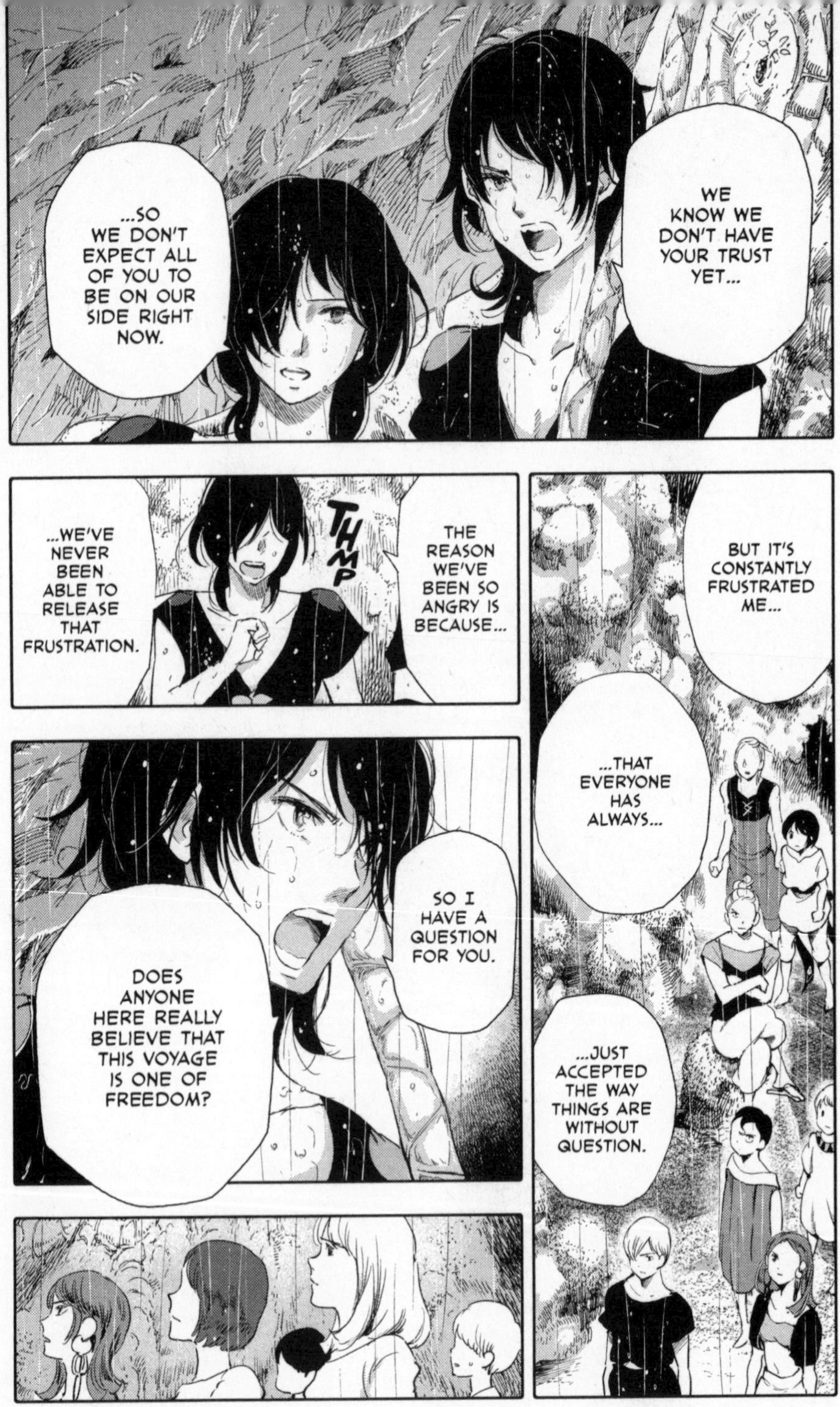
WE KNOW WE DON'T HAVE YOUR TRUST YET...
...SO WE DON'T EXPECT ALL OF YOU TO BE ON OUR SIDE RIGHT NOW.
BUT IT'S CONSTANTLY FRUSTRATED ME...
...THAT EVERYONE HAS ALWAYS...
...JUST ACCEPTED THE WAY THINGS ARE WITHOUT QUESTION.
THE REASON WE'VE BEEN SO ANGRY IS BECAUSE...
THMP
...WE'VE NEVER BEEN ABLE TO RELEASE THAT FRUSTRATION.
SO I HAVE A QUESTION FOR YOU.
DOES ANYONE HERE REALLY BELIEVE THAT THIS VOYAGE IS ONE OF FREEDOM?

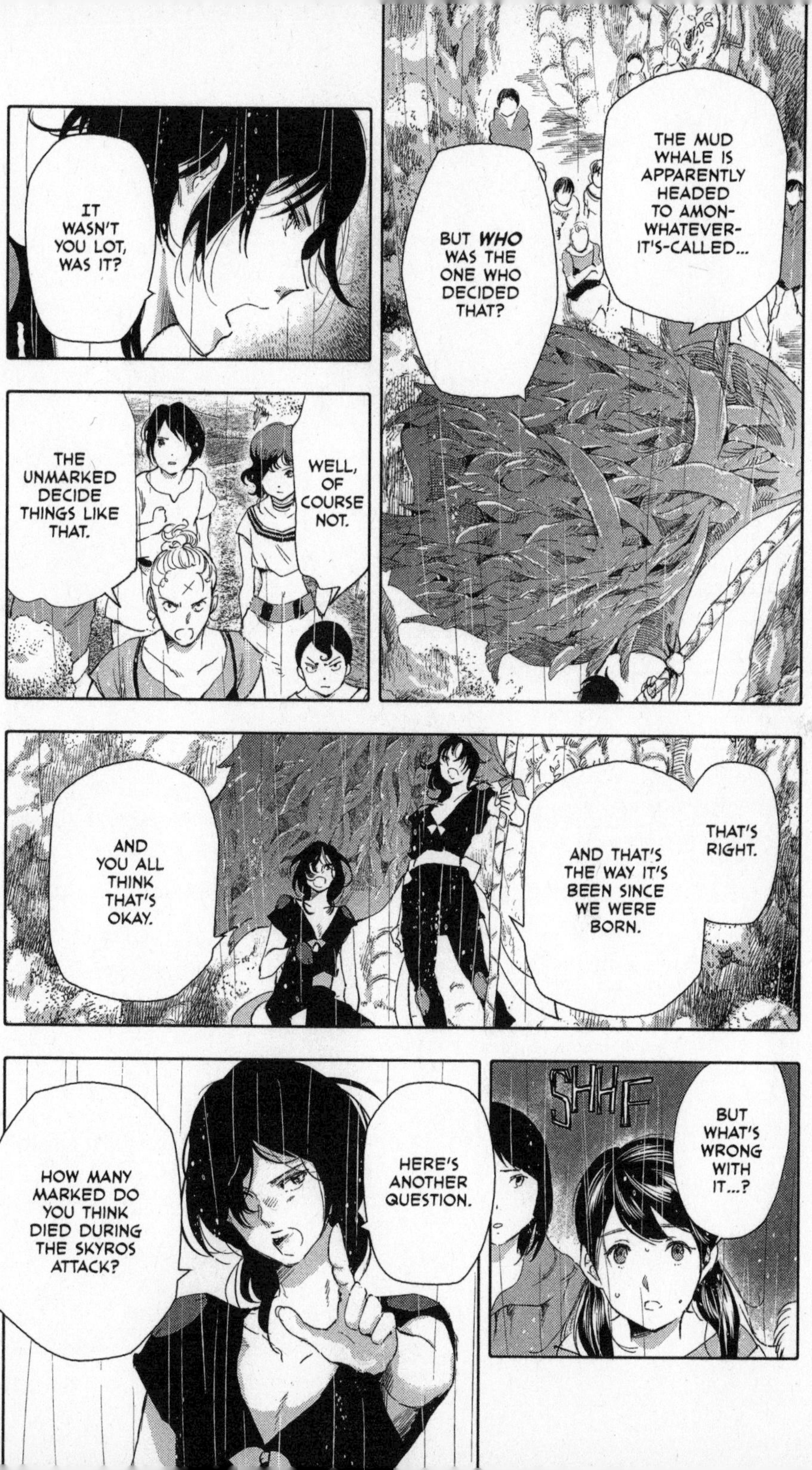
THE MUD WHALE IS APPARENTLY HEADED TO AMON-WHATEVER-IT'S-CALLED...
BUT *WHO* WAS THE ONE WHO DECIDED THAT?
IT WASN'T YOU LOT, WAS IT?
WELL, OF COURSE NOT.
THE UNMARKED DECIDE THINGS LIKE THAT.
THAT'S RIGHT.
AND THAT'S THE WAY IT'S BEEN SINCE WE WERE BORN.
AND YOU ALL THINK THAT'S OKAY.
SHHF
BUT WHAT'S WRONG WITH IT...?
HERE'S ANOTHER QUESTION.
HOW MANY MARKED DO YOU THINK DIED DURING THE SKYROS ATTACK?

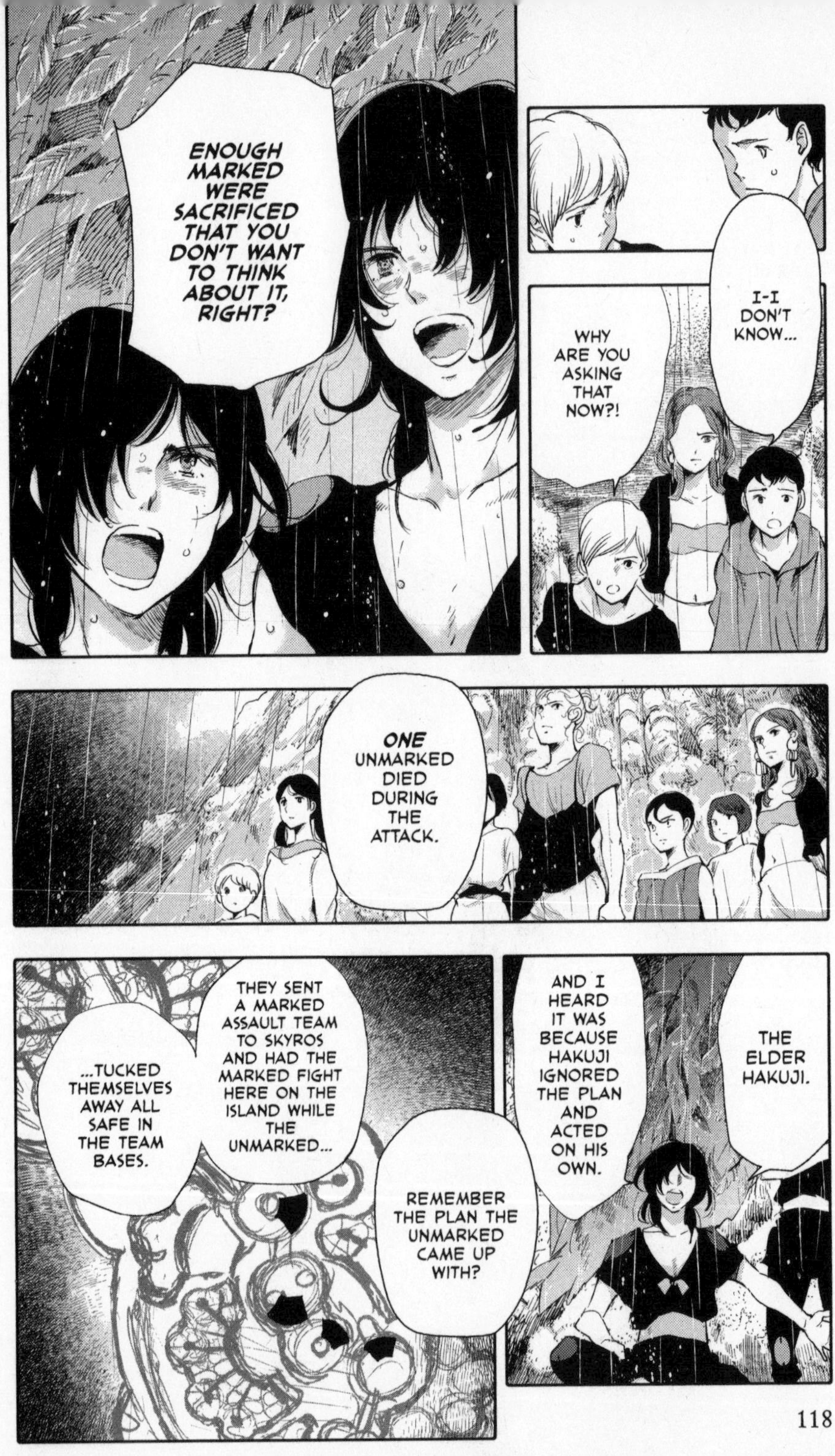
I-I DON'T KNOW...
WHY ARE YOU ASKING THAT NOW?!
ENOUGH MARKED WERE SACRIFICED THAT YOU DON'T WANT TO THINK ABOUT IT, RIGHT?
ONE UNMARKED DIED DURING THE ATTACK.
THE ELDER HAKUJI.
AND I HEARD IT WAS BECAUSE HAKUJI IGNORED THE PLAN AND ACTED ON HIS OWN.
REMEMBER THE PLAN THE UNMARKED CAME UP WITH?
THEY SENT A MARKED ASSAULT TEAM TO SKYROS AND HAD THE MARKED FIGHT HERE ON THE ISLAND WHILE THE UNMARKED...
...TUCKED THEMSELVES AWAY ALL SAFE IN THE TEAM BASES.

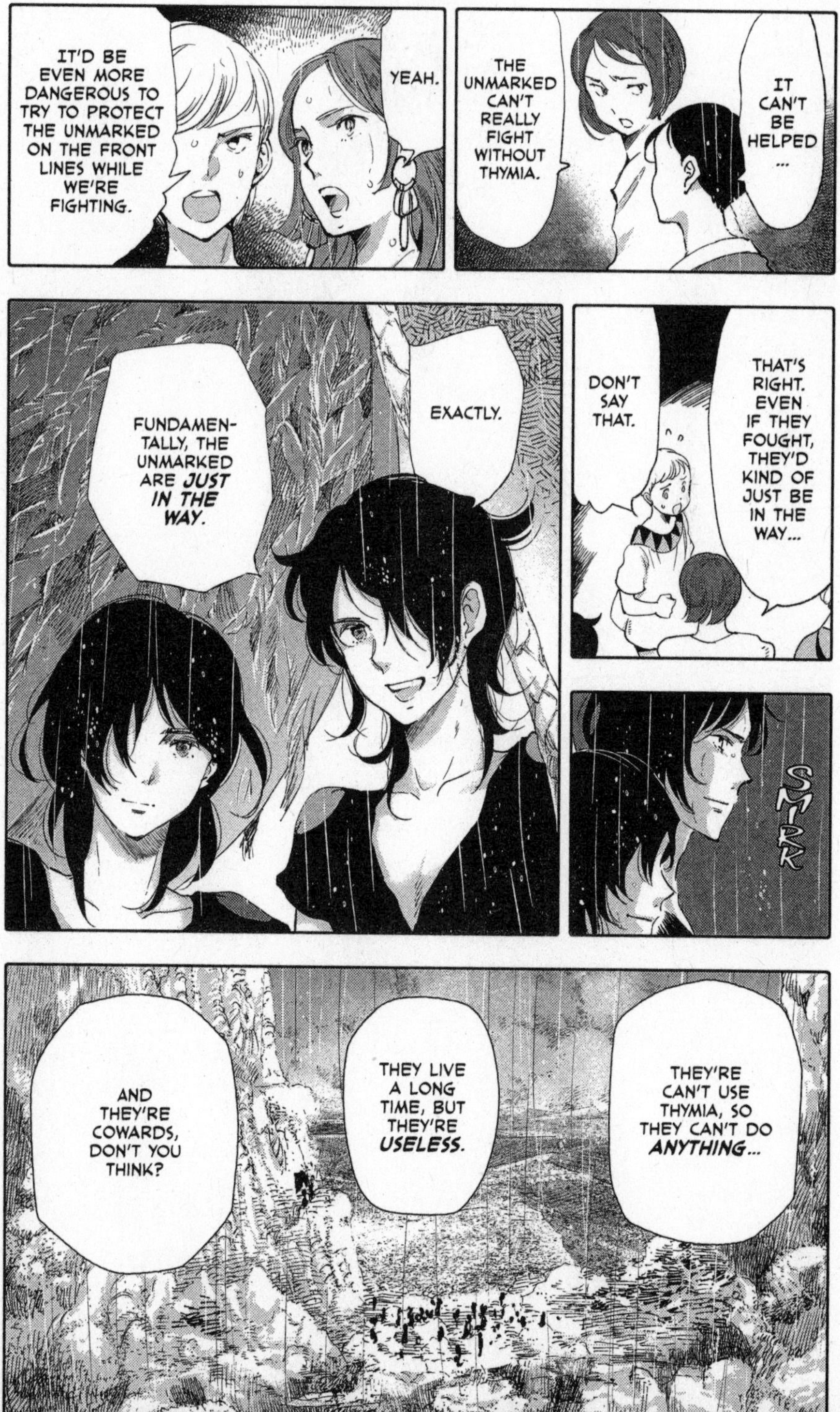
IT CAN'T BE HELPED ...
THE UNMARKED CAN'T REALLY FIGHT WITHOUT THYMIA.
YEAH.
IT'D BE EVEN MORE DANGEROUS TO TRY TO PROTECT THE UNMARKED ON THE FRONT LINES WHILE WE'RE FIGHTING.
THAT'S RIGHT. EVEN IF THEY FOUGHT, THEY'D KIND OF JUST BE IN THE WAY...
DON'T SAY THAT.
SMIRK
EXACTLY.
FUNDAMENTALLY, THE UNMARKED ARE *JUST IN THE WAY*.
THEY'RE CAN'T USE THYMIA, SO THEY CAN'T DO *ANYTHING*...
THEY LIVE A LONG TIME, BUT THEY'RE *USELESS*.
AND THEY'RE COWARDS, DON'T YOU THINK?

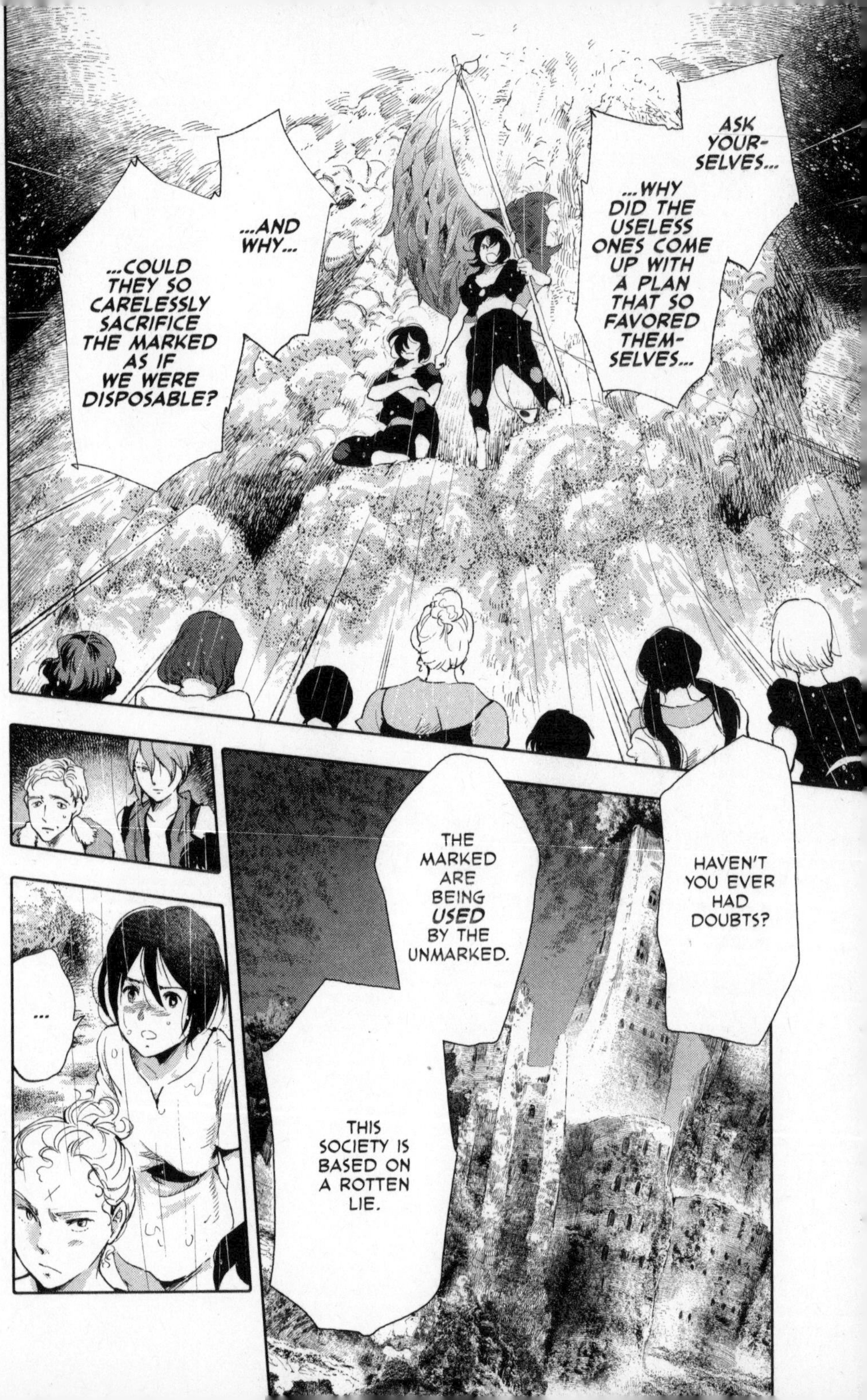
ASK YOURSELVES...
...WHY DID THE USELESS ONES COME UP WITH A PLAN THAT SO FAVORED THEMSELVES...
...AND WHY...
...COULD THEY SO CARELESSLY SACRIFICE THE MARKED AS IF WE WERE DISPOSABLE?
HAVEN'T YOU EVER HAD DOUBTS?
THE MARKED ARE BEING *USED* BY THE UNMARKED.
THIS SOCIETY IS BASED ON A ROTTEN LIE.
...

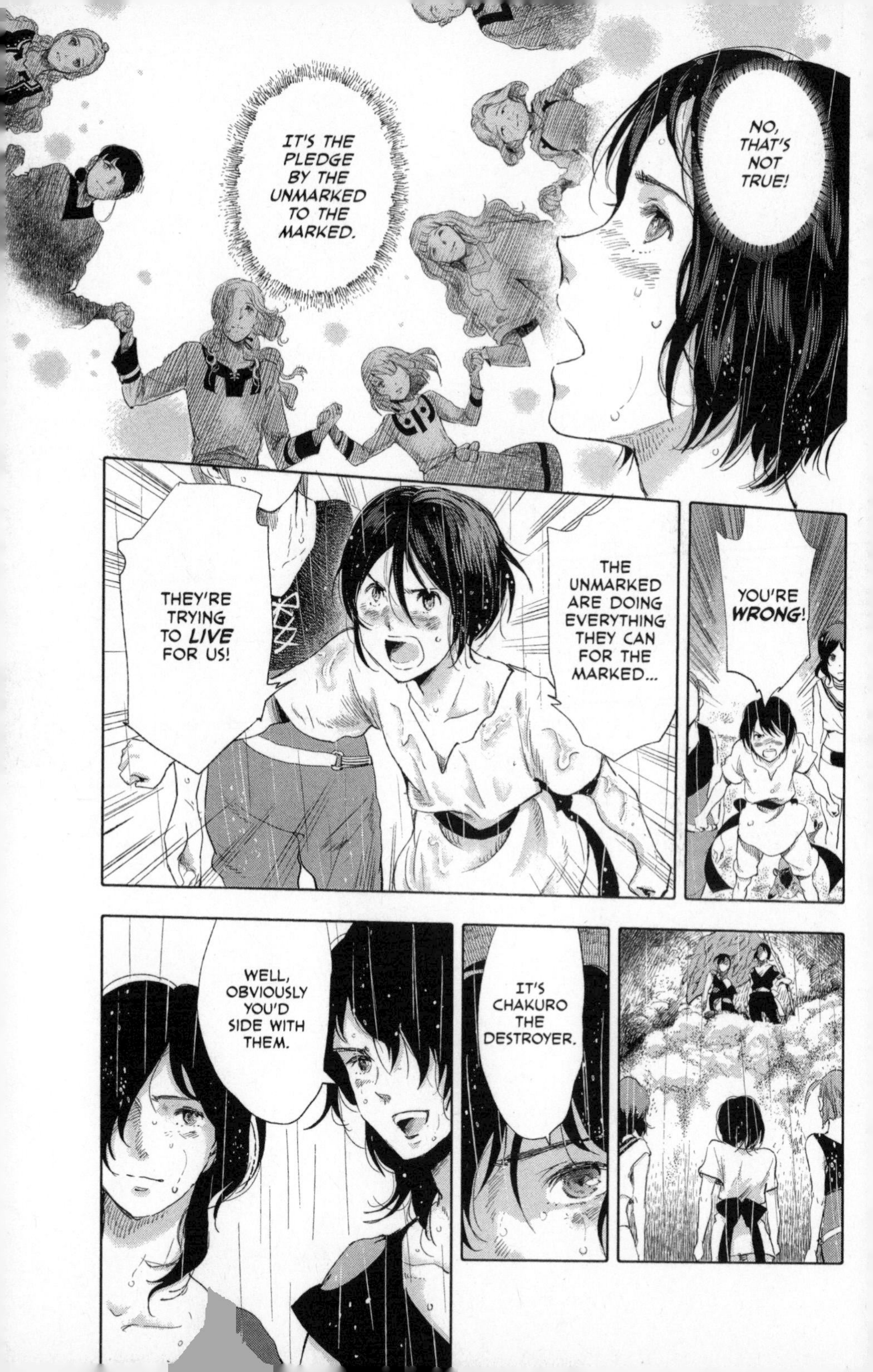
NO, THAT'S NOT TRUE!
IT'S THE PLEDGE BY THE UNMARKED TO THE MARKED.
YOU'RE WRONG!
THE UNMARKED ARE DOING EVERYTHING THEY CAN FOR THE MARKED...
THEY'RE TRYING TO LIVE FOR US!
IT'S CHAKURO THE DESTROYER.
WELL, OBVIOUSLY YOU'D SIDE WITH THEM.

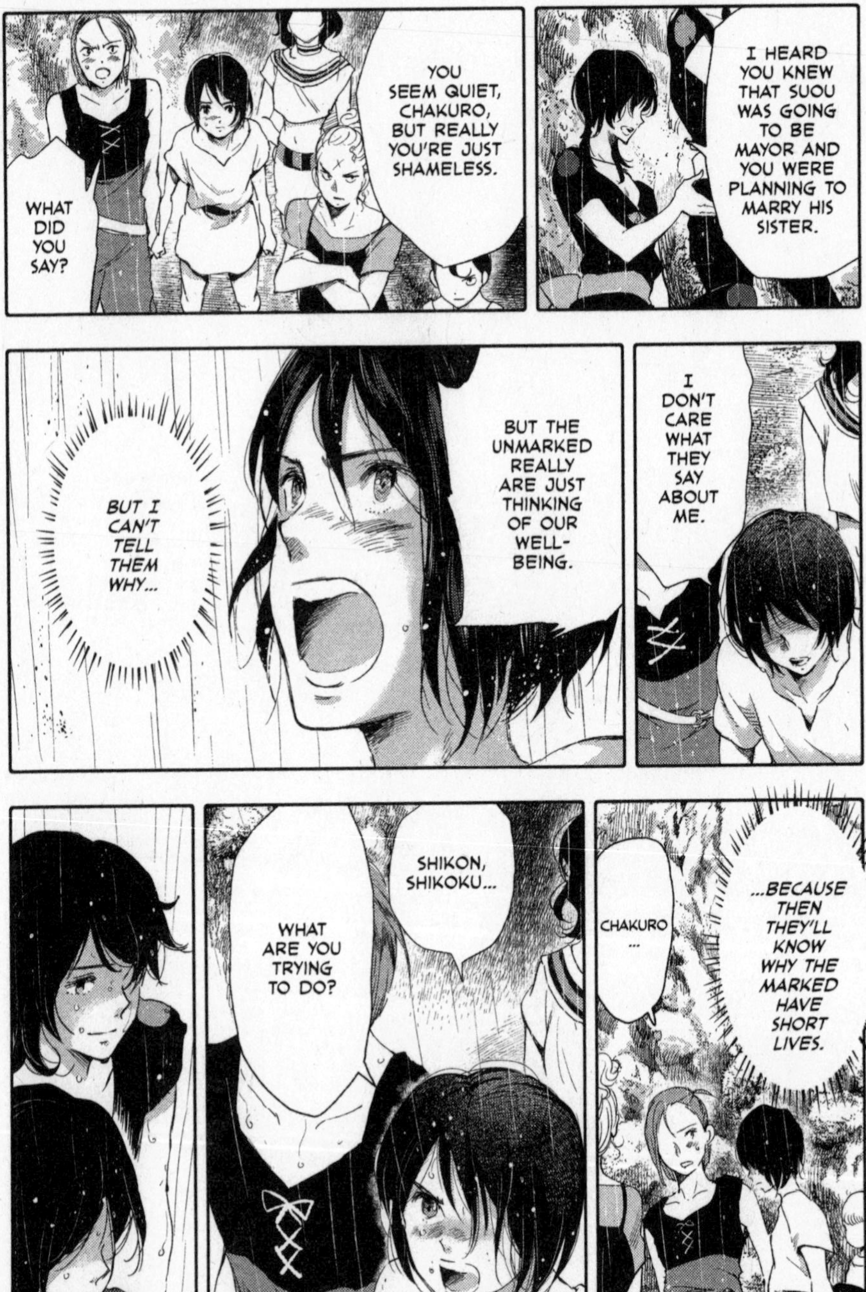
I HEARD YOU KNEW THAT SUOU WAS GOING TO BE MAYOR AND YOU WERE PLANNING TO MARRY HIS SISTER.
YOU SEEM QUIET, CHAKURO, BUT REALLY YOU'RE JUST SHAMELESS.
WHAT DID YOU SAY?
I DON'T CARE WHAT THEY SAY ABOUT ME.
BUT THE UNMARKED REALLY ARE JUST THINKING OF OUR WELL-BEING.
BUT I CAN'T TELL THEM WHY...
...BECAUSE THEN THEY'LL KNOW WHY THE MARKED HAVE SHORT LIVES.
CHAKURO ...
SHIKON, SHIKOKU...
WHAT ARE YOU TRYING TO DO?

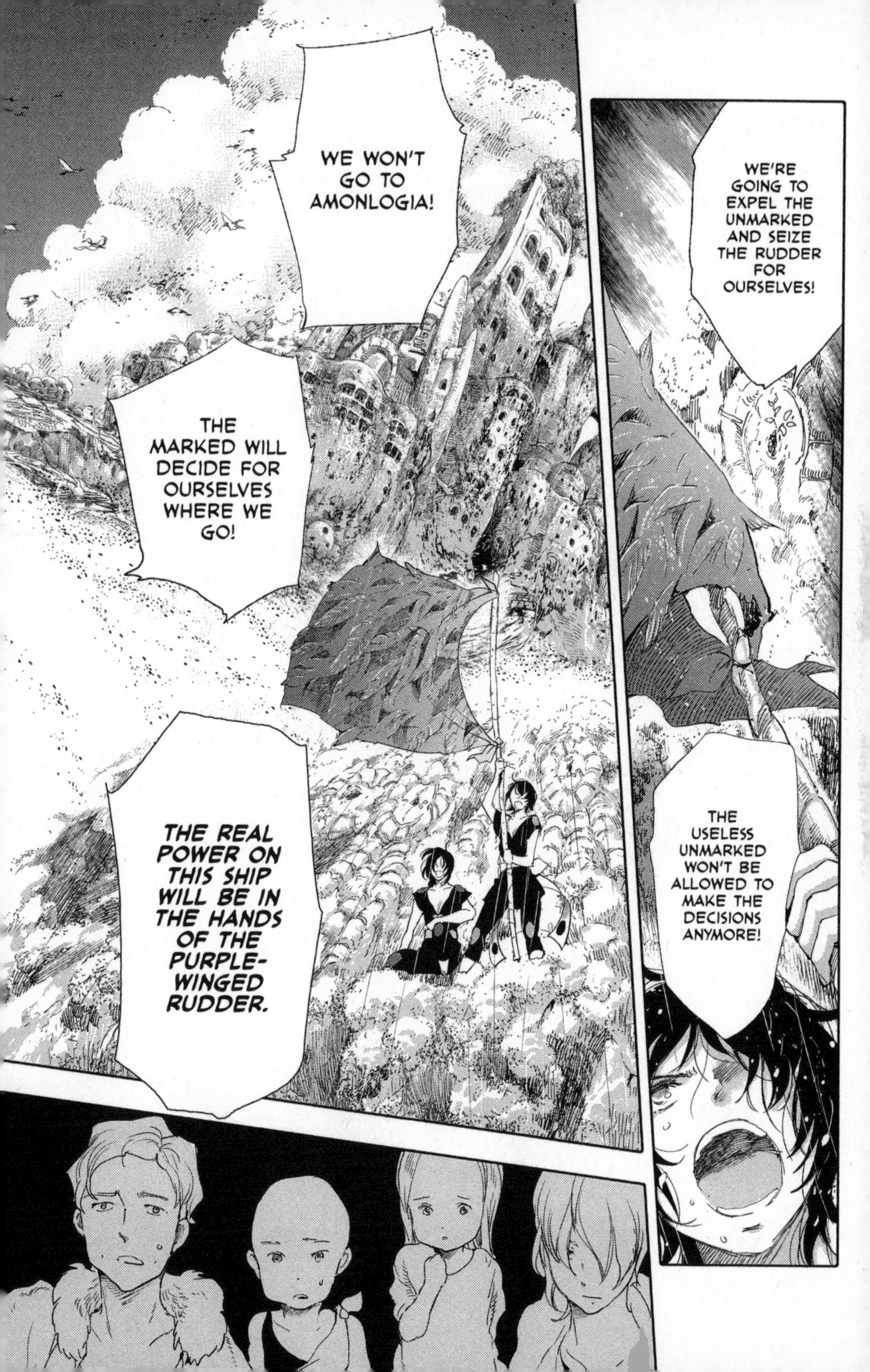
WE'RE GOING TO EXPEL THE UNMARKED AND SEIZE THE RUDDER FOR OURSELVES!
THE USELESS UNMARKED WON'T BE ALLOWED TO MAKE THE DECISIONS ANYMORE!
WE WON'T GO TO AMONLOGIA!
THE MARKED WILL DECIDE FOR OURSELVES WHERE WE GO!
THE REAL POWER ON THIS SHIP WILL BE IN THE HANDS OF THE PURPLE-WINGED RUDDER.

SHFF
SHFF
WHY NOW?
SUOU AND THE OTHERS JUST PLEDGED...
...TO KEEP THE SECRET UNTIL WE REACH AMONLOGIA.
I WON'T LET THAT HAPPEN.
I HAVE TO PROTECT THE WISHES OF THE UNMARKED.
ALL OF YOU, DON'T LISTEN TO THEM!
SHFF
SHUT UP...

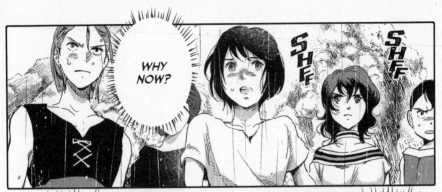

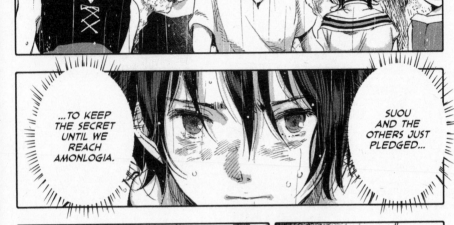

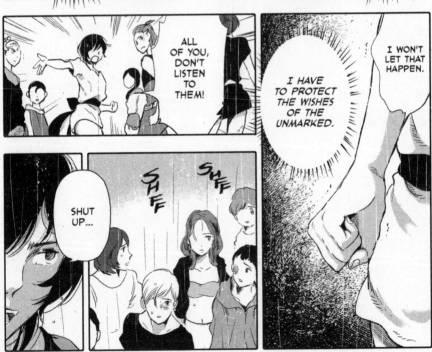

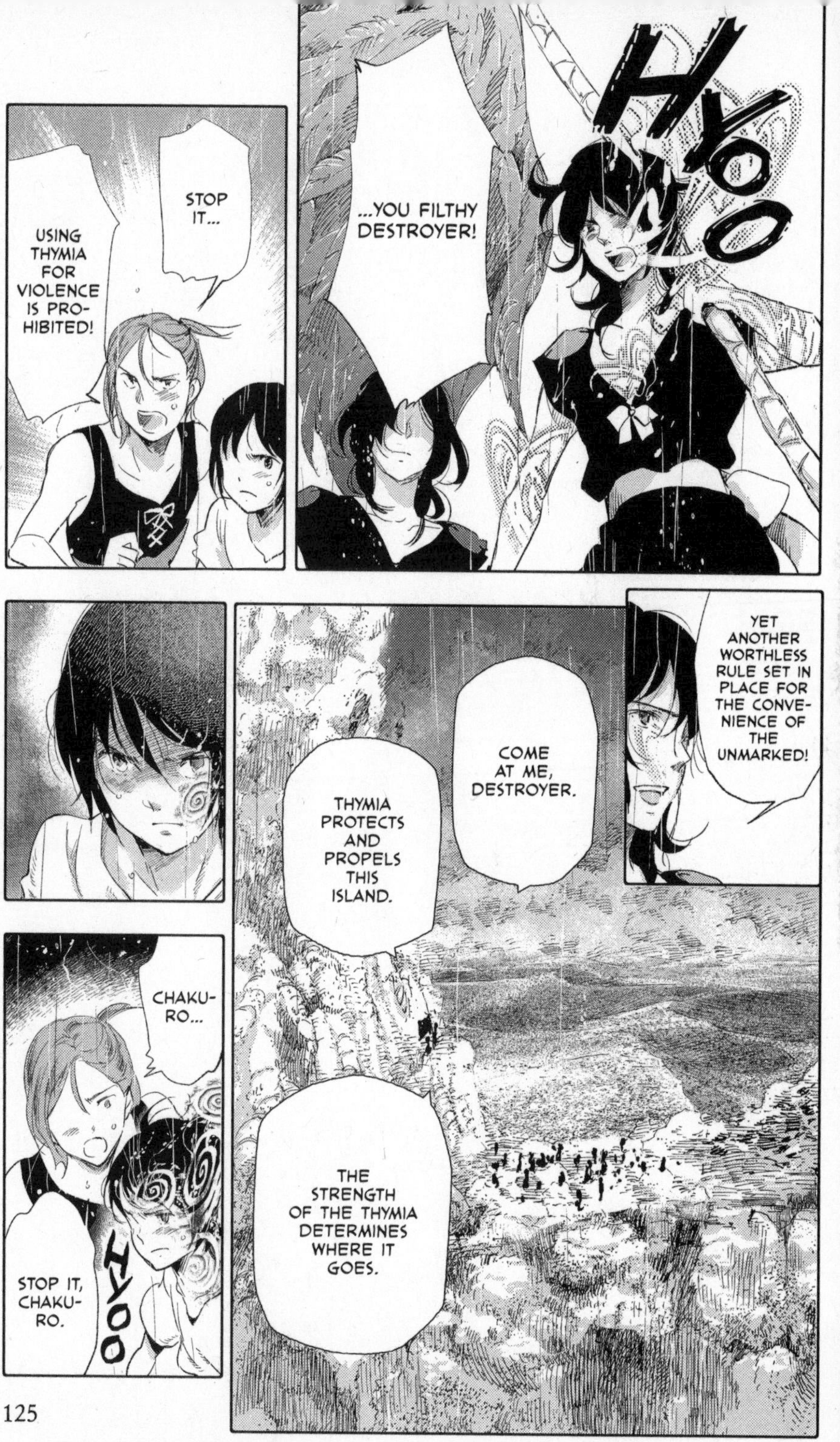
HYOO
...YOU FILTHY DESTROYER!
STOP IT...
USING THYMIA FOR VIOLENCE IS PROHIBITED!
YET ANOTHER WORTHLESS RULE SET IN PLACE FOR THE CONVENIENCE OF THE UNMARKED!
COME AT ME, DESTROYER.
THYMIA PROTECTS AND PROPELS THIS ISLAND.
THE STRENGTH OF THE THYMIA DETERMINES WHERE IT GOES.
CHAKURO...
HYOO
STOP IT, CHAKURO.

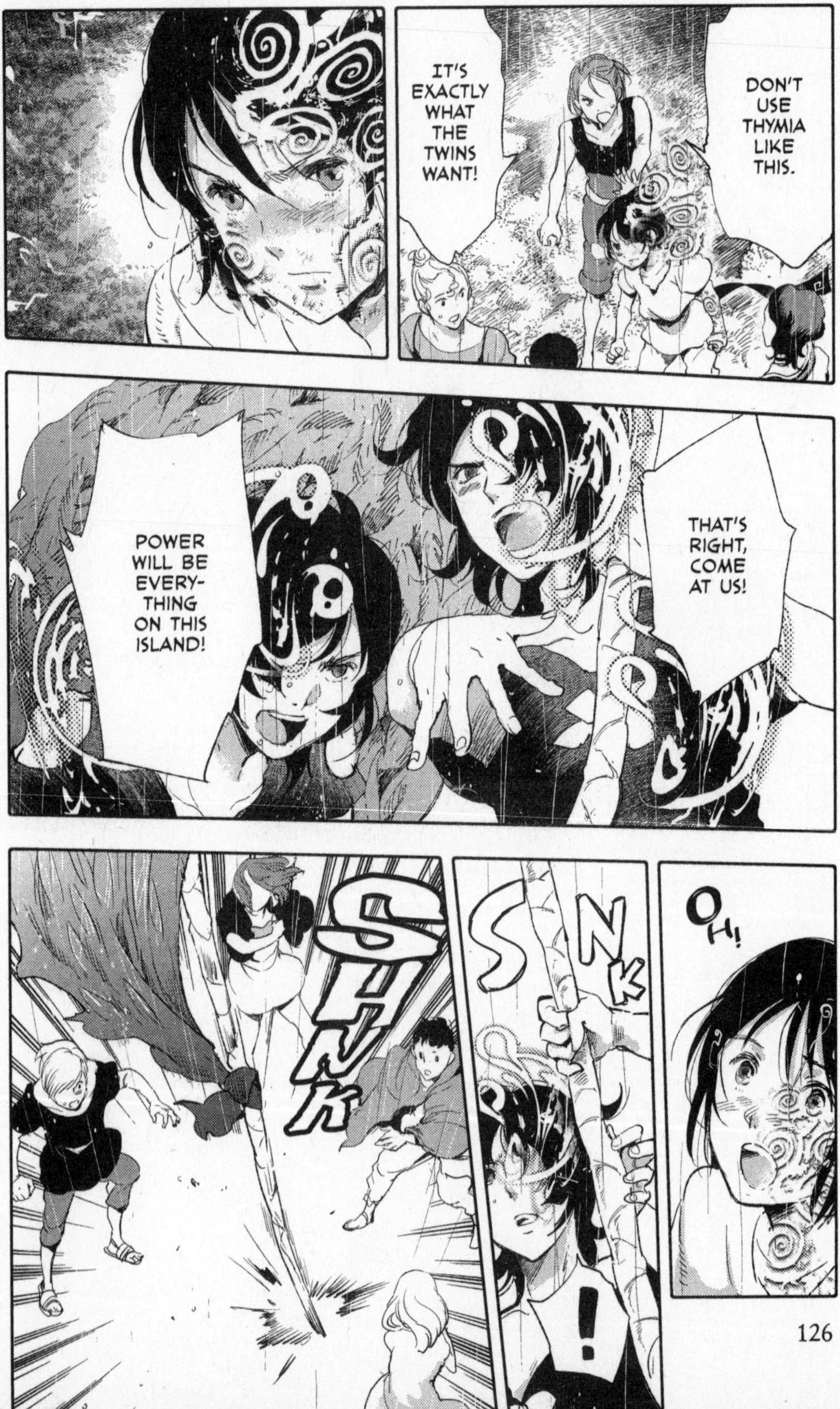
DON'T USE THYMIA LIKE THIS.
IT'S EXACTLY WHAT THE TWINS WANT!
THAT'S RIGHT, COME AT US!
POWER WILL BE EVERY-THING ON THIS ISLAND!
OH!
SNK
!
SHHNK

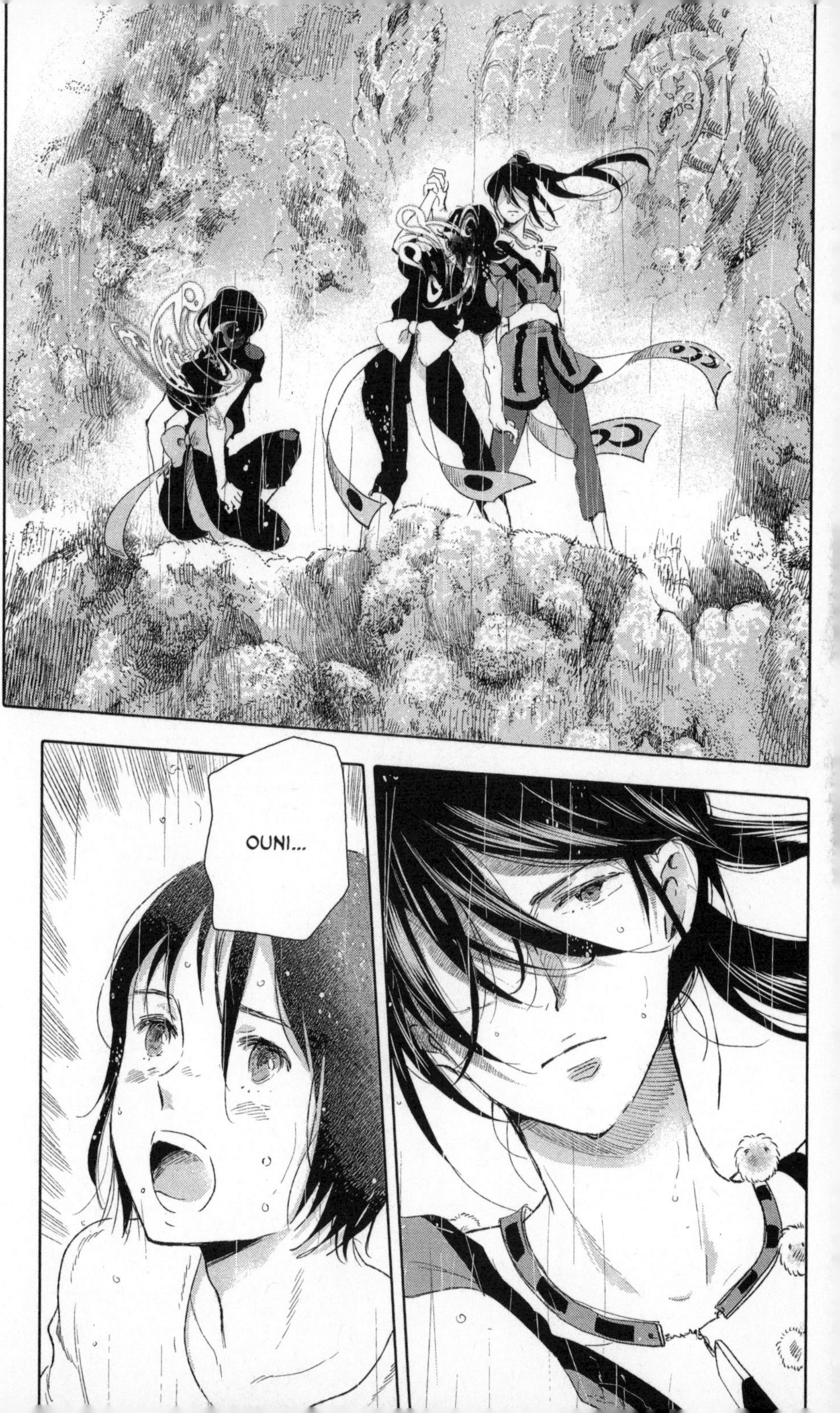
OUNI...

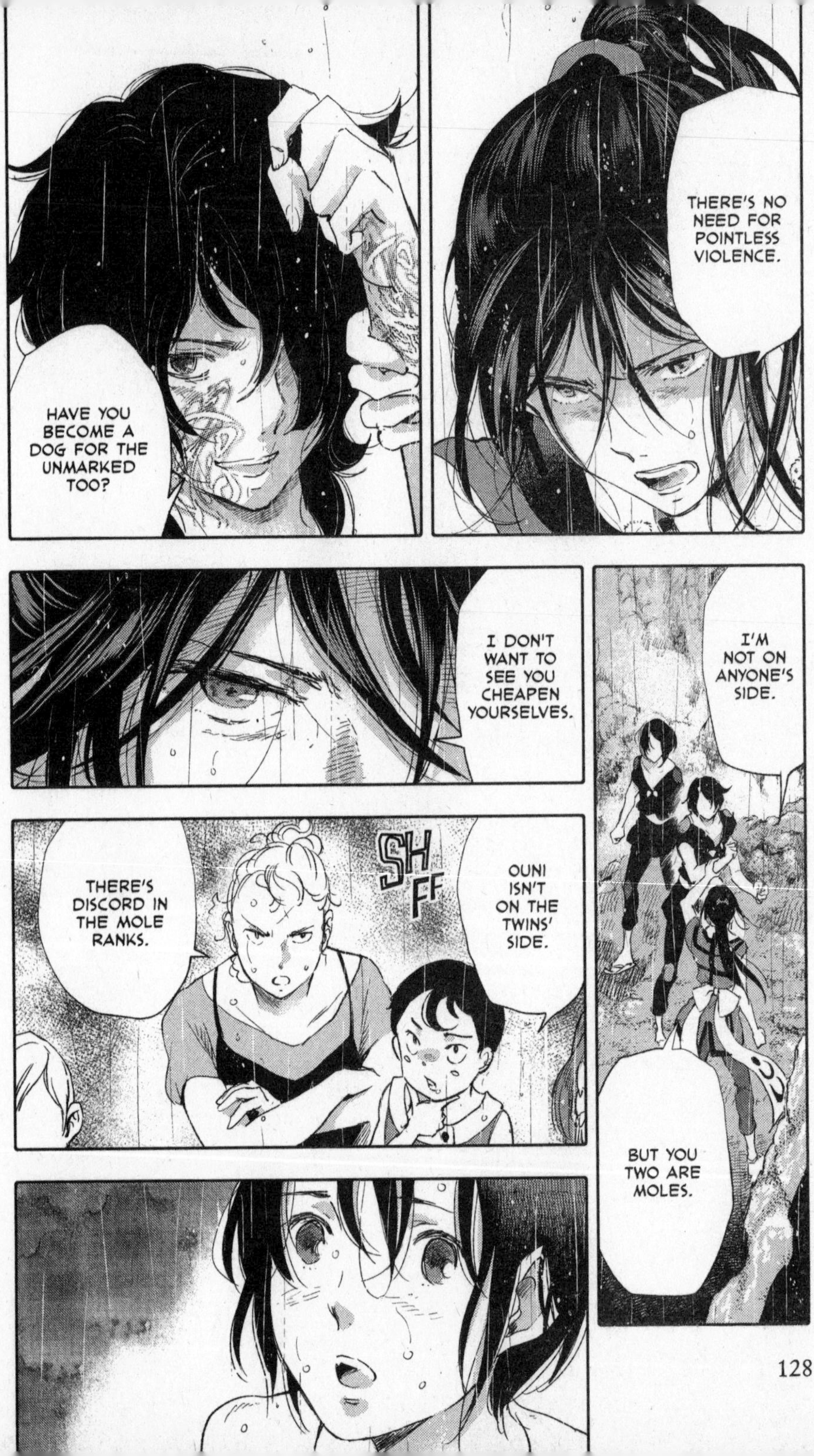
THERE'S NO NEED FOR POINTLESS VIOLENCE.
HAVE YOU BECOME A DOG FOR THE UNMARKED TOO?
I'M NOT ON ANYONE'S SIDE.
BUT YOU TWO ARE MOLES.
I DON'T WANT TO SEE YOU CHEAPEN YOURSELVES.
OUNI ISN'T ON THE TWINS' SIDE.
SHFF
THERE'S DISCORD IN THE MOLE RANKS.

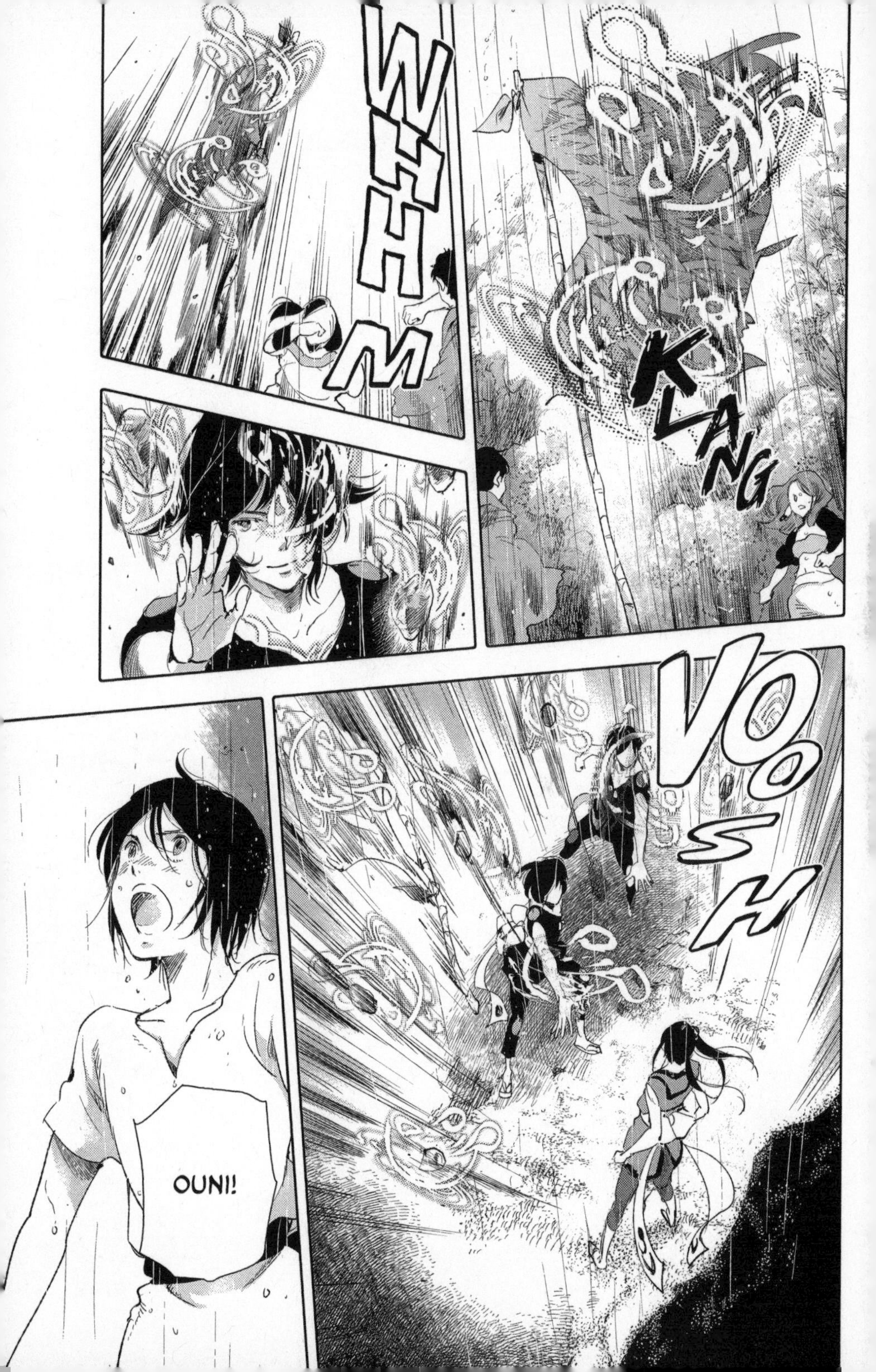
KLANG
WHHM
VOOSH
OUNI!

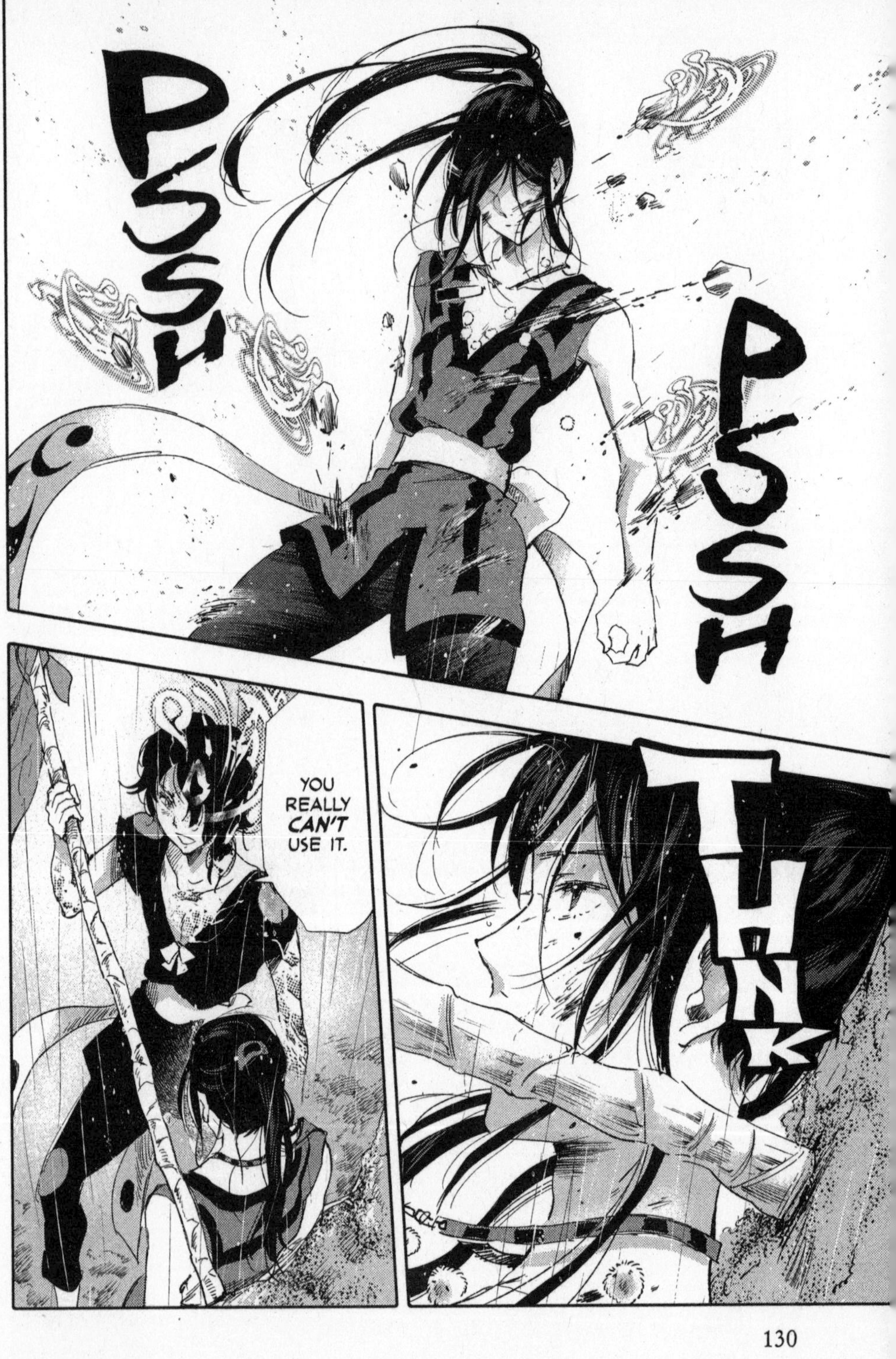
PSH
PSH
THUNK
YOU REALLY CAN'T USE IT.

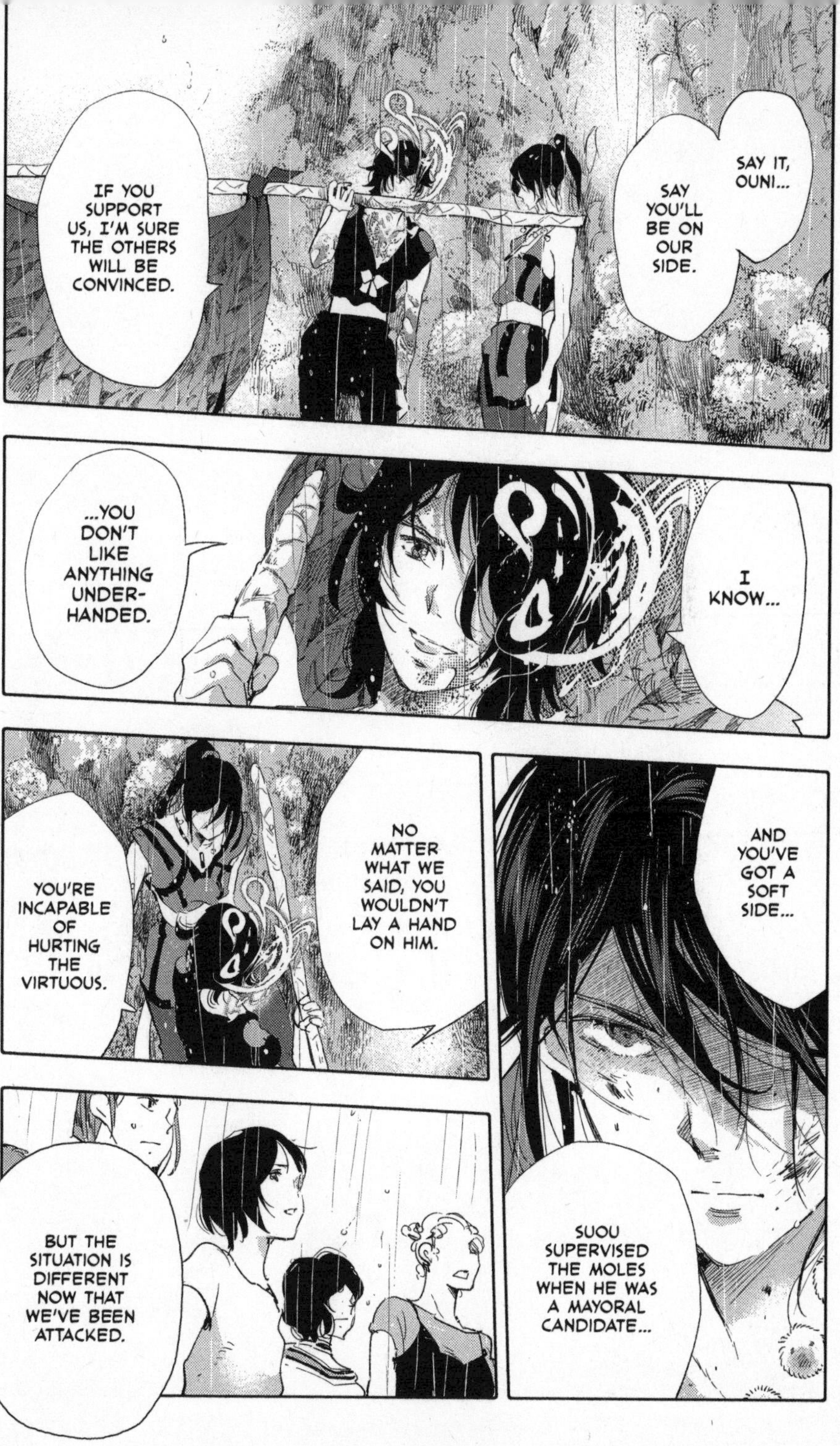
SAY IT, OUNI...
SAY YOU'LL BE ON OUR SIDE.
IF YOU SUPPORT US, I'M SURE THE OTHERS WILL BE CONVINCED.
I KNOW...
...YOU DON'T LIKE ANYTHING UNDER-HANDED.
AND YOU'VE GOT A SOFT SIDE...
SUOU SUPERVISED THE MOLES WHEN HE WAS A MAYORAL CANDIDATE...
NO MATTER WHAT WE SAID, YOU WOULDN'T LAY A HAND ON HIM.
YOU'RE INCAPABLE OF HURTING THE VIRTUOUS.
BUT THE SITUATION IS DIFFERENT NOW THAT WE'VE BEEN ATTACKED.

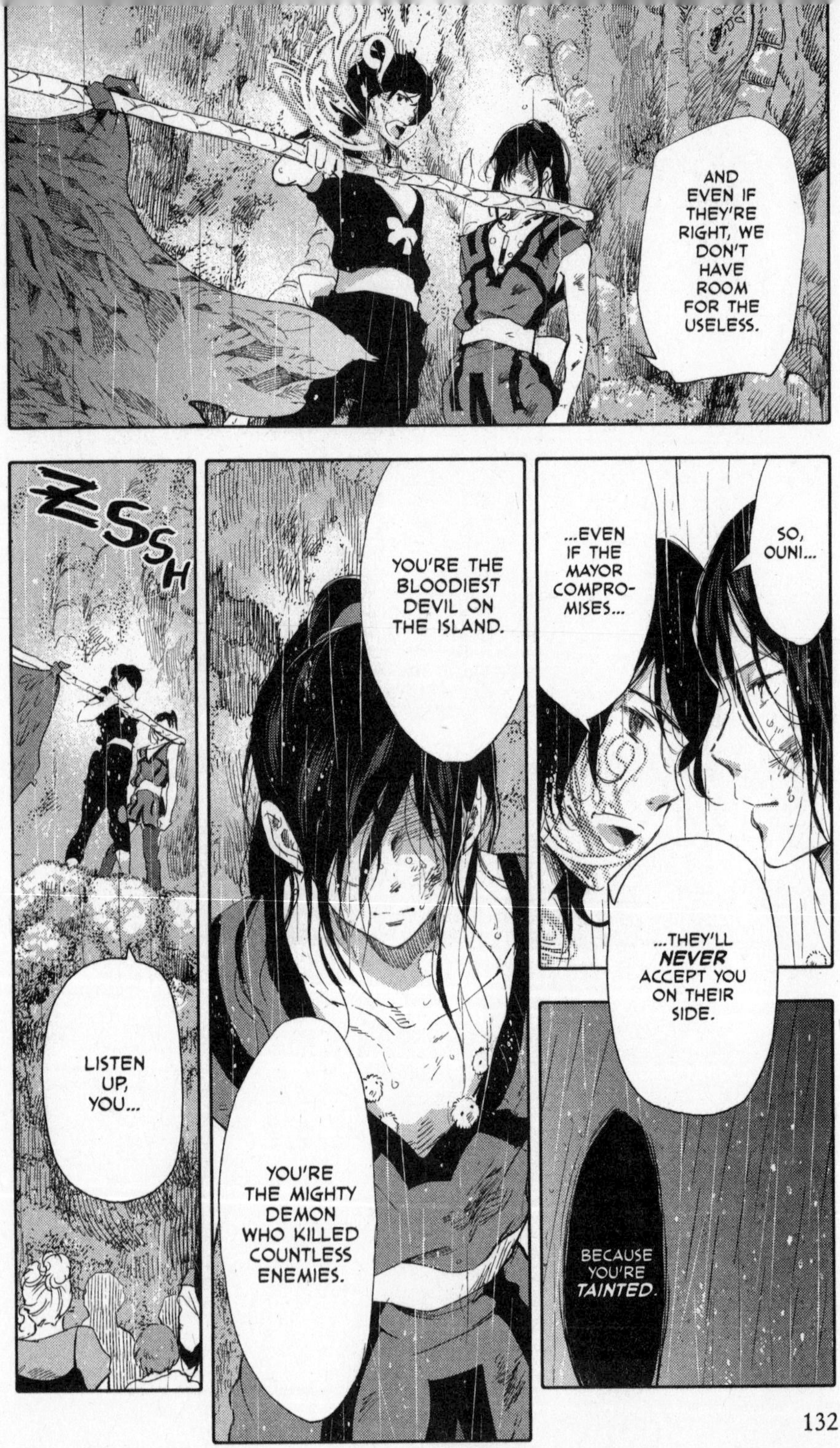
AND EVEN IF THEY'RE RIGHT, WE DON'T HAVE ROOM FOR THE USELESS.
SO, OUNI...
...EVEN IF THE MAYOR COMPRO-MISES...
...THEY'LL *NEVER* ACCEPT YOU ON THEIR SIDE.
BECAUSE YOU'RE *TAINTED*.
YOU'RE THE BLOODIEST DEVIL ON THE ISLAND.
YOU'RE THE MIGHTY DEMON WHO KILLED COUNTLESS ENEMIES.
ZSSH
LISTEN UP, YOU...

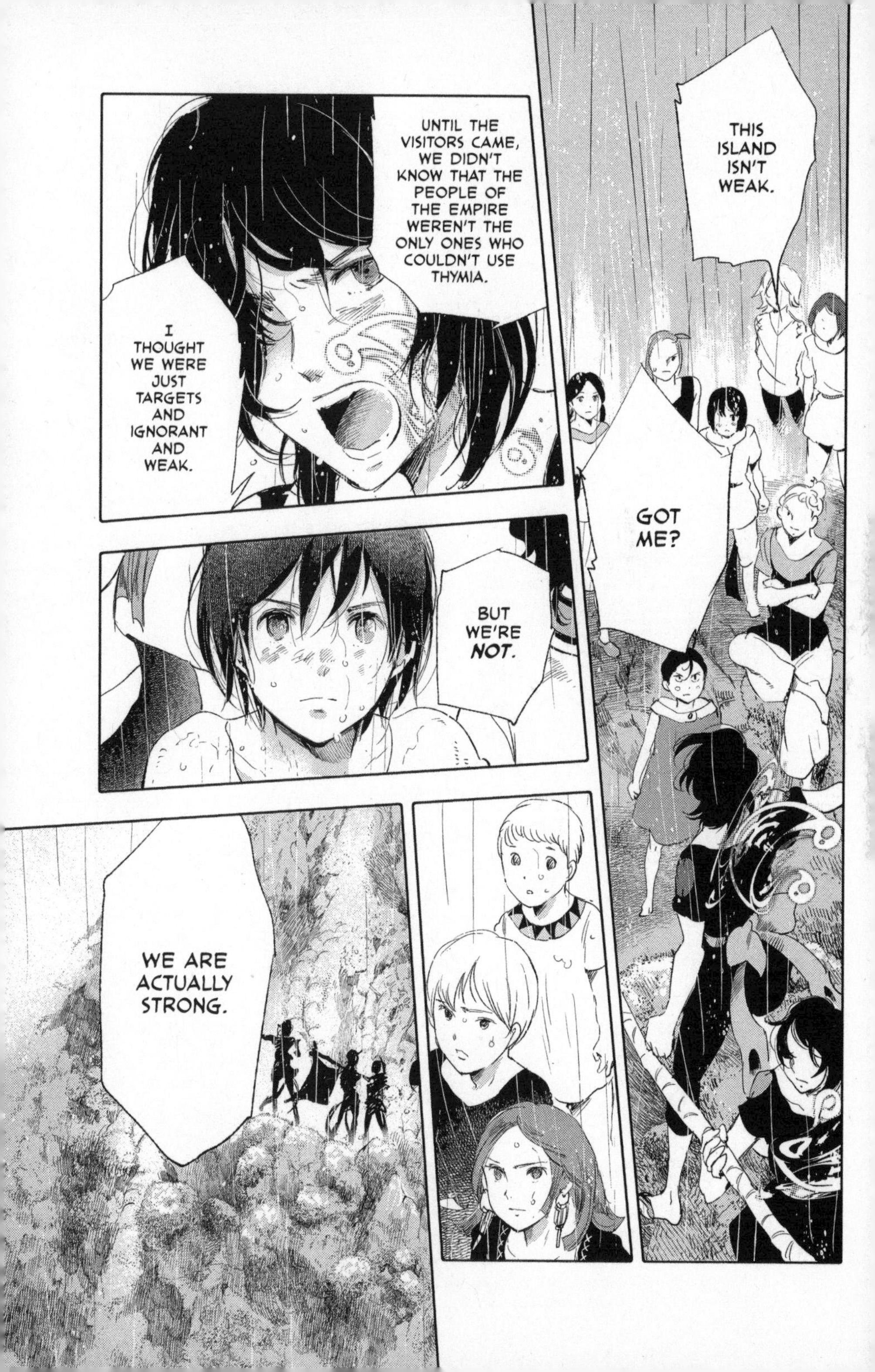
THIS ISLAND ISN'T WEAK.
GOT ME?
UNTIL THE VISITORS CAME, WE DIDN'T KNOW THAT THE PEOPLE OF THE EMPIRE WEREN'T THE ONLY ONES WHO COULDN'T USE THYMIA.
I THOUGHT WE WERE JUST TARGETS AND IGNORANT AND WEAK.
BUT WE'RE NOT.
WE ARE ACTUALLY STRONG.

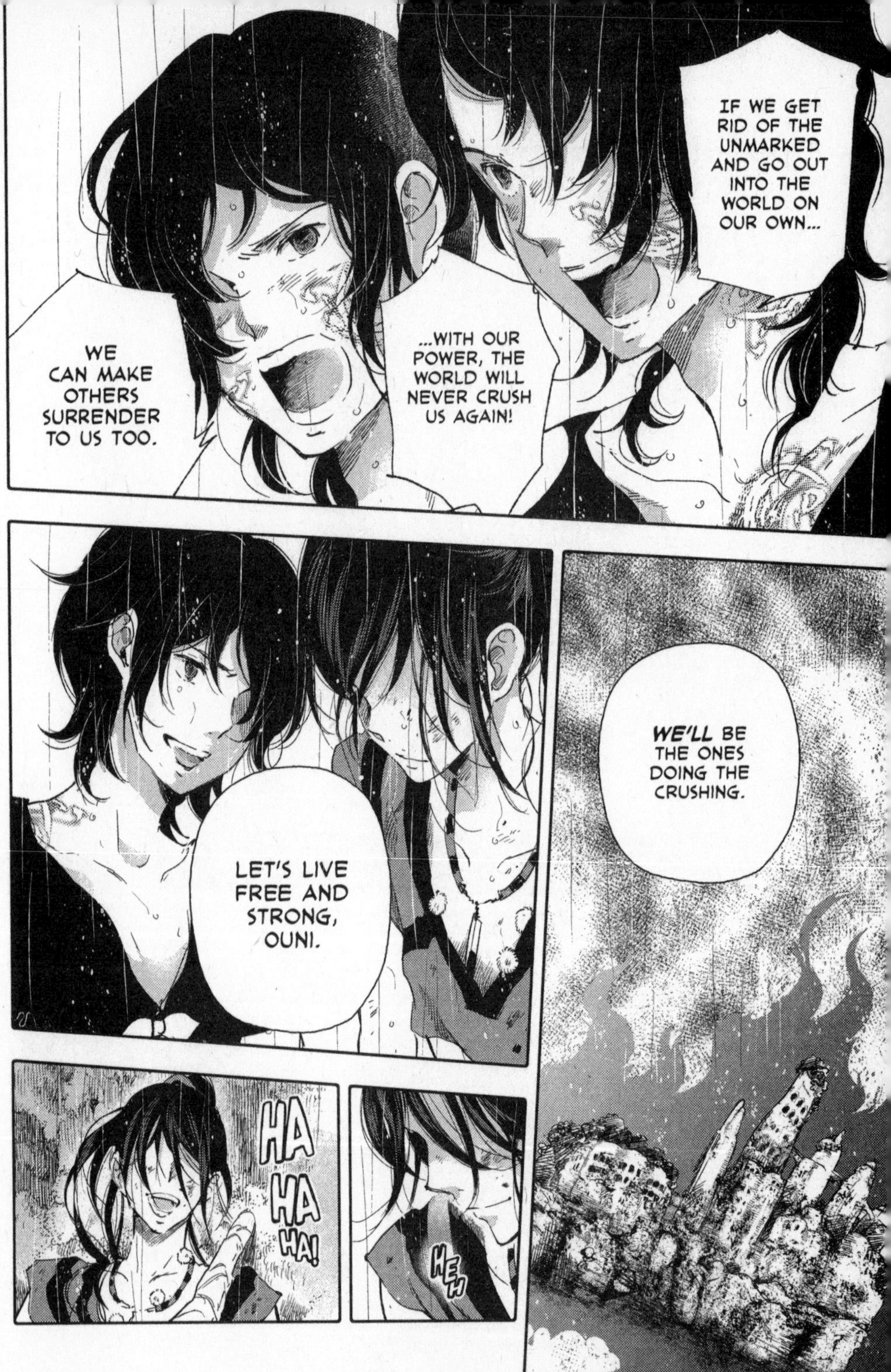
IF WE GET RID OF THE UNMARKED AND GO OUT INTO THE WORLD ON OUR OWN...
...WITH OUR POWER, THE WORLD WILL NEVER CRUSH US AGAIN!
WE CAN MAKE OTHERS SURRENDER TO US TOO.
WE'LL BE THE ONES DOING THE CRUSHING.
LET'S LIVE FREE AND STRONG, OUNI.
HEH
HA HA HA!

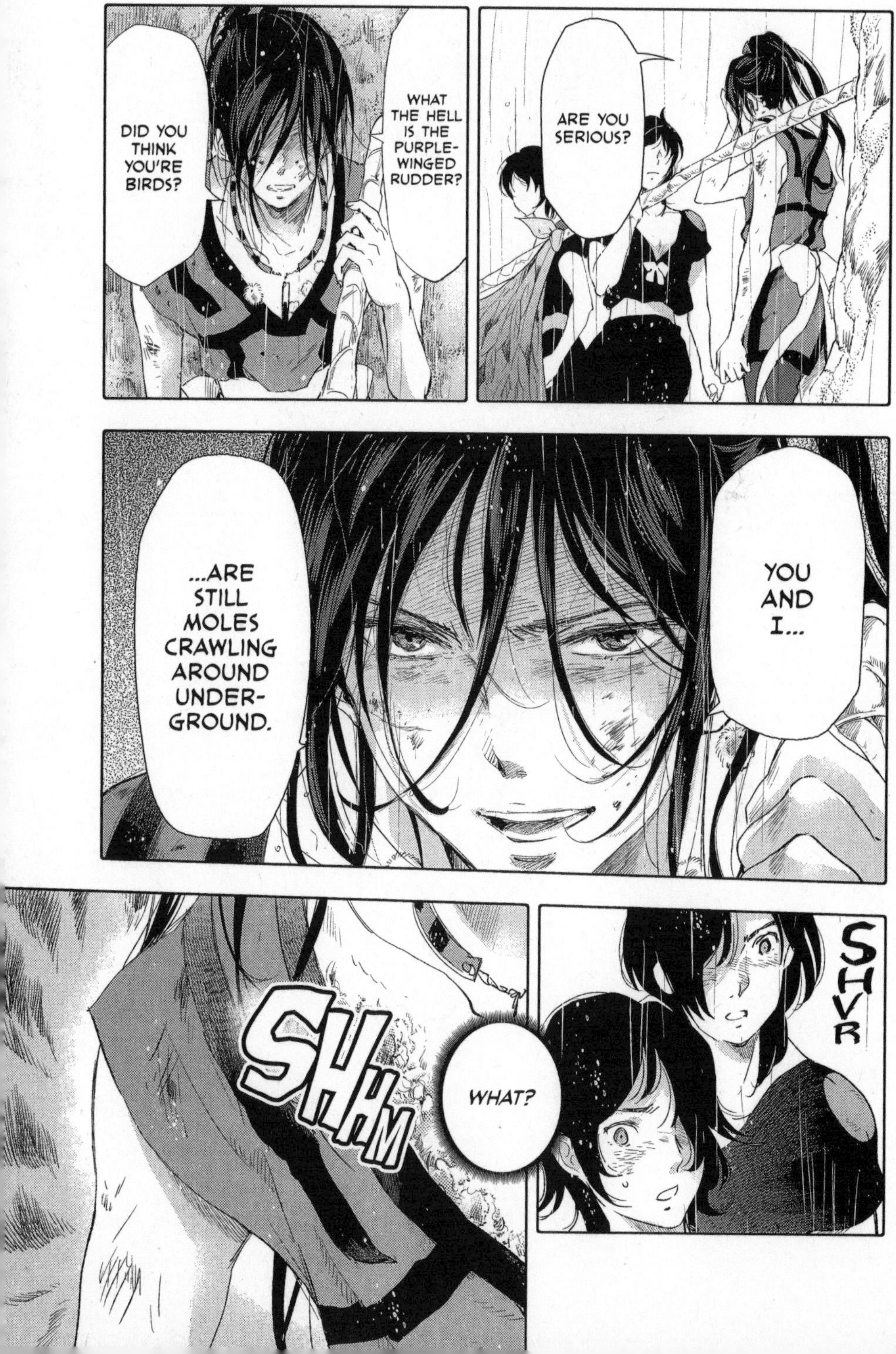
ARE YOU SERIOUS?
WHAT THE HELL IS THE PURPLE-WINGED RUDDER?
DID YOU THINK YOU'RE BIRDS?
YOU AND I...
...ARE STILL MOLES CRAWLING AROUND UNDER-GROUND.
SHVR
WHAT?
SHHM

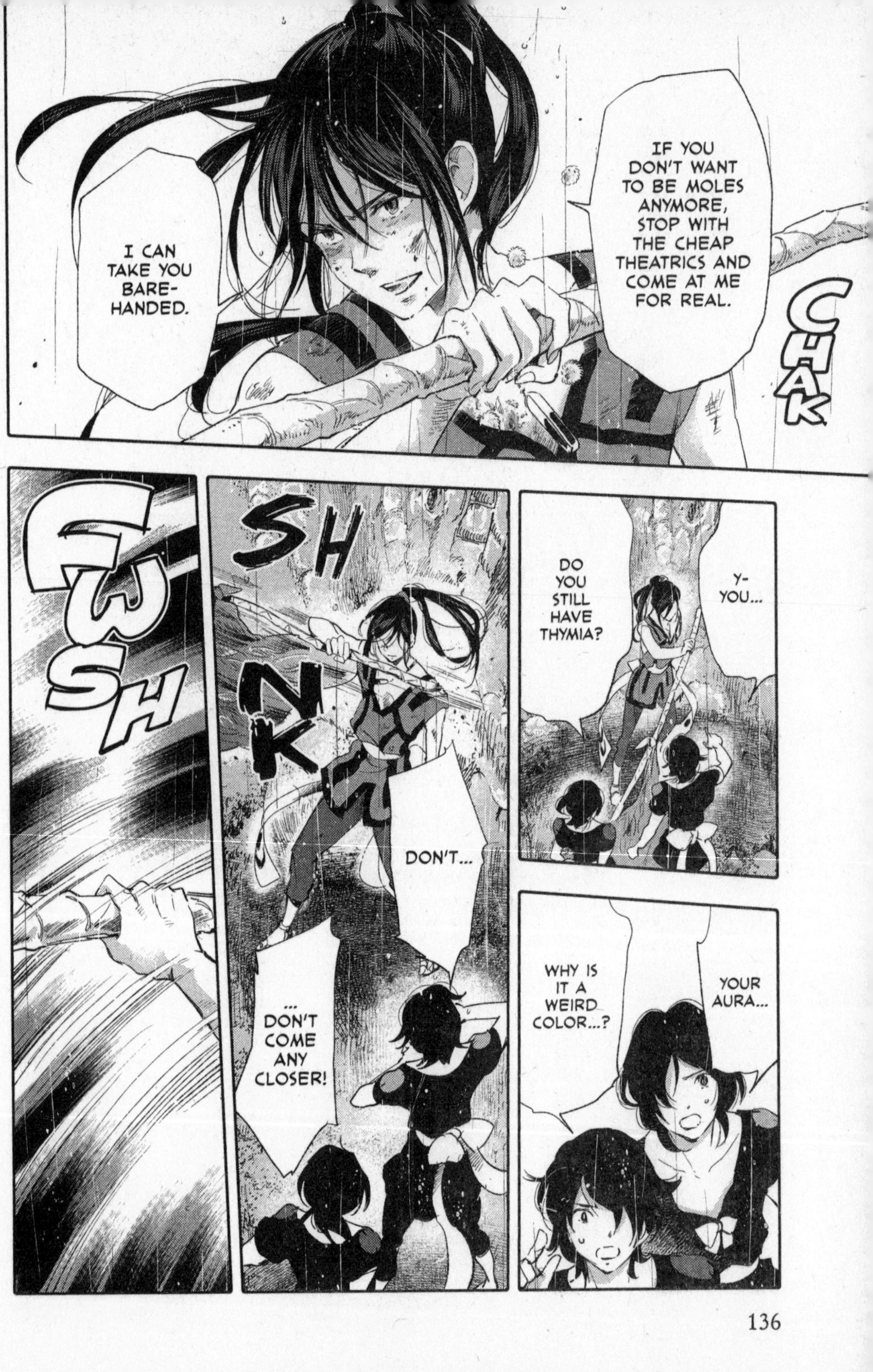
IF YOU DON'T WANT TO BE MOLES ANYMORE, STOP WITH THE CHEAP THEATRICS AND COME AT ME FOR REAL.
CHAK
I CAN TAKE YOU BARE-HANDED.
Y-YOU...
DO YOU STILL HAVE THYMIA?
YOUR AURA...
WHY IS IT A WEIRD COLOR...?
SHNK
DON'T...
... DON'T COME ANY CLOSER!
FWSH

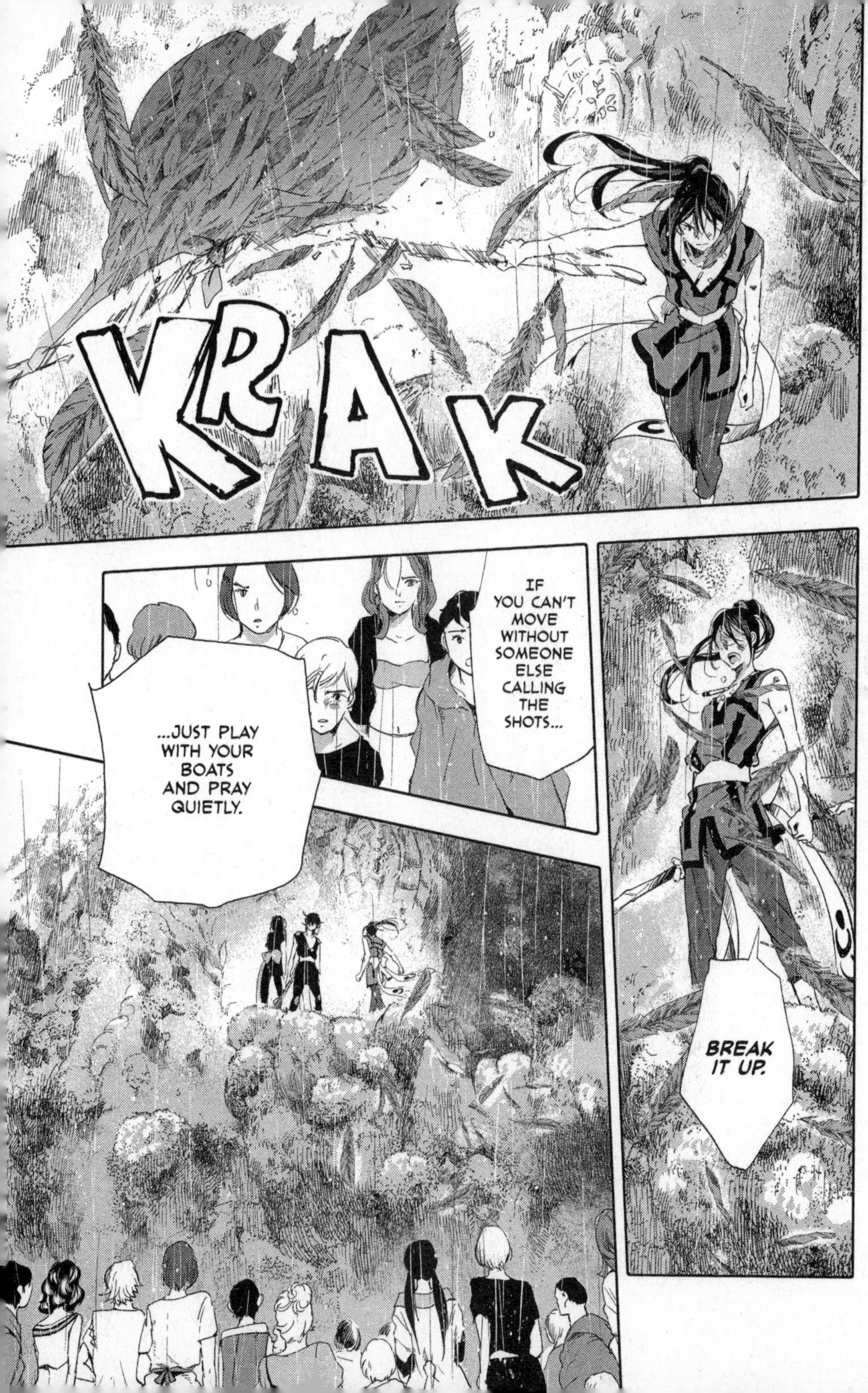
KRAK
BREAK IT UP.
IF YOU CAN'T MOVE WITHOUT SOMEONE ELSE CALLING THE SHOTS...
...JUST PLAY WITH YOUR BOATS AND PRAY QUIETLY.

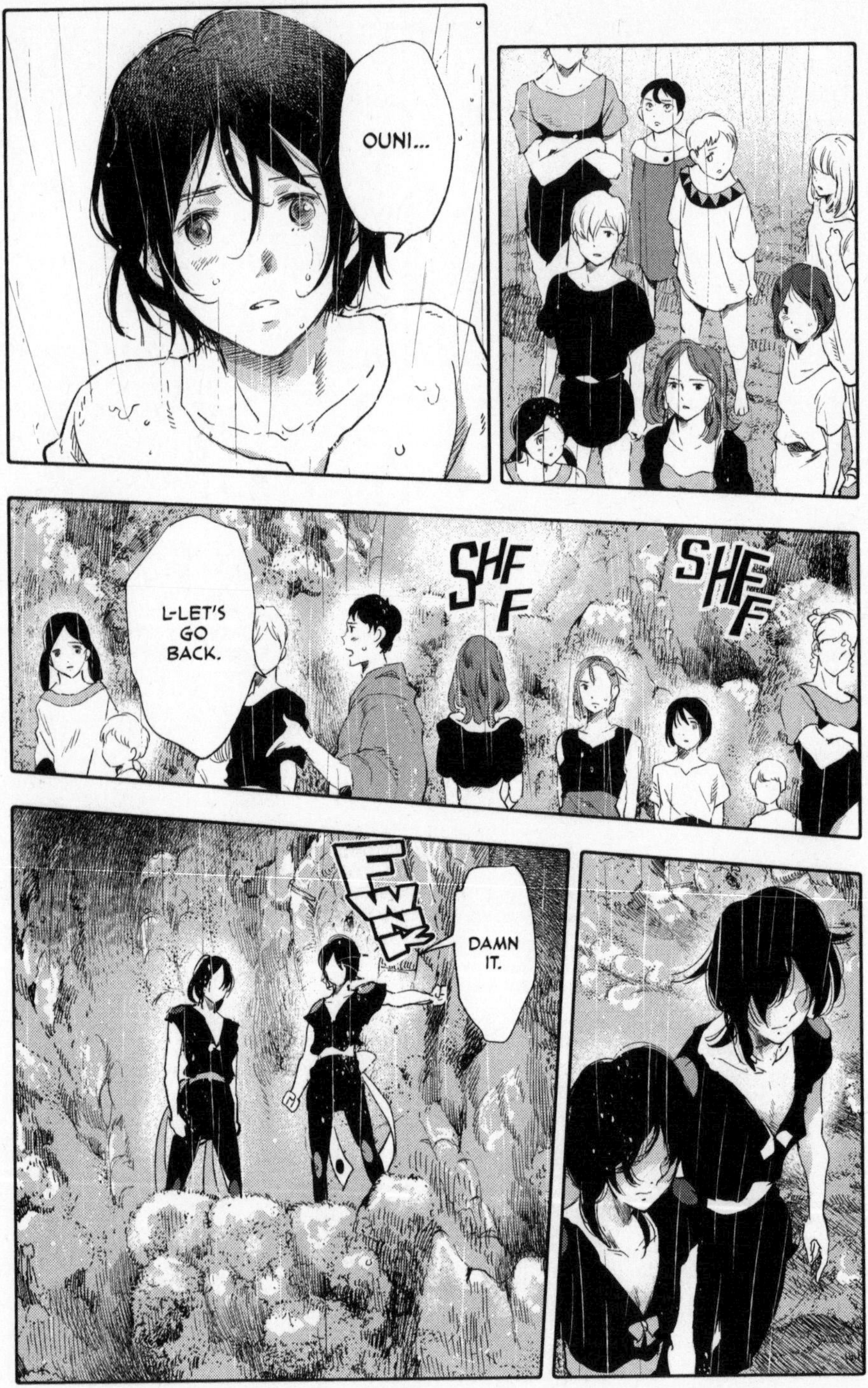
OUNI...
SHFFF
SHFF
L-LET'S GO BACK.
FWAK
DAMN IT.

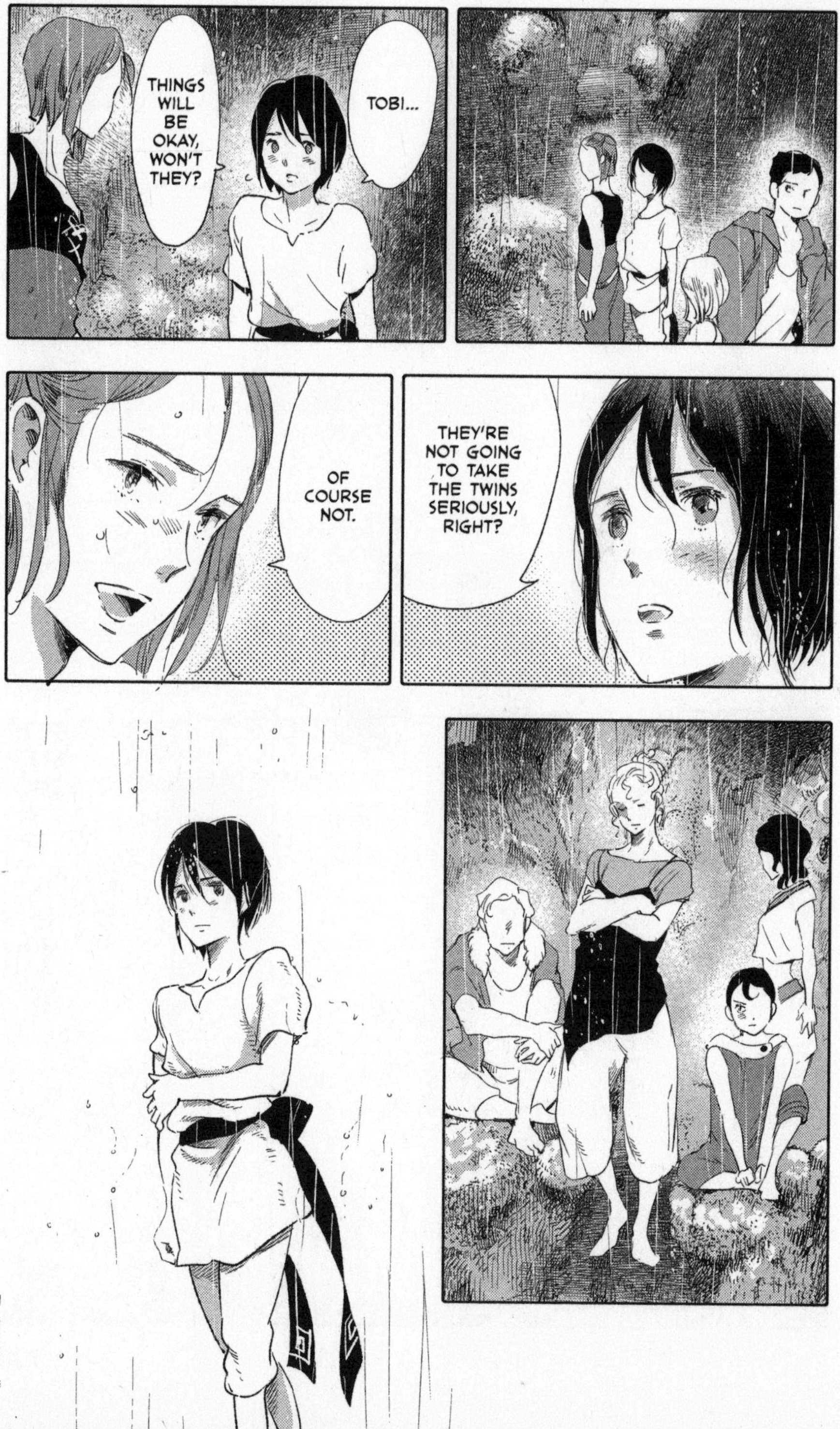
TOBI...
THINGS WILL BE OKAY, WON'T THEY?
THEY'RE NOT GOING TO TAKE THE TWINS SERIOUSLY, RIGHT?
OF COURSE NOT.

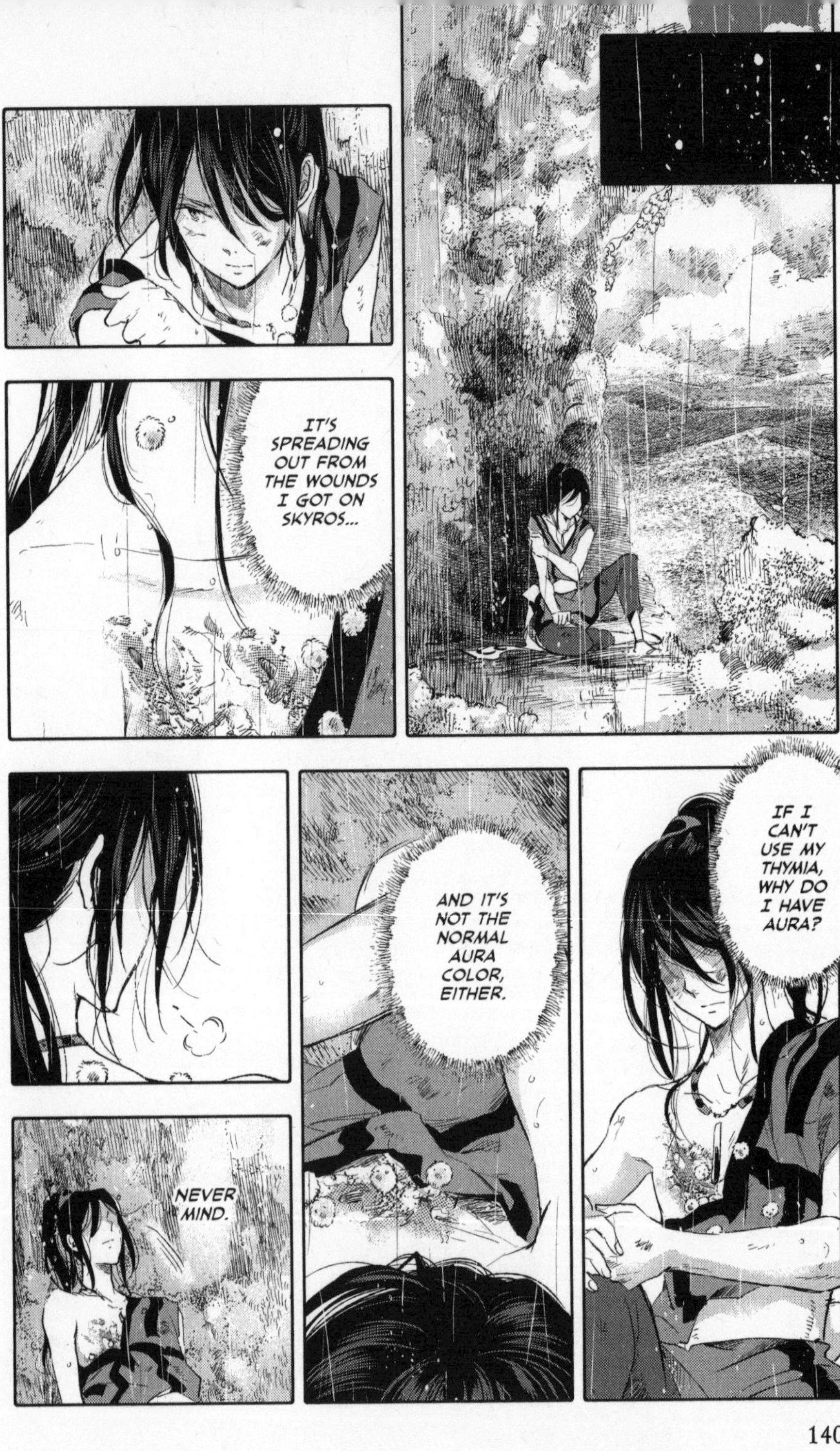
IT'S SPREADING OUT FROM THE WOUNDS I GOT ON SKYROS...
IF I CAN'T USE MY THYMIA, WHY DO I HAVE AURA?
AND IT'S NOT THE NORMAL AURA COLOR, EITHER.
NEVER MIND.

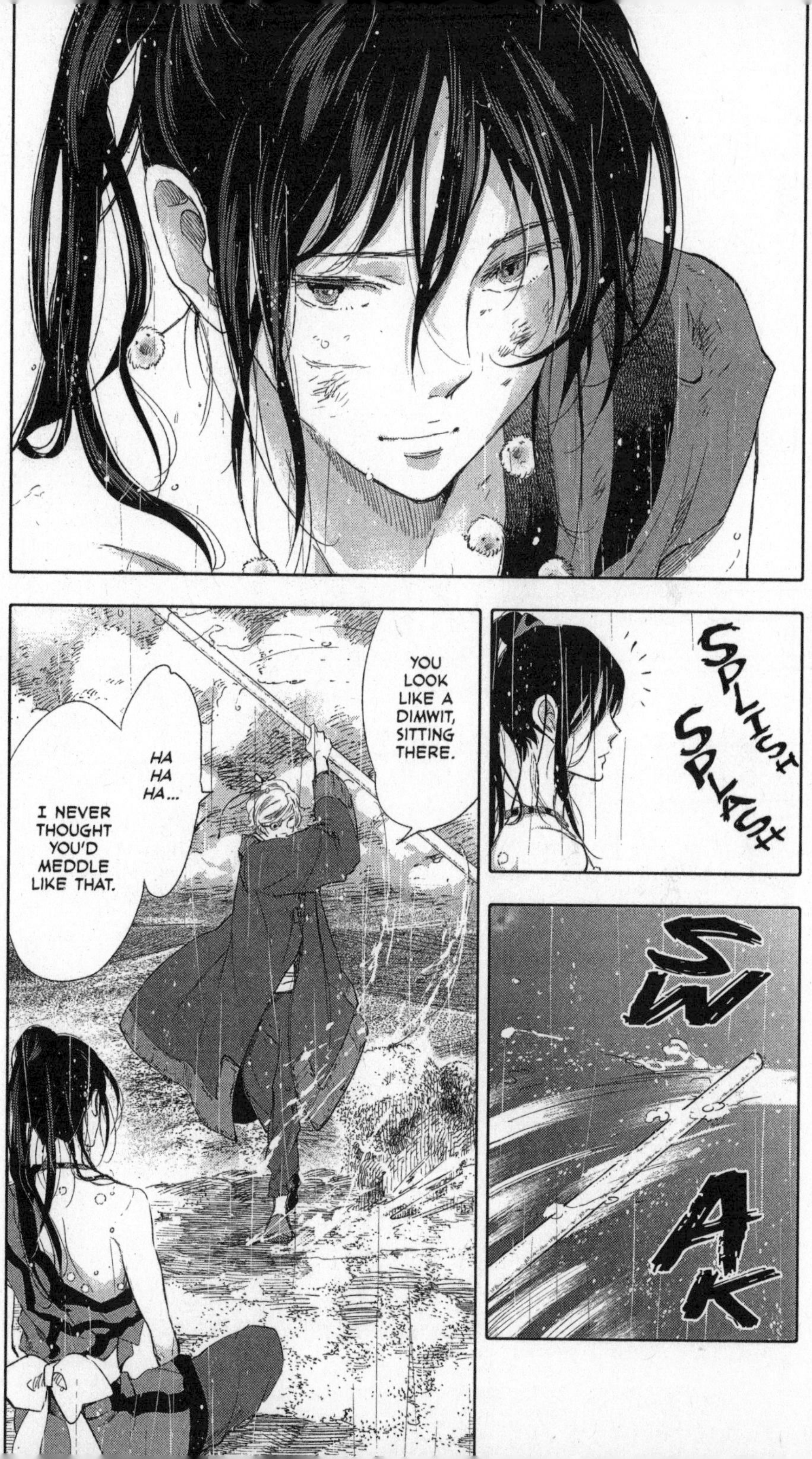
SPLISH
SPLASH
SWAK
YOU LOOK LIKE A DIMWIT, SITTING THERE.
HA HA HA...
I NEVER THOUGHT YOU'D MEDDLE LIKE THAT.

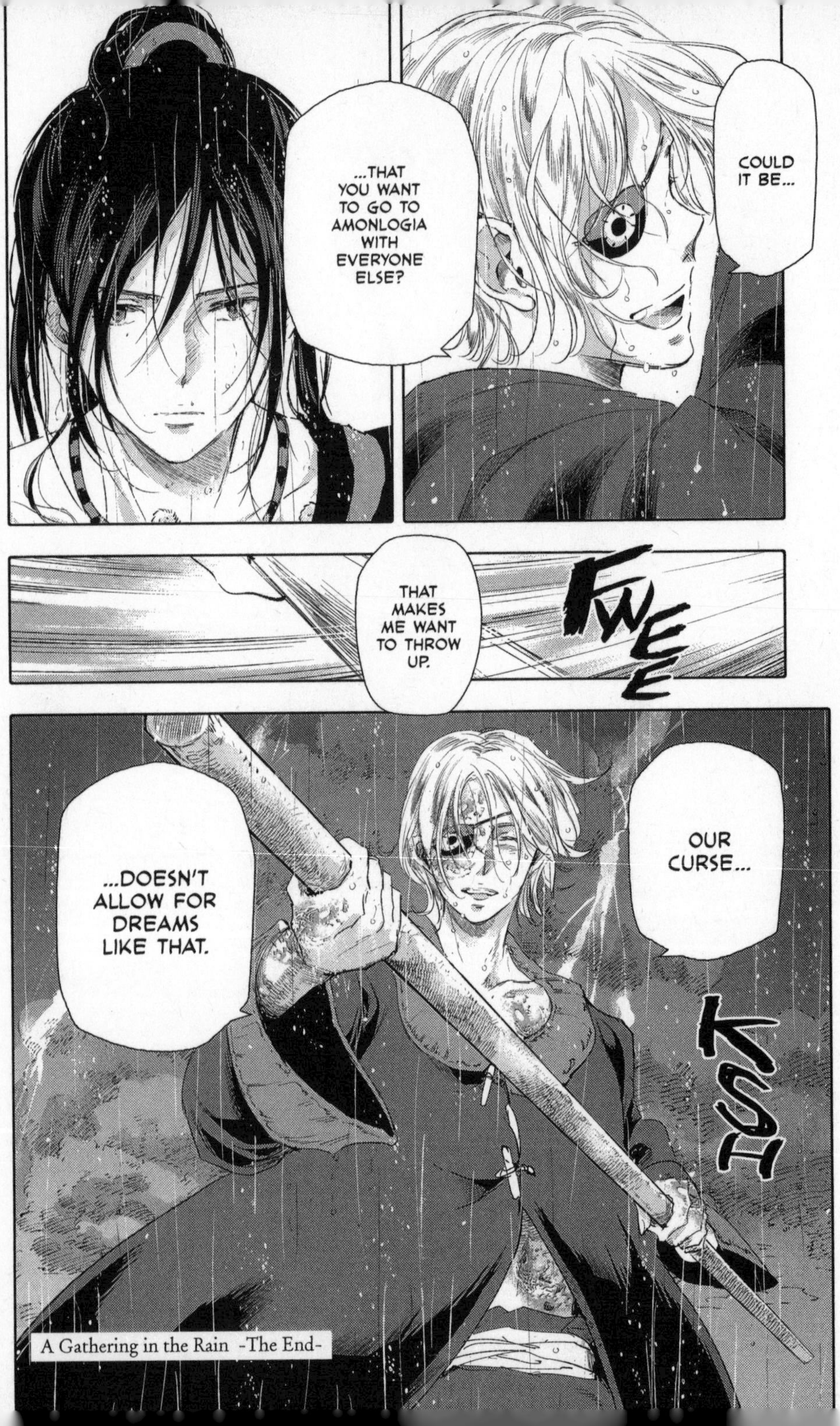
COULD IT BE...
...THAT YOU WANT TO GO TO AMONLOGIA WITH EVERYONE ELSE?
THAT MAKES ME WANT TO THROW UP.
FWEE
OUR CURSE...
...DOESN'T ALLOW FOR DREAMS LIKE THAT.
KSH
A Gathering in the Rain -The End-

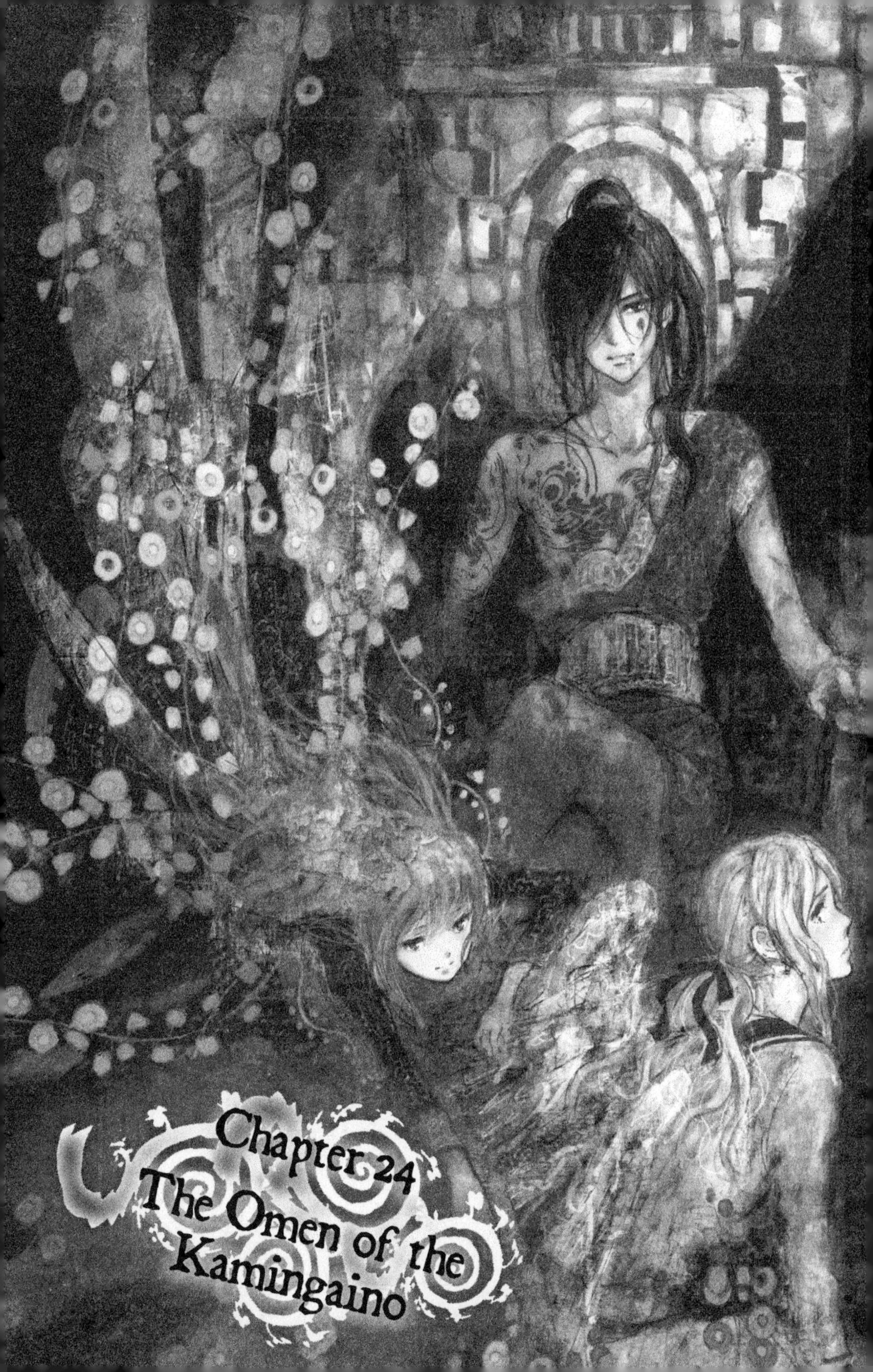
Chapter 24
The Omen of the
Kamingaino

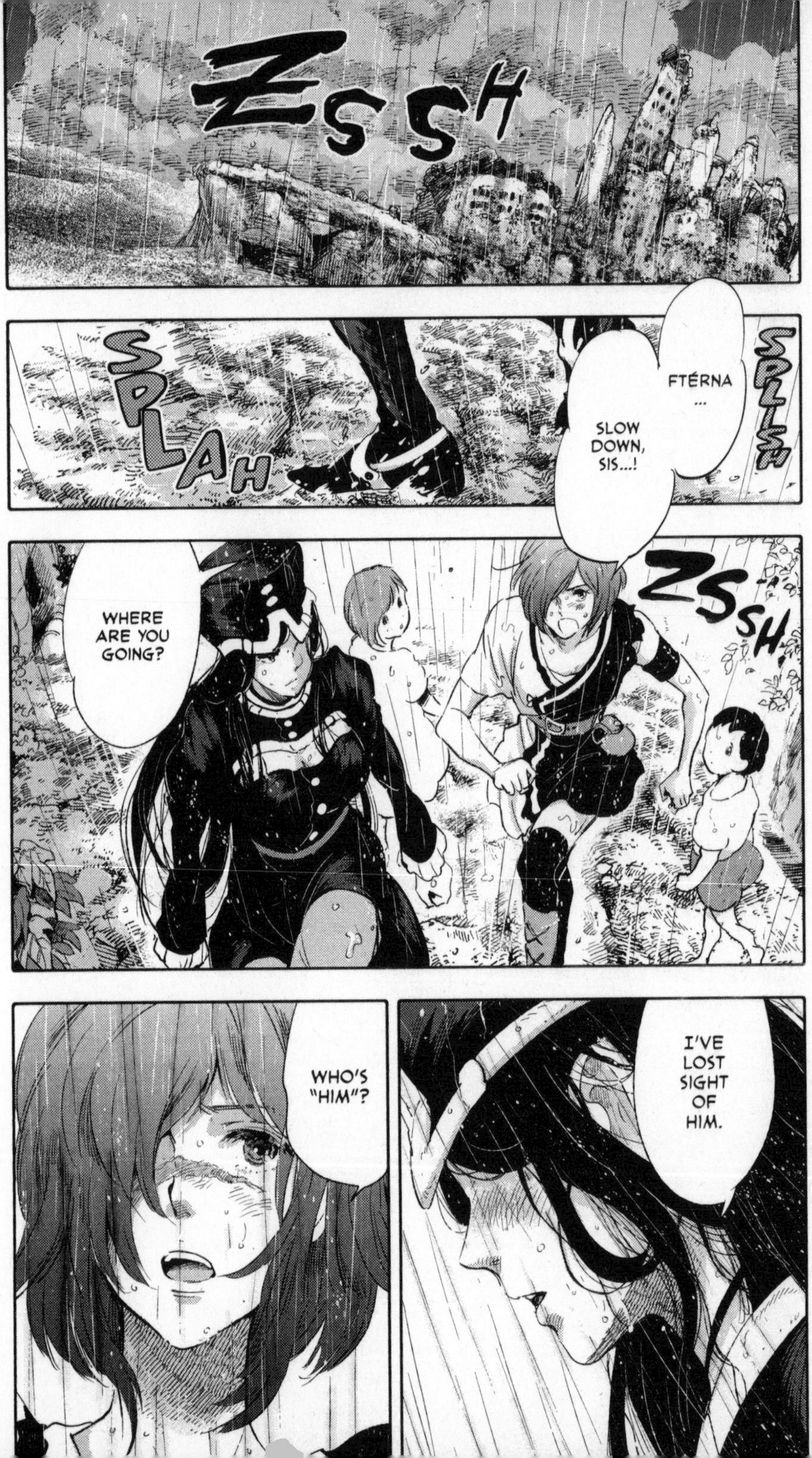
ZSSH
SPLISH
FTÉRNA ...
SLOW DOWN, SIS...!
SPLAH
ZSSH
WHERE ARE YOU GOING?
I'VE LOST SIGHT OF HIM.
WHO'S "HIM"?

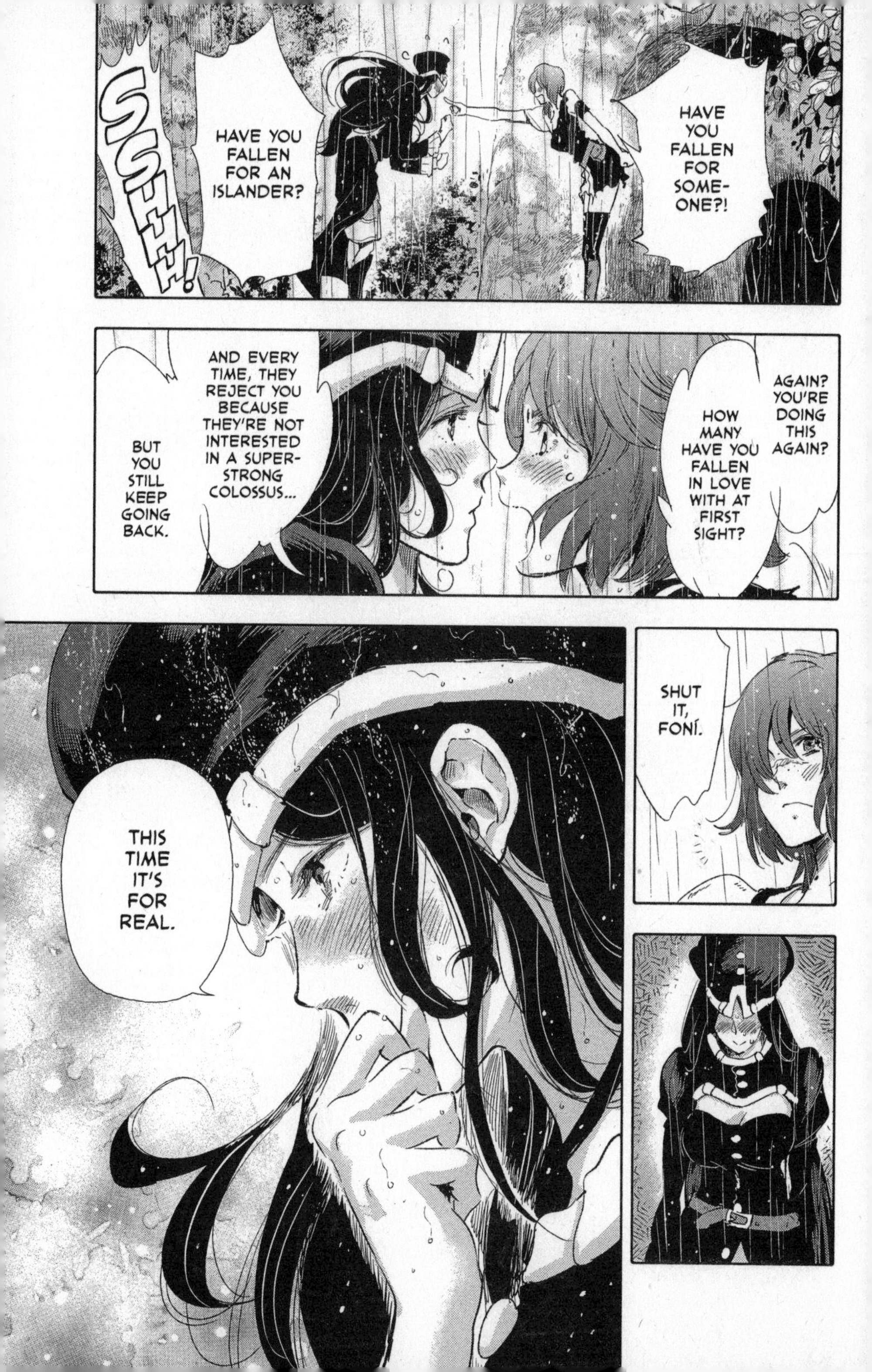
HAVE YOU FALLEN FOR SOME-ONE?!
HAVE YOU FALLEN FOR AN ISLANDER?
SSHHHH!
AGAIN? YOU'RE DOING THIS AGAIN?
HOW MANY HAVE YOU FALLEN IN LOVE WITH AT FIRST SIGHT?
AND EVERY TIME, THEY REJECT YOU BECAUSE THEY'RE NOT INTERESTED IN A SUPER-STRONG COLOSSUS...
BUT YOU STILL KEEP GOING BACK.
SHUT IT, FONÍ.
THIS TIME IT'S FOR REAL.

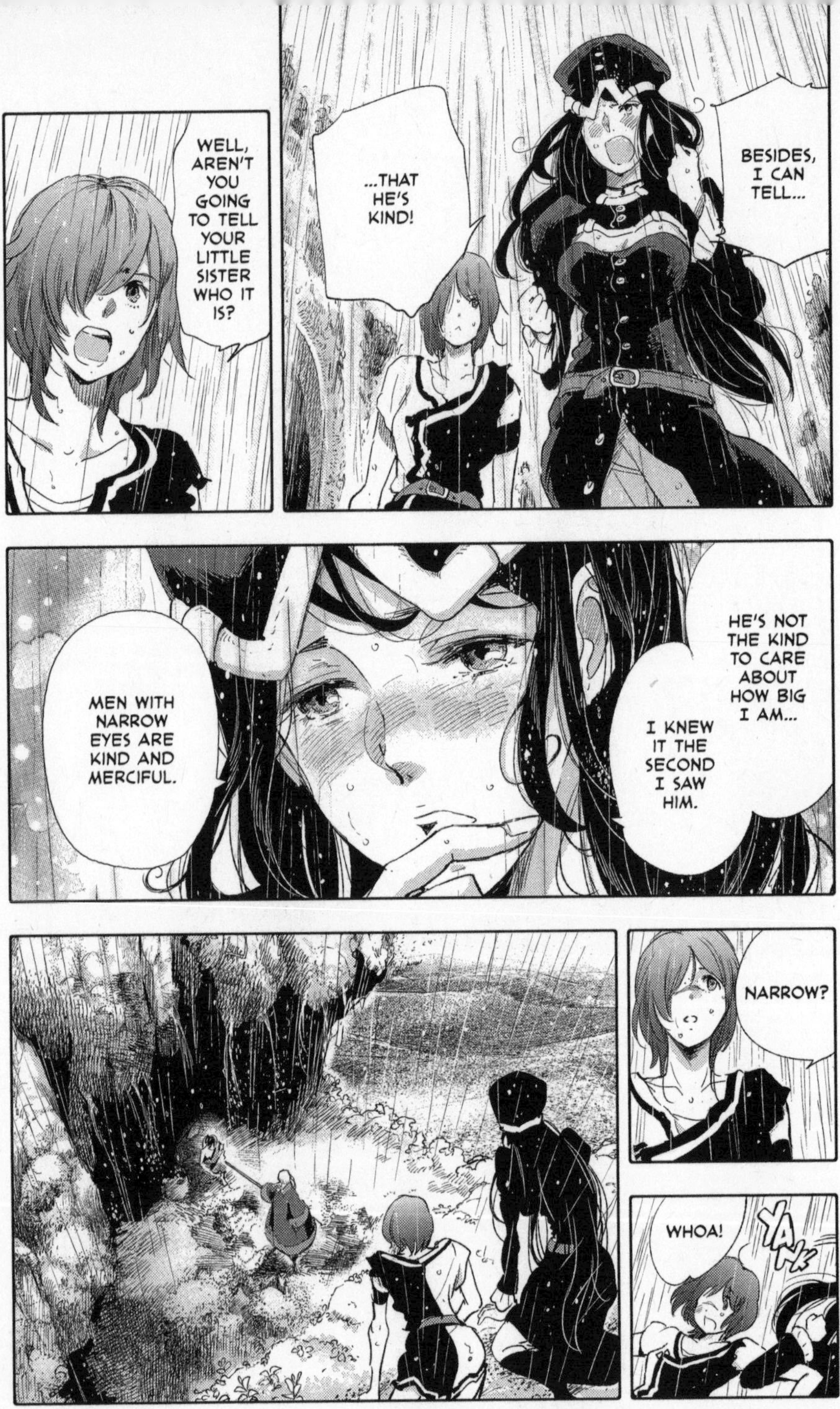
BESIDES, I CAN TELL...
...THAT HE'S KIND!
WELL, AREN'T YOU GOING TO TELL YOUR LITTLE SISTER WHO IT IS?
HE'S NOT THE KIND TO CARE ABOUT HOW BIG I AM...
I KNEW IT THE SECOND I SAW HIM.
MEN WITH NARROW EYES ARE KIND AND MERCIFUL.
NARROW?
YANK
WHOA!

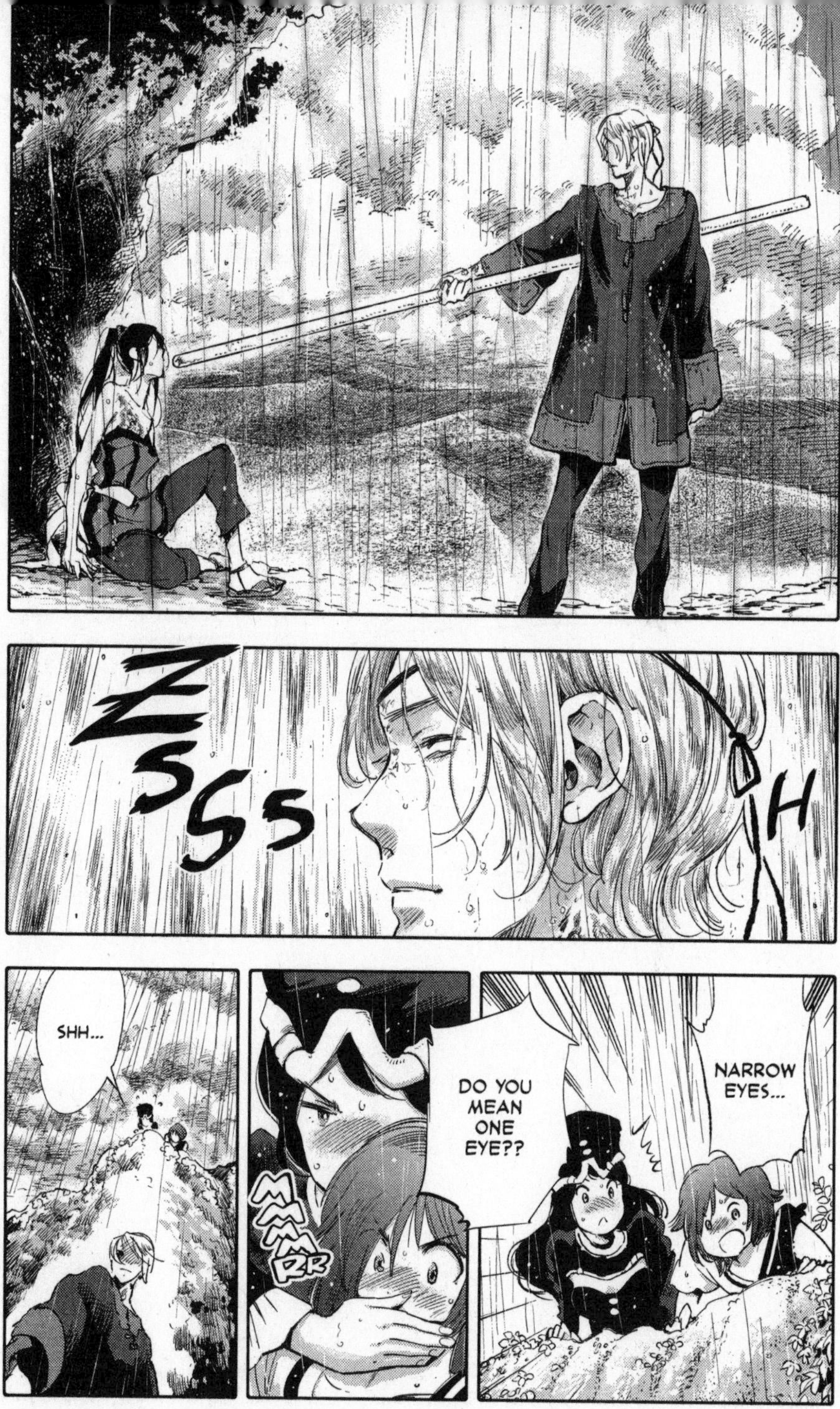
ZSSSH
NARROW EYES...
DO YOU MEAN ONE EYE??
MMMMRR
SHH...

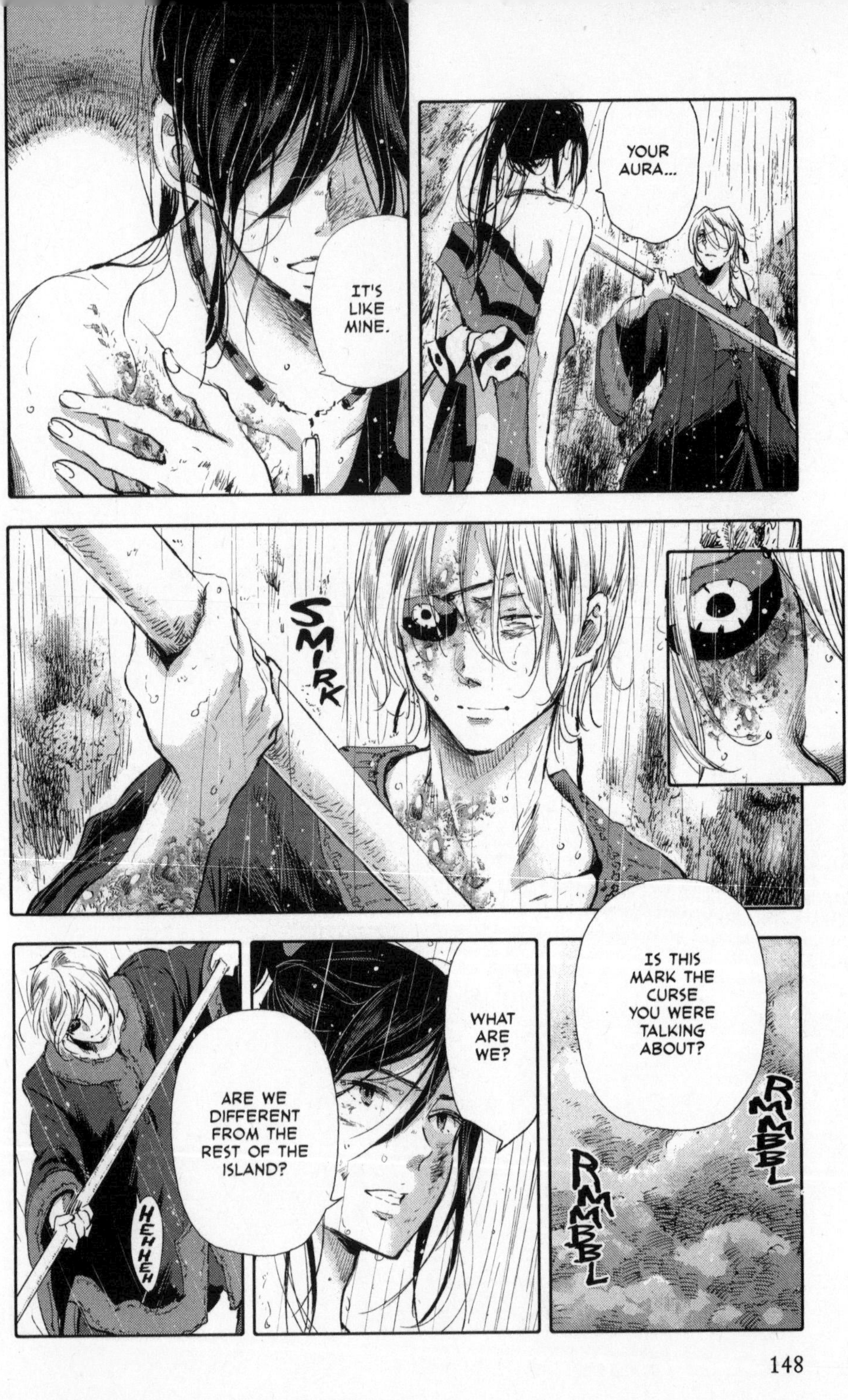
YOUR AURA...
IT'S LIKE MINE.
SMIRK
IS THIS MARK THE CURSE YOU WERE TALKING ABOUT?
RMMBBL
RMMBBL
WHAT ARE WE?
ARE WE DIFFERENT FROM THE REST OF THE ISLAND?
HEHHHEH

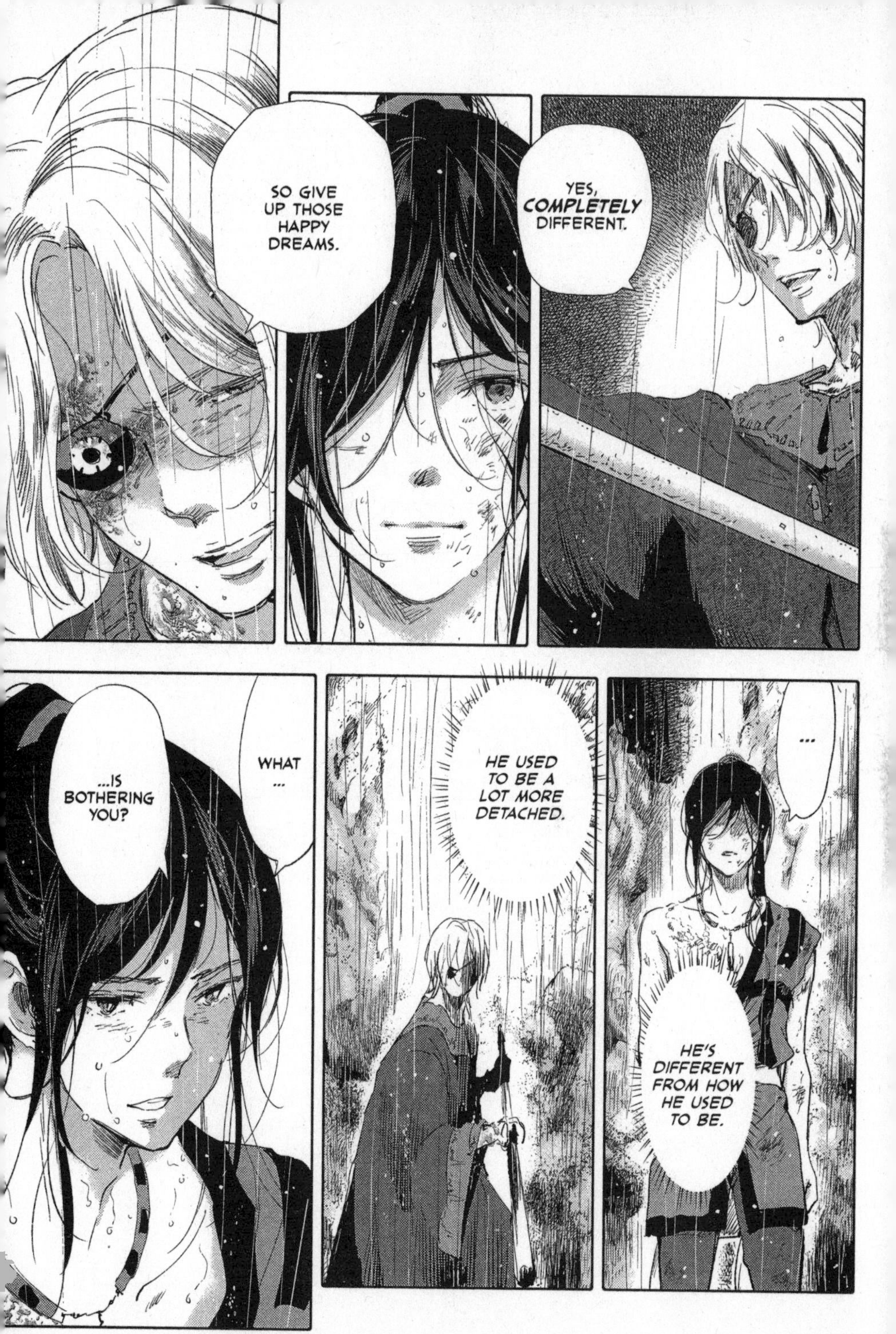
YES, COMPLETELY DIFFERENT.
SO GIVE UP THOSE HAPPY DREAMS.
...
HE'S DIFFERENT FROM HOW HE USED TO BE.
HE USED TO BE A LOT MORE DETACHED.
WHAT ...
...IS BOTHERING YOU?

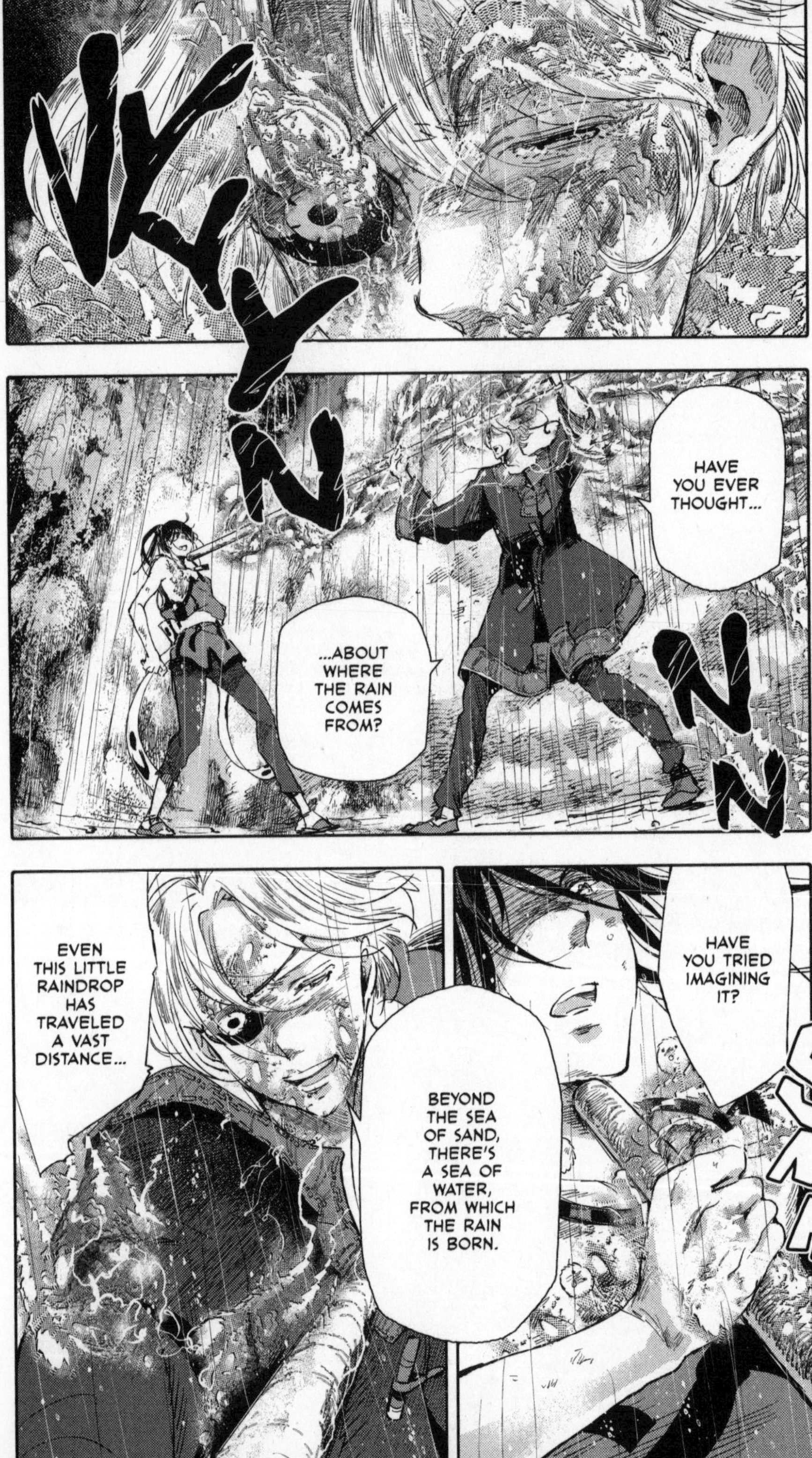
HAVE YOU EVER THOUGHT...
NNN
...ABOUT WHERE THE RAIN COMES FROM?
SMK
HAVE YOU TRIED IMAGINING IT?
BEYOND THE SEA OF SAND, THERE'S A SEA OF WATER, FROM WHICH THE RAIN IS BORN.
EVEN THIS LITTLE RAINDROP HAS TRAVELED A VAST DISTANCE...

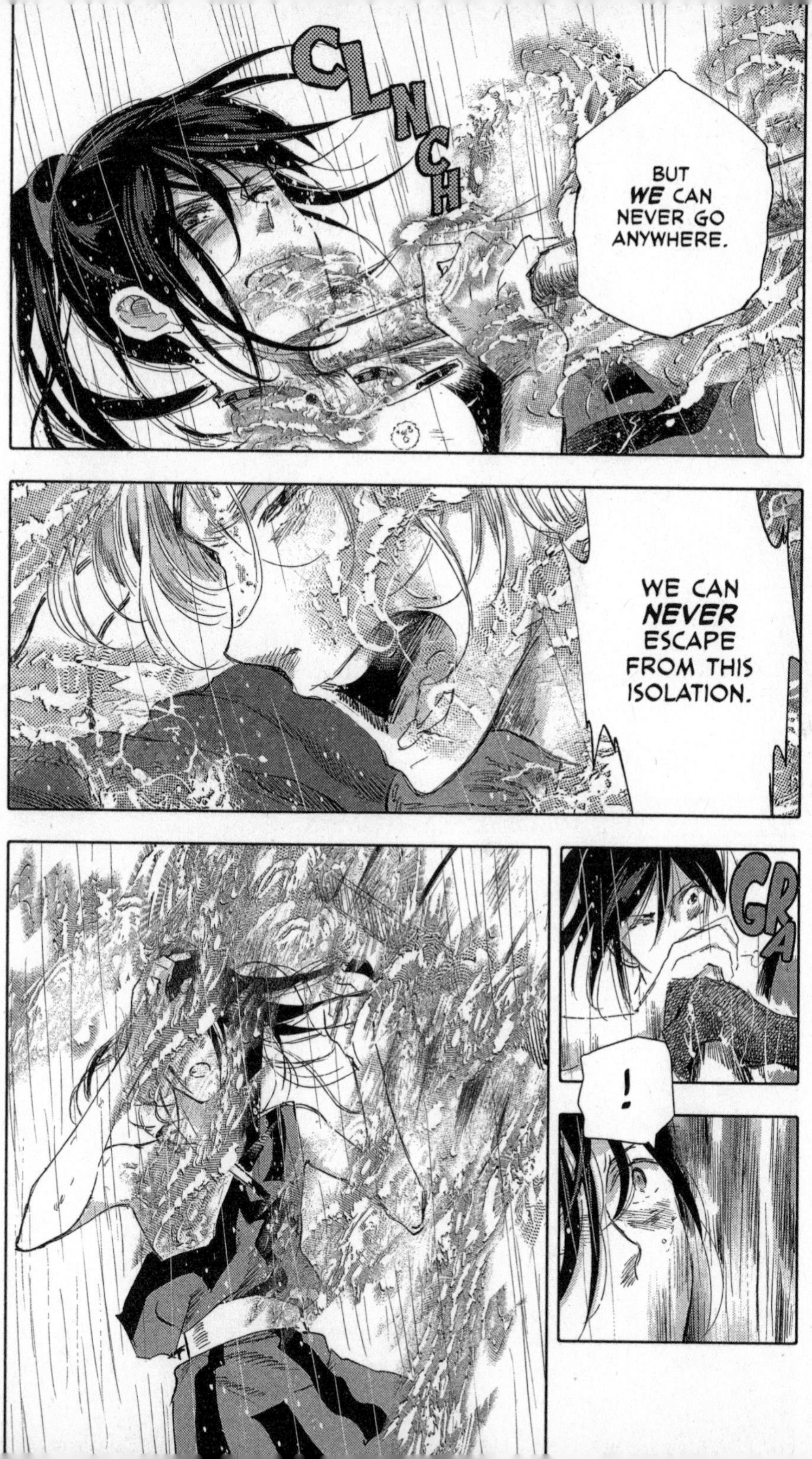
BUT **WE** CAN NEVER GO ANYWHERE.
CLNCH
WE CAN **NEVER** ESCAPE FROM THIS ISOLATION.
GRA
!

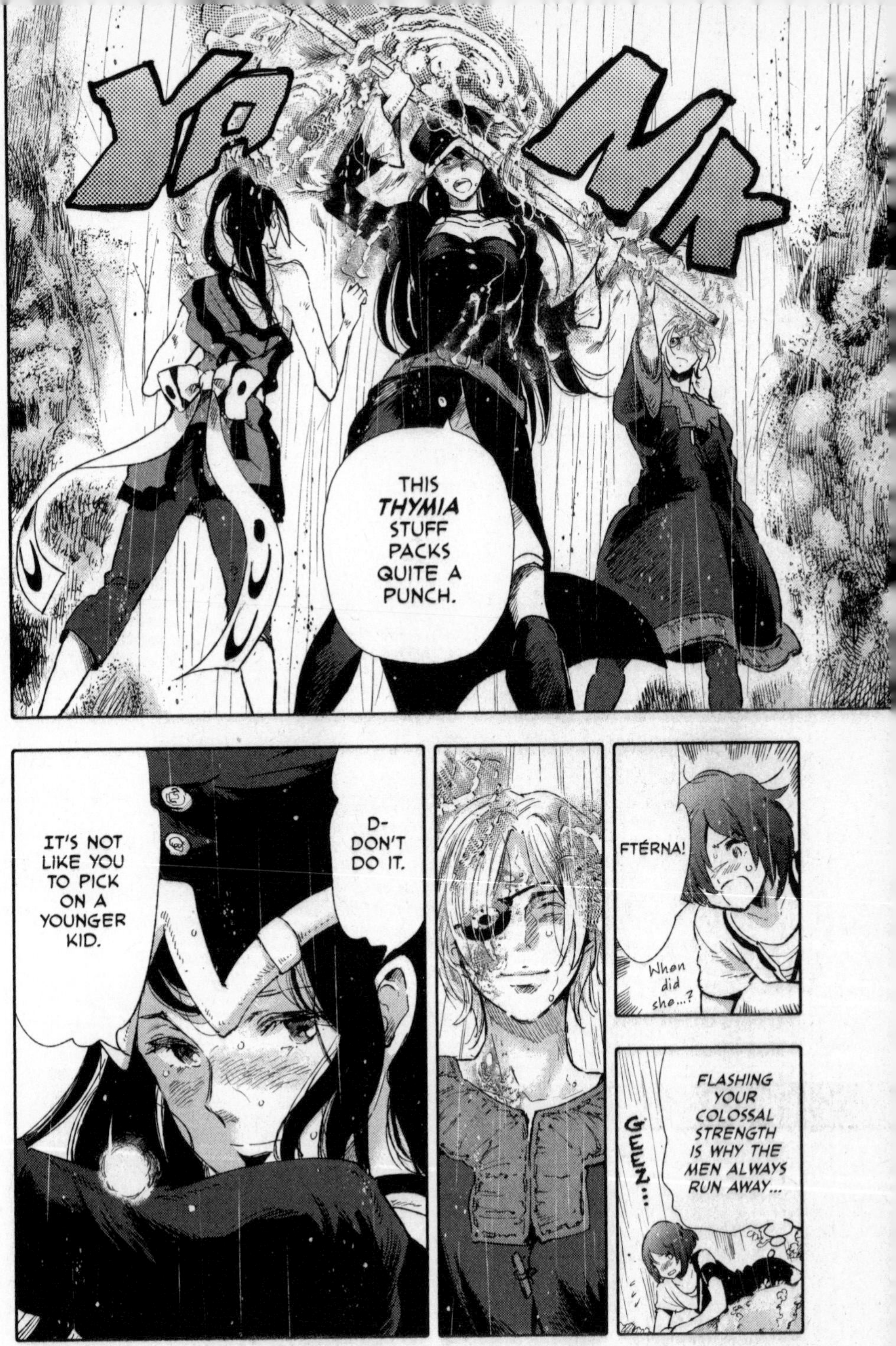
YA
NK
THIS THYMIA STUFF PACKS QUITE A PUNCH.
FTÉRNA!
When did she...?
FLASHING YOUR COLOSSAL STRENGTH IS WHY THE MEN ALWAYS RUN AWAY...
GEEZ...
D-DON'T DO IT.
IT'S NOT LIKE YOU TO PICK ON A YOUNGER KID.

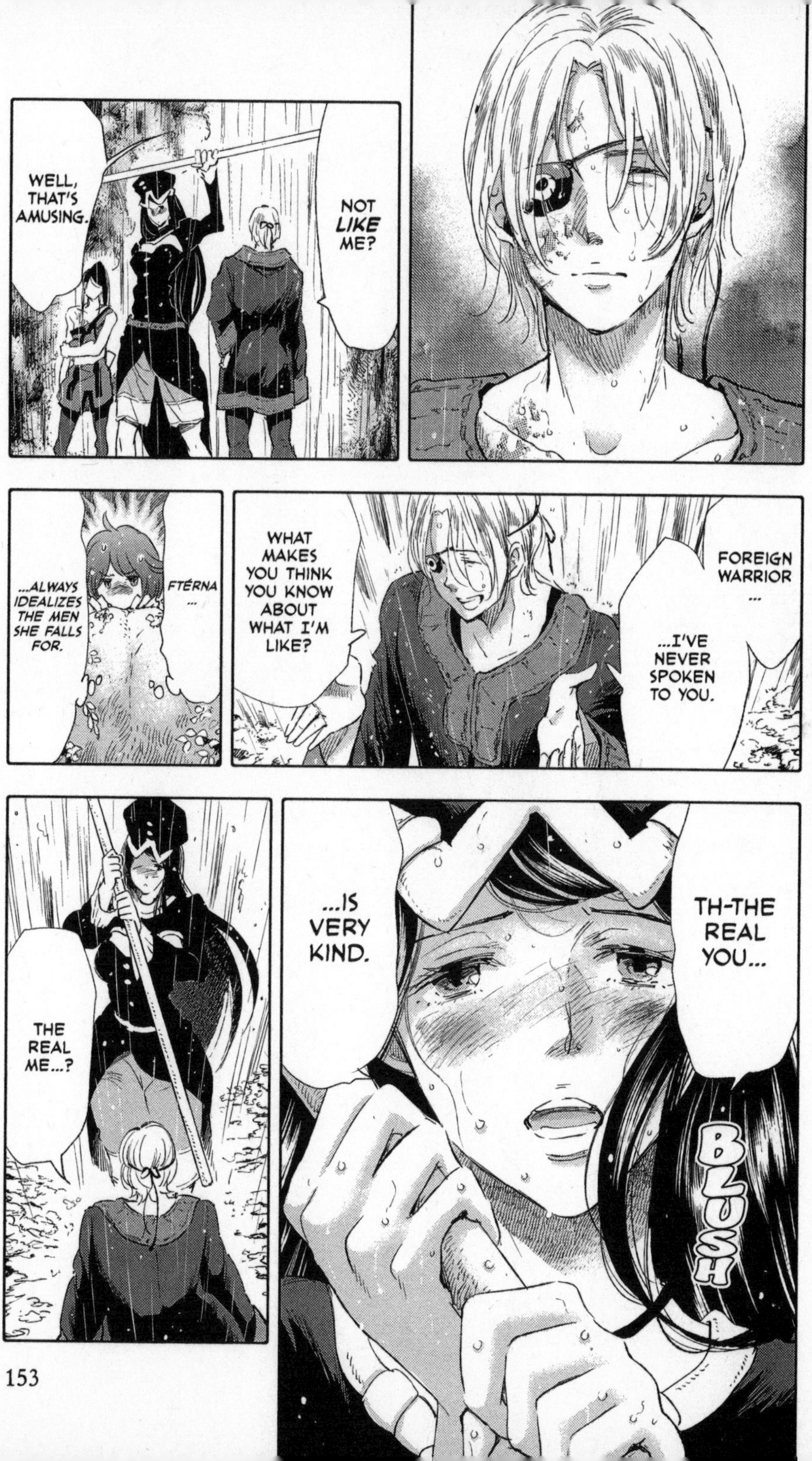
NOT *LIKE* ME?
WELL, THAT'S AMUSING.
FOREIGN WARRIOR...
...I'VE NEVER SPOKEN TO YOU.
WHAT MAKES YOU THINK YOU KNOW ABOUT WHAT I'M LIKE?
FTÉRNA...
...ALWAYS IDEALIZES THE MEN SHE FALLS FOR.
TH-THE REAL YOU...
...IS VERY KIND.
BLUSH
THE REAL ME...?

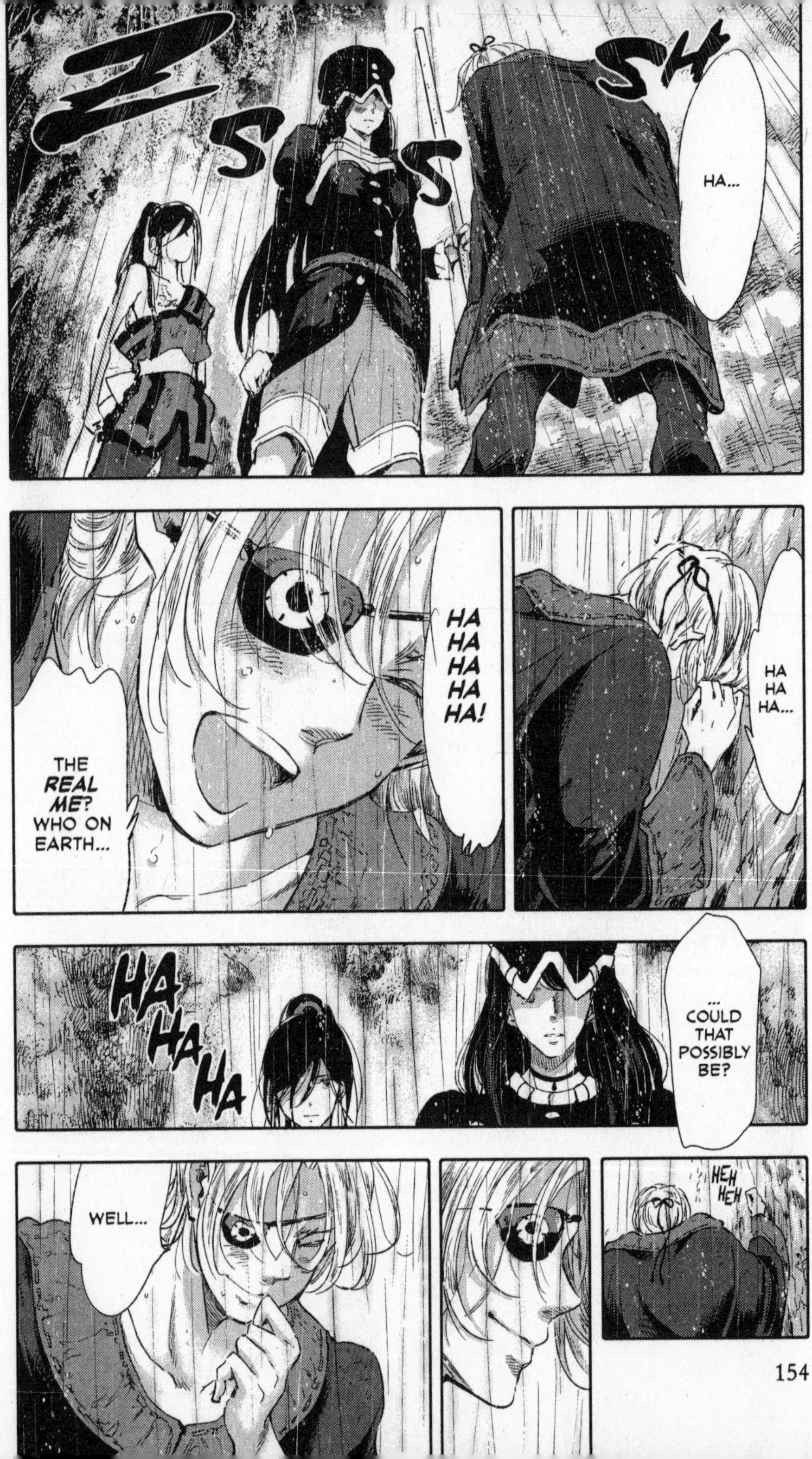
ZSSSH
HA...
HA HA HA...
HA HA HA HA HA!
THE *REAL ME*? WHO ON EARTH...
... COULD THAT POSSIBLY BE?
HA HA HA HA
HEH HEH
WELL...

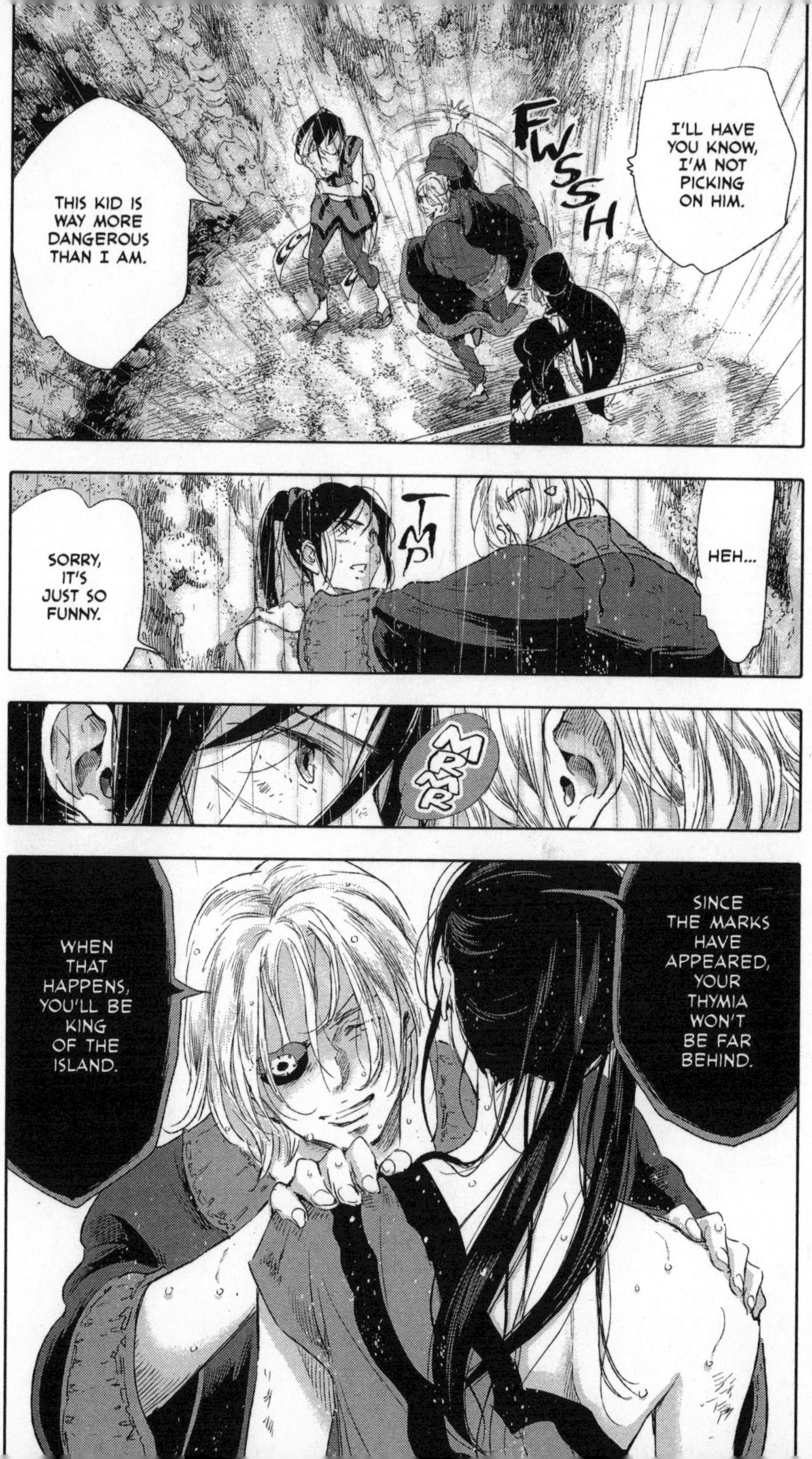
I'LL HAVE YOU KNOW, I'M NOT PICKING ON HIM.
FWSSH
THIS KID IS WAY MORE DANGEROUS THAN I AM.
HEH...
TMP
SORRY, IT'S JUST SO FUNNY.
MRMR
SINCE THE MARKS HAVE APPEARED, YOUR THYMIA WON'T BE FAR BEHIND.
WHEN THAT HAPPENS, YOU'LL BE KING OF THE ISLAND.

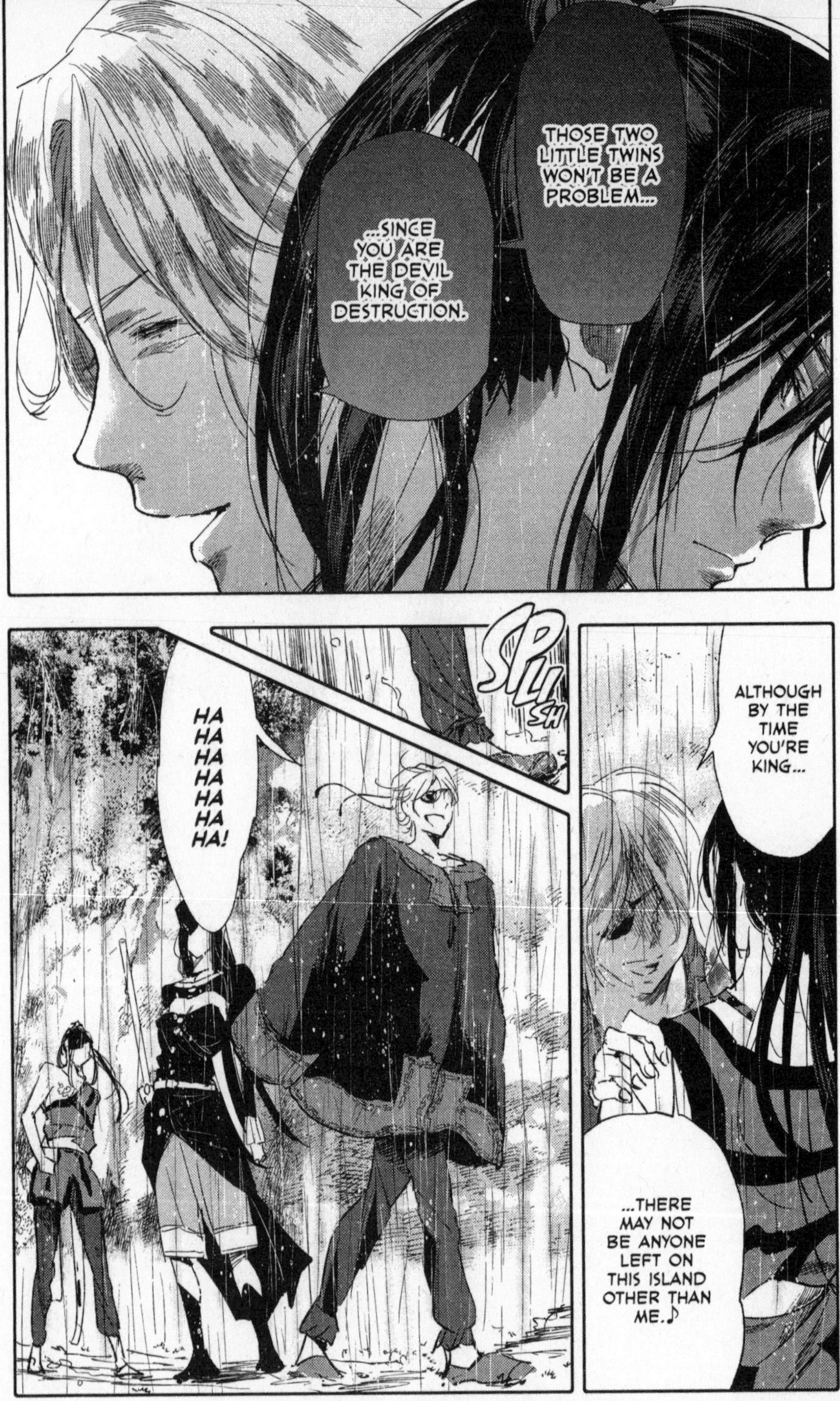
THOSE TWO LITTLE TWINS WON'T BE A PROBLEM...
...SINCE YOU ARE THE DEVIL KING OF DESTRUCTION.
ALTHOUGH BY THE TIME YOU'RE KING...
...THERE MAY NOT BE ANYONE LEFT ON THIS ISLAND OTHER THAN ME.♪
SPLISH
HA HA HA HA HA HA HA!

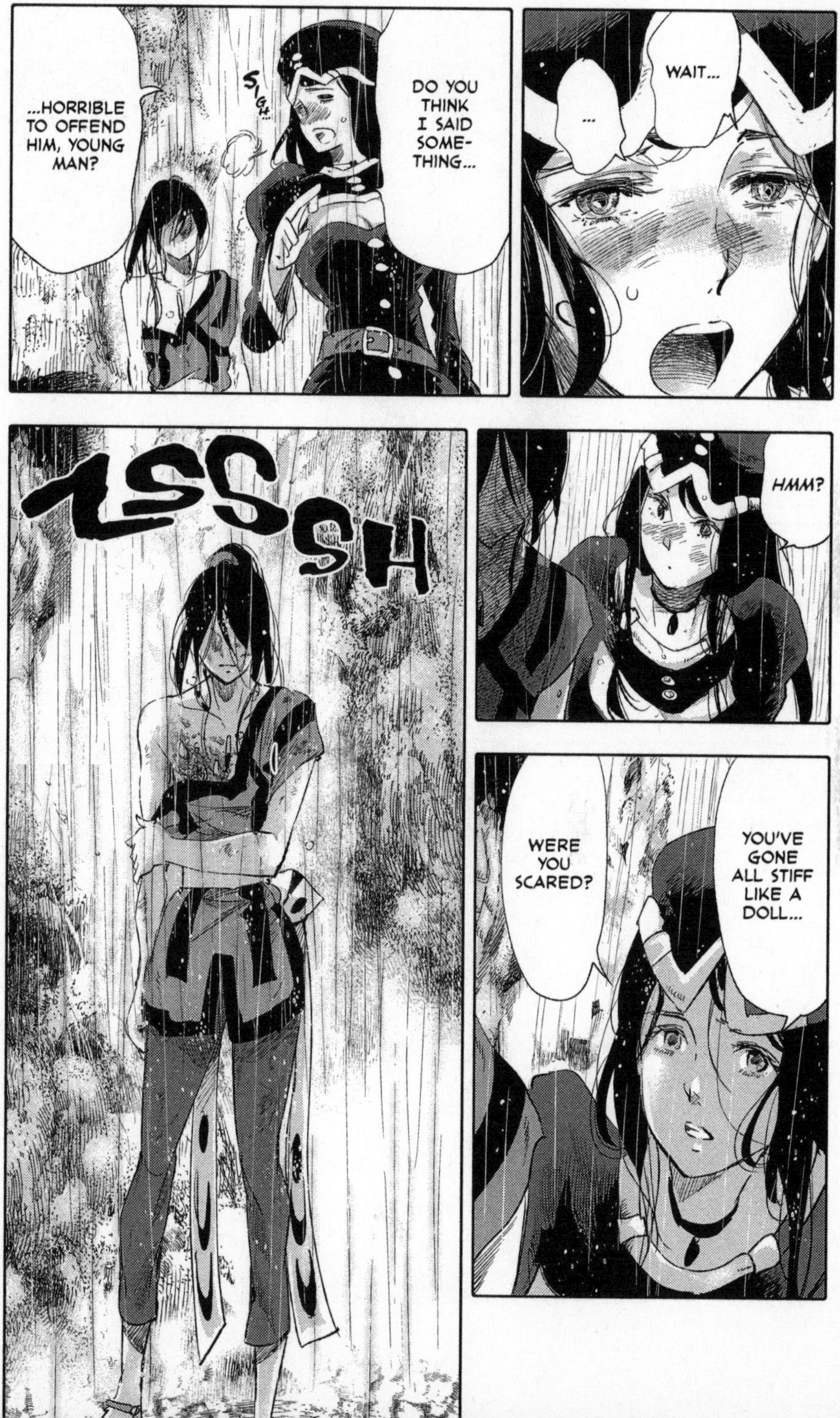
WAIT...
...
DO YOU THINK I SAID SOMETHING...
SIGH...
...HORRIBLE TO OFFEND HIM, YOUNG MAN?
HMM?
YOU'VE GONE ALL STIFF LIKE A DOLL...
WERE YOU SCARED?
TSSSH

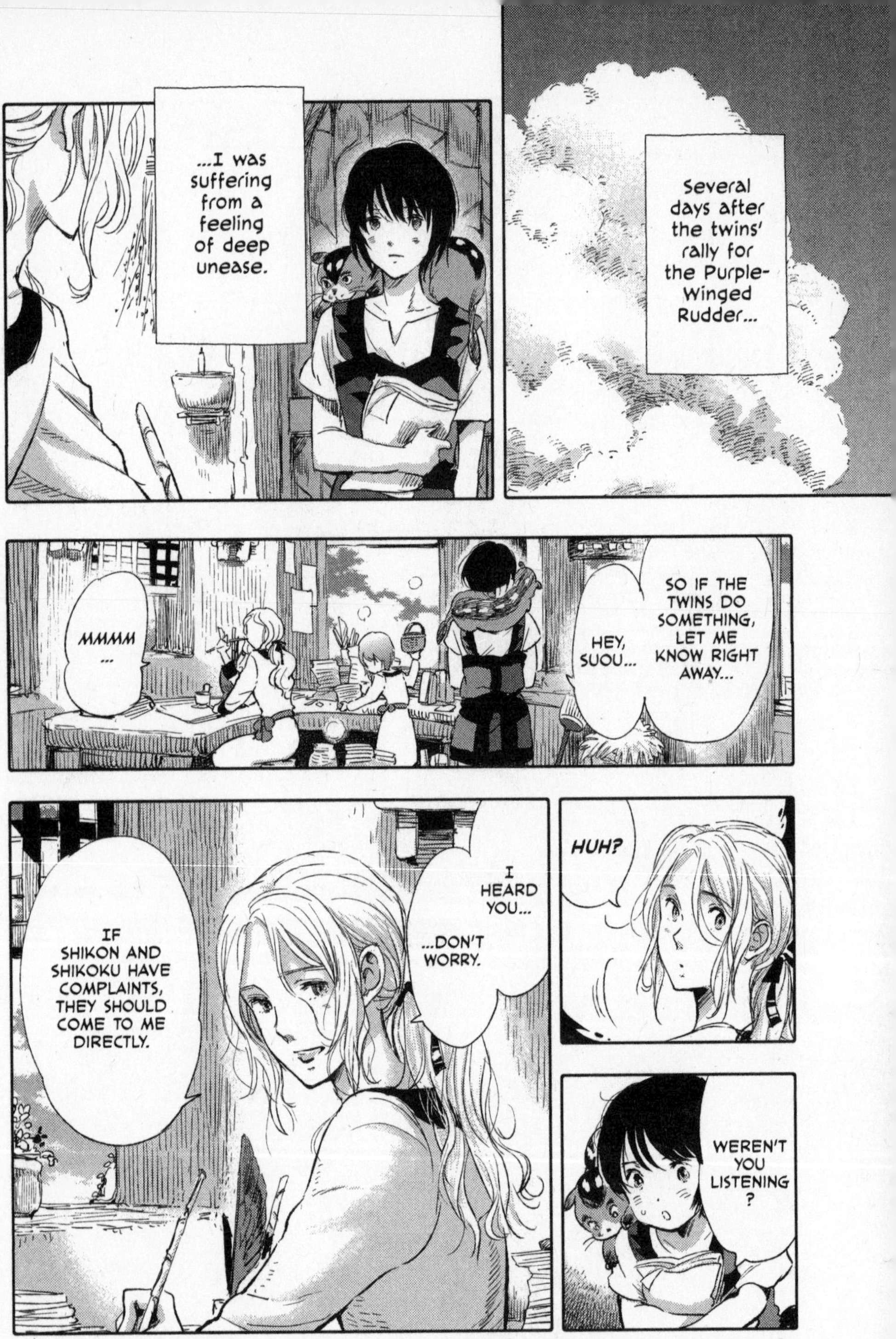
Several days after the twins' rally for the Purple-Winged Rudder...
...I was suffering from a feeling of deep unease.
SO IF THE TWINS DO SOMETHING, LET ME KNOW RIGHT AWAY...
HEY, SUOU...
MMMM ...
HUH?
WEREN'T YOU LISTENING ?
I HEARD YOU... ...DON'T WORRY.
IF SHIKON AND SHIKOKU HAVE COMPLAINTS, THEY SHOULD COME TO ME DIRECTLY.

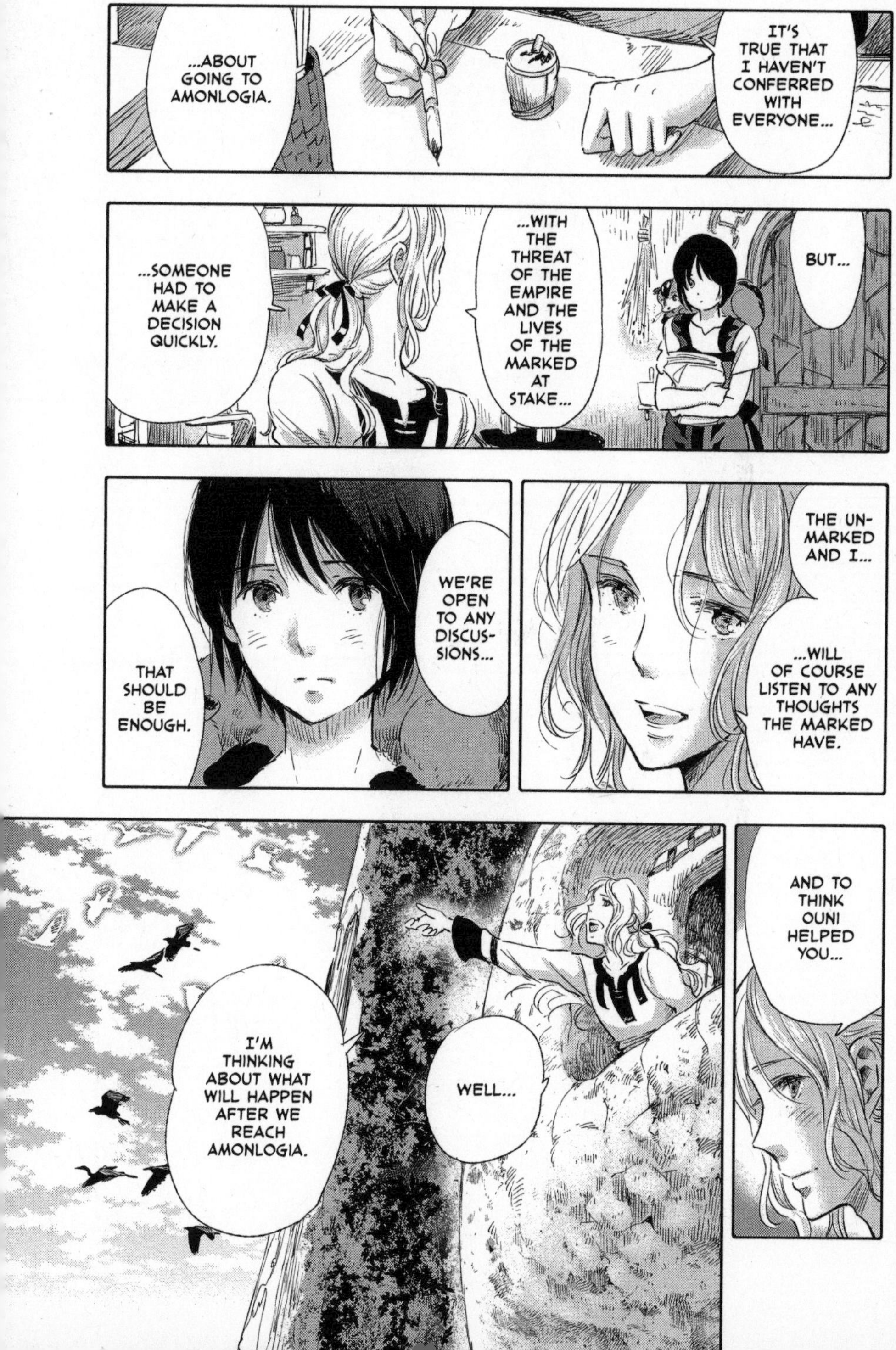
IT'S TRUE THAT I HAVEN'T CONFERRED WITH EVERYONE...
...ABOUT GOING TO AMONLOGIA.
BUT...
...WITH THE THREAT OF THE EMPIRE AND THE LIVES OF THE MARKED AT STAKE...
...SOMEONE HAD TO MAKE A DECISION QUICKLY.
THE UNMARKED AND I...
...WILL OF COURSE LISTEN TO ANY THOUGHTS THE MARKED HAVE.
WE'RE OPEN TO ANY DISCUSSIONS...
THAT SHOULD BE ENOUGH.
AND TO THINK OUNI HELPED YOU...
WELL...
I'M THINKING ABOUT WHAT WILL HAPPEN AFTER WE REACH AMONLOGIA.

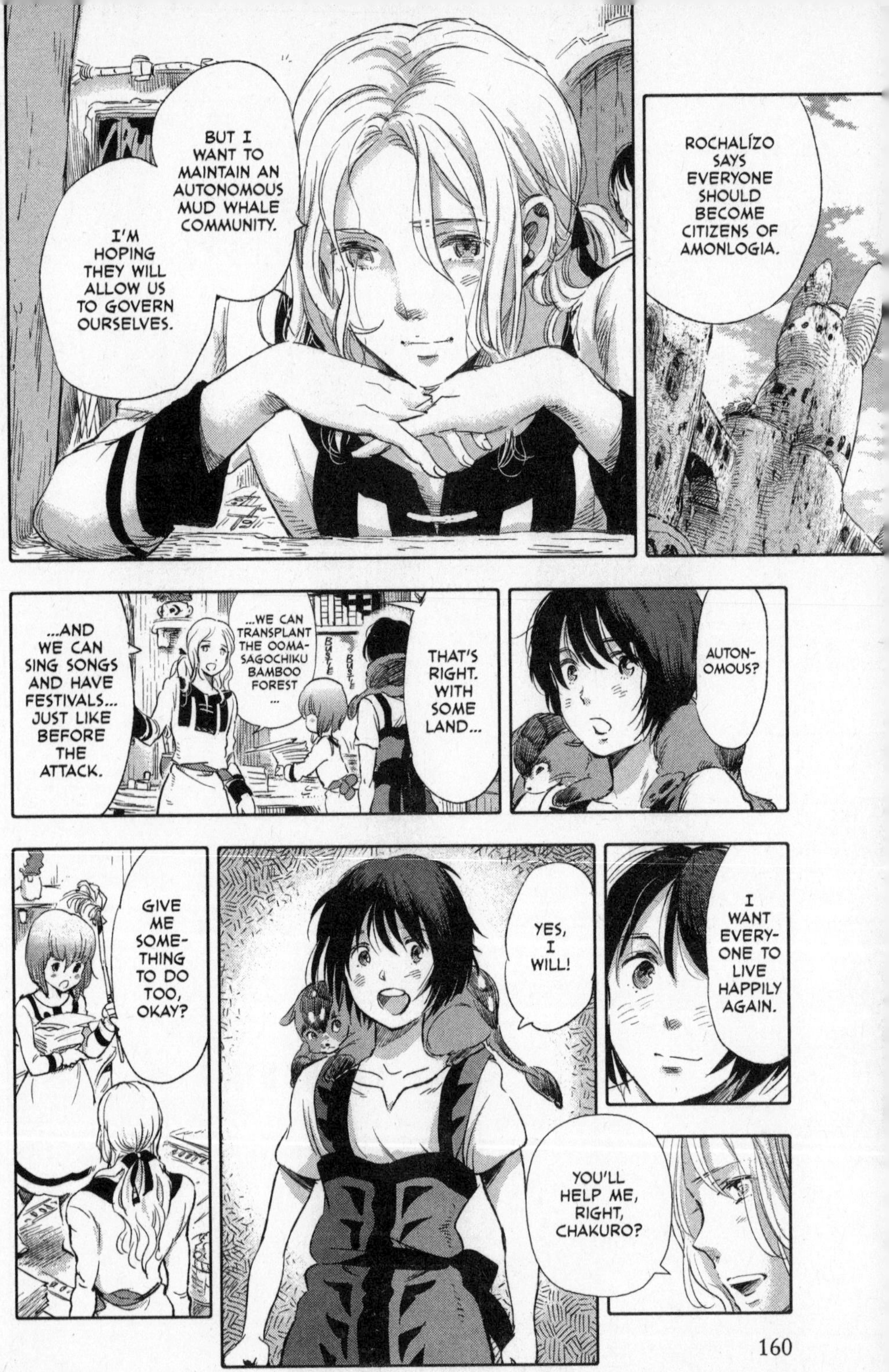
ROCHALÍZO SAYS EVERYONE SHOULD BECOME CITIZENS OF AMONLOGIA.
BUT I WANT TO MAINTAIN AN AUTONOMOUS MUD WHALE COMMUNITY.
I'M HOPING THEY WILL ALLOW US TO GOVERN OURSELVES.
AUTON-OMOUS?
THAT'S RIGHT. WITH SOME LAND...
...WE CAN TRANSPLANT THE OOMA-SAGOCHIKU BAMBOO FOREST...
BUSTLE
BUSTLE
...AND WE CAN SING SONGS AND HAVE FESTIVALS... JUST LIKE BEFORE THE ATTACK.
I WANT EVERY-ONE TO LIVE HAPPILY AGAIN.
YOU'LL HELP ME, RIGHT, CHAKURO?
YES, I WILL!
GIVE ME SOME-THING TO DO TOO, OKAY?

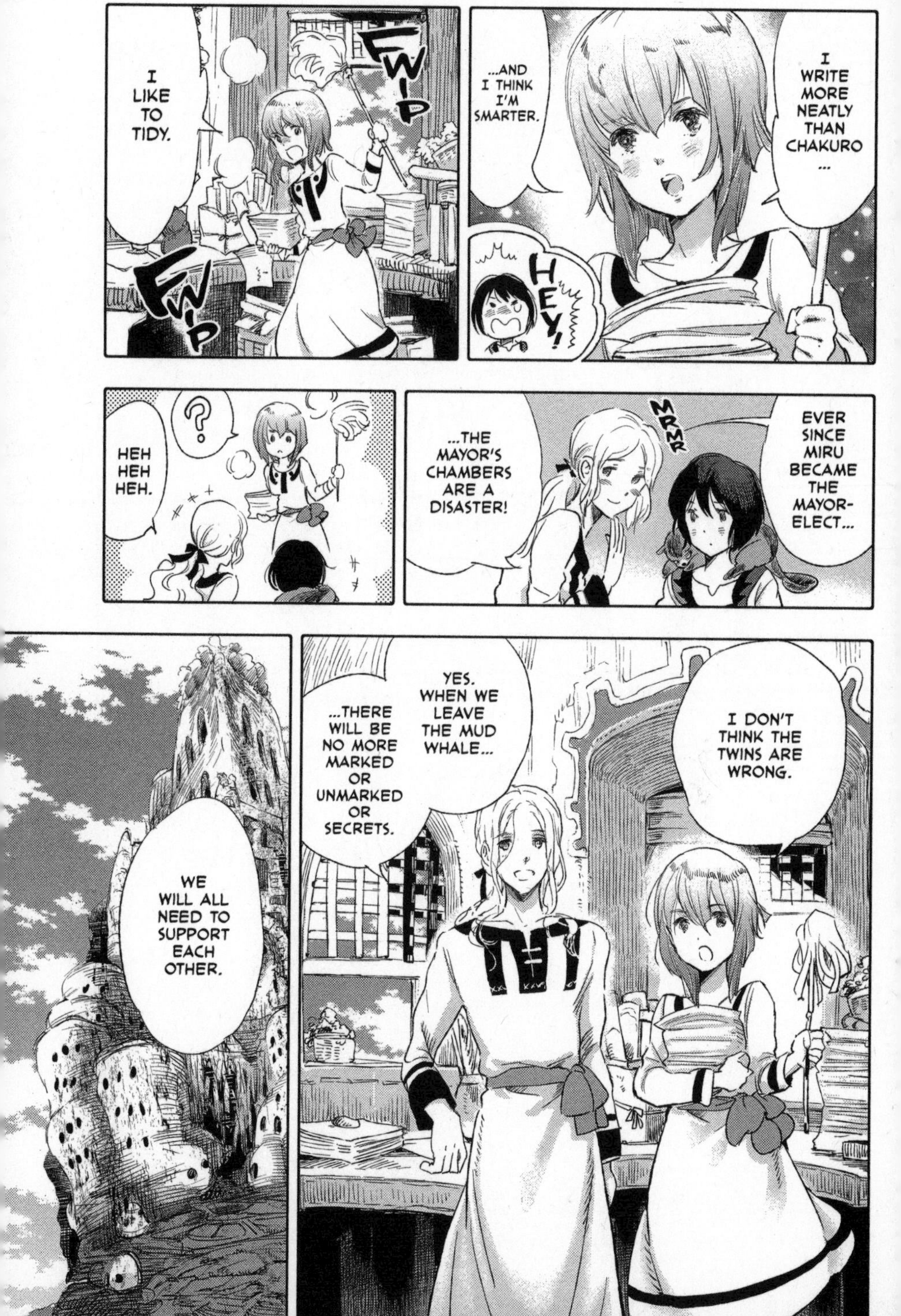
I WRITE MORE NEATLY THAN CHAKURO ...
...AND I THINK I'M SMARTER.
HEY!
FWIP
I LIKE TO TIDY.
FWIP
EVER SINCE MIRU BECAME THE MAYOR-ELECT...
MRMR
...THE MAYOR'S CHAMBERS ARE A DISASTER!
?
HEH HEH HEH.
I DON'T THINK THE TWINS ARE WRONG.
YES. WHEN WE LEAVE THE MUD WHALE...
...THERE WILL BE NO MORE MARKED OR UNMARKED OR SECRETS.
WE WILL ALL NEED TO SUPPORT EACH OTHER.

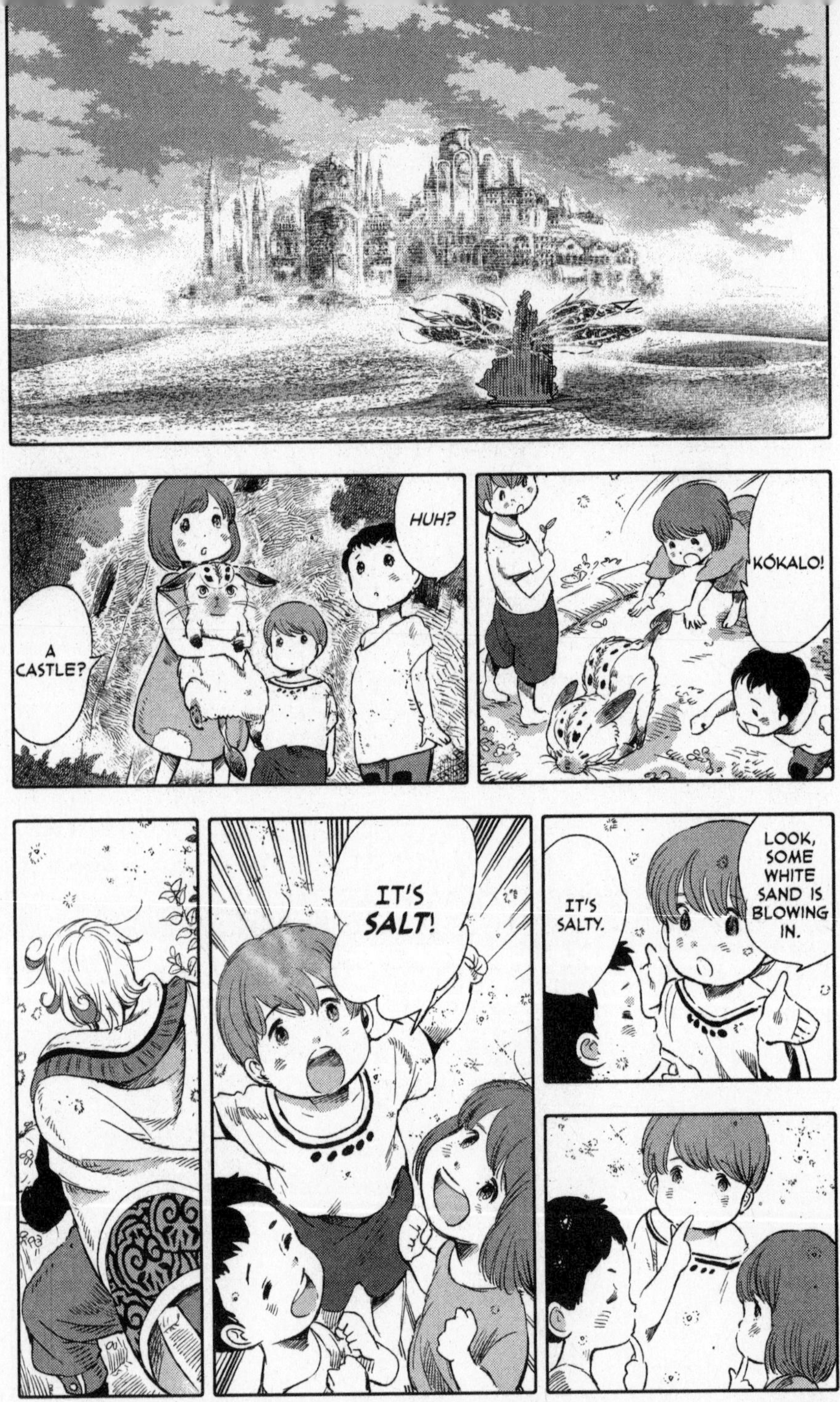
KÓKALO!
HUH?
A CASTLE?
LOOK, SOME WHITE SAND IS BLOWING IN.
IT'S SALTY.
IT'S SALT!

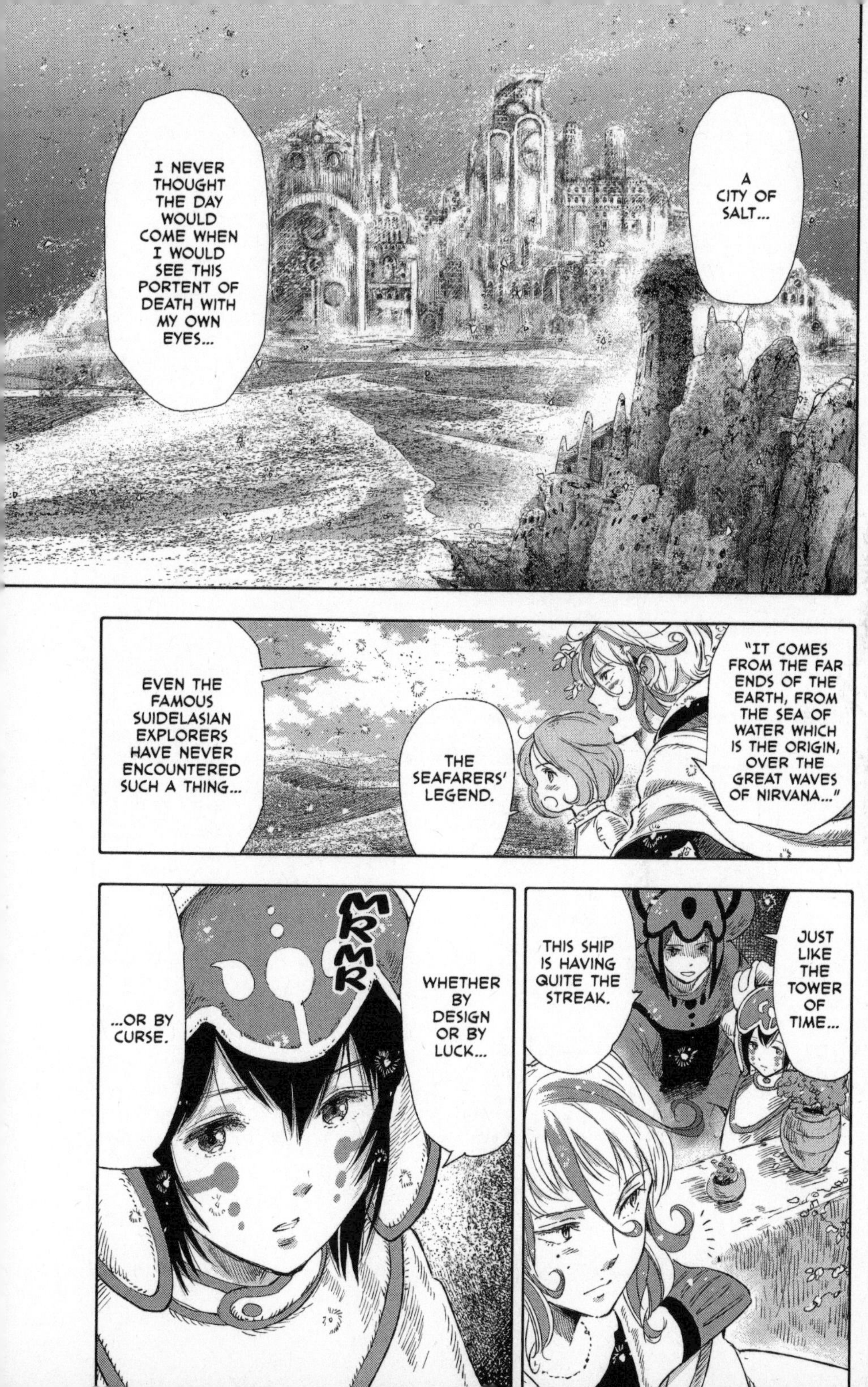
A CITY OF SALT...
I NEVER THOUGHT THE DAY WOULD COME WHEN I WOULD SEE THIS PORTENT OF DEATH WITH MY OWN EYES...
"IT COMES FROM THE FAR ENDS OF THE EARTH, FROM THE SEA OF WATER WHICH IS THE ORIGIN, OVER THE GREAT WAVES OF NIRVANA..."
THE SEAFARERS' LEGEND.
EVEN THE FAMOUS SUIDELASIAN EXPLORERS HAVE NEVER ENCOUNTERED SUCH A THING...
JUST LIKE THE TOWER OF TIME...
THIS SHIP IS HAVING QUITE THE STREAK.
WHETHER BY DESIGN OR BY LUCK...
MRMR
...OR BY CURSE.

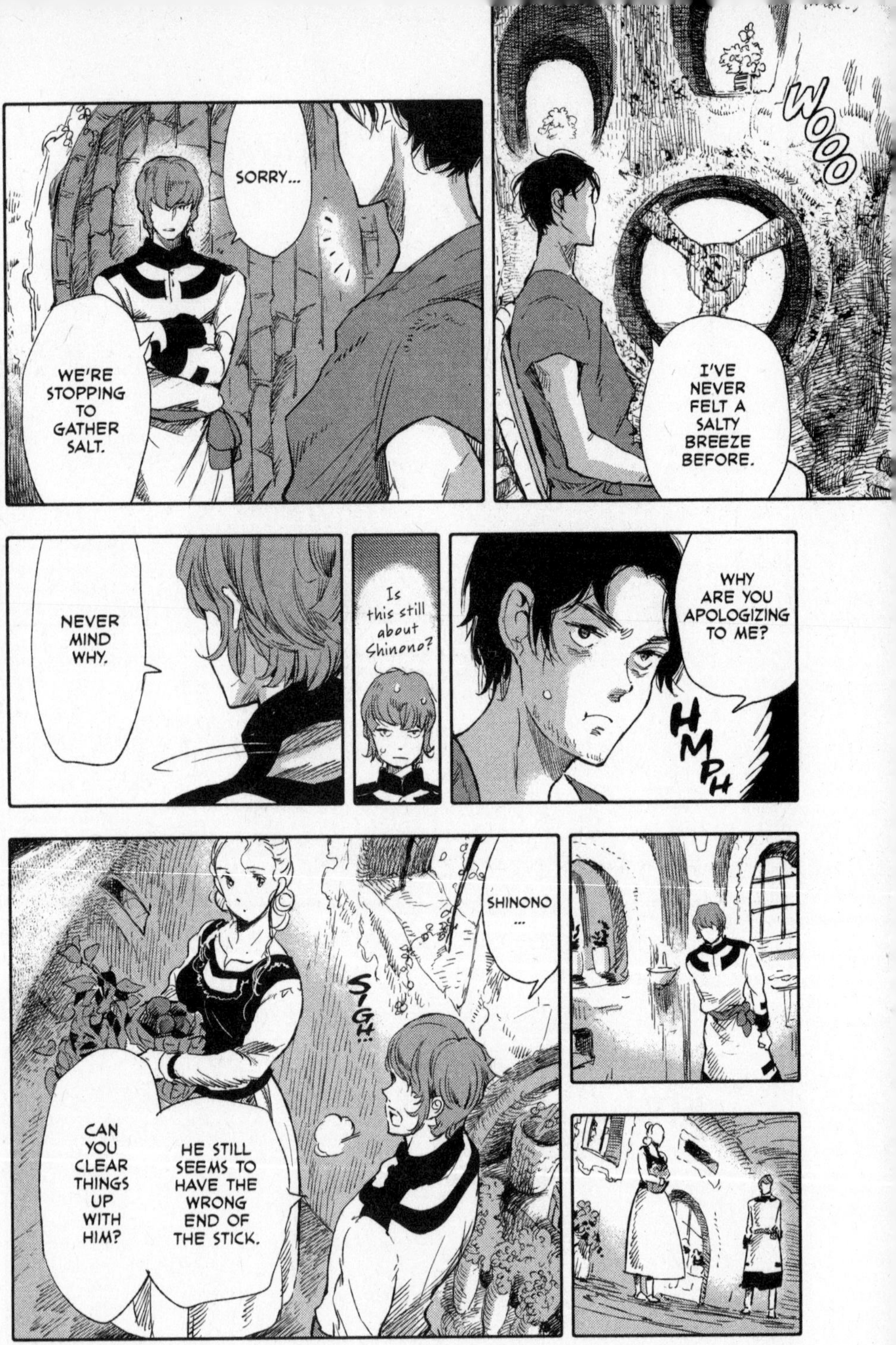
WOOO
I'VE NEVER FELT A SALTY BREEZE BEFORE.
SORRY...
WE'RE STOPPING TO GATHER SALT.
WHY ARE YOU APOLOGIZING TO ME?
HMPH
Is this still about Shinono?
NEVER MIND WHY.
SHINONO...
SIGH!!
HE STILL SEEMS TO HAVE THE WRONG END OF THE STICK.
CAN YOU CLEAR THINGS UP WITH HIM?

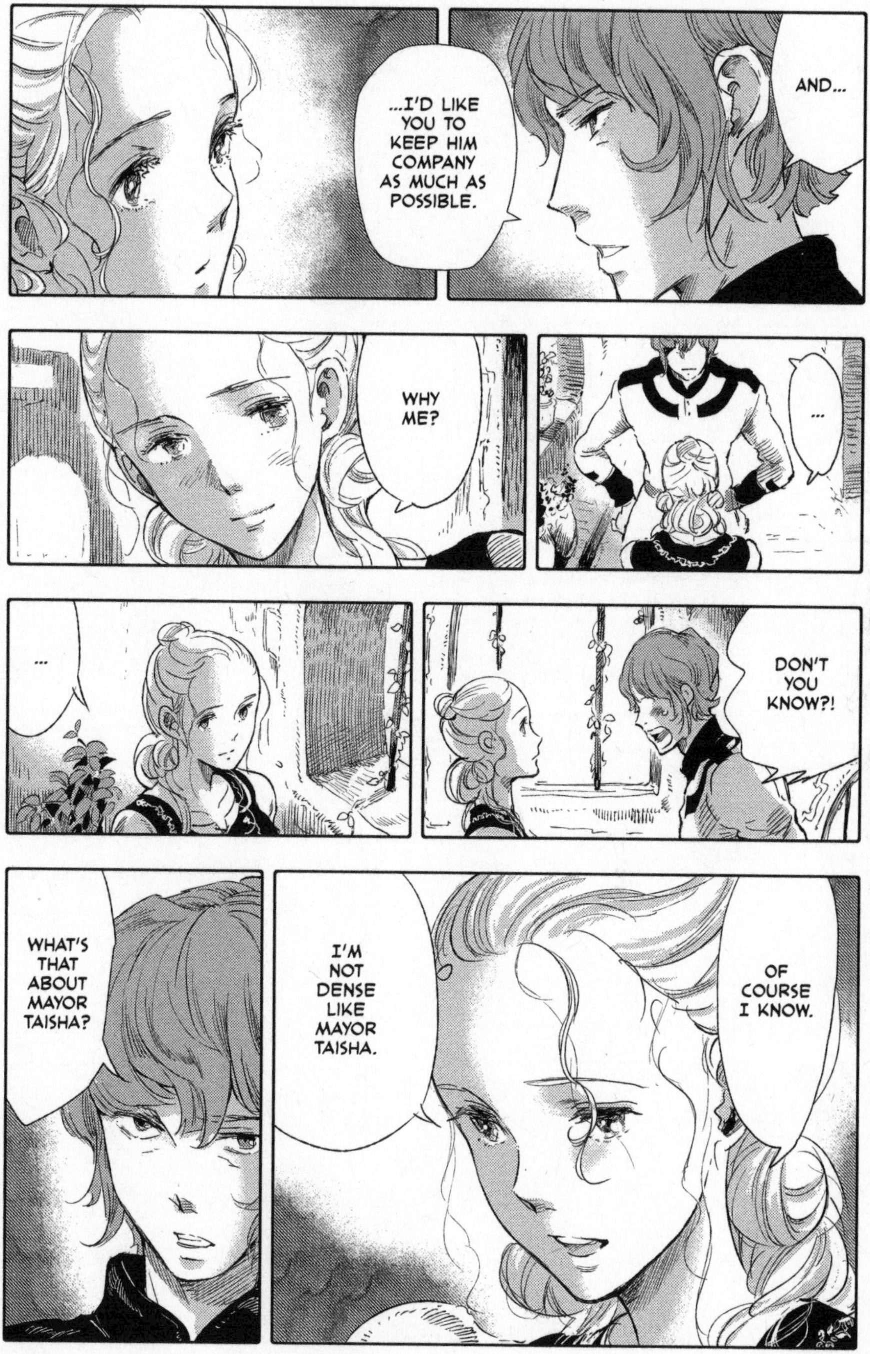
AND...
...I'D LIKE YOU TO KEEP HIM COMPANY AS MUCH AS POSSIBLE.
...
WHY ME?
DON'T YOU KNOW?!
...
OF COURSE I KNOW.
I'M NOT DENSE LIKE MAYOR TAISHA.
WHAT'S THAT ABOUT MAYOR TAISHA?

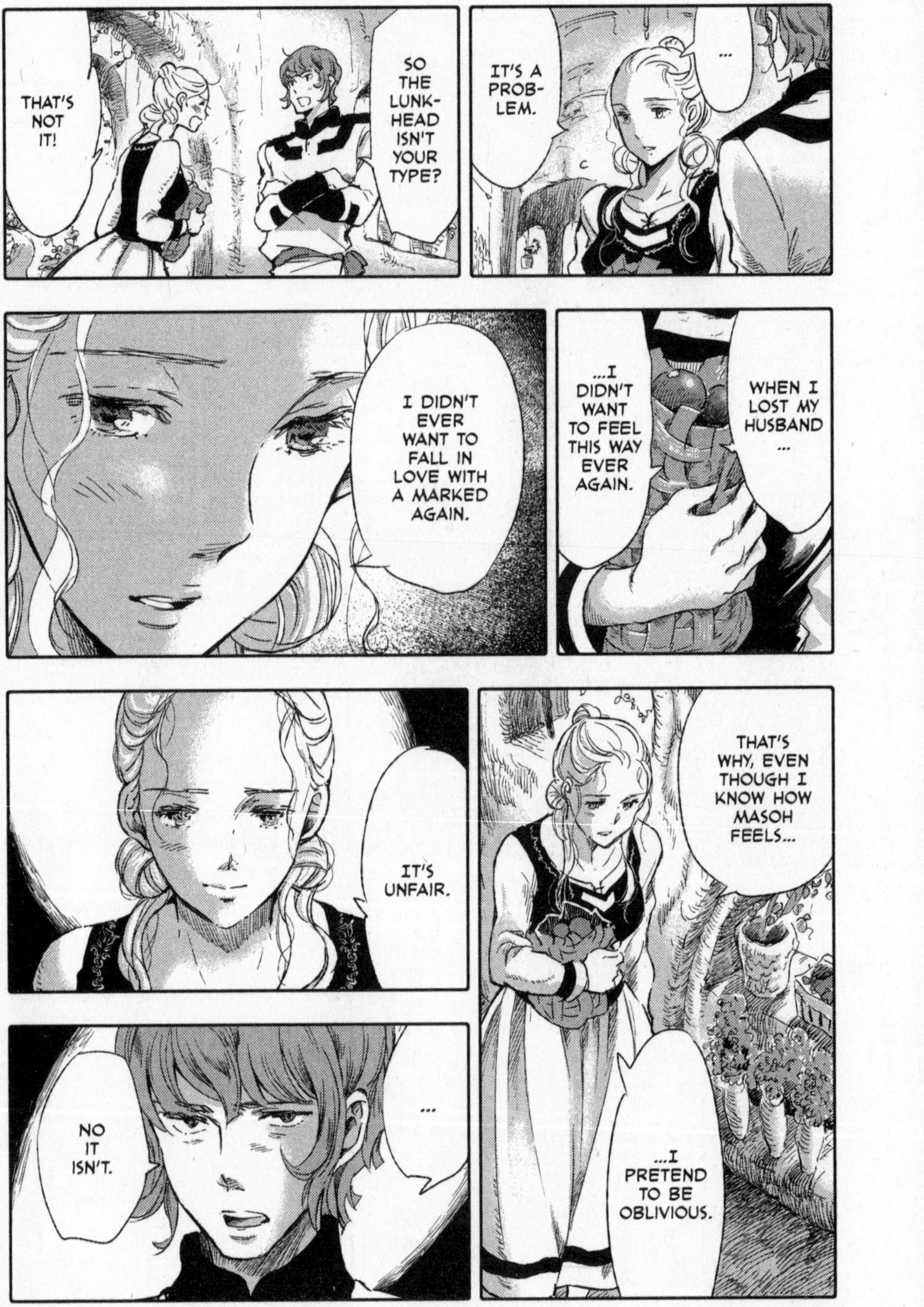
...
IT'S A PROBLEM.
SO THE LUNKHEAD ISN'T YOUR TYPE?
THAT'S NOT IT!
WHEN I LOST MY HUSBAND ...
...I DIDN'T WANT TO FEEL THIS WAY EVER AGAIN.
I DIDN'T EVER WANT TO FALL IN LOVE WITH A MARKED AGAIN.
THAT'S WHY, EVEN THOUGH I KNOW HOW MASOH FEELS...
...I PRETEND TO BE OBLIVIOUS.
IT'S UNFAIR.
...
NO IT ISN'T.

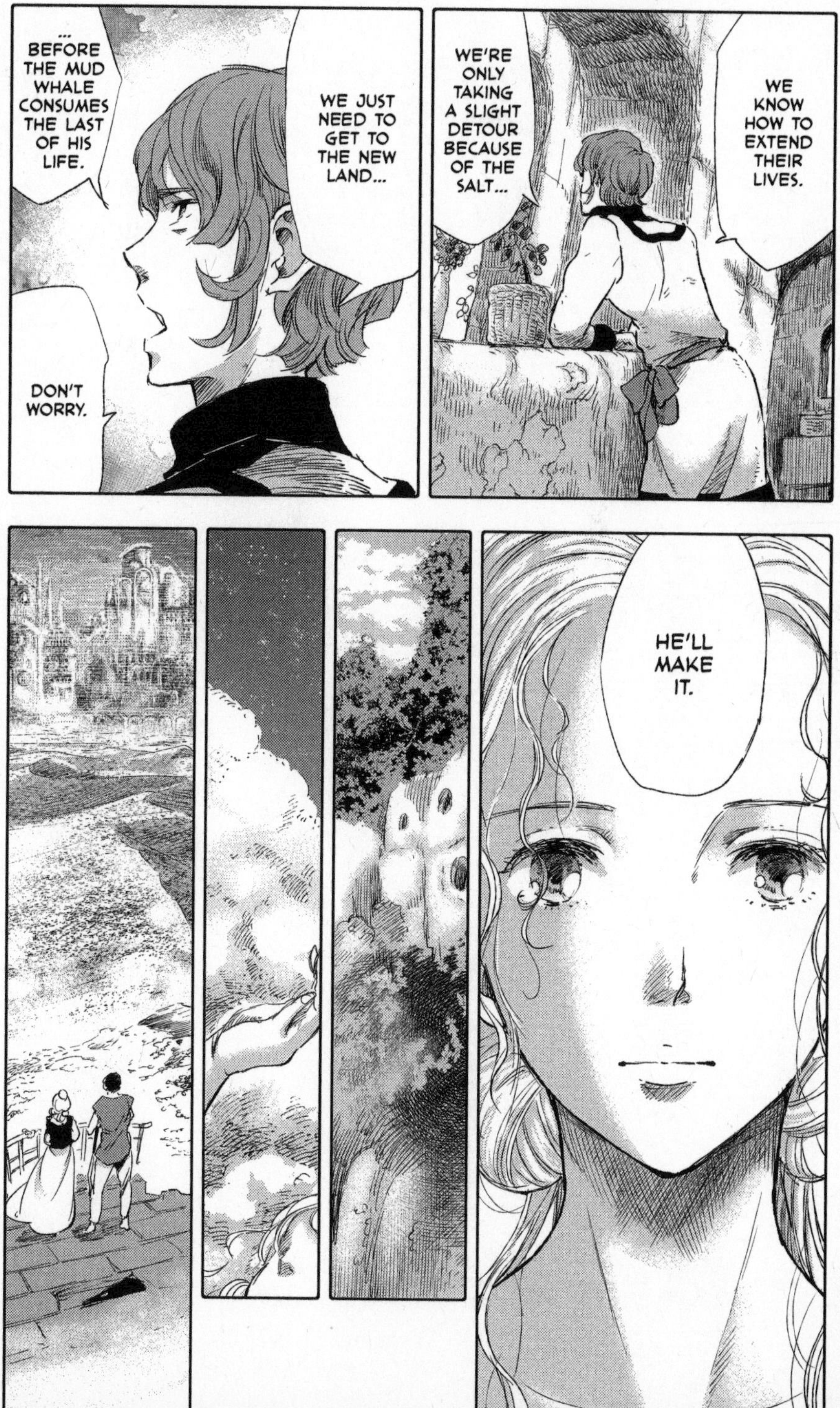
WE KNOW HOW TO EXTEND THEIR LIVES.
WE'RE ONLY TAKING A SLIGHT DETOUR BECAUSE OF THE SALT...
WE JUST NEED TO GET TO THE NEW LAND...
...BEFORE THE MUD WHALE CONSUMES THE LAST OF HIS LIFE.
DON'T WORRY.
HE'LL MAKE IT.

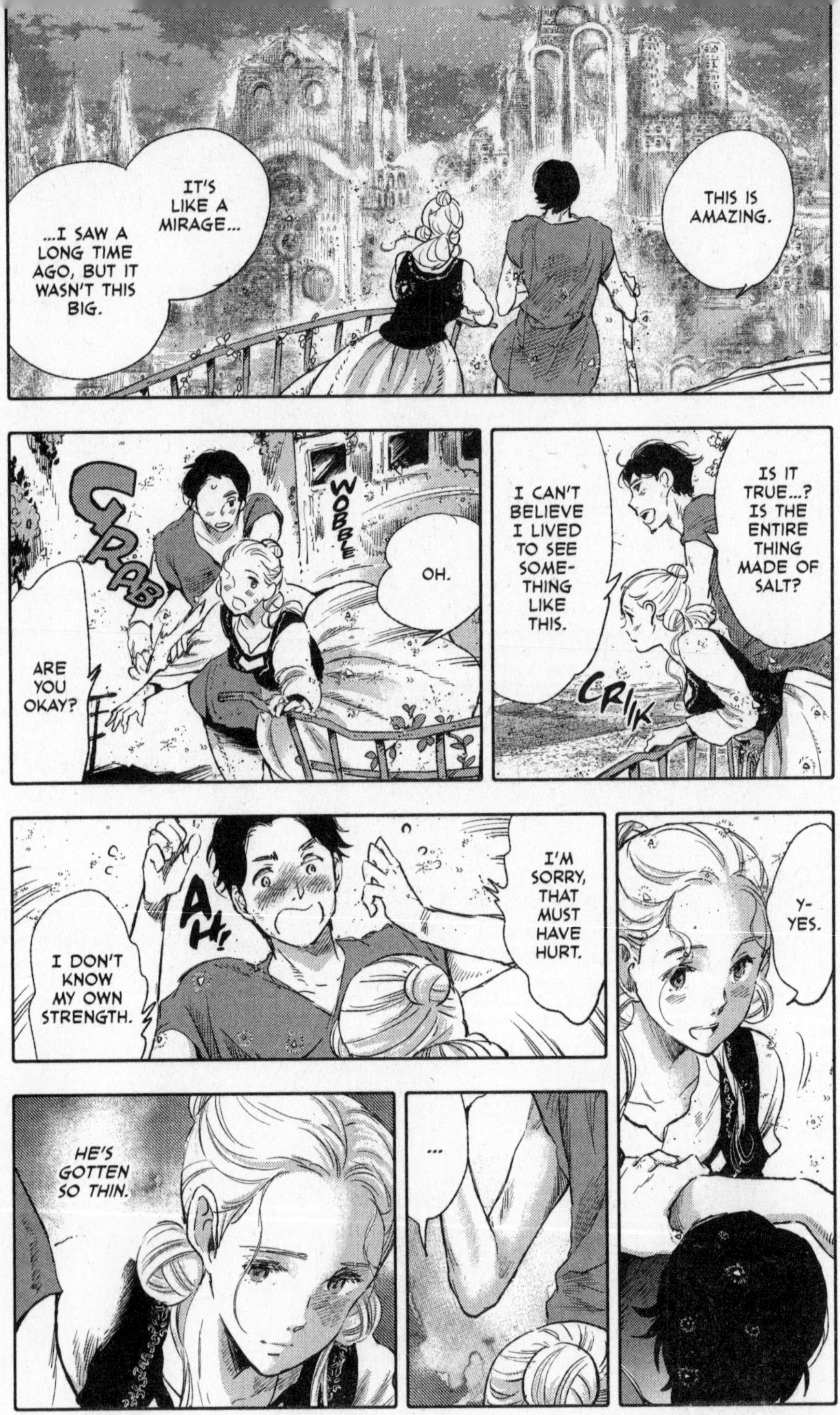
THIS IS AMAZING.
IT'S LIKE A MIRAGE...
...I SAW A LONG TIME AGO, BUT IT WASN'T THIS BIG.
IS IT TRUE...? IS THE ENTIRE THING MADE OF SALT?
I CAN'T BELIEVE I LIVED TO SEE SOME-THING LIKE THIS.
CRIIK
OH.
WOBBLE
GRAB
ARE YOU OKAY?
Y-YES.
I'M SORRY, THAT MUST HAVE HURT.
AH!
I DON'T KNOW MY OWN STRENGTH.
...
HE'S GOTTEN SO THIN.

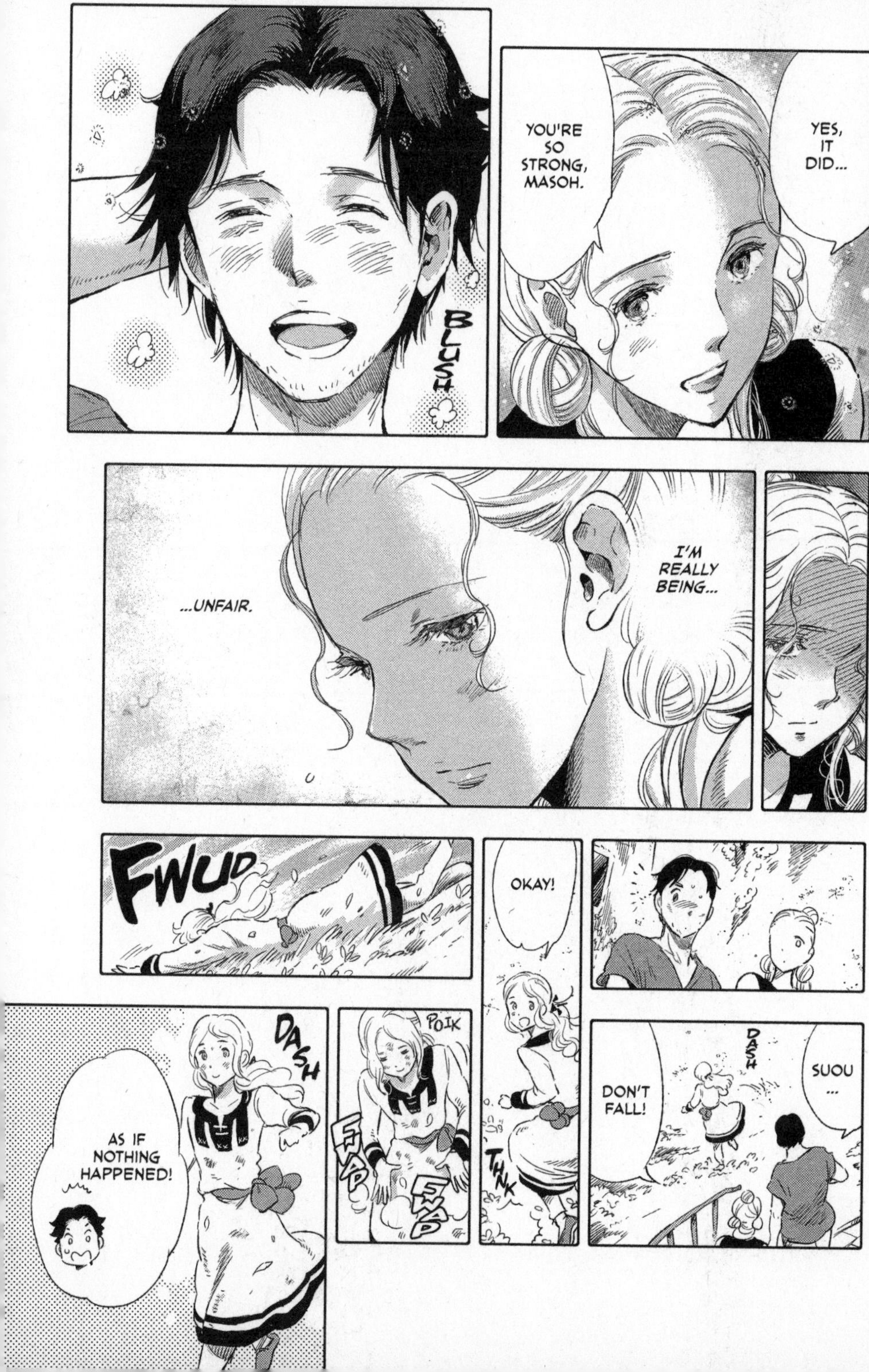

YES, IT DID...
YOU'RE SO STRONG, MASOH.
BLUSH
I'M REALLY BEING...
...UNFAIR.
SUOU ...
DASH
DON'T FALL!
OKAY!
THNK
FWUD
POIK
SWAP
FWAP
DASH
AS IF NOTHING HAPPENED!

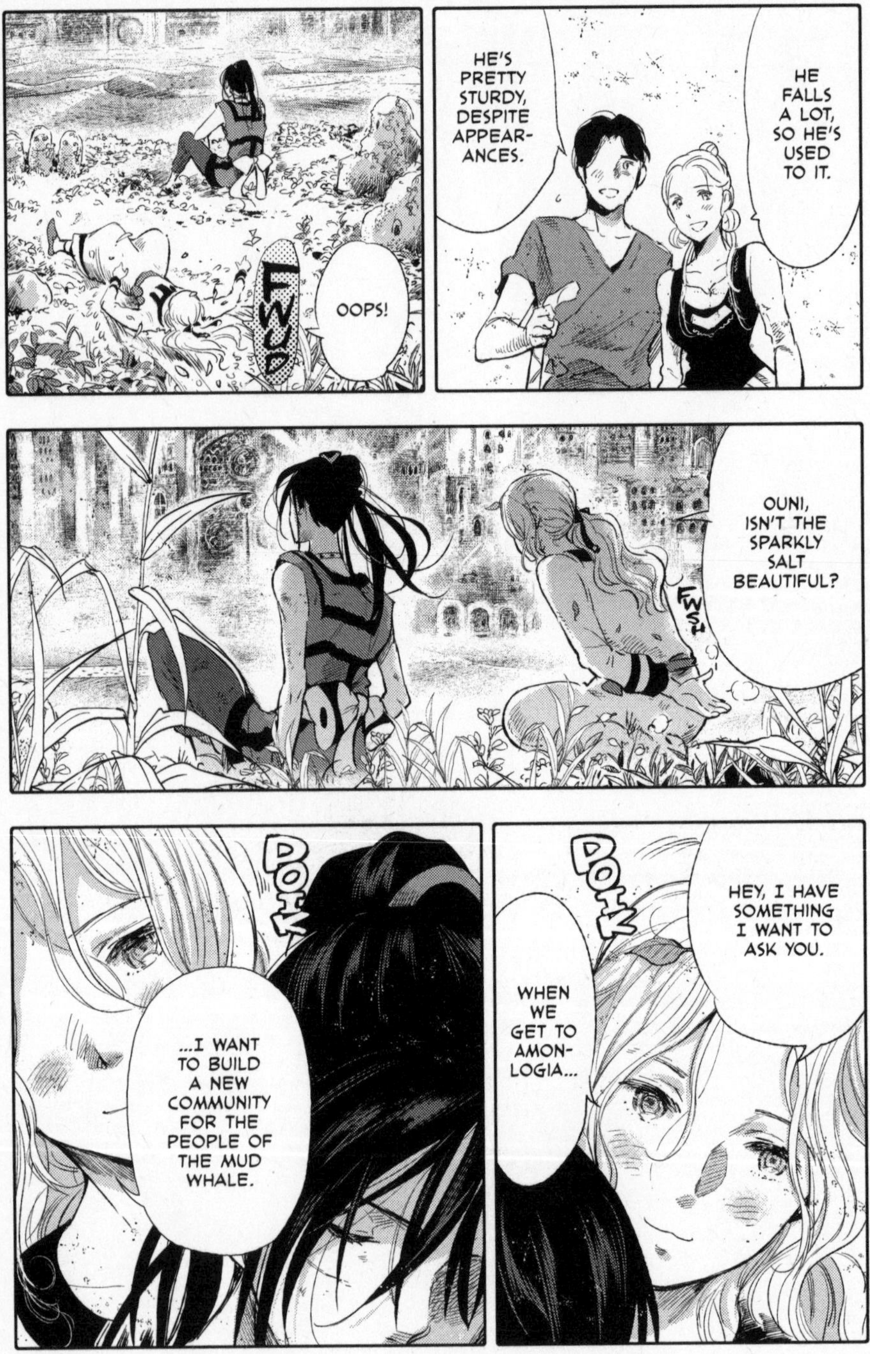
HE FALLS A LOT, SO HE'S USED TO IT.
HE'S PRETTY STURDY, DESPITE APPEARANCES.
OOPS!
FWUD
OUNI, ISN'T THE SPARKLY SALT BEAUTIFUL?
FWSH
HEY, I HAVE SOMETHING I WANT TO ASK YOU.
DOIK
WHEN WE GET TO AMONLOGIA...
DOIK
...I WANT TO BUILD A NEW COMMUNITY FOR THE PEOPLE OF THE MUD WHALE.

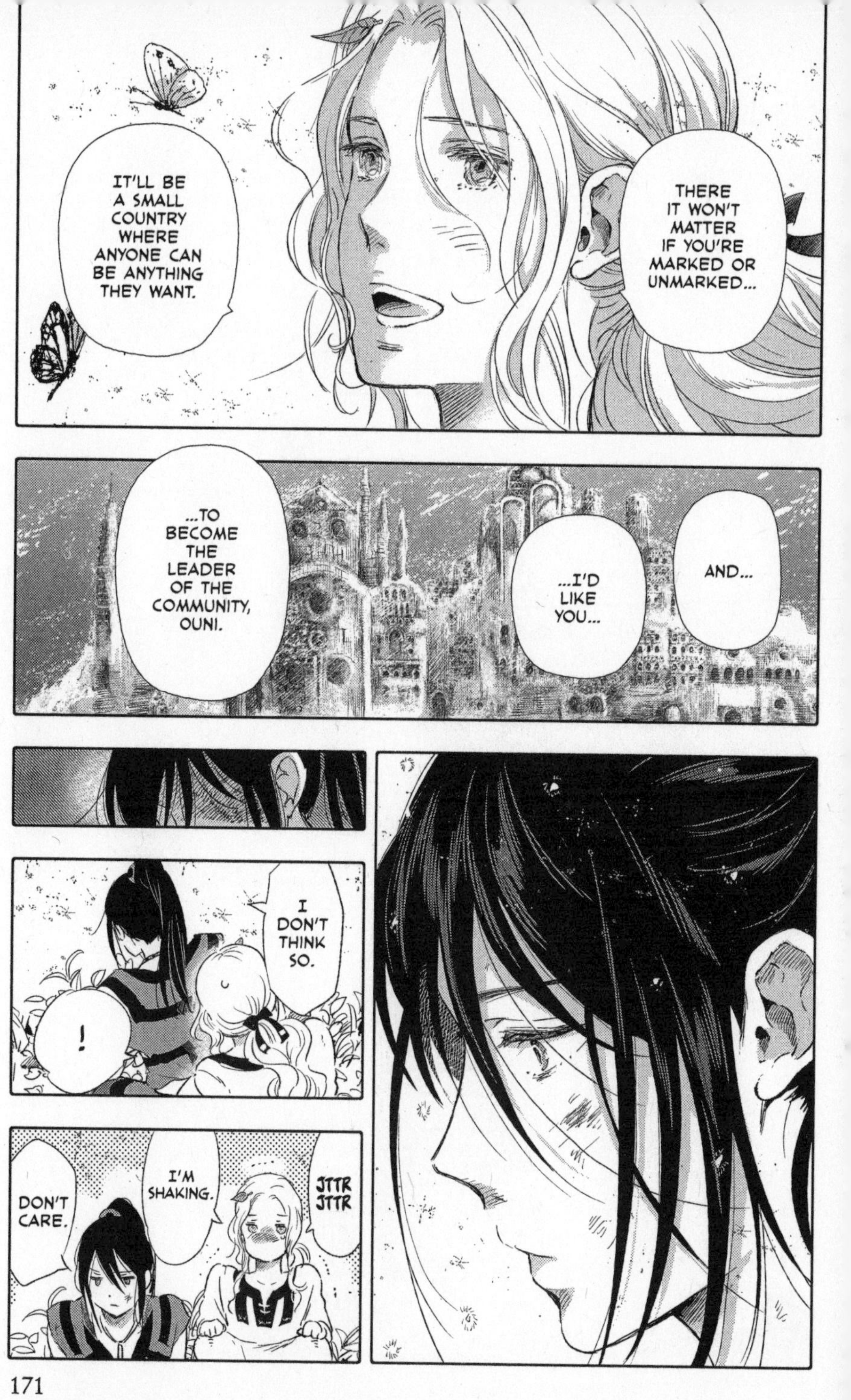
THERE IT WON'T MATTER IF YOU'RE MARKED OR UNMARKED...
IT'LL BE A SMALL COUNTRY WHERE ANYONE CAN BE ANYTHING THEY WANT.
AND...
...I'D LIKE YOU...
...TO BECOME THE LEADER OF THE COMMUNITY, OUNI.
I DON'T THINK SO.
!
JTTR JTTR
I'M SHAKING.
DON'T CARE.

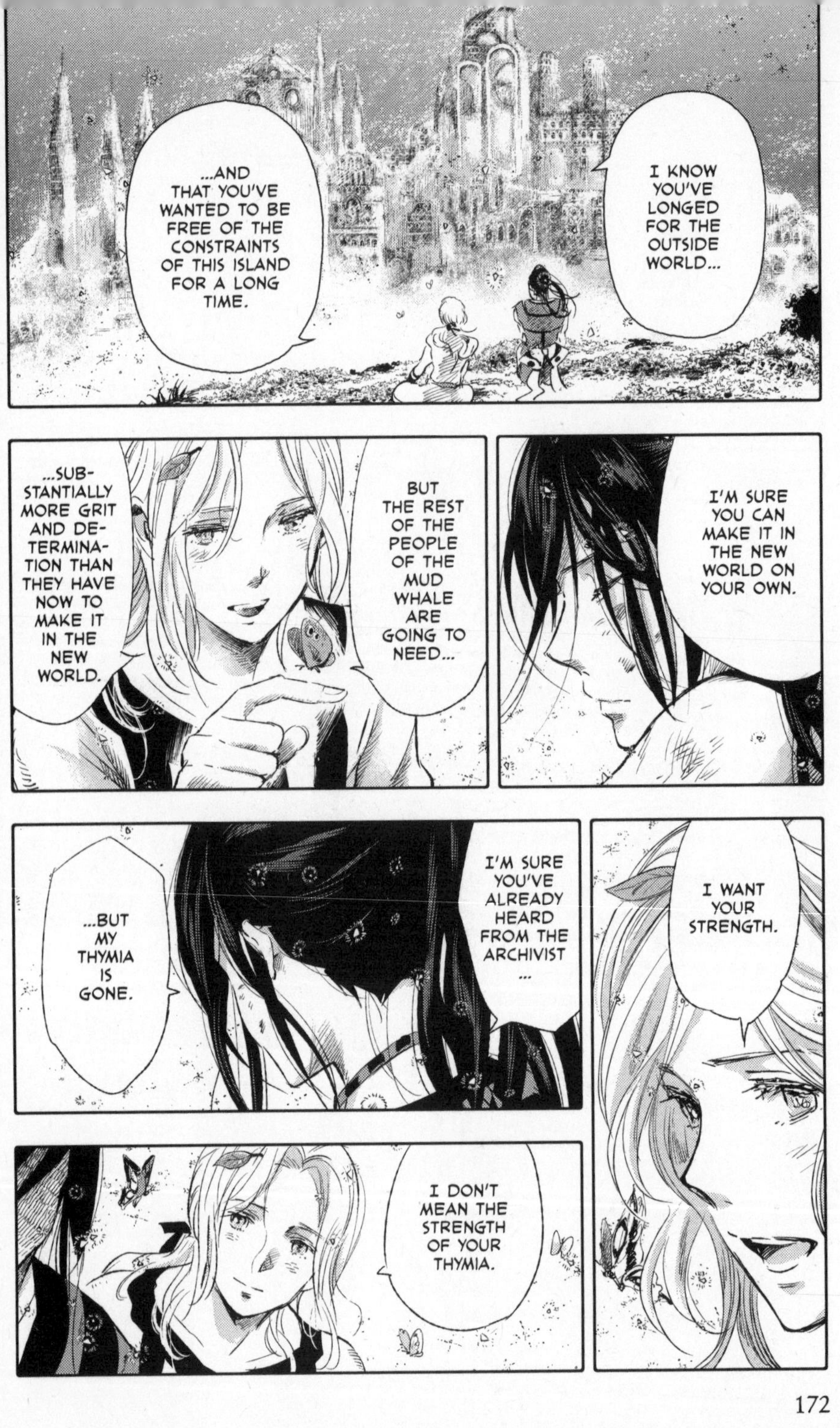
I KNOW YOU'VE LONGED FOR THE OUTSIDE WORLD...
...AND THAT YOU'VE WANTED TO BE FREE OF THE CONSTRAINTS OF THIS ISLAND FOR A LONG TIME.
I'M SURE YOU CAN MAKE IT IN THE NEW WORLD ON YOUR OWN.
BUT THE REST OF THE PEOPLE OF THE MUD WHALE ARE GOING TO NEED...
...SUB-STANTIALLY MORE GRIT AND DE-TERMINA-TION THAN THEY HAVE NOW TO MAKE IT IN THE NEW WORLD.
I WANT YOUR STRENGTH.
I'M SURE YOU'VE ALREADY HEARD FROM THE ARCHIVIST ...
...BUT MY THYMIA IS GONE.
I DON'T MEAN THE STRENGTH OF YOUR THYMIA.

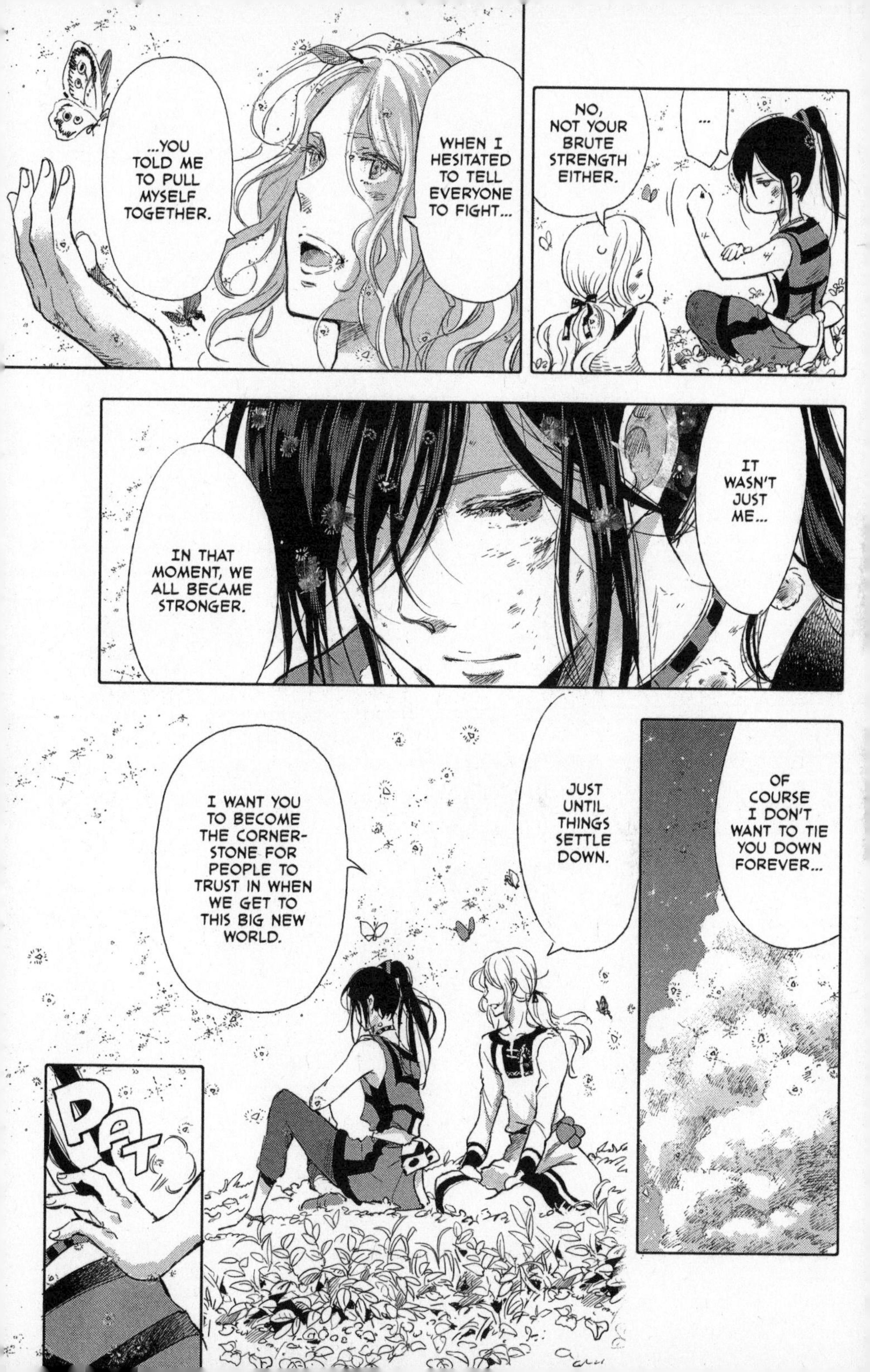
...
NO, NOT YOUR BRUTE STRENGTH EITHER.
WHEN I HESITATED TO TELL EVERYONE TO FIGHT...
...YOU TOLD ME TO PULL MYSELF TOGETHER.
IT WASN'T JUST ME...
IN THAT MOMENT, WE ALL BECAME STRONGER.
OF COURSE I DON'T WANT TO TIE YOU DOWN FOREVER...
JUST UNTIL THINGS SETTLE DOWN.
I WANT YOU TO BECOME THE CORNER-STONE FOR PEOPLE TO TRUST IN WHEN WE GET TO THIS BIG NEW WORLD.
PAT

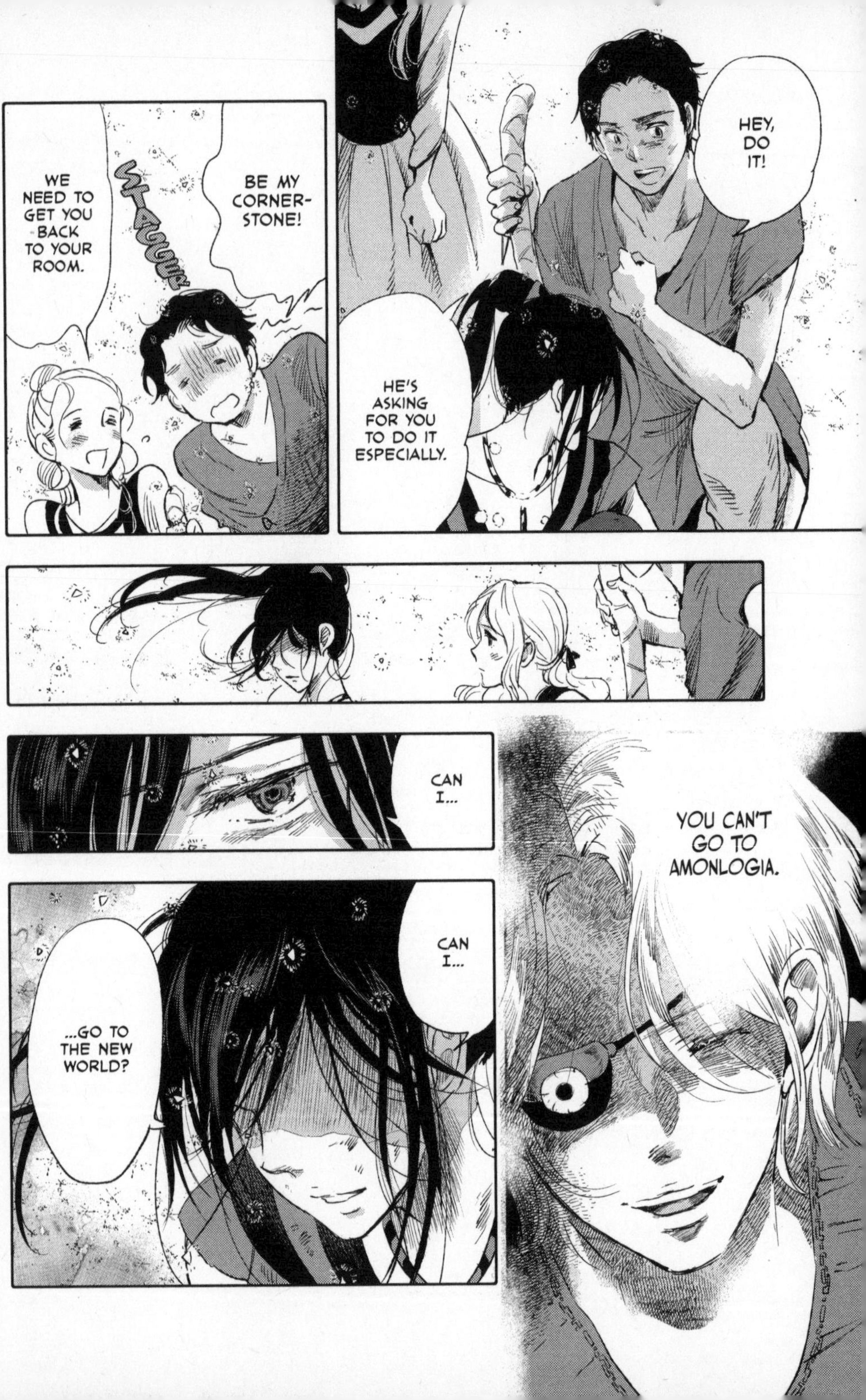
HEY, DO IT!
HE'S ASKING FOR YOU TO DO IT ESPECIALLY.
BE MY CORNER-STONE!
STAGGER
WE NEED TO GET YOU BACK TO YOUR ROOM.
YOU CAN'T GO TO AMONLOGIA.
CAN I...
CAN I...
...GO TO THE NEW WORLD?

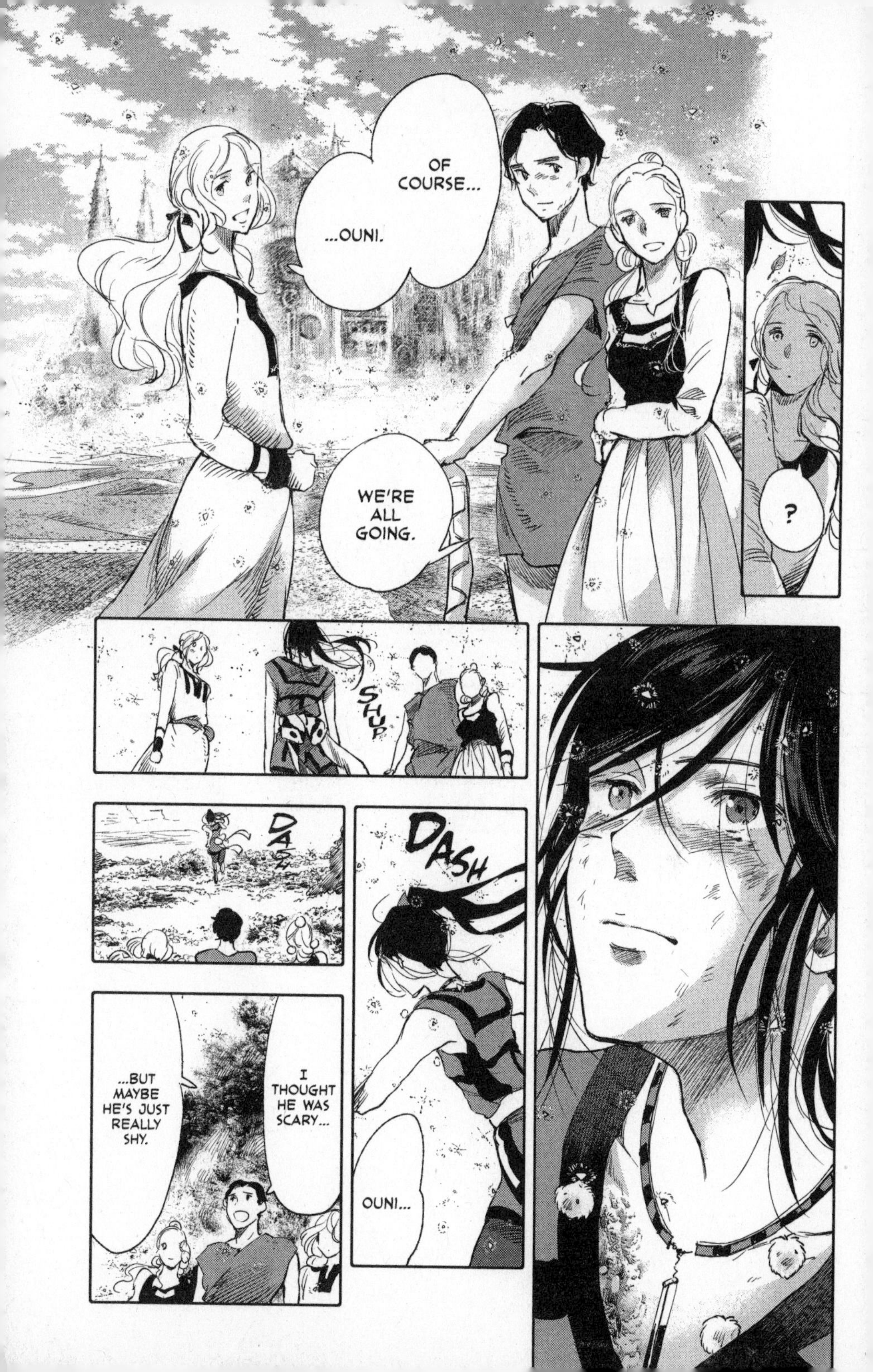
OF COURSE...
...OUNI.
WE'RE ALL GOING.
?
SHUP
DASH
OUNI...
DASH
I THOUGHT HE WAS SCARY...
...BUT MAYBE HE'S JUST REALLY SHY.

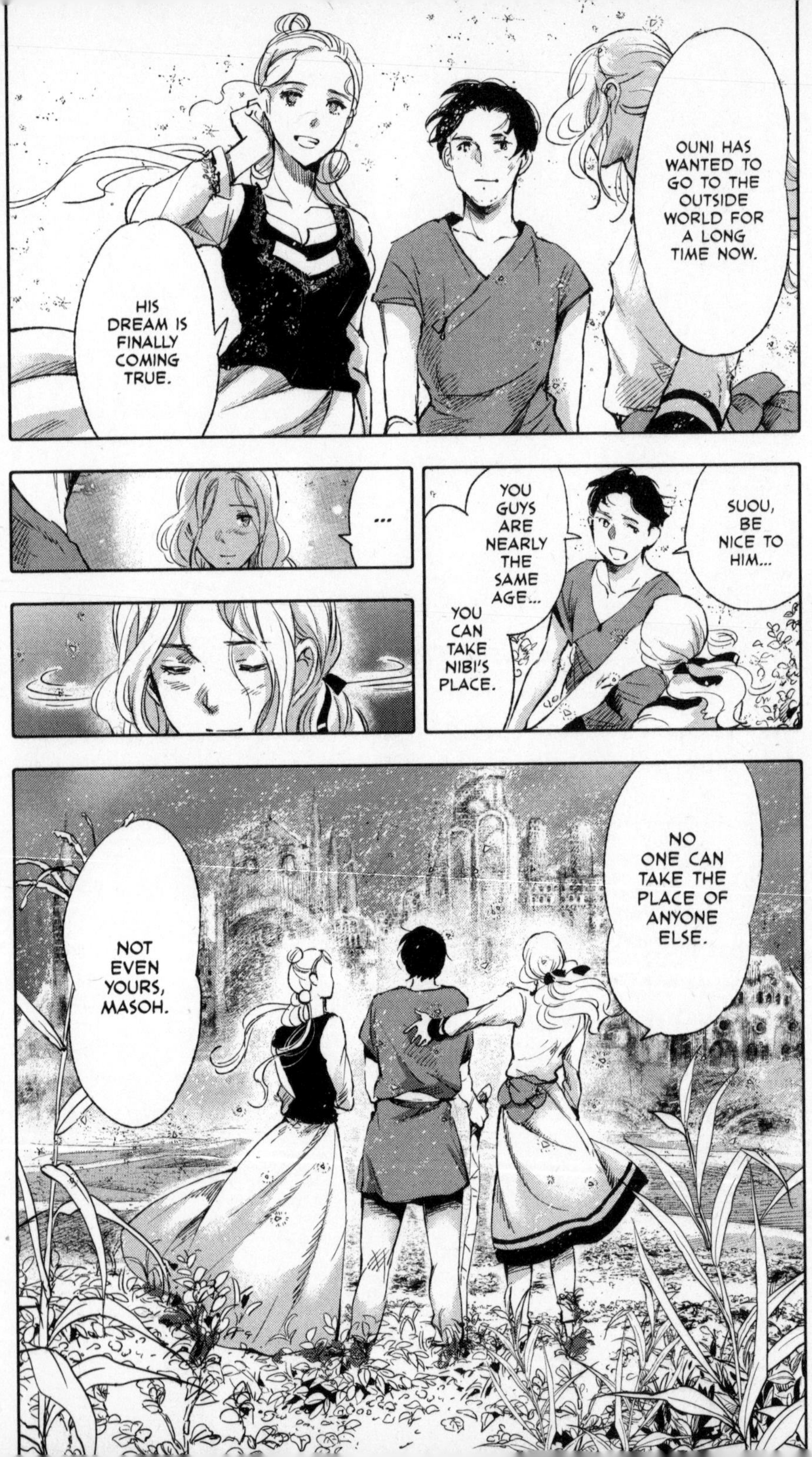
OUNI HAS WANTED TO GO TO THE OUTSIDE WORLD FOR A LONG TIME NOW.
HIS DREAM IS FINALLY COMING TRUE.
SUOU, BE NICE TO HIM...
YOU GUYS ARE NEARLY THE SAME AGE...
YOU CAN TAKE NIBI'S PLACE.
...
NO ONE CAN TAKE THE PLACE OF ANYONE ELSE.
NOT EVEN YOURS, MASOH.

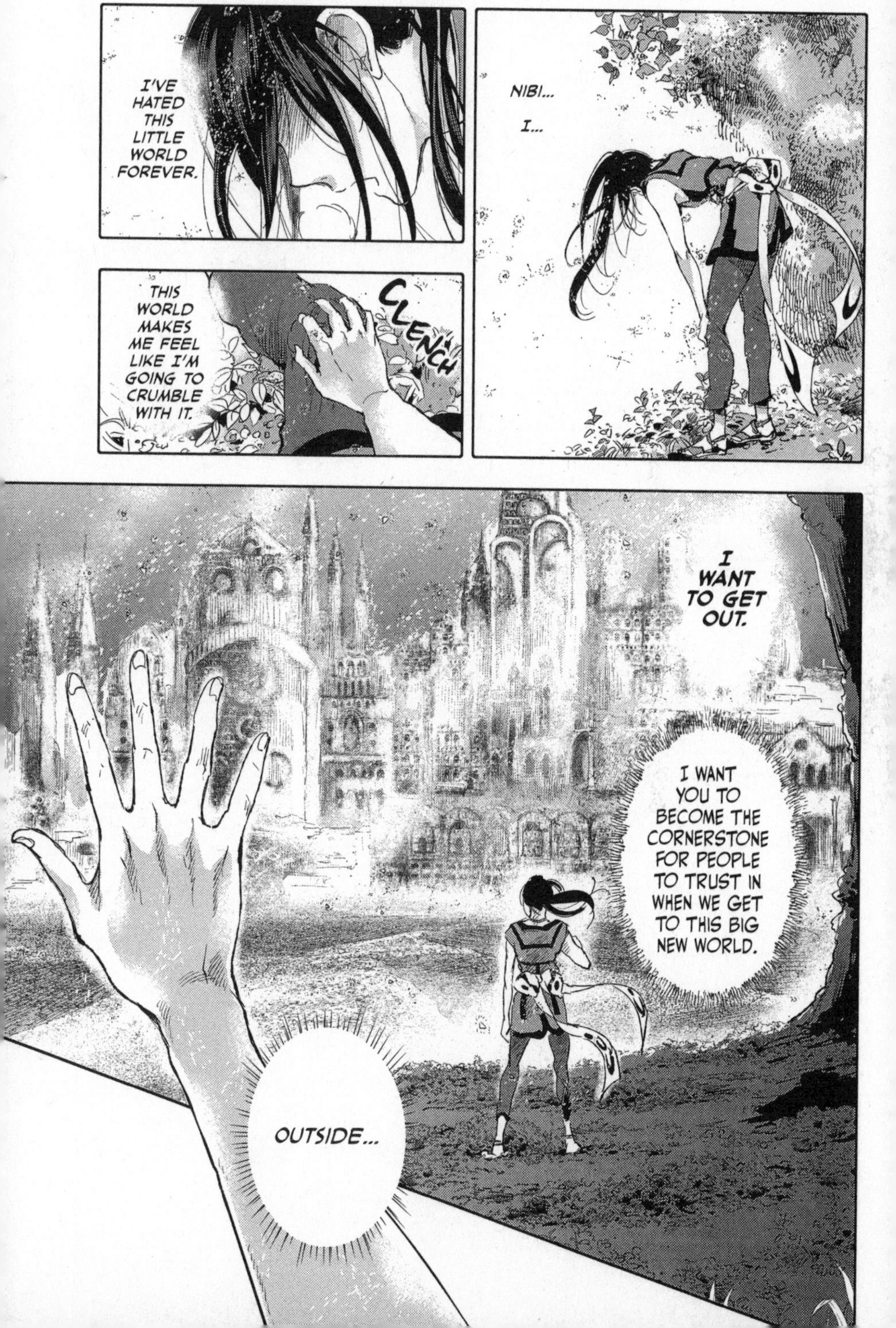
NIBI...
I...
I'VE HATED THIS LITTLE WORLD FOREVER.
THIS WORLD MAKES ME FEEL LIKE I'M GOING TO CRUMBLE WITH IT.
CLENCH
I WANT TO GET OUT.
I WANT YOU TO BECOME THE CORNERSTONE FOR PEOPLE TO TRUST IN WHEN WE GET TO THIS BIG NEW WORLD.
OUTSIDE...

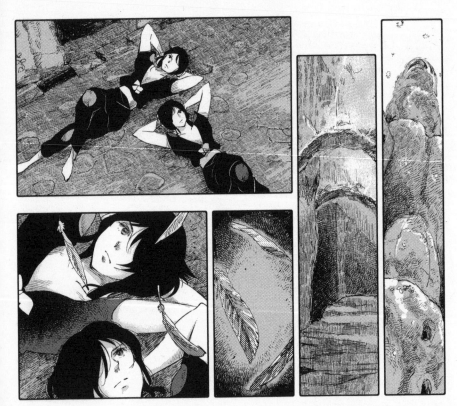

178

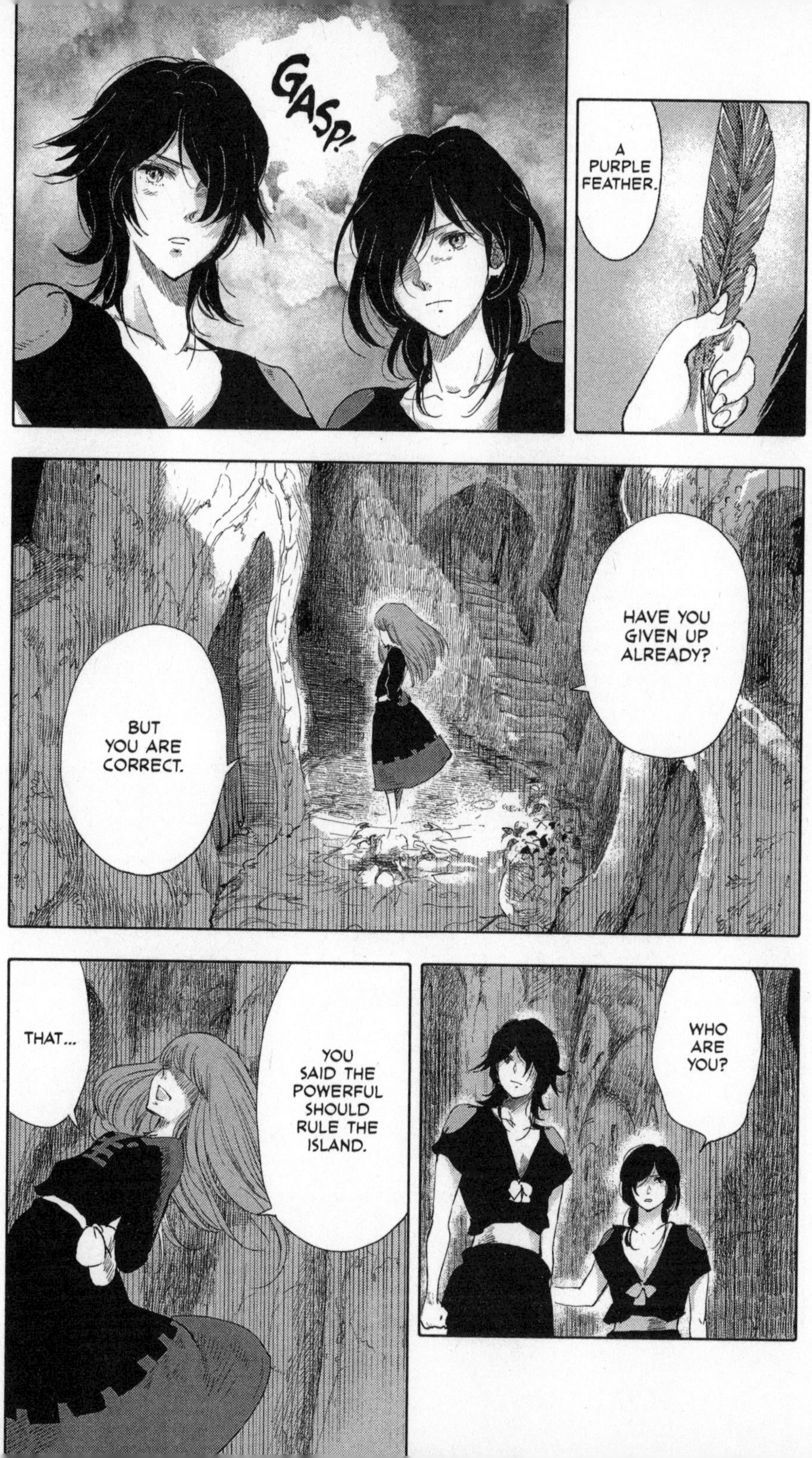
A PURPLE FEATHER.
GASP!
HAVE YOU GIVEN UP ALREADY?
BUT YOU ARE CORRECT.
WHO ARE YOU?
YOU SAID THE POWERFUL SHOULD RULE THE ISLAND.
THAT...

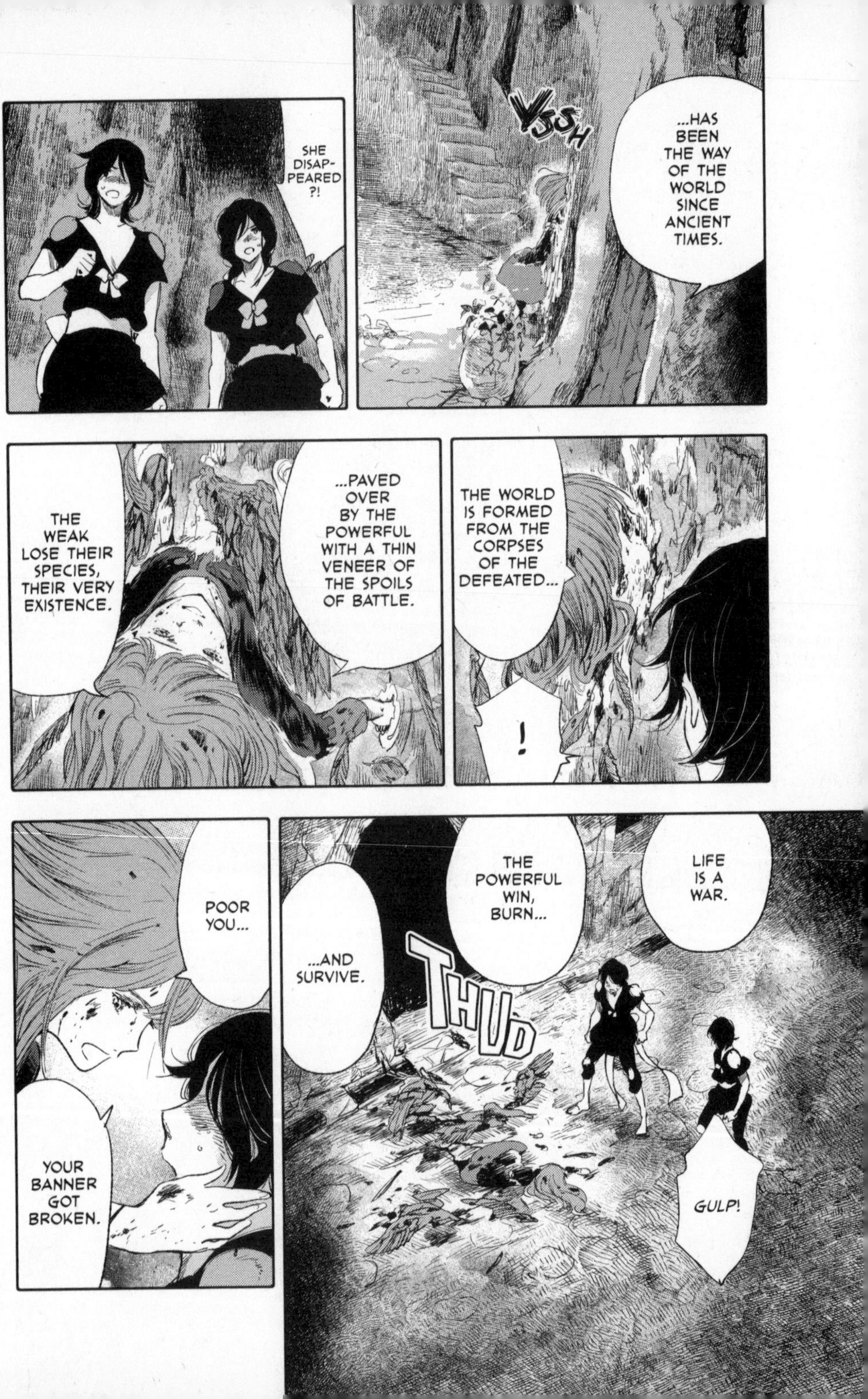
VSSH
...HAS BEEN THE WAY OF THE WORLD SINCE ANCIENT TIMES.
SHE DISAP-PEARED?!
THE WORLD IS FORMED FROM THE CORPSES OF THE DEFEATED...
!
...PAVED OVER BY THE POWERFUL WITH A THIN VENEER OF THE SPOILS OF BATTLE.
THE WEAK LOSE THEIR SPECIES, THEIR VERY EXISTENCE.
LIFE IS A WAR.
THE POWERFUL WIN, BURN...
...AND SURVIVE.
THUD
GULP!
POOR YOU...
YOUR BANNER GOT BROKEN.

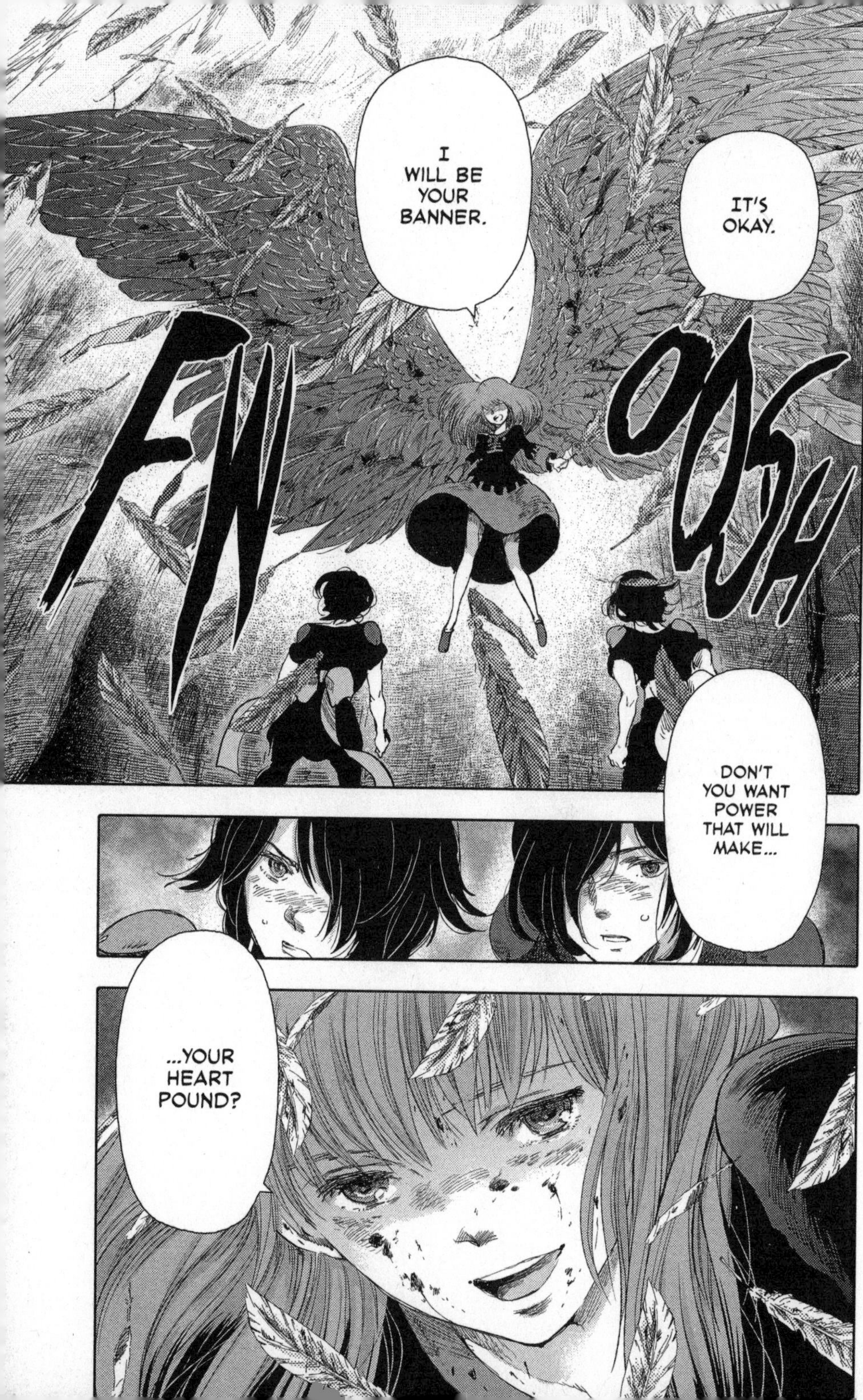
IT'S OKAY.
I WILL BE YOUR BANNER.
FWOOSH
DON'T YOU WANT POWER THAT WILL MAKE...
...YOUR HEART POUND?

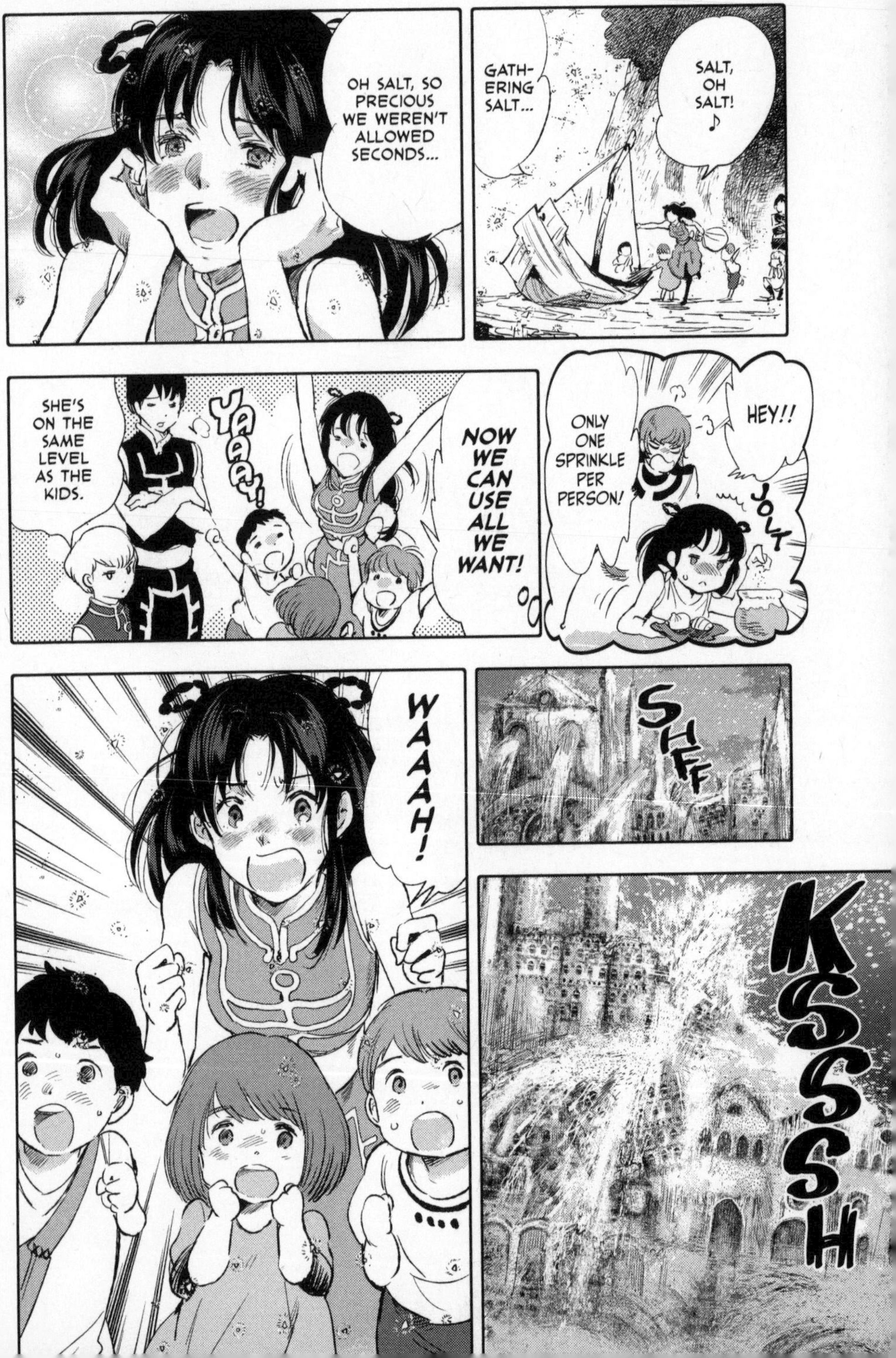
SALT, OH SALT! ♪
GATH-ERING SALT...
OH SALT, SO PRECIOUS WE WEREN'T ALLOWED SECONDS...
HEY!!
ONLY ONE SPRINKLE PER PERSON!
JOLT
NOW WE CAN USE ALL WE WANT!
YAAAY!
SHE'S ON THE SAME LEVEL AS THE KIDS.
SHFF
KSSSH
WAAAAH!
....

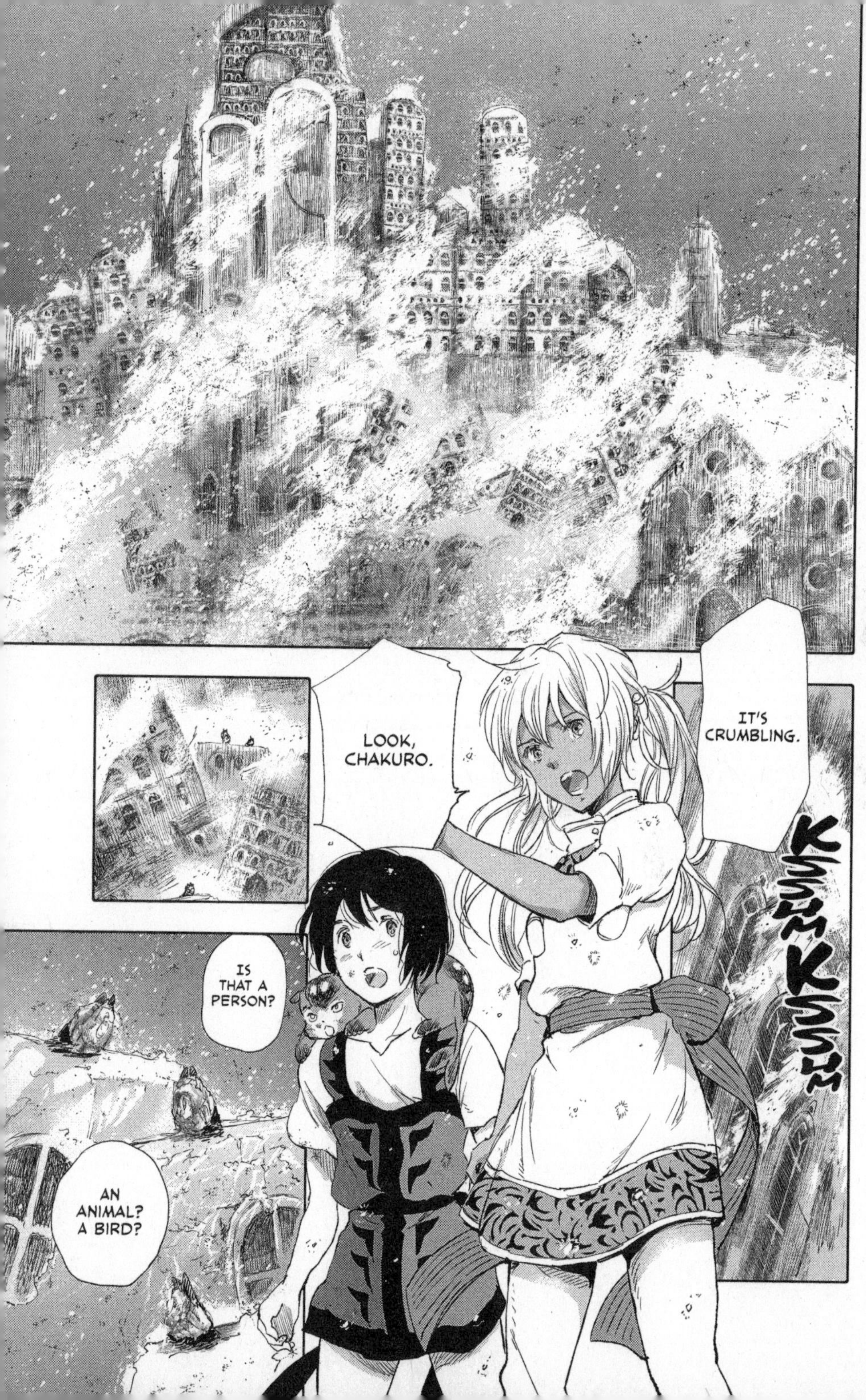
IT'S CRUMBLING.
LOOK, CHAKURO.
KSSHM KSSHM
IS THAT A PERSON?
AN ANIMAL? A BIRD?

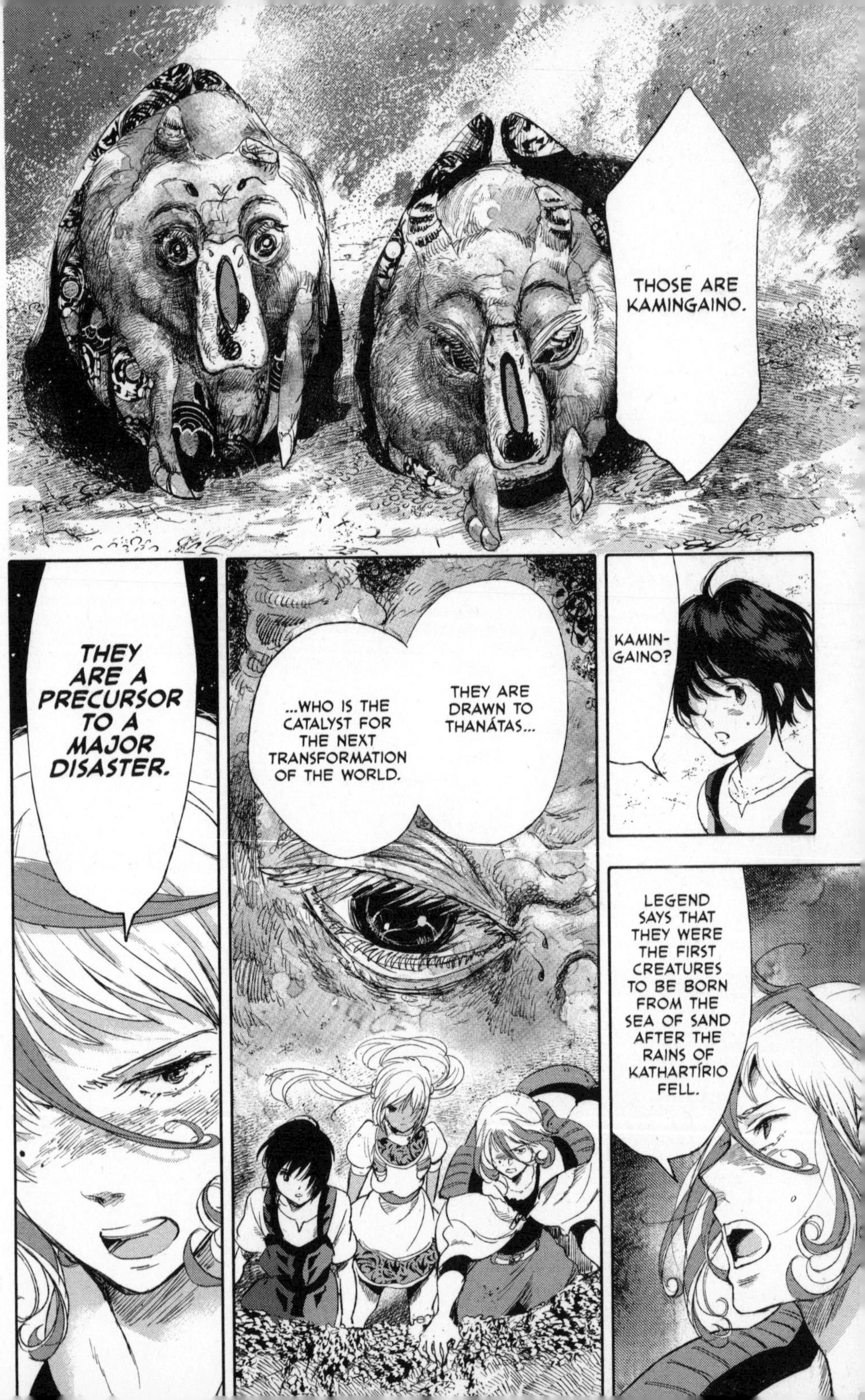
THOSE ARE KAMINGAINO.
KAMIN-GAINO?
LEGEND SAYS THAT THEY WERE THE FIRST CREATURES TO BE BORN FROM THE SEA OF SAND AFTER THE RAINS OF KATHARTÍRIO FELL.
THEY ARE DRAWN TO THANÁTAS...
...WHO IS THE CATALYST FOR THE NEXT TRANSFORMATION OF THE WORLD.
THEY ARE A PRECURSOR TO A MAJOR DISASTER.

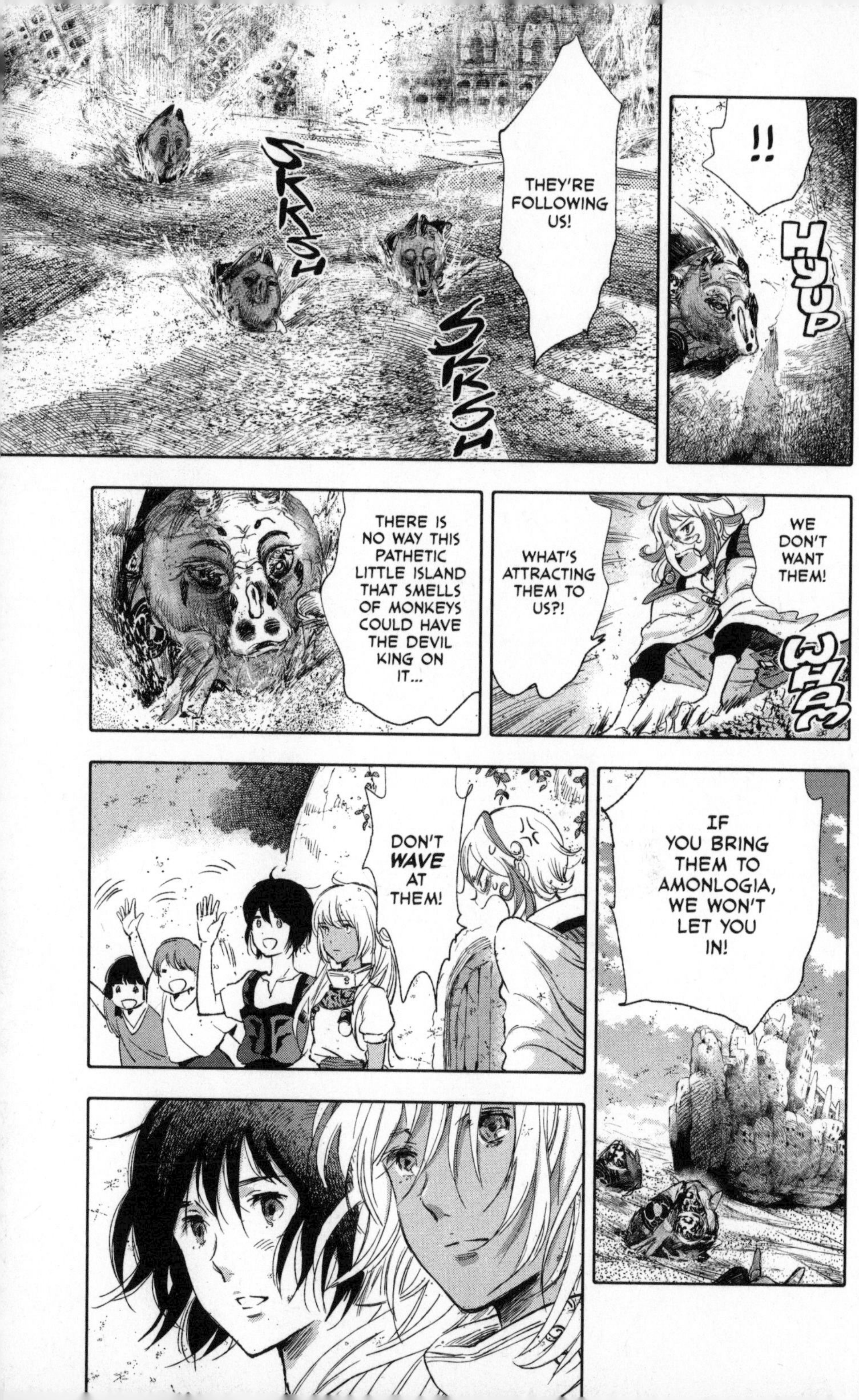
!!
HYUP
THEY'RE FOLLOWING US!
SKRSH
SKRSH
WE DON'T WANT THEM!
WHAM
WHAT'S ATTRACTING THEM TO US?!
THERE IS NO WAY THIS PATHETIC LITTLE ISLAND THAT SMELLS OF MONKEYS COULD HAVE THE DEVIL KING ON IT...
IF YOU BRING THEM TO AMONLOGIA, WE WON'T LET YOU IN!
DON'T *WAVE* AT THEM!

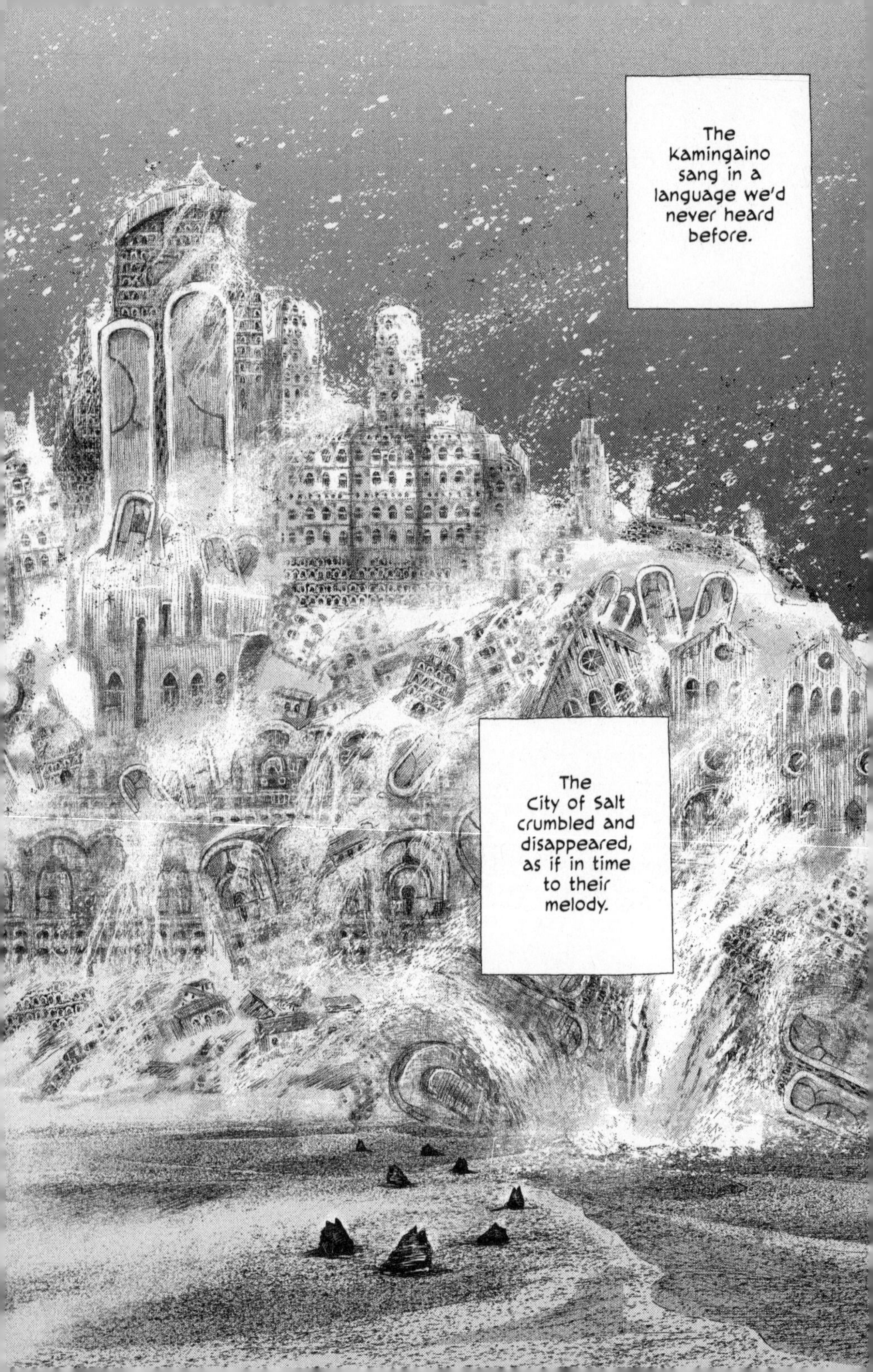
The kamingaino sang in a language we'd never heard before.
The City of Salt crumbled and disappeared, as if in time to their melody.

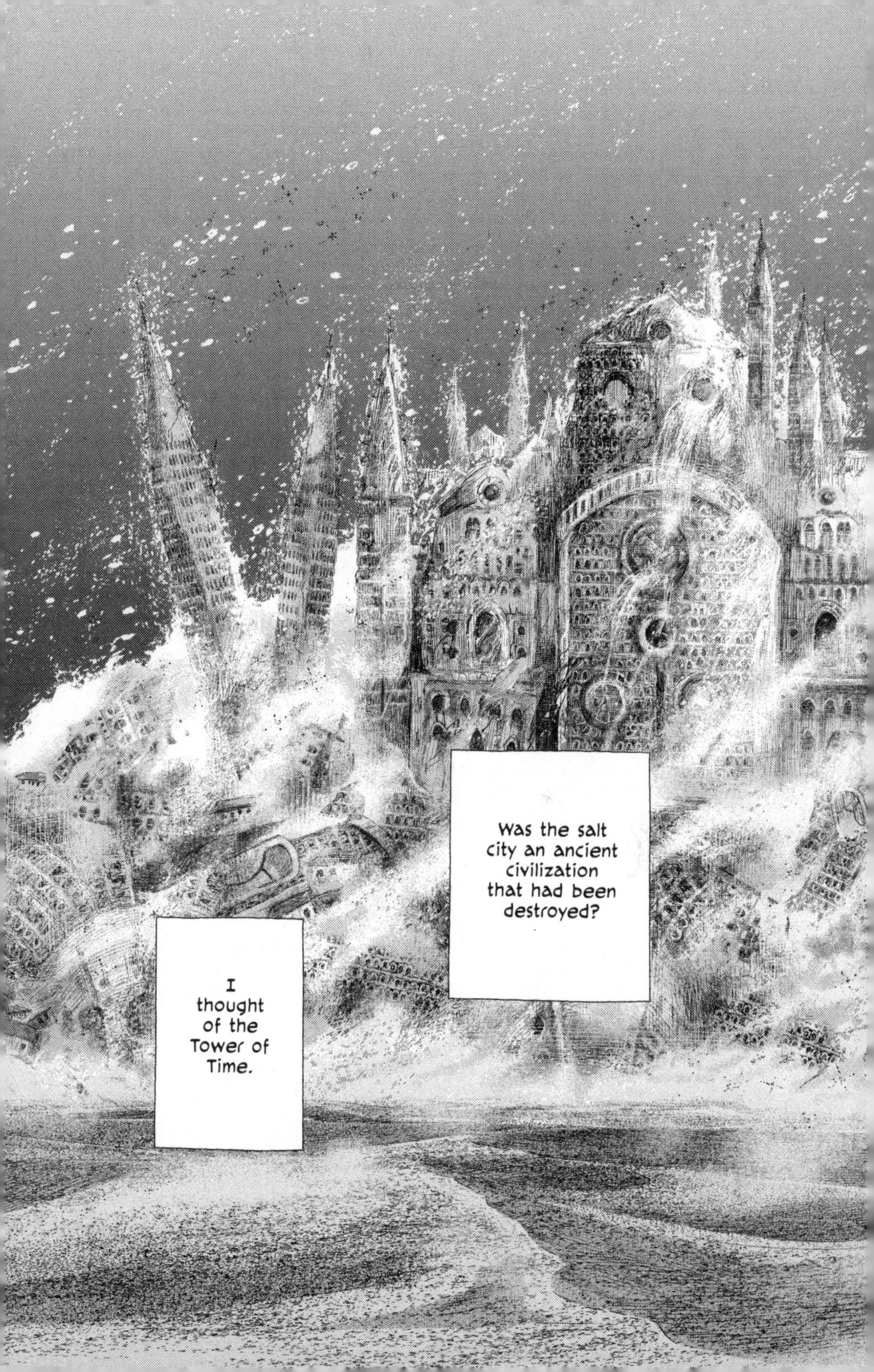
Was the salt city an ancient civilization that had been destroyed?
I thought of the Tower of Time.

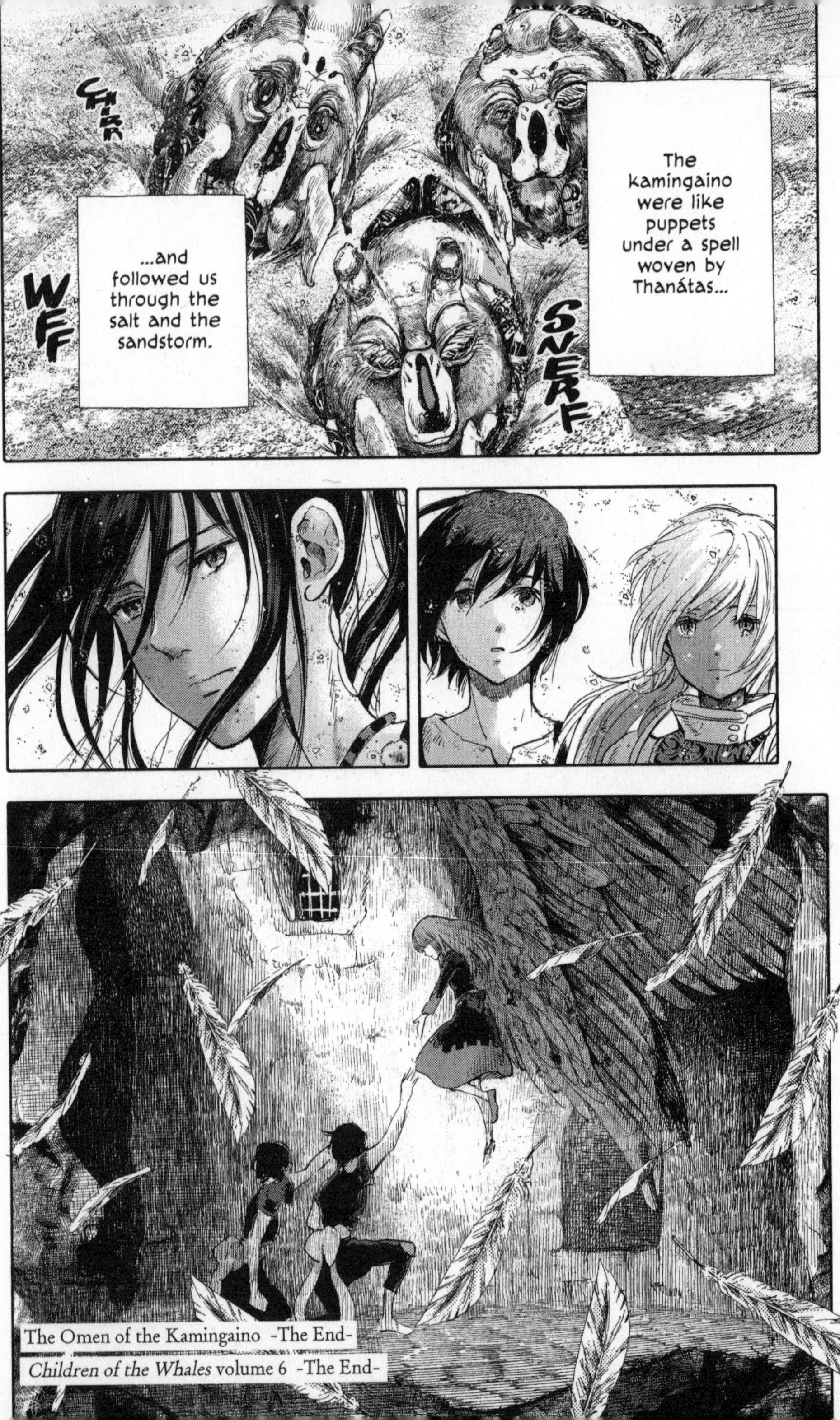
The kamingaino were like puppets under a spell woven by Thanátas...
SNERF
CHIRR
...and followed us through the salt and the sandstorm.
WFF
The Omen of the Kamingaino -The End-
Children of the Whales volume 6 -The End-

Afterword

The Journeys of the Children of the Whales

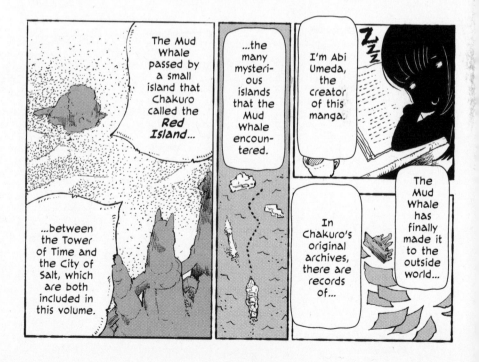

ZZZ
I'm Abi Umeda, the creator of this manga.
The Mud Whale has finally made it to the outside world...
In Chakuro's original archives, there are records of...
...the many mysterious islands that the Mud Whale encountered.
The Mud Whale passed by a small island that Chakuro called the *Red Island*...
...between the Tower of Time and the City of Salt, which are both included in this volume.

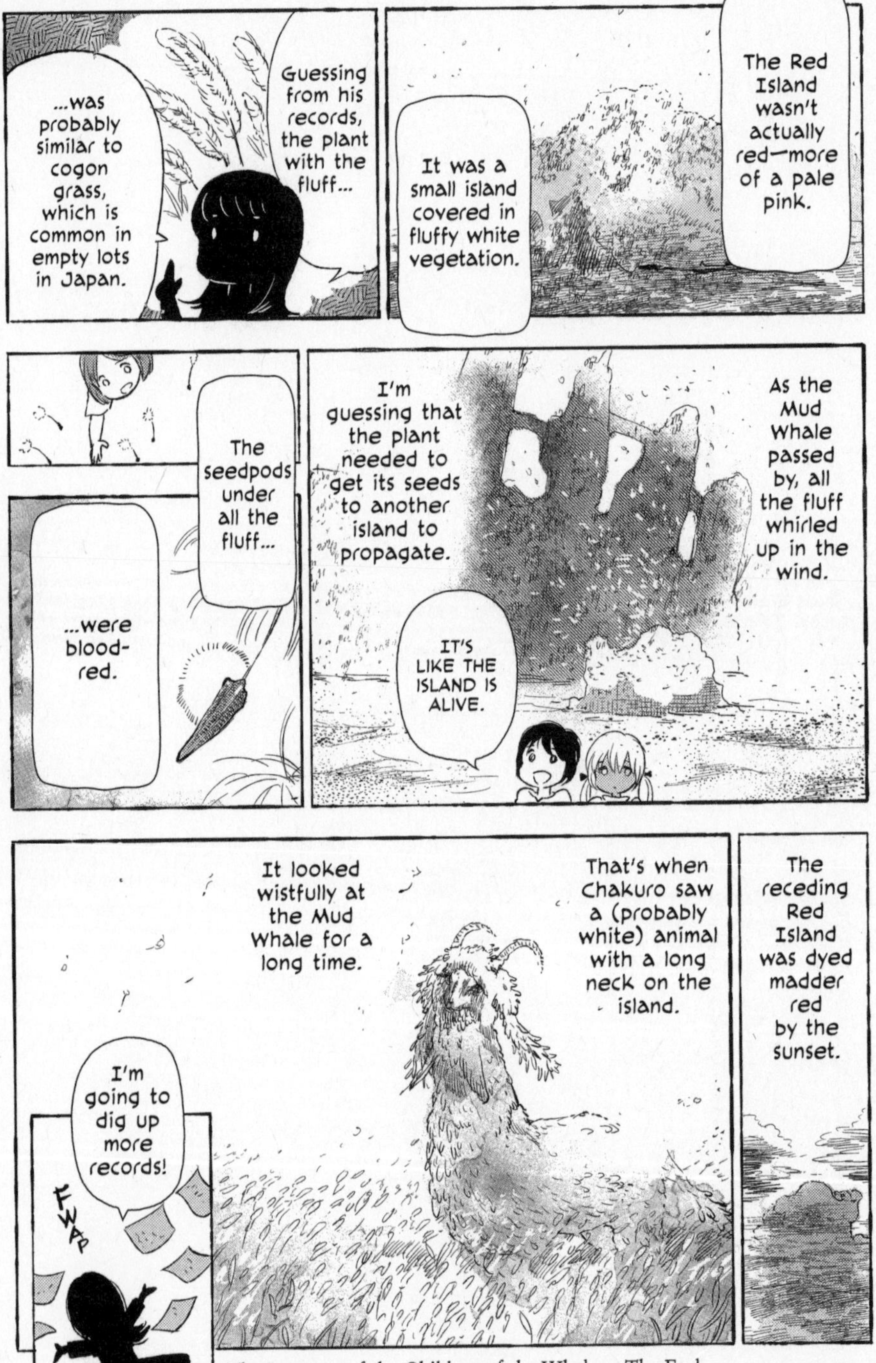
The Red Island wasn't actually red—more of a pale pink.
It was a small island covered in fluffy white vegetation.
Guessing from his records, the plant with the fluff...
...was probably similar to cogon grass, which is common in empty lots in Japan.
As the Mud Whale passed by, all the fluff whirled up in the wind.
I'm guessing that the plant needed to get its seeds to another island to propagate.
IT'S LIKE THE ISLAND IS ALIVE.
The seedpods under all the fluff...
...were blood-red.
The receding Red Island was dyed madder red by the sunset.
That's when Chakuro saw a (probably white) animal with a long neck on the island.
It looked wistfully at the Mud Whale for a long time.
I'm going to dig up more records!
FWAP

The Journeys of the Children of the Whales -The End-

A Note on Names

Those who live on the Mud Whale are named after colors in a language unknown. Abi Umeda uses Japanese translations of the names, which we have maintained. Here is a list of the English equivalents for the curious.

Aijiro	pale blue
Benihi	scarlet
Buki	kerria flower (*yamabuki*)
Byakuroku	malachite mineral pigments, pale green tinged with white
Chakuro	blackish brown (*cha* = brown, *kuro* = black)
Ginshu	vermillion
Hakuji	porcelain white
Jiki	golden
Kicha	yellowish brown
Kikujin	koji mold, yellowish green
Kogare	burnt muskwood, dark reddish brown
Kuchiba	decayed-leaf brown
Masoh	cinnabar
Miru	seaweed green
Neri	silk white
Nezu	mouse gray
Nibi	dark gray
Ouni	safflower red
Rasha	darkest blue, nearly black
Ro	lacquer black
Sami	light green (*asa* = light, *midori* = green)
Shikoku	purple-tinged black
Shikon	purple-tinged navy

Shinono	the color of dawn (*shinonome*)
Shuan	dark bloodred
Sienna	reddish brown
Sumi	ink black
Suou	raspberry red
Taisha	red ocher
Tobi	reddish brown like a kite's feather
Tokusa	scouring rush green
Urumi	muddy gray

I like watching nature shows. But drawing animals is so hard... I want to draw them quickly and make them cute.

—Abi Umeda

ABI UMEDA debuted as a manga creator with the one-shot "Yukokugendan" in *Weekly Shonen Champion*. *Children of the Whales* is her eighth manga work.

CHILDREN OF THE WHALES

VOLUME 6
VIZ Signature Edition

Story and Art by **Abi Umeda**

Translation / JN Productions
Touch-Up Art & Lettering / Annaliese Christman
Design / Julian (JR) Robinson
Editor / Pancha Diaz

KUJIRANOKORAHA SAJOUNIUTAU Volume 6
© 2015 ABI UMEDA
First published in Japan in 2015 by AKITA PUBLISHING CO., LTD., Tokyo
English translation rights arranged with AKITA PUBLISHING CO., LTD. through
Tuttle-Mori Agency, Inc., Tokyo

Printed in the U.S.A.

Published by VIZ Media, LLC
P.O. Box 77010
San Francisco, CA 94107

10 9 8 7 6 5 4 3 2 1
First printing, September 2018

viz.com

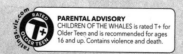
PARENTAL ADVISORY
CHILDREN OF THE WHALES is rated T+ for
Older Teen and is recommended for ages
16 and up. Contains violence and death.

vizsignature.com

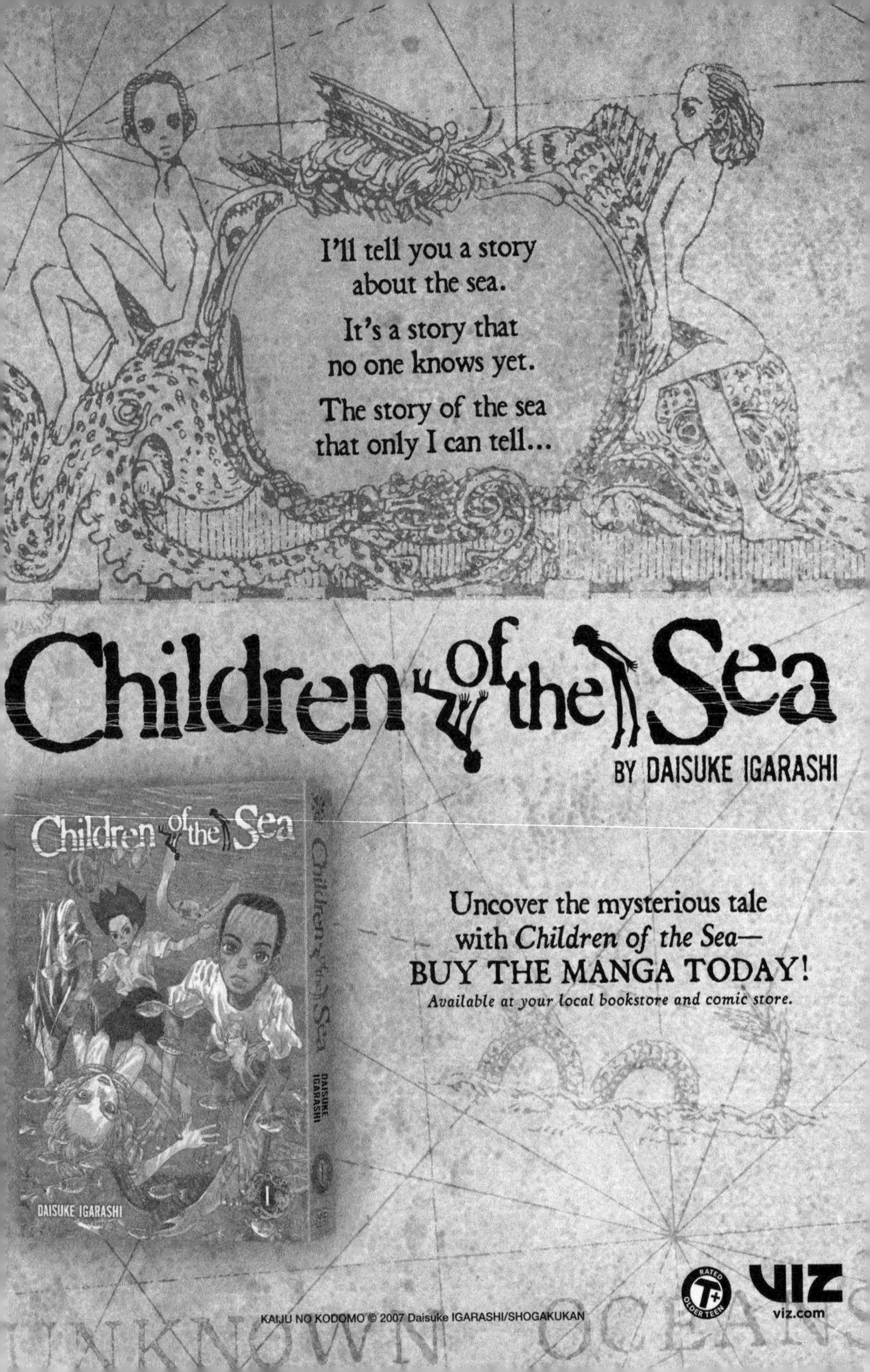
I'll tell you a story
about the sea.
It's a story that
no one knows yet.
The story of the sea
that only I can tell...
Children of the Sea
BY DAISUKE IGARASHI
Children of the Sea
DAISUKE IGARASHI
1
Uncover the mysterious tale
with *Children of the Sea*—
BUY THE MANGA TODAY!
Available at your local bookstore and comic store.
RATED T+ OLDER TEEN
VIZ
viz.com
KAIJU NO KODOMO © 2007 Daisuke IGARASHI/SHOGAKUKAN
UNKNOWN OCEANS

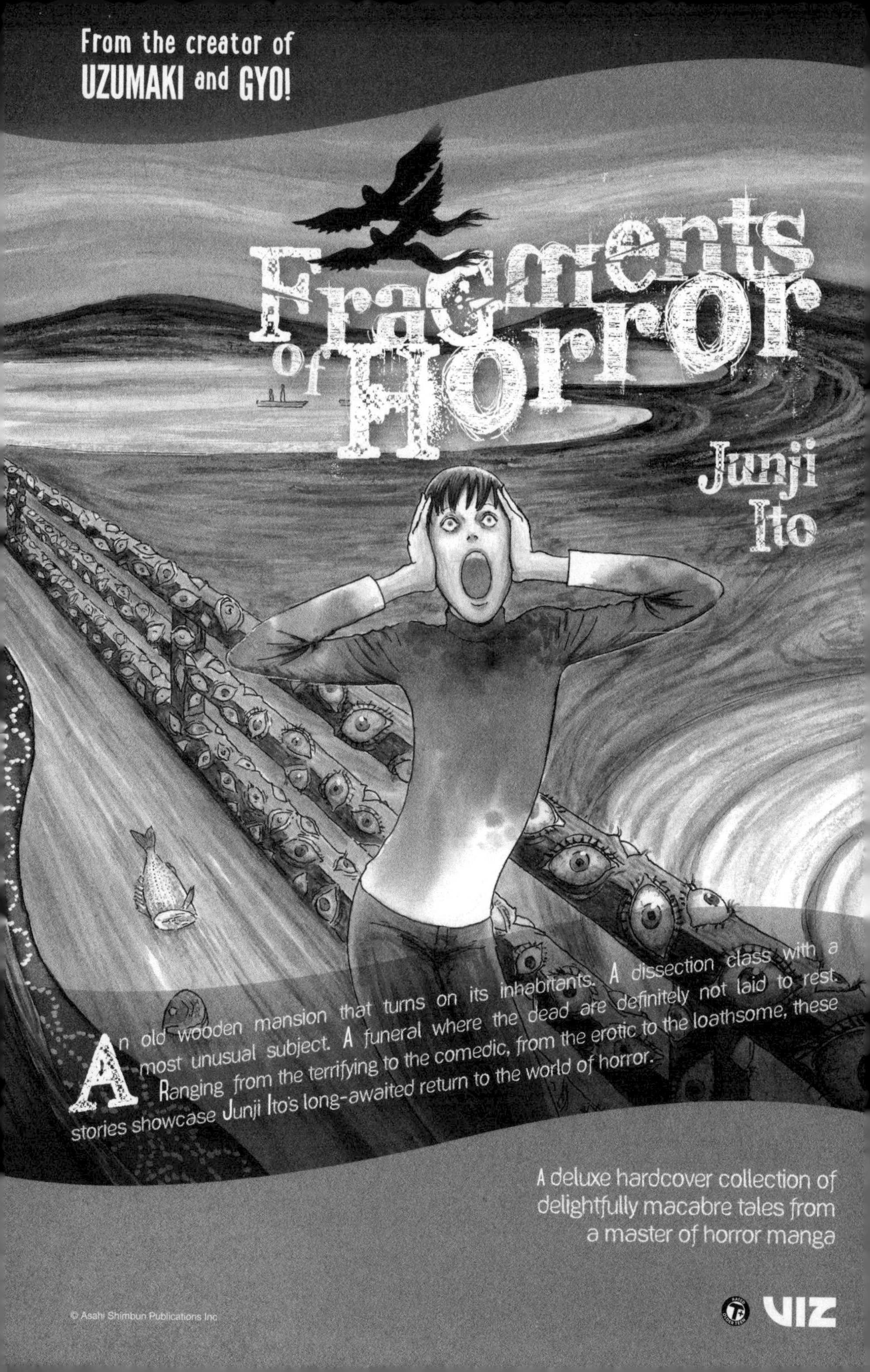

Fragments of Horror

Junji Ito

An old wooden mansion that turns on its inhabitants. A dissection class with a most unusual subject. A funeral where the dead are definitely not laid to rest. Ranging from the terrifying to the comedic, from the erotic to the loathsome, these stories showcase Junji Ito's long-awaited return to the world of horror.

A deluxe hardcover collection of delightfully macabre tales from a master of horror manga

VIZ

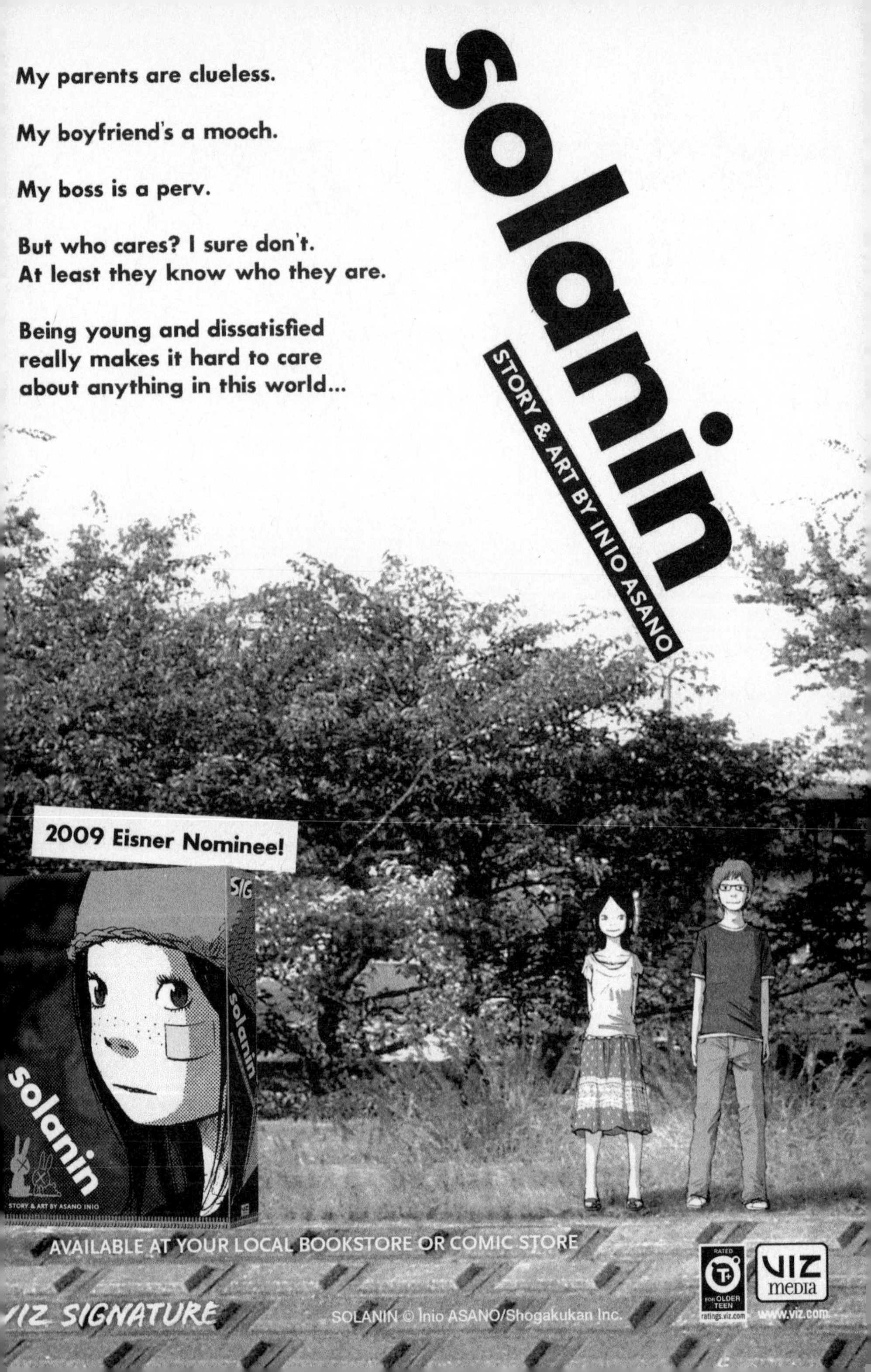
My parents are clueless.
My boyfriend's a mooch.
My boss is a perv.
But who cares? I sure don't.
At least they know who they are.
Being young and dissatisfied
really makes it hard to care
about anything in this world...
solanin
STORY & ART BY INIO ASANO
2009 Eisner Nominee!
SIG
solanin
solanin
STORY & ART BY ASANO INIO
AVAILABLE AT YOUR LOCAL BOOKSTORE OR COMIC STORE
VIZ SIGNATURE
SOLANIN © Inio ASANO/Shogakukan Inc.
RATED T+ FOR OLDER TEEN
ratings.viz.com
VIZ media
www.viz.com

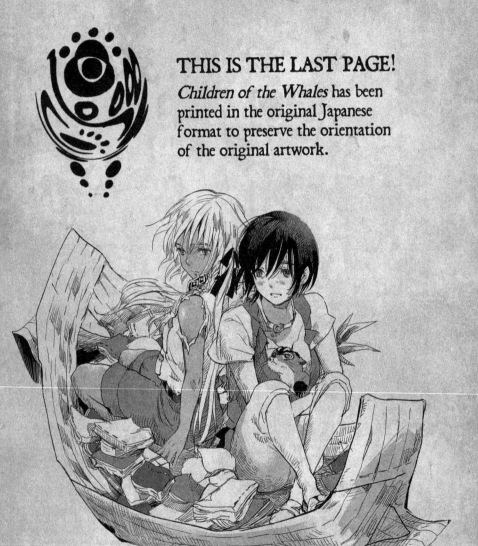

THIS IS THE LAST PAGE!

Children of the Whales has been printed in the original Japanese format to preserve the orientation of the original artwork.

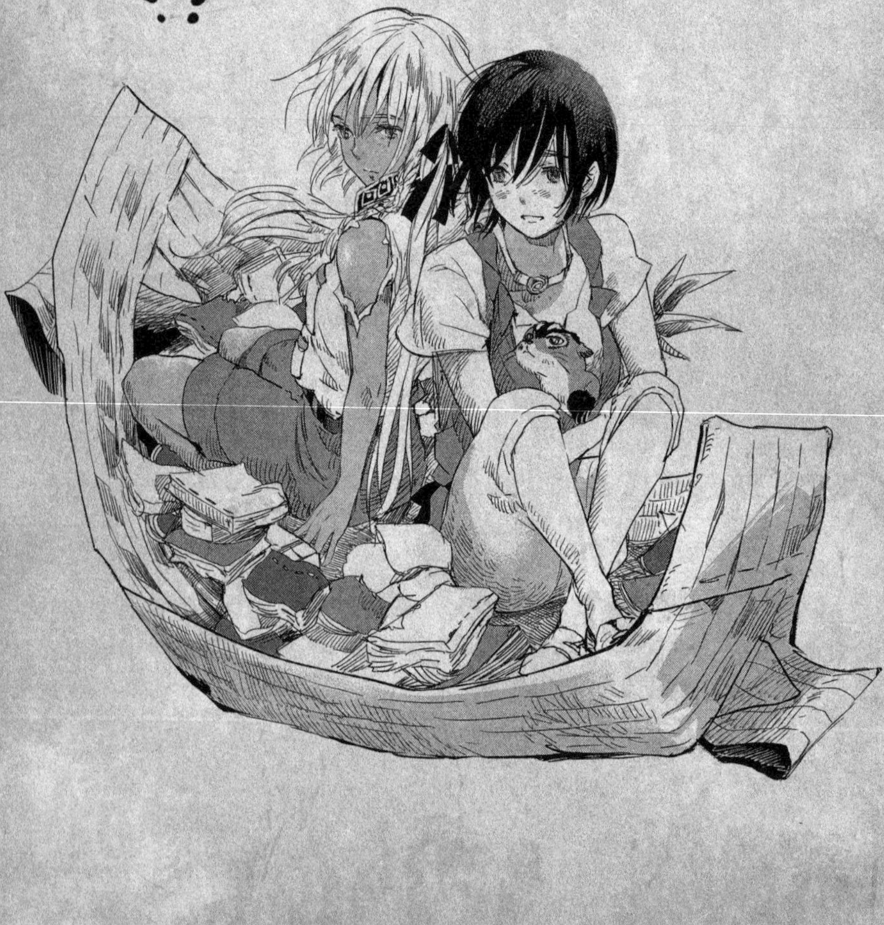